THE LIFE OF THE HEART

George Sand and Her Times

THE LIFE
OF THE HEART

George Sand and Her Times

A Biography by

Frances Winwar

Harper & Brothers *Publishers*

New York *and* London

10-5   THIRD EDITION   M-U

TO
JANE PERRY VANDERCOOK
"Non sanguine, corde . . ."

CONTENTS

ILLUSTRATIONS

THE LIFE OF THE HEART
George Sand and Her Times

Chapter I: The Eagle's Shadow

FROM the window of an inn near Vitoria, a young French-woman, Sophie Dupin, was watching the horses being watered before the *calèche* went on toward Madrid. It was a sultry day early in May, 1808. Sophie, big with child, stood heavily beside her companion, Madame Fontanier, the wife of a purveyor to the French army which, since the beginning of the year, had been going on steadily in its invasion of Spain. Through Madame Fontanier, Sophie had been able to obtain a place in the carriage with her daughter Aurore, not quite four. Soon she would be rejoining her husband, stationed for an indefinite period in Madrid as aide-de-camp to Marshal Murat who, by Napoleon's order, had assumed command in Spain.

The journey had been a foolhardy undertaking for Sophie in her condition. The country seethed with rancor against the French, like another Sicily before the outbreak of the famous Vespers. Only a few days earlier, on the second of May, the people of Madrid had risen in insurrection when a carriage stopped in front of the royal palace to carry off to France the young prince, Don Antonio, the last of the Bourbon family, who had fled. Attacking Murat's guards, they abducted the prince and carried their struggle to Puerta del Sol and the central square. Two battalions of French soldiers, sent as reinforcements, were slaughtered. Neither the regiments of infantry, marching through the city and firing volleys into the cross streets, nor a detachment of armed men who took possession of the arsenal and pointed the cannon on the irate Spaniards, succeeded in quelling the tumult. Only the Spanish garrison which had been confined to barracks finally restored order, but at a heavy cost in dead to the French.

Far from dying down, the people's anger against the French and their own cowardly monarchs, smoldered in desperation. At any time, anywhere, resentment might break out. However, Madame Fontanier's coachman had followed the lines protected by the French army, so that except for a harmless encounter with a family of bears on a mountain pass and nervous stops for relays at equally nervous villages, the party whose other member

1

was Madame Fontanier's twelve-year-old jockey, had an unadventurous though not an unexciting time of it. To watch Sophie Dupin pointing out the landscape to her daughter—"See the lovely bindweed on the rocks!—Look, there, that wonderful sight! You must remember what you see here, Aurore!"—one might have thought they were out on a pleasure jaunt. "The shape of that cloud there, Aurore! The sun—see how it shines through it. Don't ever forget this, Aurore."

"Really, Madame Dupin! How odd you are with your little girl!" Madame Fontanier exclaimed.

Aurore saw nothing odd in her mother's behavior. Ever since she could remember, Sophie had told her what to look at, what to bear in mind. Aurore's slow eyes whose brooding concentration made Aunt Lucie hint that the child might not be "all there" would brighten at Sophie's voice. Then, as if by an effort of will, she would rouse herself and look where the finger pointed.

There was nothing that finger missed, directed as it was by the curiosity of a Parisian daughter of the people, a curiosity which devoured with like avidity the newest mode of the next-door neighbor and the emperor's latest show. An indefatigable gadabout, Sophie had covered all of Paris, not to mention a good part of Italy and now, Spain, thanks to that same emperor whose shadow had fallen over half the world. Had it not been for the emperor she would not have found herself as a general's mistress in Italy during the campaign, and she would not have met Maurice Dupin. She would not now be on her way to Madrid and to Maurice who still loved her with the wild impetuosity that had made him oppose his aristocratic mother to marry her, the daughter of a bird seller of Paris' Left Bank. The Emperor Napoleon. Who could do anything beyond the shadow of his awful hand?

With no precise feeling about Napoleon except for an awareness that he was there like the sun or a destructive storm, Sophie, shortly before leaving Paris, had pointed him out to Aurore like any other phenomenon of nature. Napoleon was reviewing his troops on the boulevard, not far from the Madeleine. The ubiquitous Sophie, with the help of Pierret, a sort of family retainer, elbowed her way to the edge of the crowd, and had Pierret hold Aurore aloft in his arms.

"Look, Aurore, over there—the emperor!" she cried, as the child found herself above a line of shakos and almost face to face with a pale, stocky man whose eyes frightened her. "He has looked at you!" exclaimed Sophie. "Remember, he has looked at you and it will bring you luck." It seemed to Aurore as if at that instant the ice in Napoleon's gaze melted and the face warmed in a smile. She did not understand her mother's words.

2

Luck? What was luck, and how could that pale man's look bring it to her?

In the courtyard of the inn near Vitoria, Aurore was more concerned with the wonder of a talking magpie in a cage, and with the sunflowers that looked for all their foreignness like those in Aunt Lucie's garden at Chaillot, than with Napoleon's charmed eye. Yet just as the magpie was starting up again its truculent shrieking of *Muera, muera Godoy!* [1] a huge coach lumbered into the innyard, bearing a woman whose whole future, whose very life, was controlled by Napoleon's baleful power.

"The queen! The queen!" shouted the townsfolk who had followed the coach to the gate.

"No, it is not the queen," contradicted the innkeeper. He sent some of his men to keep out the mob and others to change the horses, all of which happened so quickly that it looked like magic to the little girl gaping by. There was no need for Sophie to admonish her to look and remember. Aurore, who had seen an emperor but never a queen, stood by the carriage, her large eyes made larger by fairy tale come true, as a woman came down the coach steps, followed by a girl of nine or ten. Slowly, disappointment dulled Aurore's expectancy. That plain dark woman in the white dress yellowed with dust, that ugly little girl in her skimpy frock—was that a queen, was that a princess? The fairy world of radiant beings lost its magic before those two drab creatures standing there, unhappy and frightened, separated from the throng by the barrier of their terror.

Soon they crawled back into their carriage. The coachman cracked his whip, the horses champed, the crowd parted, and the vehicle sped down the road in a panic of dust.

"Another queen running away," commented Sophie from her window to the world in general. The magpie screamed, *Muera, muera!*

And so the infanta, daughter of Charles IV, fled from her own people to put herself, like her father and mother and her brother Ferdinand, under the treacherous protection of Napoleon at Bayonne.

The prime minister, Don Manuel de Godoy, Prince of Peace, had long been pursuing a policy of appeasement. But with Charles IV his master and Queen Maria Luisa, his mistress in more senses than one, he had found himself at last under Napoleon's heel. If only, like the rulers of Portugal, they had all sailed to the New World and safety! After the troops of General Duhesme marched into Barcelona, the king had indeed planned an escape to Mexico. Everything was in readiness for the preliminary foothold at Seville when the people, discovering the

[1] Spanish. "Death, death to Godoy!"

plan, rushed out of their houses, cut the traces of the royal carriage and implored their monarch not to quit his country.

"Dearly beloved subjects," he addressed them that night in a proclamation, "calm your spirits. We assure you that the army of our dear friend, the Emperor of the French, is marching through our states only in peace and amity, to protect the points threatened by the landing of an enemy on the coast of Spain. Our guards have not been called out either to defend our person or to escort us on a journey," he lied.

The disillusioned people found relief in riots and violence, sacked Godoy's palace in Madrid, and demonstrated against the king. Terrified, Charles IV abdicated in favor of his son. On March 20 Ferdinand was proclaimed the new king and when, two days later, Murat entered Madrid with a vanguard of cavalry and banners flying, the people cheered wildly the man whom they assumed to be their young monarch's ally and protector.

Alas, too soon both Ferdinand and his subjects learned that Napoleon's support was nothing but a trick. Ferdinand, however, in spite of warnings from all sides, crossed the Pyrenees to Bayonne to obtain in person the emperor's recognition. Far from granting it, Napoleon made him understand that he must surrender the crown of Spain in exchange for the meaningless one of Etruria. For a time the duped Ferdinand refused. But he was virtually the emperor's prisoner, and a prisoner must submit, especially after the king, the queen and Godoy came to sue for Napoleon's protection and overwhelmed him, Ferdinand, with contumely for his stubbornness.

Then followed the events of the second of May. Napoleon was in no mood to compromise with an exasperated people. His army seized the key Spanish citadels of Pampeluna, Barcelona, Figueras, and San Sebastian. Both Charles IV and Ferdinand— so briefly the Seventh—renounced the Spanish throne and yielded their crowns to the conqueror for the Judas price of palaces in France and annuities of millions of francs. The son of a Corsican notary knew how to profit even after his colossal triumph over the Spanish Bourbons: the annuities were to be squeezed from the betrayed people of Spain.

Madrid, when Sophie arrived, was a desolate city but for Murat's soldiers, ready to repress any stirring on the part of the Spaniards who, during that perilous time, thought it wiser to keep under cover. From dawn till night the squares sounded to the tramp of marching feet and the clang of cavalry. Only when the iron echoes died could one hear the splashing of the fountains.

One such fountain occupied the center of the square commanded by the palace of Manuel de Godoy—his when it had sheltered his intrigue with Queen Maria Luisa, but now the

4

domicile of Murat and his aide-de-camp. For some mornings the copper-skinned Mamelukes who watered their horses at the basin had seen a diminutive spectator watching them from between the balusters of an upper balcony. Sometimes she touched the sun-baked marble, then quickly drew her hand away, as if she were playing a game. Sometimes she called out words, listened for the echo, and called again in a tireless pastime. No one ever played with her, but she seemed to want no one. She was living in her own world with her invisible companions.

For that matter, the world of reality into which Aurore was born possessed all the bizarre elements of the romantic novels that she was later to write. Indeed, her life was itself to be her best novel. License distinguished her ancestral line. Had family escutcheons figured the truth, the bar sinister would have covered a wide space.

The pertinent pedigree on the paternal side began with the two hundred or more bastards of Frederick Augustus, elector of Saxony and King of Poland. One of them, a son born to him by a Swedish noblewoman, Aurore Countess Königsmark, was to become the famous Maurice de Saxe, marshal of France, as renowned for his exploits at Fontenoy as for his adventures in the boudoir. A vulgar, exuberant yet indubitably intelligent man, Maurice de Saxe spent his time coveting a crown and sublimating his failure to attain it by planning paper utopias in which marriage was abolished, social distinction leveled, and woman made the equal of man. In practice he abided by some of his theories. He dispensed with the formality of marriage wherever possible, and overlooked class if the woman offered beauty. So it happened that he chose as one of his mistresses a young actress, Marie Rinteau, a humble name which Marie changed to the euphonious Victoire de Verrières, also adopted by her sister Geneviève. The liaison resulted in a daughter who appeared on the marriage register as "Marie Aurore, daughter of Jean Baptiste de la Rivière . . . and Marie Rinteau, his wife."

For fifteen years no one troubled to uncover the marshal's incognito, until Marie Aurore was ready to be married. Unofficially, however, she had been recognized by none other than the Dauphine of France as the daughter of Maurice de Saxe. She had placed the girl at Saint-Cyr, and had now found her a husband in Antoine, Count de Horn, himself fathered without benefit of clergy by Louis XV. Marie Aurore, a girl of strong will and stronger principles, saw no reason why she should not bear her father's illustrious name. At her behest she was allowed by parliamentary decree to be known as Marie Aurore de Saxe, and under that name she was married.

The marriage was one in name only, as if legitimacy brought

5

a curse with it. Then, hardly three weeks after the wedding, the Count de Horn was killed in a duel. The last thing the young girl saw was his large white dead hand dangling from the bed.

Marie Aurore was thirty when she married again. This time she chose Claude Dupin de Francueil, a comfortable farmer-general past sixty who had been an intimate at her mother's house and a lover of her Aunt Geneviève's. Before that he had had a passionate and much talked about liaison with the celebrated Madame d'Épinay, with an exchange of correspondence of so warm a nature that the presses of the day fairly sizzled when it was published in the form of a romance. The son born of the affair was reared on a farm and then placed in holy orders where, in the large tolerance of the times, he eventually rose to an archbishopric.

The De Verrières ladies, besides holding a salon, "cultivated the muses," particularly music, which Dupin loved. Perhaps he had been attracted by Marie Aurore when she sang Colette in Rousseau's *Le Devin du Village* at one of their amateur performances. Perhaps his author's vanity was flattered to hear his lines from her lips, for he had collaborated with the great Jean Jacques on his opera. However it was, the two were married and lived harmoniously together, even though the word love never crossed Marie Aurore's lips. But if she made no verbal professions, neither did she fall into the least error, so much was she the living reaction from her mother's laxity. When, therefore, a son was born to Dupin de Francueil, he knew beyond a doubt that the child was his own. Marie Aurore called him Maurice after the Marshal de Saxe.

The name held its own destiny. Almost from the moment Maurice was born, Madame Dupin knew he belonged more to the marshal than to Francueil. She adored the boy. When her husband died after ten years of marriage, she took stock of her assets which were considerable, chose a tutor for her son in the person of François Deschartres, and devoted herself to his education.

The boy early revealed his complex heredity. In vain Deschartres imposed the rigid discipline of a pedant and an ex-abbé. Maurice remained self-willed and uncontrolled. His alert intelligence, inherited from his mother, together with the Rousseauistic sensibility and Voltairian principles, he turned to his own uses, with unexpected results. Unexpected at least, to Madame Dupin. But as Maurice was as much absorbed in her as she was in him, she reasoned herself out of all doubt with her usual logic. Maurice could do no wrong.

He was in many ways a more than satisfactory son. During the Terror, while Madame Dupin was imprisoned at the convent

6

of Les Anglaises for secreting papers and valuables, it was Maurice who cheered her captivity with almost loverlike letters and later, when the citizens permitted, with daily visits. Maurice too, it was, who comforted her when she lost most of her fortune. Adversity drew them closer. More than ever they lived by and for each other.

But it was not to continue for long. Nature and the Republic conspired to destroy her dream, nature by its assertion in Maurice's vigorous manhood, and the Republic by its law of the second Vendémiaire (September 23, 1798) which made conscription obligatory. Madame Dupin lived in a fever of anxiety. Maurice was twenty. The Republic called for two hundred thousand conscripts. Maurice had been restless. He needed only an interview with De La Tour d'Auvergne, leader of the glorious "infernal column" for the blood of the marshal to prove itself. From 1798 on Maurice was on active duty. "I hate glory," Madame Dupin cried in her anguish. "I would reduce to ashes all those laurels on which I am always seeing the blood of my son."

Before that the marshal's heredity had asserted itself in still another way, although its fruits were not apparent until April of 1799, some six months after Maurice had left Nohant. Tactfully Madame Dupin wrote her son that she had established a *petite maison* close to her own manor. In the *little house* lived a wet nurse and a fine newborn baby boy, Hippolyte. The mother was a certain young domestic whom Maurice had known well. She did not live at Nohant now, but she, Madame Dupin, had provided for her and was assuming responsibility for the rearing of the infant. After all, she too had been a natural child.

In his reply to his mother Maurice unlocked the floods of sentimentality. "Women are born to comfort us for all the world's ills," he wrote with strange illogic. "You taught me as much, dear Mother, when I was with you, and now you are repairing my follies. Oh, if only all mothers were like you . . . No! We must not abandon this helpless creature. I know you will not." He closed with a Rousseauesque stanza wherein a nestful of fledglings is made to rejoice that their mother would rear and cherish them—

> Whereas if human babies we,
> In an asylum we might be!

It was characteristic of Maurice to withdraw from an awkward situation with a song or a pirouette. Graceful, elegantly trim, he wore his uniform well and rode his horse with distinction, though inclined to sudden recklessness. Women found him irresistible, so typical was he of the military ideal emblazoned in the popular engravings: aquiline of nose, dashing, with a black line of mustache over a sensual mouth, and fine black arches shading the questing eyes. He was a man of feeling rather than intellect, the feeling itself translated to sentimentality rather than sentiment. He could go through experiences that made heroes of other men and yet remain unchanged, almost untouched. How, otherwise, could he have described the tremendous Battle of Marengo in the accents of *opéra bouffe*? *"Pin, pan, pouf, patatras* —forward! Sound the charge! Retreat, now! . . . We are lost! Victory! Every man for himself. Flee to the right! To the left! . . . Watch out for the shells! Gallop away! . . ."

Nevertheless, partly because of his courage, but more because the tradition of the army kept alive the name of Marshal de Saxe, Maurice was advanced by Murat, not quite to the rank that Madame Dupin had hoped for him—but Maurice was young. He might distinguish himself. Better, he might make an advantageous marriage. Even the longest war must have an end. Governments come and go. She knew several willing young ladies, daughters of fine families of the old régime.

In her dreams for her son, however, Madame Dupin did not reckon with the captivating presence of one Sophie Victoire Antoinette Delaborde who was doing the Italian campaign, like Maurice, though in quite other ranks. Since Sophie's line sprang simply and directly from the first toiler Adam, it offered no such fascinating divergences as Maurice's. Neither Sophie nor anyone else could think back beyond her maternal grandmother, known as Mother Cloquart. Her own mother she scarcely remembered. As for her father, Antoine Delaborde, she recalled him vaguely among cages and twittering birds, more vaguely as the keeper of a billiard room. Orphaned with her sister Lucie when they were still infants, they were brought up by Mother Cloquart, a good but ignorant woman, possessed of all the fanaticisms and prejudices of the poor.

Oddly, when the Revolution broke out, Mother Cloquart who should have had nothing to fear because she had nothing to risk, became a Royalist, and brought up her two granddaughters according to her lights. Sophie and Lucie could make nothing of it all. But once, when they saw the head of the Princesse de Lamballe at the end of a pike, the long hair matted with blood, they compared the sight with the gay celebrations carried on in the squares, and they knew that the people could be as terrible as they were wonderful.

To the two girls, especially to Sophie who was the beauty of her quarter, the honest citizens had shown particular favor. She never forgot the day—she was just sixteen—when the women dressed her in white and led her to the Hôtel de Ville, where she

8

presented a wreath and declaimed some verses to Lafayette. Still less did she forget the great man's words, "Lovely child, these flowers become your face better than mine," as he placed the roses on her hair, to the frantic cheering of the citizens.

The compliment and the applause may have turned Sophie's head, for from then on she determined to have more of both. For three or four years she obtained them in ways more or less legitimate, what with her beauty and the impudent verve she gave to her small rôles in the popular theater. She was nineteen when the people again singled her out, this time, however, with disfavor, for singing a broadside that pricked republican susceptibilities. Like Madame Dupin, Sophie Delaborde, daughter of the people, served a term in the cloisters of Les Anglaises.

What happens to attractive young women of no definite occupation and no means of support in a social upheaval happened to Sophie. For a time she was neither seen nor heard of. Finally she turned up at Marengo, first as a camp follower and then as the mistress of an aging general. She had a baby daughter with her, Caroline, of father unknown.

It was then that Maurice had met Sophie and fallen in love with her. At first he had taken her for a lady and the general's wife, so well had the adaptable Parisian mastered the tone expected of her. When he discovered the true relationship, Maurice had already become so enslaved by her small, vital, tempting person that what she was made no difference, provided she was his. It did not matter that she was four years older than he, that she had an illegitimate daughter—did he not have his *petite maison?*—that she could scarcely read and write, and that her known pedigree could be traced only to her father, the bird seller. The general was the only obstacle. Sophie gave him up for Maurice's sake.

Much as he loved her, Maurice did not marry her. He was too much afraid of his mother whose portrait as the Chaste Diana, painted in her youth, represented with formidable clarity her rigorous moral qualities. As successfully as he could, Maurice kept his affair from her. For four years Sophie followed him from camp to camp, bearing him children that died almost as soon as they were born. She resented her state of concubinage, yet she understood Maurice's reluctance to alienate Madame Dupin. Moreover, she had the practicality of the needy. Madame Dupin. would be better as a friend than as an enemy. But Madame Dupin, when she heard of Sophie, made open battle. Sophie knew that they would never be reconciled. It was then, perhaps, that she insisted on marriage.

She was eight months gone with child when Maurice, who was in Paris, set off for Nohant to obtain his mother's consent.

"Ah, you love another more than you love me!" Madame Dupin cried passionately. "Why did I not die like so many others in '93? Then you would have kept me in your heart and I would never have had a rival."

Defeated, Maurice returned to Paris and to Sophie who was waiting in the small apartment they had taken at 46 Rue Meslay. Madame Dupin's inflexibility only strengthened Sophie's determination. This child of hers must be born legitimate. She won.

One month exactly after their marriage, the Dupins were giving a party to celebrate the engagement of Sophie's sister Lucie to one of Maurice's friends. They were all very young and very gay, and made the most of the brief respites that Napoleon allowed in his conquest of power and more power. Maurice, an accomplished musician, was playing the violin for a quadrille. The rest were dancing.

In the midst of the dance Sophie quietly retired to her room. A little later Lucie followed her and came out crying, "Maurice! Maurice! Come, you have a baby girl."

"She will be named Aurore after my mother," he said.

Sophie was more ambitious. She called the child, born legitimate and to the sound of music, Amantine Aurore Lucile Dupin. And so the future George Sand arrived on the first day of July, 1804,[2] in the last year of the Republic and the first of the Empire.

Even the birth of a legal grandchild named after her failed to soften Madame Dupin. In fact, with the help of Deschartres she endeavored to have the marriage annulled. But the citizens who had once abolished church marriage respected the civil ceremony, so that Madame Dupin's efforts came to nought, and with them her dreams of a noble marriage for her son. Again the blood of Marshal de Saxe had triumphed—Marshal de Saxe who for the favors of a lady-in-waiting had betrayed the Duchess Anna Ivanovna. "He might have been the Emperor of Russia," said Anna Ivanovna, then empress. "That woman cost him dear."

[2] In *Histoire de Ma Vie* George Sand gives the date erroneously as July 5, 1804.

Chapter II: Mother and Son

AURORE found so much to delight her in the palace of Godoy that she gave hardly a thought to the house and friends she had left in Paris. The house had been squalid enough, a small apartment in a plebeian quarter, furnished meagerly but kept spotless by Sophie's tireless scrubbing. There was no money for luxury. Even though Madame Dupin had become reconciled to her son's marriage, she had never accepted her daughter-in-law. The allowance she gave Maurice she therefore expected him to employ in keeping up appearances, rather, the appearance, of the grandson of Marshal de Saxe, a costly business which army pay would never have covered without her help.

Friends were few in the modest household, and there was little time for friendship in the brief furloughs between campaigns. Aurore's childhood had been invaded by men in uniform who would arrive with her father. There would be dancing and music and good things to eat. After the men had left, Mama and Aunt Lucie would again be alone. Then Aurore and her cousin Clotilde, Aunt Lucie's daughter, would re-enact what they had heard their fathers tell. They became cavalrymen and staged mock battles, striding chairs for horses, dismembering their dolls for realism and even, with the macabre fancy of children, scattering about shreds of red cloth for the blood of the battlefield. Sophie and Lucie were too busy to pay much attention to them. Maurice, however, who came in unexpectedly on one of those games, had such a shock at the gruesome play that he begged Sophie to sweep up that mock shambles.

Aurore's half sister, Caroline, was too big a girl for such pastimes. A quiet child, her position when she was not boarding out, was rather that of Sophie's helper. Although Aurore loved her, she did not share with the older girl that world of the imagination which is the true realm of childhood, and in which she was most at home.

The palace of the Prince of Peace resembled nothing Aurore had ever known. Now she had no need to escape into the fairy tale world as in Paris, when she had spun out stories by the hour, to the entertainment of Clotilde and the worried perplexity of

Aunt Lucie. Here enchantment lay all about, from the gilded globe-and-cross of the cathedral spire, multiplying itself wherever she turned her sun-dazzled eyes, to the white rabbit that had found its way to the bedroom and chose to camp behind the psyche mirror. Had it escaped from the kitchen, up those three marble flights to safety, or had someone left it there for her? Soon she had other pets, for with only the eyes of the royal portraits to reprimand them, a variety of domestic animals had made free of audience chamber and salon. One night Aurore awoke at the sound of voices, to find the huge Murat beside her bed, holding a tiny fawn in his arms. Half asleep, she saw him lay it beside her on the pillow. For a few days she loved it and played with it, and then it disappeared. Sophie said it had gone back to its mother in the woods—for what did the little child know of death?

Another night Aurore trembled with terror as a tremendous roaring shook the palace. It was Murat, Prince Fanfarinet, as she called him for his gay uniform. Were the assassins trying to murder him? Without stopping to dress Papa dashed down to Murat's apartment. The roaring continued, now louder, now cut short by a hideous yelp. When Maurice came back he said *Le Prince* was in great pain—something in his entrails. Perhaps the Spaniards had poisoned him. But in a few days Murat recovered and was up and about, looking bigger and more frightening than ever. No Frenchman felt safe, however. Maurice talked of attempts and uprisings. He wished Sophie had stayed at home.

In the immense rooms with their damask hangings and gilt furniture, and the toys of the fleeing Spanish princes for her own, Aurore had no wish for the novel life to end. Dream and reality coalesced. Sophie, whose untutored imagination had turned bizarre from her taste of the theater, fostered Aurore's already overdeveloped sense of play. At home she had frowned upon Lucie's efforts to bring Aurore down to earth like her own Clotilde. Here, amid the convulsions of war and insurrection, Sophie indulged in fantastic masquerade, dressing herself in the black satin of the Madrilena, and Aurore in a miniature uniform, item for item the duplicate of Maurice's.

"Meet my little aide-de-camp," Murat would laugh as he introduced the child. And Aurore would hold herself with military dignity, her vivid little face high, her white cashmere cape jauntily off the shoulder, her spurred red morocco boots planted on the ground and one hand on the hilt of her saber, so much too big for her that it screeched along the tessellated floors. She liked her trousered uniform that made her look so much like her father. Sophie made her another costume besides, a Spanish gown of black silk like her own, with a hem of net caught up

12

at the knee and a mantilla bordered with velvet. In that fancy dress the child danced before the long mirror, marveling that she could be so many selves and yet remain Aurore.

Sophie had been in Madrid a month when she gave birth to a son, Louis. Usually Sophie was delivered with little pain. This time, perhaps because of the fatigue of the journey, she was in labor many hours before the Spanish doctor, the only one they could find, at last brought forth the child. Dazed with suffering and mistrustful of the Spaniard, Sophie watched him. In her stupor it seemed to her that he pressed his thumbs on the baby's eyes, muttering something whose full meaning for the moment eluded her.

Louis was a pretty child, but sickly. He turned on the world a pair of pale blue eyes whose glassiness began to worry Sophie. Maurice, when she spoke to him about it, also found it singular. There had never been such eyes in the family. Finally they learned the worst: the child was blind. In her despair Sophie's suspicions fixed on the Spanish doctor. He had blinded the baby in his revenge on the French. She had seen him crushing the little one's eyeballs. Had she not heard him, in her agony, mutter: "Here is one who'll never see the light of Spain?"

Was it fact or the fantasy of a mother distraught with grief and rage? Maurice tried to reason with her. No human being could have been capable of such a crime. She had imagined what she heard and saw. More likely the hardships of the journey by coach in her advanced state, with Aurore often sitting on her lap, had contributed both to the difficult labor and to the baby's blindness. Besides, suppose the doctor were guilty, what proof had they on which to convict him? Perhaps— he held out a futile hope—Louis was not incurably blind. In France, with the help of Deschartres who knew so much about medicine, something might still be done. Murat could not now incite an already frenzied people by a court martial.

Even if Murat had decided to prosecute the doctor, it was too late. He, the man who had been welcomed with flying banners a few months earlier, now found himself fleeing with his army before the Spaniards, prepared to expel the intruder or die. In every part of the country a Frenchman seen on the street was killed at sight. Murat realized he had to contend with a people which neither asked quarter nor gave it. "Your monarchy is old. My mission is to rejuvenate it," said Napoleon. The Spaniards gave him their answer with sword and pickax.

Maurice joined the ranks of the retreating army across the Pyrenees, now in the wake of Murat, now watching over his family which shared the perils of the soldiers in flight. The mid-July heat baked the roads and sent up a stench of corrup-

13

tion from the unburied dead. Holding one child in her arms and the other by the hand, Sophie begged places on wagons met on the way. She shared her bread with the famished soldiers; they gave her water from their flasks. At every turn they ran the risk of a surprise attack.

Filth and vermin, and finally scabies, afflicted them all. Aurore lay half conscious in a constant fever. Toward the end they knew thirst and hunger, an animal hunger that gripped them like a physical ill. But the thirst was worst of all. Past smoldering farmhouses, across fields sown with dead, Sophie went with the rest in search of water. They would find it at the bottom of a pit. Then suddenly sickness came over them as dark clots rose to the surface. The earth was choked with blood.

Sometimes Sophie managed to find a room for herself and the children. One night she took the languid Aurore to the window and pointed to the sky, booming with incessant thunder. "Look, there, Aurore. That's a battle. Your father is probably in it." The child widened her eyes at the curves and rockets of fire, and then bit thoughtfully into an apple someone had given her. "How lucky children are not to understand anything," sighed Sophie.

When they reached the seaboard at last Sophie insisted on making the rest of the voyage by water. They crossed the rough Bay of Biscay without mishap, but the sloop struck a reef as it entered the mouth of the Gironde, and the voyagers who had braved death by war barely escaped it by shipwreck.

The Spanish venture had been wholly disastrous. Maurice had returned in flight. Louis was born, or made, blind. Aurore had been reduced to a shadow by her fever. Sophie felt nothing but hate for the country and its people. She mistrusted even the horse, Leopardo of Andalusia, which Ferdinand VII had presented to Murat's aide-de-camp before leaving for Bayonne and dishonor. "I warn you, he meant you no good when he gave you that beast," Sophie cautioned. "Be very careful. I don't trust it."

Maurice smiled at her fears while admitting that Leopardo was the only horse he had ever mounted which gave him a sense of an indomitable will of its own. All the more reason for his wishing to break it, Sophie knew. At any rate, next to his saber, Maurice owned nothing that he prized more. Both had carried him through the thick of battle; both had preserved him.

In their precipitate flight the Dupins had still found time to carry off a few souvenirs from Spain, among them several statuettes in painted wood which Aurore had discovered in the clutter of broken dolls left behind by the royal children. One had both fascinated and frightened her. It was a figurine of an old

14

man in rags whose face was emaciated by hunger, hand reached out from among its tatters in sup menace. A strange plaything to have found its way toys of princes! What monitory chance had thrown it symbol of an unhappy land, starved and despoiled, abandoned by its kings?

Once in France, the sick, harassed little troupe went by coach toward Nohant and Madame Dupin. Maurice tried to hide his nervousness as they approached his mother's house, and almost wished himself with Murat, off to Italy to receive the crown of Naples—Napoleon's reward to his former brother-in-arms, now his brother-in-law, for his part in the Spanish tragedy.

Sophie sat beside her husband, tight-lipped and defiant. She had never been admitted to Nohant, and the only token of recognition she had ever received from her mother-in-law was a ruby ring, sent to her in Aurore's little fist the first time Maurice had prevailed upon Madame Dupin to look upon his child. Sophie hated her with the deep hate of the plebeian for the aristocrat, aggravated by the resentment of a woman who knew that if the man she loved felt through her, he was nevertheless made to think by another. They had lived in want to spare the rich woman the responsibility of looking after Maurice's family, since she had already assumed the care of one illegitimate member. How old would Hippolyte be now? Nearly nine, the same age as her own Caroline. Well, they were now sick and homeless, and the old woman would have to do something about them. Sophie was too tired to fight, at least for the present.

As for Madame Dupin, she awaited their arrival with conflicting emotions, although anyone looking at her placid face framed in the blond wig correctly poised, might have thought nothing more ruffling than abstract speculation could ever have disturbed it. She was only five feet tall, but she held herself with a dignity that gave the illusion of greater height. The slimness of her Diana portrait was gone. Under the folds of her wide, long-waisted brown silk dress, a fashion of the old régime which she had never abandoned, one guessed at heavy legs, unused to exercise. She walked with almost the ponderousness of a stone statue endowed with motion. Her face had distinction, perhaps beauty, had there not been too much pride in her eyes, too much the suggestion of scorn in the upturned corners of her mouth. The hands were beautiful. One imagined them, however, inclined to clutch too firmly at the reins.

She was fearful for her power over her son, now that she had to contest it with a young and pretty woman who had managed to hold him for almost eight years with and without a legal tie. The marriage had been a grave blow to her, as hard to bear as

15

idelity, so close had she been to Maurice. And he to her, for that matter. The letters he had sent her at Les Anglaises—she had kept every one—spoke with such devotion that they might have been written by a lover. "I kiss you as I used to kiss you at the same hour when we were together. How I long for those days! How happy they were! Now we are scattered like leaves in the wind, who knows why! . . . I see you always in my dreams," the fifteen-year-old boy had once written. "If sleep is the image of death, and if, while lying dead, I could forever see you in my dreams, I would quickly sink into that long sleep to enjoy such happiness."

But that was all over, and perhaps it was best so. Enough that her son had been spared to her through many perilous years. If she, the deist, could pray, she would pray that he be saved as many years again. It was happiness to know that she would have him with her for a month, two months, perhaps.

Discreetly in the background another waited with equally mixed feelings. François Deschartres, Maurice's tutor, had good reason to wonder what sort of greeting he would receive from that high-spirited young person, Madame Sophie Dupin, whose acquaintance he had once sought out under circumstances that reflected no glory upon him, considering the turn of events. Briefly, during Sophie's stay at an inn near Nohant while Maurice was visiting his mother, before the two young people were married, Deschartres had attempted to have the scarlet woman run out of town. With the caution of the pedant he sought authority for the act by enlisting the help of a number of respectable citizens to shame the Jezebel in her lair. Unfortunately for the pillars of virtue, Jezebel, besides being more than commonly attractive, had the air of a lady—Sophie was no mean actress when she chose—and put on such a show of injured innocence, running the gamut of tears and indignation, that the good burghers, simple and of a susceptible middle age, behaved like a herd of Balaam's asses. Deschartres himself, who had gone to damn, remained, if not to pray, at least to offer apology, unwillingly and with ill grace, but an apology.

The act was typical of the man. Serious to a fault, he often put himself into highly comical situations without appreciating their ridiculousness, and always because he acted on principle and through high motives. Science was his god, the only god he believed in after the Revolution had made him hastily throw off his abbé's collar, to become, at least outwardly, a sansculotte. The scientific method ruled him, and he in turn ruled by it everyone who came under his influence. With him the head was mightier than the heart, an organ which he recognized as an anatomical necessity but only to mistrust it. It may be that

16

some harsh early experience had turned him against love. Perhaps, a born misogynist, he had eagerly adopted St. Paul's view of women during his theological studies. However it was, the mention of the silly passion roused him to a fury, expressed in booming periods and enforced by the artillery of classical quotations. Severe with himself, he was intolerant of others. Yet he had a churlish sympathy with frail human nature which made him perform many kindnesses, particularly to the peasants round about Nohant, even if, as often as not, he capped the good deed with an insult.

He held a unique position in that part of Berry. Since 1793 when Madame Dupin had snatched enough of her fortune from the Revolution to buy the manor and property of Nohant, Deschartres had become a familiar figure to the people of that small, almost feudal community. They accepted him first as the major-domo of Madame Dupin and the tutor of her son, then as the doctor, half physician and half magician, of the district. A product of the late eighteenth century which had deified knowledge, Deschartres's inquiring mind had found nothing alien to it. Together with Latin and Greek, theology and logic, he had also studied medicine and its more primitive sister, magic, so that side by side, on the bookshelves of Nohant, whither he had removed his few household gods, one would find a treatise on reason and a black letter tome on how to raise the devil. He had his anatomical charts and his herb garden from which he brewed electuary and simple; he had his skull—he had helped to desiccate guillotined heads in the Paris hospitals during the Terror—and his cabalistic symbols. He was the product of a period of transition that took on the new without shedding the old.

By the miracle of personality Maurice had passed through Deschartres' tutelage and emerged as unscathed as through the Napoleonic campaigns. He was fond of the old eccentric. As for Deschartres, he would have given up his life—in the name of reason—for Maurice or Madame Dupin, the only beings toward whom his heart had ever betrayed human weakness.

Whatever Madame Dupin and the tutor had dreaded on the arrival of the refugees from Spain vanished in the emotion of the meeting. Mother and son embraced, then Madame Dupin kissed Sophie and took Aurore in her arms. "You had better rest with your son, *ma fille*," she said to Sophie, "while I take care of the little girl."

The sharp words Sophie had rehearsed died on her lips at Madame Dupin's welcome, and she retired meekly, glad to lie down with her little Louis who was half dead with scabies and fever.

In her grandmother's bedroom Aurore felt herself transported to the palace in Spain whose memory had become a dream in the hardships of the journey home. The walls, as in the palace, were hung with flowered draperies; the furniture glistened with gold. Lace cushions and *bibelots* lay scattered about, and a great bed, as large as a hearse and with plumes like a hearse at the four corners, crowded everything out. Aurore, when her grandmother laid her upon it, shrank in humiliation. Madame Dupin looked so beautiful, while she, in her filth and her loathsome red spots which Sophie had tried in vain to cure with even more loathsome sulphur, felt as if she could not make herself small enough in her misery. But Maman, as Madame Dupin taught Aurore to call her, soon quieted her with unexpected tenderness.

A little later Aurore saw a big awkward boy come in with a bunch of flowers. "This is Hippolyte," Madame Dupin informed her. "Come and kiss, children."

Hippolyte threw the bouquet at Aurore's head in clumsy play and kissed her. Hippolyte? Aurore had no idea who he was, but she took a liking to the boy. Just then Maurice came in with Sophie. He held the boy by the hand and, introducing him to her, said, like Maman, "This is Hippolyte."

Sophie showed no surprise. "Well," she said, "he will be my child, just as Caroline is yours." In a vague way Aurore understood that she and Hippolyte were related, as she and Caroline were. Not until many years later did she know the nature of the relationship.

Under the care of Deschartres the two sick children began to improve, but neither medicine nor magic availed to restore Louis' sight as Maurice, and even more Sophie, had hoped. In her disappointment, Sophie was less willing to forgive past insult. Besides the Spanish doctor she now held Madame Dupin and Deschartres responsible. If Madame Dupin had accepted them earlier, if the old tutor, instead of upholding his mistress, had taken Maurice's part, it would not have happened that she now had a blind child. Then, too, she chafed under the strain of maintaining her best behavior among "the old countesses" and the gentlemen in their high stocks who paid court to her mother-in-law, who by her very reserve, showed up her own lack of breeding. She would take her revenge, however, like the *gamine* she was, in maliciously clever burlesques of those eccentric aristocrats, performed for Maurice and the delighted Aurore. But these private revenges did not satisfy her hurt vanity and she made public scenes which Madame Dupin treated with the arrogant aloofness she bestowed upon a tantrum in the kitchen.

The rivalry between the two women increased. Sophie dressed lavishly to make herself more than ever alluring to Maurice.

Madame Dupin observed the most graceful decorum to expose by contrast Sophie's vulgarity. Long ago, on discovering that the hated marriage was a *fait accompli,* she had unburdened herself once for all to Maurice, using a word for Sophie that cut him to the quick. She had kept his answer.

"No, mother, a man suffers no dishonor in loving a woman. And a woman is not a *fille* if she is loved by a man who is willing to atone to her for the injustices of fate. You know that better than I do, for my sentiments, formed by your teachings . . . are only a reflection of your soul. By what strange whim do you now blame me for being the man you made me?"

The feelings his letter had stirred in her remained unaltered. She adored Maurice for being her son and her creation, and admired him for his defense of the woman he had married. But to her Sophie was still a *fille.* Mother and daughter-in-law possessed the irreconcilable enmity of the two major forces of the Revolution. Between them Maurice was caught, dreading to propitiate the one for fear of the other. At times, no doubt, he thought nostalgically of the comparative tranquillity of his life in the army, and took to going out at night to the neighboring town of La Châtre, tearing through the tree-shaded roads on the fiery Leopardo.

Sophie, however, soon had other cares to occupy her. Poor little blind Louis had fallen sick again. Deschartres brewed herbs and administered remedies. Sophie watched him, a prey to hope and suspicion. The child seemed to respond to the treatments but, after a favorable day, he would again sink into the lethargy of fever and lie for hours across Sophie's knees, scarcely breathing. Deschartres stubbornly wrestled for the baby's life. During successive days Louis showed improvement and Sophie, in her relief, almost forgave the grim old man all past injuries. Suddenly, one night, Louis went into convulsions. When his tiny body quieted at last, it was forever.

He died the night of September 8, 1808. On the ninth they buried him in the Nohant cemetery, divided from the Dupin garden by a low wall. The wearing emotions of the child's prolonged sickness, the blindness which had made his suffering more afflicting, his death in the midst of hope and, finally, the sight of the coffin being lowered into the grave, proved too much for Sophie. She went into a kind of hysterics peculiarly her own, a passion of self-accusation and penance in which one thing followed another. Herself, Deschartres, Madame Dupin, the Spanish doctor, Maurice, the war, everyone, everything came in for a measure of blame in the baby's death. By the time she and Maurice went to bed that night, she was in a state of such morbid excitement that she was convinced Louis had been buried alive.

"Your Deschartres!" she flung at Maurice. "Your Deschartres with all his learning! How do you know he isn't just an ignoramus who can't tell the difference between coma and death?" The baby had been well before those convulsions. He had laughed all day and was playful. In his little coffin he had looked no different from when he was asleep. Hadn't Maurice ever heard of premature burials? They had not waited long enough before burying Louis. Not even twenty-four hours. Louis was alive. He was alive and he must be saved or she would lose her mind.

After hours of futile remonstrance Maurice had no choice but to go to the cemetery and dig up the body that had barely been laid in the ground. He worked in a frenzy, for by the time he started out, Sophie had convinced him that the baby was alive. The soil resisted, considering how recently it had been turned. Groping his way in the darkness—he knew too well the superstitious nature of the peasants to risk being caught molesting a corpse—he heard at last the hollow sound of wood against his spade. When he tried to lift the coffin, however, he could not. He had dug the mound of a man who had been buried a few days earlier. The child's coffin lay beside it, he remembered. But he had to do his work all over again before he found it.

On leaning forward to dislodge the small wooden box, he planted his foot for support on the corner of the larger coffin which sank under him and, rising up from behind, smote him and flung him into the hollow upon the body of his son. Chilled with horror at being struck down by a corpse, he had an impulse to abandon the gruesome exploit and endeavor to convince Sophie that the child was dead. But was Louis really dead? Sophie's doubt, his own too, now, must be dispelled. Lifting up the child's coffin he laid it down beside him on the ground and carefully filled in the graves. They had been so recently made that no one would ever know they had been disturbed.

In their room the two, in mingled hope and dread, opened the coffin. Louis was dead. They could hope no longer. But Sophie would not let Maurice nail down the lid so soon. Her morbid sentimentality must batten on emotion. With her own hands she washed and anointed the stone-cold body which had been so hastily buried to spare her pain, by order of the too rational Madame Dupin. Then dressing it in fresh white linens, Sophie laid it in its cradle and watched over it all night, pretending Louis was asleep.

What secret duty she was fulfilling in that ritual no one knows. Perhaps in the shock of her sudden loss she was disputing

20

Maurice's heir, her only son, to death itself, and must convince herself in her own way that death had won. Maurice, always weak where she was concerned, humored her, even if in humoring her he committed an act he condemned.

All of the following day Sophie kept to her room. Madame Dupin respected her grief and left her alone. Aurore, busy laying out a new garden with Hippolyte, did not miss her, especially since Papa came now and then to help them. Late that night Sophie laid Louis in his coffin and covered the corpse with flowers before Maurice nailed down the lid for the last time.

He did not go back to the graveyard with it. Perhaps the blow of the coffin had affected him more than he had admitted to Sophie. He buried it instead at the foot of a pear tree in the children's garden, with an inscription between two plates of glass giving his son's brief biography. Every day, for over a week, he and Sophie worked with the children, raising a seat of turf under the pear tree, laying out flower beds and walks, all the while keeping their secret. Outwardly it seemed as if everyone had put off mourning, even they. Calmly Madame Dupin watched them from a bench and approved. She never walked. It was too great an effort for her small, tightly shod feet.

But she walked all of a mile on the midnight of September 17, in a rainstorm that blinded her more than the dark, in a pair of slippers and a dressing gown, to recover the body of her son, lying on the road off La Châtre. When she came to it, she found Deschartres bending over it and, tied to a tree, the ill-omened Leopardo who had thrown Maurice and killed him.

Again the ground was opened in the cemetery beyond the garden wall and Maurice filled the grave from which he had taken his son.

For a while the two women were more united in their grief than they had been by the death of Louis, but now their rivalry reasserted itself over Aurore, Maurice's only legitimate heir. The child felt the difference in their behavior without comprehending the reason. Her grandmother had only to ask Aurore to do something for Sophie to insist on the contrary. She became the pendulum between them, drawn to the one by a quiet force, compelled by the other with passionate demonstrations which, just as violently, turned to unreasonable punishments.

Only vaguely Aurore understood that her father was dead. Of death itself, of its finality, her child's mind had no conception. "Is Papa still dead today?" she would ask Sophie. Or, seeing her mother's sorrow, she cheered her with "When Papa is done being dead, he will come to see you again—won't he?"

She had seen him so seldom, that handsome soldier in his

21

brilliant uniform, who used to amuse her at the dinner table with the jumping rabbits he made out of the *serviettes*. She understood that he had been very dear to her *maman* and that somehow she, Aurore, was linked with him in the old woman's fancies. "Maurice," Madame Dupin would call to Aurore when they were alone. "Come here to me, my son."

Chapter III: Awakening of Wonder

FOR three years after the death of her husband Sophie remained at Nohant as her mother-in-law's guest, but not because of any growth of love between them. Each looked on Sophie's stay as a measure of expediency. Madame Dupin the elder wanted Aurore. She would educate her in a manner worthy of the mistress of Nohant and eventually make the child her heir. Of course, the eighteenth century rationalist argued, Sophie could keep Aurore. But what could she offer for the future, with her meager pension, which had also to provide for her other daughter Caroline? What connections did she have? What sort of marriage prospects could she muster for the descendant of Marshal de Saxe? True, Sophie had managed to marry well, in spite of her origin. But Aurore did not promise to develop into a beauty. An interesting woman, yes, and one with a quality that went deeper than beauty. But men, unfortunately, were attracted through the senses, and as for that other quality, call it soul, spirit, what you will, it remains as dull as a jewel in its veinstone without the light of education to make it shine. Would Sophie, on her small means, be able to undertake that intellectual mining and polishing?

Sophie was too shrewd not to feel the force of such argument. Hating the snobbery of her mother-in-law, she was still enough of a realist to see Aurore's advantage as well as her own and even Caroline's, poor child, who in her life of ten years had known almost as many boarding mistresses. If Sophie gave up Aurore, she could take back Caroline. They could live together in Paris which she loved with the passion of one brought up under the shadow of Notre Dame. Moreover, she would not really be giving up Aurore, for even Madame Dupin knew that no mother ever wholly surrenders her child. She would simply be placing Aurore with a superior kind of foster mother who would provide her with luxuries of breeding and education which she herself could never afford. Sometimes as she gazed at the child, sitting upon a hassock in one of her moods of abstraction, her eyes staring, her lips parted and her plump arms hanging limp, Sophie would think aloud: "Would Aurore really

23

be happier here than with me? I'm ignorant, I know, and I wouldn't have the means to teach her much of anything. Besides, if the old woman shouldn't see her constantly she might lose interest and leave her nothing. But then who can say that money and talents necessarily make for happiness?"

Such words had their effect upon the child. She was fond of her grandmother who spoiled her in her disciplined way, but she adored Sophie. It was from Sophie that she had learned her first nursery song about the white hen that laid a silver egg, and heard of fairies and enchanted princesses. Long before the formal gardens of Nohant had become her playground, it was Sophie who had shown her the wonders of Paris, the river and boats, the streets full of people, the shops, the Chinese shadow-play theater, the giants and the dwarfs on show, the military parades and the emperor's celebrations. Sophie had taught her the alphabet and told her about the saints and made her feel the peace of falling asleep to the words, "Dear God, I give Thee my heart." Sophie, too, it was, who understood her fits of *stupidity* and explained them to Madame Dupin. "Aurore has always been like that, ever since I can remember. It's not that she's stupid. Once she used to tell us all sorts of queer things that she made up in her moods. Now she's quiet and doesn't say a thing, but it doesn't mean that she thinks any less, as her poor father used to say."

"That may be," Madame Dupin answered. "But it is not good for a child to brood so much. . . . She's got to be shaken out of her apathy and distracted in spite of herself. We're overburdening her with our troubles. She feels them, even if she does not understand them."

The better to distract her, Madame Dupin found her a playmate in Ursule, the niece of Mademoiselle Julie, the chambermaid. There might have been another solution nearer home, in Caroline. But Madame Dupin, who accepted Hippolyte and gave him the privileges of a legitimate grandson, had only loathing for the inoffensive Caroline. Sophie felt the discrimination and, as with all her grievances, poured the new complaint into Aurore's ear. In the generous loyalty of childhood the little girl drew still closer to her mother. "Don't give me away to Maman for money," she cried, sobbing, after one of Sophie's outbursts.

"I daresay you'd rather be back in your garret and eat beans!" Mademoiselle Julie taunted her from the other camp.

Ursule, who had arrived suitably dressed in mourning to the bereaved but prosperous household, did not hesitate to take sides. Somewhere, somehow, she had picked up the phrase, "the golden age." Whenever she found Aurore in tears, torn between her mother and her grandmother, she would reason with the common sense of the poor, "It's rather nice to have a big house and a garden like this to play in, and a carriage and frocks, and good things to eat every day. How do you think you get them? Why, it's the *richness* that gives them to you. If you stay with your nice grandmamma you'll always have your golden age and your *richness*."

As a matter of fact the *richness* of Madame Dupin was only the residue of her late husband's original fortune. A dilettante, blessed or cursed with a plurality of talents, Dupin de Francueil had cultivated them all. He played the violin, he painted, he embroidered with greater skill than any woman. He reasoned with the best eighteenth century minds and patronized Jean Jacques Rousseau who rewarded him with a small theft, later acknowledged in the famous *Confessions*. Not content with playing the violin, Dupin also made his own instruments and furnished himself with a small orchestra. Reasoning alone failed to satisfy his ambitions; he must set down his deductions for posterity. Hence, at the time Rousseau had come into his life, Dupin de Francueil had a good part of a refutation of Montesquieu to read him. He was a patron of the opera and the Maecenas of poets and composers, who came to him in a constant stream. In a constant stream his substantial fortune flowed away. At his death Madame Dupin inherited a large circle of grateful friends and a much diminished capital. The Revolution diminished it still further.

Out of her funds she invested two hundred and thirty thousand livres in the substantial property of Nohant. It was solid and rooted. Not even the Terror had succeeded in shaking it. Four hundred years earlier an obscure nobleman, Charles de Villalumini, had raised a feudal castle there. When time and the wars had laid it in ruins, the Seigneur de Serennes built the house of Nohant on the foundations. The low, rambling building with its steep mansard roof had little beauty to recommend it. But the grounds, thanks to the pliability of nature and the love of gardens of the period, rewarded the enterprise of Madame Dupin. She tore down boundary walls that obstructed her view of the sunrise. She filled in moats and leveled hillocks. With the compass art of the century she measured alleys and lined them with trees, described precise flower beds, laid out beauty spots and populated them with gorgeous peacocks. She cut down trees that crowded the landscape. She planted poplar, chestnut, elm and pine for shade.

In spite of its vicissitudes, Nohant retained an anachronistic air, a feudal self-sufficiency scarcely affected by the upheavals that, like a social earthquake, had altered the whole structure of France. The village of Nohant and near-by La Châtre, might still have been part of the Middle Ages in habits and tradition, so little had they been aired by the winds of doctrine which had ripped away cobwebs of superstition and false thinking, and cleansed the social system of corruption—not without a rain of blood. Like many other isolated communities, they had seen the storm coming. Not being in the center of it, they had shaken this way and that during the worst of it, suffered casualties in life and property, but when it was over, settled back on their rock of custom. Nohant had seen the Revolution sweep past like a pageant, and remained faithful to its usages. After all, it was still a three days' journey on ill-made roads from Nohant's prefecture to Paris.

While clinging to the old, Madame Dupin kept a finger on the pulse of the times, and maintained an apartment in Paris on the Rue Neuve des Mathurins. The furnishings, strictly of the old era, decorated salon and bedchamber, and harmonized with her antique styles and tufted wig, topped by the lace-frilled cap which she wore even in bed. She held soirées for her aristocratic friends as if the Revolution had never been and anathematized the Corsican upstart, while watching with alert eye every change in the political horizon. She had remained strangely consistent in her inconsistencies. A reader of the Encyclopedists, she had intellectually accepted their theories of equality; in practice she adhered to established categories. She approved in the abstract the triumph of the masses; in her circle she condoned no overstepping of barriers. Intolerant of every infraction of the code of honor, she had a consistent leniency toward human frailty and, always, what her head condemned her heart forgave.

To Sophie alone she showed herself invariably rigorous, but only because in her daughter-in-law she saw a being dominated by passions she herself had never felt. A frigid woman whose first unconsummated marriage had been fraught with horror— (on the eve of her wedding she was admonished, *Never, never be alone with your husband!*) —she had only repugnance for any physical demonstration. Duty, rather than desire, had made her the mother of her only son. She therefore looked upon Sophie as the incarnation of everything she abhorred. Sophie was fire to her ice. The natural antipathy could never be overcome.

She must, however, keep the evil from influencing the child of her son. Strengthened by faith in Rousseau's *Émile*, she hoped to succeed by the right education. For the present she needed Sophie in her scheme for the child. Two or three years, and the fledgling would emancipate itself. Then she, Madame Dupin, would be everything to Aurore. Meanwhile she put Aurore, as long ago Maurice, in Deschartres' care.

The old man grudgingly accepted his charge. He had never

26

taught "a female" before, as he did not believe in the education of women, and he felt he had fallen on evil days. Of what use to a girl were the treasures of Latin and Greek, philosophy and his cherished science? Aurore, fortunately, was still too young to learn anything but her letters, which could be taught her by the ladies; therefore he concentrated on her health, starting out on the traditional principle of a sound mind in a sound body.

The poor child had a wretched time of it. If she looked pale, if she showed no enthusiasm for the rough games with Hippolyte, if she refused a dish at table, Deschartres rushed for his sovereign remedy, an emetic. For some reason, perhaps because of the olive skin she had inherited from her mother, Deschartres concluded Aurore suffered from bile and made it his duty to rid her of it at any cost—to her. Sophie, on the other hand, believed in powerful vermifuges which she administered on her own account and from her private knowledge of household medicine. Between the cures of the two, Aurore suffered more than from disease, and early developed a stoicism toward pain that finally rescued her from their hands. Both claimed the cure and both desisted, satisfied.

It was Sophie, whose barbarous orthography horrified the literary Madame Dupin who, on Deschartres' unwillingness, taught Aurore to write. The great man agreed to take on the cultivation once the ground was prepared. Long before the Spanish journey Sophie had begun to teach Aurore and Clotilde their alphabet, and enjoyed repeating how Aurore stubbornly insisted, "I can say *A* but I don't think I can say *B*." She resumed her teaching where she had left off. But Aurore became impatient practicing the light and dark strokes of the formal calligraphy—Sophie made up for her lack of grammar by the beauty of her handwriting—and devised her own method by copying print, learning to read and write at the same time.

Now the magical world of childhood opened before her, the world she had heard of from Sophie but which became hers the moment she turned over the pages of a book. Greedily she devoured the tales of Perrault and Madame d'Aulnoy. Over and over she read about the Blue Bird and Hop O'My Thumb, the Green Serpent and the Happy Warrior, making them part of her imaginative life until she knew them better than Hippolyte or Ursule. Later, in a book of Greek mythology, she came upon another continent of what to her was the same world. Beings of whom her mother had never told populated this realm, nymphs and zephyrs and goat-footed fauns, dryads who lived in trees, Echo, mocking and invisible, whom she had discovered for herself when she had called and an unseen playmate answered on the balcony of Godoy's palace. She looked for them, and her stimulated imagination found them in the still pools after rain, or crouching behind the rock piles, rustling among the reeds, running their fingers through her hair in the wind, breathing their breath on her body in the summer sun. She recognized them in the wallpaper of her bedroom where they twined, dryads and bacchantes, and strange naked men beckoning with goblets, in a static dance among the vine leaves. At night, as the mice scampered behind the linen-lined paper, the figures came alive. But her fancy had made them live long before this, in marvelous adventures of her own creation.

As always in the imaginative child, the borderland vanished between dream and reality and the figments of one mingled with the characters of the other without doing violence to credibility. There were times when Maman and Sophie, Deschartres and even Hippolyte became phantoms of her mind. The gentle Nohant donkey whom Maman had retired and allowed the freedom of the place—was it not a creature of fairy tale? Surely, no ordinary donkey had that knack of raising the latch and finding his way to the loveliest room in the house— at least to the child—to dream in bliss, its nose over Maman's powder box. And the peacocks, spreading their fanlike tails—she knew about them, the children of Argus with a hundred eyes.

Then there was the rock garden they built, she and Hippolyte and Ursule, under Sophie's direction. What storybook palaces rose up under their hands in their fanciful landscapes! Here, from the colored stones of the stream bed, they built the castle of the Sleeping Beauty, there a magic grotto peopled with shy beings who would not come out, even for Aurore, but whom nevertheless she knew. Under those mosses, transplanted from oak roots, the elves danced by moonlight. A fairy curled in each flower cup at night. Aurore saw them there; she sometimes made others see them. Only Maman would not be drawn into the play. Whenever she was there the castles tumbled and turned to heaps of stone. Maman refused to see anything except with her eyes, always clear and sharp and matter-of-fact. Aurore never forgot the day when she ceremoniously escorted Maman to inspect the fish pool and cascade that Sophie magically made to play with three strokes of her willow wand. "Why, that's only Nurse hiding behind there with the watering pot, making that waterfall," she said. "And what's this pool?" She laughed a mocking little laugh at Sophie. "If it isn't our old lye basin!"

But Madame Dupin wove a magic of her own for her grand-child after grief over her son's death had abated and the period of formal mourning had passed. (It was never to be over in her heart.) For two years her harpsichord had been shrouded and as silent as a coffin. Now she would occasionally shut herself up alone with it in the small Louis XVI drawing room and commune with the spirits that had once brought joy to her youth. Thin sighs of music would then come through the closed door. The harpsichord had been recalled to life and the whole house breathed again.

One day she took Aurore in with her and played. Her fingers were stiff from age and its ailments, but the scores had been too often read for her to falter. Pergolesi, Piccini, Gluck, Mozart —she played them all, and to Aurore's amazement, sang the arias in a sweet, quavering voice that filled the child with the same strange sadness she had known when for the first time she heard her playmates singing the old song:

> *Nous n'irons plus au bois,*
> *Les lauriers sont coupés . . .*

She had then but dimly understood the words, yet that wood, whose laurels were cut down, became the first landscape of her imaginary land.

Madame Dupin began to teach her music by making her feel its spell. While Aurore sat on the floor with the dog, Brillant, Maman would play for hours, finding nothing too difficult for the child's comprehension. Aurore was transported. Here was another magic, a magic of sound that gave her as much joy as the tales of Perrault and the stories of the Greeks. The words Maman sang, most of them from the Italian of Porpora and Piccini, had no meaning and therefore held all meaning for the child, leading her to the melancholy laurel wood. She loved her grandmother then, and found her the most wonderful being in the world, especially when Maman allowed her to join her in the duet:

> *Non mi dir bel idol mio,*
> *Non mi dir ch'io son ingrato.*

The sound of the Italian thrilled her as much as the music.

Except for Hippolyte and Ursule and the children of the peasants, Aurore saw none but Madame Dupin's friends who spoke to her formally as if she were their age, and whom she had to address in the third person. "Would Madame la Comtesse like to walk in the garden?—Monsieur le Comte is very kind to pick up my gloves,"—those gloves which the seven-year-old had to wear like a dowager.

Among the old folk there was one Aurore liked, the portly, white-haired, jolly Abbé de Beaumont—Uncle Beaumont, as she called him, after sensing a family relationship. The Abbé de Beaumont, in fact, was a half brother of Madame Dupin's, another child of that same *dame de l'Opéra*, Mademoiselle Vic-

toire de Verrières, by the Marshal de Turenne. Victoire, possibly
to live up to her adopted name, had favored military men.

The world spun round when Uncle Beaumont arrived, the
cooks in the kitchen—for he loved nothing better than food
except his bachelor freedom—the chambermaids whom he was
not too much the abbé to pinch, the gardeners who brought
him their best produce. It became a round of feasting and good
times, an unseasonable carnival which for a few days gave life
to the sad house. Sophie, who always attracted men, got along
well with the old abbé, and spared him the merciless satire she
had for Madame Dupin's female retinue, too ready with tongue
and claw toward an alluring and still young member of their
sex. Aurore was delighted with him. In his quaint, well-powdered
pigeon's-wing peruke, dressed in his black satin breeches, silver-
buckled shoes and purple quilted dressing gown, he made a
companion piece for Madame Dupin. Smaller, they would have
looked charming on a mantel shelf.

What Madame Dupin had of austerity melted to human kindness in her brother, that human kindness in turn becoming
tolerance which bordered dangerously upon license. Live and
let live, he might have cried with the liberated spirits of his age.
But he reserved for himself the additional provision that he live
well. He carried that well-being so much with him that it spread
like a benevolent contagion. During one of his visits at Nohant
he accomplished the miracle of organizing the household in a
celebration honoring Madame Dupin. In it Hippolyte and
Ursule declaimed Racinian couplets for which the abbé had
burned several cruses of midnight oil, Aurore danced a bolero,
and Deschartres, the flint-faced Deschartres, played the flageolet,
one of his accomplishments. Most wonderful of all, Madame
Dupin laughed for the first time since her son's death.

Although time can soften sorrow, only death can heal incom-
patibility. At the end of three outwardly restrained but secretly
turbulent years, the chatelaine of Nohant made a momentous
decision. The time had come for her to be sole guardian of
Aurore. Sophie must go.

Madame Dupin had not expected Sophie to accede without
a struggle. But with the calm confidence of the intellectual in
the final victory of will over passion, Madame Dupin bided her
time. She knew Sophie. She had observed her with the detachment of a scientist, had seen the emotional woman's veering
from one extreme to the other, now insolent, now repentant,
now prodigal to extravagance, now counting the pennies like a
miser. Money, Madame Dupin had noted, was to Sophie another
outlet for her exigent nature. Money, therefore, must enter into
the final settlement. Then there were other exigencies, of the

flesh. Sophie's infernal temperament demanded its satisfactions. Madame Dupin did not like to dwell on them. In Paris Sophie would doubtless make some arrangement satisfactory to her. Madame Dupin could only hope it would be discreet.

In the end everything turned out as she had anticipated. For the consideration of a specified allowance, Sophie signed over Aurore's guardianship to Madame Dupin and left Nohant for Paris. From Sophie's point of view leaving Aurore had been a sacrifice no other mother could have borne. Her suffering did not matter. Aurore would be a lady.

Chapter IV: Aurore in Search of a God

"AURORE, stand up straight. You're holding yourself like a hunchback.—Aurore, you walk like a peasant.—Ah, my child, you've mislaid your gloves again. You're too big a girl to do such things, Aurore."

In that tempered voice which not even a cataclysm would have raised, Madame Dupin kept reminding Aurore of her new dignity as her grandmother's ward and heir. No more whispering in corners henceforth with Ursule; she must remember Ursule was a servant. No more horseplay with Hippolyte. No more loitering in the kitchen, either, to babble with the help. Moreover, she must insist on their addressing her in the formal *vous*. The future mistress of Nohant must learn to make herself respected.

"Here you are, amuse yourself quietly," Madame Dupin would say, taking Aurore into her sitting room and giving her an album of engravings to study.

In the thick atmosphere of the room whose windows never let in sun or air for fear of what ills they might bring to the delicate old woman, Aurore gasped for breath. The smell of powder and patchouli made her sick. The closeness gave her headaches. It was as if Maman had shut her up in a quilted, perfumed box, the sort of box she made of the Nohant house, of the whole world, with her frail health and her rigid prejudices. Aurore was terrified that she might become like her. Already she had the migraines that laid Maman inert on her bed, looking like a corpse, and blinded the child with their dizzying pain. There was something of the dead about Maman's stillness. She was pale; the blood was sluggish in her. Whenever she had to be bled the doctor had a hard time drawing the blood from her torpid veins. "Amuse yourself quietly. Don't make any noise." To the sensitive child the words came as a command to learn to be dead. As she sat immobile, sometimes alone, sometimes at her grandmother's feet, the song of a bird, a dog's bark reaching her from the world outside, brought tears of envy. She would gladly have changed places with that sparrow, that dog.

She longed for Sophie and the longing intensified her love

to a championship of her mother, who became the victim of the tyrannical old woman. It was Maman who had driven Sophie away, Maman who, whenever they went to Paris, forbade Aurore's seeing Caroline. Even when Aurore visited Sophie, so that, as her grandmother said, she could see for herself the way she might have had to live, Madame Dupin made sure that Caroline would not be there. The prohibition only made Aurore fix with abnormal yearning on her mother and half sister. Their little apartment, far from the Faubourg Saint-Germain of Maman's aristocratic friends, became her rainbow's end.

At Nohant she marked the months before another trip to Paris. Grandmother traveled a great deal for those times, making the long trip back and forth in a huge berlin without once complaining of her health. The coach was equipped like a house. One had only to reach out and everything came to one's hand—food and bonbons, decks of cards, books, perfumes, for Grandmother could never travel without her smelling bottles. There were blankets and pillows, foot warmers, hassocks. Aurore wondered whether there were also pistols, the roads were so dark and dangerous. Everyone seemed nervous, especially toward sundown, and shouted to the postilion to whip up the horses toward the next town. It was most frightening crossing the long stretch of forest at Orléans. The branches met overhead, making a weird dimness even by daylight. Every moment one expected armed robbers to leap out from behind the black tree trunks. The women pretended to be very brave, but Mademoiselle Julie drew closer to Madame Dupin on their seat.

"Robberies aren't so frequent here nowadays," said Madame Dupin on one of their trips, "considering what they were before the Revolution. . . . Then the bandits committed so many murders that the authorities showed in a peculiar way that justice was done. After the robbers were caught and sentenced, they were hanged on the trees along the road, over the very spot where they had committed their crime. If you made the trip often enough you got to know those corpses and became acquainted with the new ones, which proved that the horrible examples didn't do much good, after all. I remember seeing a woman, one winter, with her long black hair blown about in the wind and the ravens wheeling round her, quarreling. . . ."

Aurore shivered with horror. She was never to cross the Orléans forest without being haunted by that wild hair in the winter wind.

From 1811 to 1814 they were often in Paris. The mischievous Hippolyte was sent to school on *demi-pension,* and the servants at Nohant enjoyed peace from his experiments, performed too literally to demonstrate the efficacy of Deschartres' teachings.

Now they could put up their *pot-au-feu* without having it hurled into the air by an exploding log into which Hippolyte had stuffed gunpowder—to study the theory of volcanoes, as he explained. They could go to bed without the smell of smoke in their nostrils, as on the night he set the house on fire by throwing flaming brands up the chimney as a tribute to the infernal deities. He gave reasons enough for raising the devil except the right one, the natural irruption of his high spirits against the unnatural restraints imposed upon him, as upon Aurore.

The Paris school curbed him somewhat. Encouraged by signs of improvement, Madame Dupin engaged a dancing master for the two children. Several times a week Aurore tripped and pirouetted while the young oaf dislocated his legs mastering the five dance positions, and strained them in the opposite direction the moment the ballet master was out of sight. Later, when his enthusiastic *changements de pieds,* his *battements* and *entrechats* brought down the ceiling, Madame Dupin decided to leave him to his own natural grace.

Aurore's education was not neglected. At Nohant, Deschartres, overcoming his misogyny by pretending she was another Maurice, taught her grammar and Latin, but as she showed no love for the dead language, abandoned it quickly. He opened her mind to first principles, introduced her to history and mathematics and, best of all, turned her loose in his library, making sure, however, that the "forbidden" books were all beyond her reach on the top shelf. Of course those were the first she read with Hippolyte, and disappointing books they were, on medicine and anatomy. Even a black letter tome which gave explicit directions on how to raise the devil, turned out to be a hoax. In spite of the circles and triangles Hippolyte chalked upon the floor, in spite of terrifying words cried out three times and three times more, Satan showed neither hoof nor tail, and Deschartres was not carried away by his diabolic majesty, as the children had carefully planned.

Aurore also studied music with the organist of La Châtre, after Madame Dupin had wakened her love for it. Monsieur Gayard, however, took a strictly practical view of the subject. Young ladies had to have accomplishments, such as playing the harpsichord, and he accordingly set about the business of "accomplishing" Madame Dupin's granddaughter. Every lesson day he appeared with a sheaf of show pieces under his arm, placed them on the music rack and told Aurore to go on and play. He was an old man, bored by a too thorough familiarity with the compositions. While Aurore played he sat by the fire munching prunes and hazelnuts, and then fell quietly asleep. Aurore did not disturb him, especially when, as it sometimes happened, she would find among the musical inanities some delightful page of Mozart, Pleyel, Steibelt or Clementi.

She learned also to play the harp, but singing, which she loved best of all, Madame Dupin neglected. Aurore made up for the lack by devising singing games for herself in the manner of an opera heroine. "Oh, pretty butterflies, come light upon my flowers," she would trill in the garden. "Grow, grow, lovely grass, from the seeds I sow." In moments of longing for Sophie, she wailed in a minor key: "Sweet Mother, dost thou hear? I pine and sigh for thee."

To round out her education, she was given lessons in drawing by a Mademoiselle Greuze who claimed to be the daughter of the painter. Aurore had a natural facility with her pencil and won Mademoiselle Greuze's praise, but she had no love for it. What she enjoyed most was to escape to that inner life which the separation from her mother and her growing unhappiness with her grandmother, forced upon her.

She was undergoing the first ferment of adolescence, doubly disturbing in her emotional disquiet, when she came across two books that were to throw her more than ever upon her imagination. The *Iliad* brought back to her, in a nobler form, the world of the Greeks, a world in which men walked with gods and sometimes became gods. *Jerusalem Delivered* vitalized for her the Christian epic. Like the other children of Berry, she had been prepared for her first communion— (Nohant was fervently Catholic and Madame Dupin believed in exposing her ward to all experience)—but as she understood nothing of the catechism, she relieved her grandmother of any fear of conversion. Homer and Tasso gave Aurore a religion and a god.

Corambé, her god-man or man-god, came to her in a semi-mystical revelation, and was born full-panoplied like Minerva from the brow of Jove. He was as radiant as the angel Gabriel, as beautiful as Apollo, less holy than Christ, more spiritual than Homer's gods. He was young and of a noble perfection that was nonetheless human, and he was tolerant, more tolerant than the priests described Christ, who forbade loving the gods and philosophers of antiquity. But Corambé had the purity and mercy of Christ. He had, moreover, an extraordinary versatility, and could turn himself into a woman whenever he chose. When George explained Corambé years later, she wrote: "The being I had loved best was a woman, my mother." Corambé had therefore to be a woman too, if only occasionally.

Once Aurore had created her god, she raised him an altar in a secret place in the wood bordering the garden. Only the rarest stones, the most delicate ferns and mosses were found worthy of her deity. Whenever she could escape, Aurore went to com-

35

mune with Corambé. One day, however, a little girl from the village followed her and saw the altar. "Ah, mam'selle, what a sweet little crib for the infant Jesus!" she exclaimed. The shrine lost all charm on its discovery. As painstakingly as she had built it Aurore now tore it down. Corambé henceforth lived only in her mind as the godlike hero of unwritten adventures, as the inner voice guiding her through her troubled growth.

The strain of her divided loyalties tormented her. Nohant became a prison and her grandmother its keeper. Madame Dupin, grieved at the girl's misery without sympathizing with its cause, humbled her pride and took Sophie as an ally. Obviously, Aurore still needed her mother. The weaning was longer and more painful than she had anticipated, but it must succeed at last if Sophie played her part. During the summers, therefore, Sophie stayed as guest at Nohant. In the winter, she visited *en famille* at Uncle Beaumont's Paris apartment, with Madame Dupin and Aurore. On Sundays she had Aurore to herself in her apartment on Rue Duphot. Sophie's task was to convince Aurore of her fortunate situation with her grandmother; her reward an increase of her allowance.

The visits to Uncle Beaumont were made bearable to Aurore only because Sophie was there, the only real person among a collection of grotesques, the *vieilles comtesses* and the worldly men with nothing spiritual about their habits or conversation, who were addressed as Abbé This and Abbé That. During the interminable dinners, prepared by Uncle Beaumont's *cordon bleu,* each dish savored, discussed and appreciated by these puppets in their pointed shoes and powdered wigs, Aurore would have perished of boredom had she not had leave to wander about Uncle Beaumont's salon. She visited it like a museum, a lighted taper in her hand, in the permanent dusk of a room that was used only on state occasions. The Louis XIV pieces glowed for a moment in their gold frames and brocade, and the portraits came to life, to return to their silence and darkness when Aurore shut the door behind her.

After dinner the guests sat down to their card games, leaving Aurore to find her own amusement. Sometimes she turned the pages of a book of engravings, exchanging smiles with Sophie, or she examined Uncle Beaumont's collection of snuff boxes, exquisite gold and ivory trinkets, painted with frolicsome nymphs unembarrassed by drapery. Most of the time she observed the old people as if they were characters in a play: Madame de Marlière, whose husband, the general, had died on the scaffold, a noisy, sharp-chinned witch who cheated at cards and kicked Madame de Maleteste's poodle under the table; Madame de Pardaillan, a mournful Versailles shepherdess who always called Aurore "poor little one"; Madame de Béranger and Madame de Ferrières, so snobbish about their birth that each waited for the other to address her first; Abbé Pernon whose face was a playground for oddly distributed warts; the Chevalier de Vinci who had such a violent nervous tic that it hurled his wig forward over his nose, sometimes almost into his soup at table; Abbé d'Andrezel who wore a spencer over his habit.

These men, so different from the good curé who had prepared her for her communion, puzzled her alert mind. "If you are not a curé," she spoke out one night to the Abbé d'Andrezel, "where is your wife? If you are a curé, where then is your mass?"

Everyone thought her observation caustic and witty and had a good laugh over it, particularly Madame Dupin who found in Aurore's irreverence encouragement for her rationalistic teachings. The child studied that assemblage of relics and remembered. Many were to reappear later in the novels of George Sand.

Very different were the hours Aurore spent with Sophie. In her somber costumes cut down from Grandmother Dupin's outworn toilettes, the despair of Sophie who complained that they made Aurore look like a little old woman, she gadded about gaily, stopping to watch the trained dogs performing on the boulevards, admiring the shopwindows, making fun of Madame de Marlière and the other ancient dames. "She says Mistouflé when she means Mephistopheles," shrieked Aurore, bold in her rapidly acquired learning. "The other night she called an *épithalame* an *épitre à l'âme.*"

"Those museum pieces," laughed Sophie.

Pretty as a figurine in her trim, short-waisted gowns, Sophie was embarrassed by the drabness of her daughter and tried to bring her up to date by combing her hair in the Chinese fashion, a style that was then the rage. The hair, drawn tightly up to the top of the cranium till the eyes slanted, was twisted into a knot, making the head look like a brioche. Aurore endured agonies with every lift of the brows, and horrified the aesthetic Madame Dupin; but for Sophie's sake she remained oriental until the next stylistic fad.

Because Aurore was growing pale and thin, Madame Dupin kept her longer in the country. Her own health was rapidly failing. She had the most serious warning one day at dinner when she fell into a dead faint and remained unconscious for more than an hour. Deschartres who treated her spoke solemnly of a stroke. The recovery left her more exacting and less patient, yet morbidly brooding over Aurore's health. She sent for Sophie.

"Oh, Mother, darling," Aurore wrote Sophie, the winter of 1815, "I kiss you, I await you, I long for you and I die of impatience to see you here. Goodness, how you worry about me! I'm in wonderful health."

The two women watched each other's empire over Aurore more jealously than ever, but they kept to their bargain. Whenever Aurore pleaded to be taken away to Paris, Sophie reasoned with her. "I don't think I can take you. Your grandmother would reduce my allowance to fifteen hundred francs—"

"Fifteen hundred francs! That's a lot of money," cried Aurore.

"Oh, you don't know. It's hardly enough for me and Caroline. We'd be so poor that if you came to live with us you'd soon be sick of it and long for your Nohant and your fifteen thousand a year."

"Never! Never! We'd be poor, but we'd be together."

"You don't know what poverty means for a young girl," Sophie said to her another time. "I know, and I don't want you and Caroline to go through what I went through when I found myself alone and starving at fourteen. . . ."

The untold story stirred the generous impulses of the growing girl. She almost blamed her grandmother for having so much while Sophie, all the Sophies in the world, had so little.

Now she adored her mother for having suffered the privations of the poor, and yearned for that poverty to make her more deserving of being her child. This time when Sophie left, Aurore's whole heart went with her, and she made her choice in her unhappy passion.

Mademoiselle Julie who hated Sophie, watched jealously the influence she had upon Aurore and threatened "to tell" Madame Dupin. Aurore's listlessness was goaded to open rebellion. She refused to study, she scarcely touched anything at meals. One day, when for the hundredth time Mademoiselle Julie flung at her that she deserved to be sent back to her mother, the tormented girl exploded: "Send me back! That's what I want more than anything in the world. . . . Send me back to her! I love her and will always love her. Now go and tell my grandmother!"

It was exactly what Mademoiselle Julie did, in the officious partisanship of the servant who knows on what side her bread is buttered. Madame Dupin was struck to the heart. She had lost. Once again, the woman who had taken from her the son she idolized, robbed her of him in her grandchild. She became bitter and vengeful. This time she would not lose without a cruel, a covert triumph. As she was sick and confined to her bed, she ordered Aurore to remain in her room for three days and not come out even for meals, or try to communicate with her in any way. She needed time to think. Aurore must be made to realize in solitude the depth of her ungratefulness.

"You'll never see your grandmother again," Mademoiselle

Julie reported. "She has given you up, since you detest her."

Aurore, stubbornly defiant, made no attempt to justify herself except to say that she loved her grandmother, but loved her mother more. "You have lied to Maman."

She kept to her room while Madame Dupin issued orders from hers. The servants were thrown into consternation, feeling sorry for Aurore yet not daring to disobey their mistress. For three days Aurore reflected on her situation and hoped that Corambé would guide her. But Corambé remained silent, like Maman, like Deschartres. Her expiation over, her door was unlocked. She went to her grandmother's room. She knocked. She was not admitted.

Aurore spent the day in the woods helping an old peasant woman to gather faggots, and at the end of her labors, she ate a crust of black bread which the woman gave her. In her weariness and exaltation, she took it as a symbol. The bread of poverty was not too bitter, after all.

At last Madame Dupin sent for her. Aurore found her propped up in bed on a heap of cushions, her lace cap with its rosette on her carefully combed hair, her special bed rings on her fingers, her snuffbox within reach. She looked hard and cold, and had no greeting for Aurore who fell on her knees beside the bed and took the old woman's hands.

"Stay there on your knees and listen to what I have to say," she began in a voice Aurore had never heard. "Listen carefully, for you've never heard what I have to tell you and you'll never hear it from my lips again."

Then without pity for the child who shuddered at the terrible words, Madame Dupin told the story of her one great love, the love of her son; she told how that son was taken from her by Sophie, and went from there to a rehearsal of Sophie's life. The narrative choked her, the words broke in her agitation, but they issued hard and cold in the final accusation: "Your mother was a lost woman and you are a blind child, bent on throwing yourself into the abyss."

Aurore mastered herself enough to rise and leave her grandmother without a word, but once out of hearing of that merciless voice, she fell into convulsions and had to be carried to her room. She was completely shattered. Many years later, when she told the story of her life, she was still embittered by the hurt Madame Dupin had inflicted on her idealized love of Sophie. "She was pitiless and without intelligence," she wrote of her grandmother's deed. "For there are in the lives of the poor temptations, heartbreaks and disasters that the rich will never understand. . . . She should have told the whole story, given the reasons for my mother's misfortunes—the corruption of the rich, the harsh bigotry of public opinion which will not take back a sinner nor accept expiation."

When she saw the futility of expecting an immediate reformation, Madame Dupin took a drastic step. If Aurore would not stay with her, neither would she be permitted to go to her mother. A return now would destroy the work of years. It would mean hurling the headstrong girl into the abyss with her own hands. She therefore turned her over to a third party—no individual who might aggravate the already complex emotional situation, but an impersonal institution. She had to swallow many prejudices to make her choice, but she made it.

During the winter of 1816–1817, therefore, Madame Dupin risked the long journey to Paris in her feeble health, to try to save Aurore. The girl's belongings had already been packed in a trunk, except for an amaranth-colored serge dress, like a uniform, which she commanded Aurore to put on. Soon a fiacre called for them, drove through the center of Paris and past it till it reached a cluster of old houses like a fortified town of another day, on the Rue des Fossés-Saint-Victor. It was Les Anglaises, no longer the prison it had been during the Terror, but the convent of the English nuns.

Madame Dupin waited in the dim parlor with Aurore. Half an hour later, Madame Dupin left alone. Until the spring of 1820 Aurore was to remain at Les Anglaises, one of a hundred or more girls enrolled in the convent school under the tutelage of the mother superior, Madame Canning, and her small staff of English sisters.

Les Anglaises had an interesting history. At the height of Cromwell's power, thousands of Catholics fled across the Channel and, in Paris alone, formed numerous communities to worship in their faith, and to pray that the Protestants be made to see the light again. Les Anglaises, founded by Augustinian nuns, began with one small building and chapel, to shelter the self-exiled women of God. When Queen Henriette of France, the wife of the unhappy Charles I, came to pray in its chapel, under whose stones Catholic martyrs were already buried, and when, with her son James II she cured the scrofulous by the royal touch, the convent gained in fame and proportions. During the Revolution which swept away many another holy place, it survived, although put to secular and unexpected uses. At one time, it is likely that the three chief persons in Aurore's life had found themselves simultaneously within its walls—Madame Dupin by order of the revolutionary tribunal, Sophie for singing an anti-popular song, and Maurice, then a fifteen-year-old boy, as a visitor.

When Aurore entered it, the convent was a congeries of buildings of various periods, set among flower and kitchen gardens, and not too far removed from the common life of the city for its sounds to penetrate the sacred precincts in the oaths and bawdy songs of the farmers taking their produce to market. Of the whole population, two-thirds were English, Scottish and Irish Catholics. The rest, like Aurore, were French girls whose guardians wished to protect them against the perils of the world during their most impressionable years, and at the same time expose them to foreign culture. Both French and English were spoken; but at stipulated hours, perhaps for the benefit of the French girls, conversations were carried on only in English. The custom of afternoon tea assumed almost ritualistic importance. Only the best-behaved students were ever allowed to drink it with the sisters.

It was not easy for the nuns to make young ladies out of their charges who, with the clannishness of the young, formed groups, the most popular of which and the most assertive, consisted of the *diables,* the devils or emancipated ones whose symbol of emancipation was their nightcap, imposed as a punishment during the day, but sported like a liberty bonnet. From the beginning Aurore was never without hers. She wore it in sullen rebellion, as a tribute to Sophie, after she threw in her lot with the *diables,* whose ringleader, a handsome, golden-haired Irish tomboy, initiated her with a tirade that would have created a commotion at the Théâtre Français.

"So mademoiselle is called Dupin? *Du pain*—some bread," punned the Irish Mary. "She is called Aurore? Rising Sun? Oh, what beautiful names! And oh, what a face! She has the head of a horse on the body of a chicken. Oh, Rising Sun, let me prostrate myself before you! Oh, I would be the sunflower to greet your first rays!"

The two became inseparable and wherever they were there was sure to be mischief. The nuns rechristened Aurore Madcap. The girls added Calepin to it because of the notebooks Aurore invariably carried to jot down ideas in flight. For now, not content with composing romances in her head, she needed evidence of her mind's activity in black and white. Corambé, neo-pagan and neo-Christian, gave way to a down-to-earth hero, Fitz Gerald, whose adventures Aurore would read to a select few. Fitz became so tediously virtuous in Aurore's efforts to make her worldly hero worthy of a still more tiresome heroine, that the girls yawned in her face. She abandoned Fitz Gerald and started another novel, a pastoral one in her homesickness for the country. For Madame Dupin would not let her come home even on vacation—not to interrupt her studies, she said.

In the not too healthful seclusion of the convent Aurore passed

41

from girlhood to womanhood. Her dull black eyes, larger than ever in her thin face, missed nothing of what went on about her. She wondered why Sister Marie-Xavier, the most beautiful woman there, had that cadaverous pallor and a devouring sorrow which she took no trouble to conceal. She was always ailing, always tormented by contrary moods that made her now love one ardently and then, in a moment, turn as cold as the grave. The girls said she had taken the veil from disappointed love. Then there was Sister Mary Alicia Spiring, young, lively, attractive, always the center of an adoring circle, the most popular nun there. Why had she turned away from the world? And Mademoiselle D—, fat untidy, cruel, vindictive, who listened behind doors and made the girls kiss the ground in penance, a violent nature craving to be loved yet bristling with antipathies: what had brought her to the convent? "You look to me like a very dissipated person," she threw at Aurore the first time she saw her, placing her at once in the category of her aversions. In frustrated maternity Mademoiselle D— made a pet of the youngest there, a thin, unhappy, sullen little girl whom she spoiled and tormented. Day and night they could hear the child shrieking hysterically.

In their concern for the spiritual welfare of their wards, the realistic nuns did not forget that most of them would have no vocation but marriage and therefore prepared them for society by teaching them "the graces." They selected Monsieur Abraham, ex-teacher of grace to the long-dead Marie Antoinette, for the girls' instruction. Aurore took her lessons in dancing and deportment with the rest, seeing in Monsieur Abraham another relic of a dead world, like the grandees of Spain whose portraits had looked on her childhood, like the splendidly garbed prince, then King Murat—executed by the Bourbons after the Eagle fell at Waterloo—like Uncle Beaumont and Grandmother Dupin.

To the dancing master in his silk breeches and lace jabots, a diamond on his finger and a kit in his hand, with his eighty years etched in fine lines on his face, the world was still the gay one of his youth, when courts were resplendent and when the ambition of every well-born damsel was to be presented to Their Majesties.

"I am the king," he would say, impersonating the unhappy monarch who had lost his head. Or, with more delicate grace, "I am the queen. Now, Mademoiselle Mary, and you, Mademoiselle Aurore, make your entrance. And now, a beautiful *révérence.*" He put as much heart into his lessons as if he expected the girls to make their bow in court. The people, the emperor, Louis XVIII, the new parliamentary government—what were they but shadows to the one reality he had known?

As Aurore played less and read more, she lost interest in her *diablerie* and spent most of her leisure time in her room at the top of one of the dormitories which her reformation had won for her. It was nothing but a cell, six by ten feet, furnished like a hermit's hut with a wooden pallet and a rush-bottom chair, except that in a corner glowed the jeweled frame of Aurore's Louis XV harp which Madame Dupin had given her. She did not play it often, for in the bustling routine of the convent she had hardly time enough for her reading.

As it was, the literary fare of the good nuns offered little variety, but it gave Aurore what she wanted. The life of St. Augustine vied in interest with the biography of St. Teresa, and that in turn gave place to the examples of St. Simeon the Stylite in her hunger for hagiographies. She burned with St. Teresa, she cultivated endurance with St. Simeon. However unworthy she might be, the fifteen-year-old girl told herself, she was not yet so lost that she could not strive for holiness.

And she strove for it with a will, fasting, disciplining herself according to the examples in her reading, and yearning for a haircloth to wear against her flesh. But since the age of haircloths had passed, she mortified her body by wearing round her neck a splintery filigree chaplet that bit into her flesh with every move. She gloried in the circlet of scars carved there by her devotion. At dusk, when the nuns had their private office of prostration before the altar, she would slip into the chapel and, hidden by the dimness, thrill mystically as one after the other the ghostly figures, shrouded in black capes, lay upon the ground in solemn humility. Then she would go back to her room and lose herself in meditation till the material self melted away and her soul quivered, ecstatic.

She went to such extremes of holiness and grew so haggard and gloomy, that the nuns began to worry about her and consulted the father confessor, Abbé de Prémord. They had had sudden conversions before, but never one so fanatical that, instead of serving as an example, it frightened the rest of the girls. Moreover, they were mistrustful of the suddenness with which the most inveterate wearer of the *bonnet de nuit* had started growing angelic wings.

Madame Dupin, too, who came to see her on visiting days when she was in Paris, at first with one or another of her countess friends, and later more and more frequently with her countess friends' sons, grew concerned at the lean face and heavy-lidded eyes, and most of all, at Aurore's indifference to the obvious attractions of the young men. She had not given up the struggle for Aurore. Knowing her days were numbered, she would have wished her grandchild safely married and so forever out of Sophie's control. She spoke her anxieties to the nuns.

Every month the girls made their confession to Abbé de Prémord. When Aurore's turn came, hers was in the manner of a heart to heart talk with the sage man whose cassock, worn before and after the Revolution, retained its semblance to the scholar's gown. He was, indeed, a learned Jesuit, a keen mind and an understanding heart human enough to admit humor.

"My child," he said, after listening to Aurore's account of mortification and austerities, "I impose as your penance—" He paused as Aurore waited for her crowning test. "I impose as your penance that you return to the pastimes and innocent amusements of your years."

Reluctantly she obeyed, and so far overcame her holiness as to make a scenario from Molière's *Le Malade Imaginaire,* which the girls acted with great success under her direction. Of course no one else at the convent knew that the scenes which provoked such laughter, that the droll characters and amusing situations, derived from a dramatist whom the nuns were forbidden to read. But Aurore knew her deception forgiven by their guileless enjoyment.

She had but a short time left at Les Anglaises, for Madame Dupin had intimated her intention of taking her back to Nohant. Aurore suffered from an intense melancholy for which she could find no reason. She still vaguely thought of becoming a nun, as vaguely envisioned a conventional life, whether at Nohant or in Paris she could not tell. It was as if she were in a state of suspension which her will had no power to affect. Like a heroine of romance, she would take her harp in her ineffable emotion, and, looking down on the roofs of Paris as the swallows flitted in the twilight, sing her wordless sadness.

Unknown to her, she had begun to suffer from the malady of the century.

Chapter V: The Malady of the Century

MADAME DUPIN looked at the young lady Aurore had become and felt herself vindicated. Whether Aurore knew it or not, she belonged to her grandmother. Those three years at Les Anglaises had accomplished it, and also, without meaning to, Sophie, who by merely being herself, had acted as her own worst enemy. The short time Aurore and Madame Dupin spent in Paris before leaving for the country had been enough for the young girl to see that between her and her mother, cruel in her vulgarity, bristling with prejudice, lay differences that not all the nostalgia of childhood memories could bridge.

Madame Dupin had invited Sophie to Nohant. "Never!" cried Sophie when she was alone with her daughter. "I'll see the old woman dead first."

Aurore had looked forward to having Sophie with her, and recalled to her the happy years they had spent there. "No, I hate the country, and Nohant most of all.—Go, go back to your Nohant," said Sophie. "You may be coming back sooner than you think."

The spiteful reference to her grandmother's death shocked Aurore and made her unwisely come to Madame Dupin's defense. "There, you see!" Sophie screamed. "Well, I'm glad you love her more than me. Go back, go back to her, since you belong to her body and soul! But I tell you one thing," she said on another occasion. "Whatever happens, you can never marry without my consent. You belong to *me,* and no matter how they try to turn you against me, your mother knows her rights!"

"Ah," sighed Madame Dupin who was not spared those storms, "why can't she let me end my days in peace? She has such a very short time to wait."

Nevertheless Madame Dupin was happier than she had ever been, if such a positive emotion as happiness could have been said to exist in her almost Hindu serenity. Yes, Aurore had turned out better than she expected. She could have wished her taller: the girl measured only four feet eleven inches, although she had attained her full development. But she had a good figure, a fine throat, rounded arms, a small but well-formed bosom, and beautiful hands and feet. The thighs could have been fuller, to suit the taste of the day, but the right clothes would help. The face was certainly arresting. Somehow Maurice's male handsomeness and Sophie's piquancy had united to give it an agreeable individuality. The eyes would have assured the beauty of any woman. Huge, black, velvety under their winglike brows, they held one by the fixity of their gaze, at once abstracted and intense, which lighted up with unexpected flashes as from the kindling of her brain. Like her high forehead, they seemed almost disproportionate in the oval of her face, giving it the look of a landscape with a too vast horizon for the foreground. Her nose had an aristocratic curve. Her mouth was perfect: the arched upper lip turned up at the corners with the roguery of a Watteau shepherdess, the lower was sensually full and slightly pouting. The general impression was one of meditation, almost of melancholy. She had, moreover, a mass of lustrous brown hair, and a skin sufficiently tinted to make one think of hotter suns and ardent blood.

Evidently, even in the shelter of the convent, probably in its parlor, Aurore's attractions had not passed unnoticed, to judge by an offer of marriage which Madame Dupin received through the rich and rather pretentious René de Villeneuve, a cousin of Aurore's on the Dupin side of the family. Madame Dupin had not mentioned it to Aurore, and had taken it upon herself to give her objections to the match. After all, a fifty-one-year-old general of the Empire, with a great saber cut across the face, hardly realized the Prince Charming dream of an imaginative girl, even if he did have "wit and wealth and everything else to assure happiness in the relationship," as Villeneuve pleaded. The marriage market was full of desirable young men, and with her dowry of five hundred thousand francs Aurore surely could do better.

Still, Madame Dupin could not refrain from a certain concern at Aurore's indifference to men. At her age most girls were already married, or at least showed as much interest as their mothers in making a match. Aurore, whenever she betrayed any emotion at all, seemed to look upon the step almost with dread. Madame Dupin watched her alternating from her books to violent exercise with Hippolyte, now a brilliant marshal of the Hussars. How different were those two children of Maurice, the one hearty, rough, "but a good lad, a good lad," the other delicate yet strong with a surprising inner strength, as if a man's spirit inhabited that woman's frame. More than before, Madame Dupin identified her granddaughter with her lost son, an identification that became unbearable whenever she saw Aurore in the boy's costume which Deschartres had insisted on her adopting, as

46

much for Aurore's comfort as for his own, not liking to be seen about the countryside with a female.

"You look so much like your father that it hurts," the old woman sighed. "Maurice, *mon fils,*" she called her, as she had long ago, after her son's death. Her mind, which had begun to cloud, helped in the self-deception.

Very early Aurore had manifested a duality that became more pronounced as she grew older. The irregularity of her upbringing which had forced her into situations beyond her years, had fostered it. With the sensibility of a woman she combined a masculine strength and a stubbornness of will that were all the more surprising for the quiet way in which she asserted them. Unconsciously, at first, she had resisted the desultory efforts to make her like everyone else. Later, instinctively aware of her unusual personality, she felt a certain vanity. Now, when normally she should have accomplished her definitive metamorphosis, circumstance and choice both contributed to emphasize her dual nature.

It was as if two equally powerful forces were struggling in her for dominion, one reckless, demanding physical play and violent adventure, the other melancholy, fond of solitude, seeking in study a cure for some indefinable malady of the soul. Deschartres, after Hippolyte left to rejoin his Hussars, permitted her with grudging magnanimity to accompany him on his rounds to his patients, some of whom lived at La Châtre. She was studying medicine with him, and he taught her how to set broken bones, dress wounds, and physic children in their minor illnesses. On the way, mounted on their horses, they carried on Socratic dialogues on ethical and philosophical themes, the fond old pedant addressing her as Mademoiselle, in spite of her costume, while Aurore roguishly dubbed him *Grand Homme,* which he accepted with humorless delight. He had been more at ease with her since her assumption of masculine clothes and, Aurore noted with amusement, less sparing of polysyllables, as if her change of garb had effected a similar transformation of her intellect.

The people of Nohant, however, did not like it. They liked it still less when Aurore was met riding late at night alone at a breakneck gallop, for what purpose they did not know, though they surmised it could not be good. After René de Villeneuve came on a visit to the manor, the whole community buzzed. That wild young woman actually practiced pistol shooting with Monsieur de Villeneuve! It was bad enough for a marriageable girl to ramble through the woods with a *distant* relative of a very green middle age. But when she also rode a horse like a man, dressed like a man, and handled firearms with the audacity of a desperado, they knew the devil was in it.

Wasn't she studying unholy arts with the unfrocked Abbé Deschartres? Where did they get their skulls and bones if not at the cemetery? That explained why she went marauding at night—to plunder graves and ride her horse right into the church, and shoot her pistols at the holy wafers. She was a witch. She and Deschartres were up to some devilish practice. And Madame Dupin had sent that brand of hell to a convent! Blood will tell. There was bad blood in the family. That young woman would come to an unholy end. One of these days they would find her dead at the foot of the tree where they had picked up her father.

Indeed, their prophecy was almost verified one night when Aurore's horse shied and threw her, either because something had frightened it in the dark, or perhaps because it felt the girl's nervousness whenever she passed the spot where her father had been killed. But beyond a bad fall and the shock to her nerves, Aurore remained unhurt. However, she kept the accident from her grandmother.

The spiritual side of her nature also found its satisfactions and, oddly, it was Madame Dupin who led her toward them. Too late a close relationship had developed between the two. Aurore had almost grown to love that impeccably formal woman who, even though she was so feeble that she had to be helped to the table, came to dinner in her long pansy-colored gown, her cheeks rouged, the diamonds shining in her ears. The girl noticed in mingled pain and admiration how vainly Madame Dupin tried to control the trembling of those poor palsied hands by the effort of a will that thought it unseemly to betray any weakness.

Madame Dupin admitted intellectual weakness even less, and was keenly distressed when she found, though Aurore tried to conceal it from her, that her mind had begun to wander. It was a strange phenomenon. Aurore would be reading to her, and to all appearances she was listening with her usual alertness, when she would suddenly make an irrelevant observation.

One evening, while Aurore was reading aloud a passage out of Chateaubriand's *Génie du Christianisme,* Madame Dupin started up saying: "That's enough, child. What you've just read seems so strange that I'm afraid I couldn't have heard aright. What's that you were saying about bells tolling?—" She caught herself at Aurore's ill-concealed amazement. "How strange, I do believe I must have dozed off," she said. "I guess I must be very tired. I can no longer read, and I can't even be read to. Get the cards, dear, and let's have a game." Then Aurore knew that the gallant old woman was secretly preoccupied with the thought of death.

The final warning came soon afterward. This time, the stroke left Madame Dupin partially paralyzed, and Deschartres prepared Aurore for the end. But Madame Dupin lingered on for months. She never left her room. Her two serving women were constantly in attendance, but it was Aurore she wanted day and night. They talked to each other as they had never talked before —death has its terrible sincerity—and at last Aurore was able to apprehend the spirit behind that cold exterior. Her conscience gave her no rest. She took the blame for past misunderstandings, for the rebellion that had caused her grandmother so much pain, and in the short time left, she made up for her failures in unceasing care.

Toward autumn Madame Dupin seemed to have lost all strength. Past and present merged in her unconscious mind, and she lived in that self-created world of those who know they are soon to leave this. She hardly slept but dozed fitfully, as if, knowing she had so little time, she must lose none of it. At night Aurore and Deschartres took turns in relieving the women. The old man broke her heart with his silent grief. He had lived for Madame Dupin, making her life his own, raising her son and her son's children, guarding her and her property like a faithful dog for whom any reward was enough. In the death of that woman, coeval with him, he saw the end of himself and his era.

During the day Deschartres and Aurore made their rounds as usual. But now another joined them in their studies, a young man of the neighborhood whose father had been a friend of Deschartres'. Stéphane Ajasson de Grandsaigne was a medical student in Paris. Tall, strikingly handsome, he sprang from one of the oldest roots of the local nobility. But the family had fallen on evil days, what with changing times and the canker of its own destruction in the reckless blood of its members, so that now it had sunk a few degrees below genteel poverty.

Stéphane was a good student, original and intelligent, with, however, a streak of that recklessness which had marked his family. Deschartres liked him and saw nothing wrong in engaging him to give Aurore lessons in physics. The gossips, however, found more food for scandal in the association of the two young people. Whatever attachment may have grown between Aurore and Stéphane during the summer had to cease, except for letters, with his return to Paris. Correspondence ceased also, after one of his epistles frightened both Aurore and Deschartres. Stéphane had begun it platonically enough with, "O truly philosophical soul," but he had ended with, "You are the truth that kills." The danger signs were there for those who understood.

Perhaps Stéphane's departure had something to do with a morbid turn in Aurore's melancholy, although even without it her life held enough lugubriousness to have made her a hypochondriac. In her atonement to her grandmother, she scarcely slept. Moreover, the dying woman had grown increasingly demanding, and there were nights when she kept Aurore reading or talking to her till dawn. Stimulated by the coffee and sometimes the *eau-de-vie* with which she dosed herself to remain awake, the girl then thought it useless to sleep at all and would go tearing down the roads on her mare, Colette. When she finally went to bed, there were enough reminders of mortality, including a child's skeleton on the commode in her room, to keep her mind dwelling on death—her father's, her grandmother's, her own.

Suicide lured her, and the books she read presented it with the attraction of immolation. Byron and Chateaubriand fed a romantic pessimism that made her know the ills of the soul without having experienced them, and filled her with life's disenchantment even before she had begun to live. Chateaubriand's *René*, that middle brother of Romanticism between the sorrowing Werther and Childe Harold, beautiful and damned, she read and reread. The miseries of that self-tortured soul she made her own. She was René. Like him she was crushed by her loathing of life, till she almost forgot Rousseau, whom until then she had worshiped for his faith in the innate goodness of man. Her heterogeneous delving into the wisdom of the eighteenth century skeptics only confirmed her in her disenchantment. What was learning but the expression of humanity's eternal anguish? Pascal and Montesquieu, Mably and Locke, denied in vain.

Suicide became an *idée fixe* and poetic melancholy its nimbus. It may be in a mood of Byronic despair that she scratched in pencil on the right side of her window at Nohant a prose elegy, in English, as she watched the sun set. *Go, fading sun. Hide thy pale beams behind the distant trees. Nightly Vesperus is comming (sic) to announce the close of the day. Evening descends to bring melancholy on the landscape. With thy return, beautiful light, nature will find again mirth and beauty; but joy will never comfort my soul. Thy absence, radiant orb, may not increase the sorrows of my heart; they cannot be softened by thy return!*

She copied the elegy in a small commonplace book bound in black morocco which she had taken with her when she left Les Anglaises. In the same gloom she transferred to its pages the Italian verses to a song of Haydn's that sighed on the eternally recurring spring which brings new fronds to the trees, and grass to the meadows, but never peace to the heart. Those sorrows, that inconsolable heart, were they the symptoms of her Byronic malady or the consequences of an actual pain, caused by Stéphane, perhaps?

Real or imagined, her anguish became so acute that she could never pass the Indre River without staring into the water in a hypnosis of self-destruction. How easy it would be, she thought. Just one step.

One day while she and Deschartres were crossing the ford on horseback, she took that step, almost without volition. A brusque movement of the reins, and she and Colette found themselves in the deepest part of the churning waters. Ah, soon it would be over! A delirious joy welled up in her. Death, at last, and peace. But that instant of intoxication past, she found herself clinging to the mane of Colette who, sensible beast that she was, fought against the current and made for the steep riverbank where Deschartres was standing, shouting in maniac terror. At the risk of his own life he helped Aurore to safety, calling her *animal* and *brute beast* as the tears streamed down his cheeks. Aurore came to her senses at the fury of the *Grand Homme*. After the adventure, she lost all desire to drown, although the temptation of suicide persisted. Sometimes as she held a phial of laudanum in her hand for her grandmother, she would be seized with such a craving to drink it that she reeled.

She had these fits of dizziness often. Also, from childhood she had suffered from terrifying recurrent dreams of fire, and curious hallucinations during which she saw everything double. The dreams would come whenever she was troubled or ailing, but the doubled vision she could bring about at will, although most of the time she had no control over it. It was as if an inner monitor chose these manifestations to warn her. She had them often during her vigils at her grandmother's bedside.

To the end Madame Dupin thought only of Aurore. "You'll be losing your best friend when I go," she would murmur.

The deist had ended in the arms of the Church, probably as a last consideration to the girl who would continue living in the strictly Catholic Nohant, in a country which the Bourbons had restored to religion and monarchy.

Even this compromise Madame Dupin accomplished with no violence to her strict rational nature. It was not that she hated religion, she explained to Aurore, but she refused to accept dogma. She was no atheist. She believed in God and nature, esteemed Christ as a great teacher and the Gospels as perfect philosophy—"The rest is absurd mummery."

The good old curé hardly knew what to make of a penitent who commented on the service, but he performed it with the simple dignity of his long experience. There were tears in his eyes when, after confession, Madame Dupin added: "I have never done or wished harm to anybody. I have always believed in God. But, heed this well, my child." She turned toward Aurore whom she insisted on having in the room. "I have not loved Him enough. I lacked real strength—that was my failing, and from

51

the day I lost my son I could neither bless the Lord nor pray to Him. It seemed to me He had been too cruel to strike a blow so much greater than I could bear. Now that He calls me, I thank Him and I pray that He forgive my weakness. . . . Let Him reunite me to my son and I shall love Him and pray with all my soul."

After the absolution, when the curé had called in the rest of the household, Madame Dupin had a flash of the old Voltairian. "I don't believe this good man has the power to absolve me of anything," she said. "But I know that God has it, and I hope He will at least favor our good intentions."

She died quietly in her sleep on the twenty-fifth of December, 1821, as the church bells were ringing in the Noël. Aurore had watched over her so long that she could not believe her grandmother was dead. Like Deschartres, she knew that indeed her best friend was gone.

The old tutor busied himself about the house to distract himself from his sorrow. The relatives must be summoned for the reading of the will, the papers set in order, the final offices arranged. No one must say at the end that there had been the least flaw in a well-ordered life. A good and faithful servant, Deschartres was as devoted to his mistress dead as he had been when she was alive.

His grim austerity let no one penetrate the depth of his bereavement. But something must have given way in that closed personality to make him do a thing so shocking in its Gothic morbidity that no extenuation could be found for him except temporary insanity. Madame Dupin had been dressed for the grave with the same care Julie would have employed to prepare her for a feast. The grave itself, alongside Maurice's, had been dug under Deschartres' supervision. In so doing, the workmen exposed the coffin. Deschartres saw that it was intact, but the lid had been loosened in the damp, and most of the nails had fallen out.

Perhaps that circumstance suggested the deed to him, or it may be he had planned it from the moment he knew that the grave would have to be opened. One of those unfortunates, self-exiled from the joys and responsibilities of ordinary humanity, he had known vicariously fatherhood and devotion to a woman. Maurice had been taken from him by a fatal accident. Now the only other being he had ever loved was to be laid beside him. In the unbalance of his bereavement, he acted upon a mad impulse to give some final token of his love to the dead. That night he pried open the lid of Maurice's coffin to gaze upon his remains, and in necrophilic attraction, he lifted the skull which dissolution had detached from the body, and kissed it.

So far one could explain the act as temporary aberration. But what motive impelled him to waken Aurore at one o'clock in the morning, and in a voice hacked by sickly exaltation, ask: "Can you be brave? Do you believe that the dead deserve more from us than prayers and tears?"

Rapidly, with the wild eyes of a maniac, he continued in that strain and concluded: "Come with me. You are going to see the man who was your father."

Aurore followed him, not knowing what to expect. It was a clear cold night, glistening with frost. The path from the house to the cemetery was so icy that they frequently lost their footing. But Deschartres led her onward till they reached a heap of stones that made a rude crypt for the coffin, and there related what he had done. "Tomorrow," he added, "this grave will be closed. Probably it will not be opened again except to receive you when your time comes. You must do as I do. You must kiss this relic that was your father. I know that wherever he may be he will see you and he will bless you."

Compelled by his insanity, Aurore did as she was told, who knows with what effect upon her psyche, already too well acquainted with pity and terror.

The following day Madame Dupin was buried and with her, Aurore's girlhood.

Chapter VI: Enter Casimir

THE year 1821 had been a significant one for France. One leader of men had died and another had been proclaimed. At Longwood in Saint Helena, Napoleon, discrowned, heartsick, a prisoner, breathed his last on the fifth of May. The audacious man who had begun, his career before the Council of Five Hundred, crying, "Make way, I am the god of the day," died, a common mortal. The usurper who had snatched the crown of empire from the hand of a pope and placed it upon his own head that no one might say, "I have crowned him," the man who had rejected communion at his coronation, had taken humbly from the officiating priest the wafer of the last sacrament. No longer would the shackled Eagle shake Europe with the thunder of his chains.

In his will Napoleon summarized his life. "I die in the Apostolical Roman faith, in whose bosom I was born more than fifty years ago. I desire that my ashes find their last resting place on the banks of the Seine, among the French people I have so dearly loved. . . . Let my son never forget that he was born a French prince, or allow himself to be made a tool in the hands of the triumvirs who are tyrannizing over the nations of Europe. Let him adopt what was always my guiding principle: *Everything for the French people.* . . . I die before my time."

The widows and orphans of his wars of aggrandizement who wept for other deaths than his had cause to think bitterly of his legacy and wonder if he had not died too late. Posterity was to make the final appraisal. An ambitious man, he fired ambition in others, to their destruction. Hypnotic, he filled the popular mind with dreams which realization turned into nightmare. A wielder of power, he made his scepter a rod in his abuse of it, subduing intellect, corrupting conscience. Across the continent of Europe the paths of his triumphant marches bogged with blood. Death and pestilence fed the laurels of his rise. "The glorious dream with which he dazzled France has vanished," Guizot epitomized. "Its memory, though dimmed, still lingers, but always it will be fatal to our unhappy country."

With Napoleon's fall in 1815, the Bourbons had again taken the reins of France, Naples and Spain, the slack hands guided by fatuous brains, till it was as if the Revolution had never been, nor the meretricious glory of Napoleon's empire, created, in a sense, as a threat to their legitimate claims. The astute usurper had known that to be King of France against Bourbon pretensions would have been out of the question. One could not usurp royal blood. Hence the Empire, and the founding of Napoleon's dynasty. The Bourbons were now having their day. "They have forgotten nothing and they have learned nothing," it was remarked of them, and the people punctuated their wisdom with revolts and assassinations. In France the fat, weak-willed Louis XVIII who had left in exile his wig but not his ideas, allowed himself and, consequently, the nation, to be ruled by his favorites, first Blacas and then Decazes, until a woman, Madame de Cayla, supplanted them and their successors.

Napoleon's fall, however, did not mean the death of his dynasty. He had left brothers and sisters besides his legitimate heir, the young King of Rome, half of whose blood, at least, was royal. Moreover, his first wife, the Creole Josephine, had seen to it that, though cast aside for Marie Louise of Austria, her own blood staked its claim on the future through the marriage of her daughter Hortense Beauharnais to Napoleon's brother Louis.

Meanwhile, the romantic period of French literature inaugurated its rule by choosing as its leader Victor Marie Hugo, who was crowned Master of Floral Games when not yet twenty. The ancient title, revived for him, had been his reward for his prize poem on Henry IV. Born in 1802, in the shadow of Napoleon, Hugo was one of those *enfants du siècle* whose portrait Alfred de Musset was to paint in his apologia for his generation.

The child was indeed conceived between two battles, for General J. L. Hugo, one of Napoleon's ablest soldiers, had little time to spend with his wife, a royalist of La Vendée. This youngest of his war-born brood seemed so discouraged with the world he found, that it took all the resources of medicine to persuade him to live. Like Sophie Dupin and other soldiers' women, who trailed the imperial camps, Sophie Hugo often followed her husband. The child Victor, therefore, found himself in Spain at the same time as Aurore Dupin. Where the little girl stored in her impressionable mind the gloomy romance of a desolated nation, the boy made a collection of epic prints.

He grew up a Catholic and, influenced by his mother, a royalist. The poems he began to write and publish when other poets had scarcely fledged, found inspiration in a fervid religion and a no less fervid royalism. It was not without warrant that Balzac made Étienne Lousteau in *Un Grand Homme de Provence à Paris*, define the two opposing literary factions as political in their implication:

"Literature is divided into several zones, but our great men fall into two opposing camps. The royalists are Romantics, the liberals, Classicists. The paradox is that the royalist Romantics uphold liberty in literature and aim to overthrow rules and conventions, whereas the liberal Classicists are determined on observing the unities and maintaining the Alexandrine and the classical subject. Thus in either case political opinions are completely at variance with literary taste . . . 'Be a Romantic,' Lousteau urges. 'The Romantics are young. The Classicists are pedants. Besides, the Romantics are sure to win the day.' "

As yet the lines were not too clearly drawn, for it was not until the 1830's that the Romantic movement came into power. In its initial period it was enough that Chateaubriand gave Hugo the accolade by hailing him as a "sublime child" in his journal, *Le Conservateur*, and that the young literary hotheads acclaimed him as the leader of their Sacred Battalion.

"Why don't you write a novel?" René de Villeneuve urged Aurore in the spirit of the day, to distract her from the family wrangles that had arisen over her guardianship. Aurore obeyed him, but her heart was not in it. What began as a romance turned into a philosophical dissertation and she gave up in disgust.

As it was, she had little desire for writing or for anything except, perhaps, the peace that seemed to have gone with her grandmother. Scarcely had Madame Dupin been buried, to a great concourse of the poor who did not trouble to dissemble that they had come more for the burial doles than out of honor to the departed, when the house bulged with relatives gathered together for the reading of the will.

Sophie too had come, true to her vow: "I'll see the old woman dead first." She embraced Aurore with the old effusiveness, but a day had hardly passed before she betrayed the rancor which even death had not softened. Oh, yes, she would be interested to hear the old woman's will, she said, darkly. Some very unusual provisions in it had already been bruited to her, and she wanted to make sure she would be present to voice her objections.

Aurore speculated in vain as to the identity of the informant of whose existence in the household she had no doubt, since Sophie always knew to the least detail whatever had taken place at Nohant. She was uneasy. She knew of a particular provision in the will, which appointed René de Villeneuve her guardian, and she hoped it was not her mother's intention to go counter to Madame Dupin's wishes.

Aurore marveled at the change four short years had made in her. What heartbreak it had been for her to part from Sophie.

To what active mutiny she had risen in her defense, and what a noble martyr she had made of her. What had brought about the change? Not in her affection—that was still constant. But now in her love of Sophie entered a rueful pity as for an irresponsible child.

Sophie's irresponsibility was not without its cunning, however. Her mind, always at the mercy of variable moods, knew when to anchor. She held her ground stubbornly, therefore, when at the reading of the will, she came to the guardianship clause. "I am Aurore's legal guardian," she insisted, "and while I live her place is with me, until she comes of age."

René de Villeneuve bowed coldly. He tried to make Sophie understand the advantages of Aurore's living with his wife and family, the suitors the girl would have, the place in society. Sophie would not be moved. René de Villeneuve had no choice but to submit. Besides, the law was with Sophie.

He tried another expedient. Aurore might go back to Les Anglaises as a resident until she came of age or till a suitable *parti* were found for her. For no respectable person would seek her out at her mother's house, he added, unnecessarily. Unfortunately, not even her old cubicle was available at the convent for the heiress of Nohant, and Aurore had no alternative but to live with her mother.

She left Nohant—for under no circumstances would Sophie consent to stay there—and the two spent a few weeks with Aunt Lucie till Madame Dupin's apartment on the Rue Neuve des Mathurins was ready to receive them. Sophie showed a strange uneasiness, Aurore might almost have thought, embarrassment, at being with her, and an ill-concealed resentment. It was as if she were taking charge of her daughter out of duty, and would rather have continued living in a freedom which gossip qualified as more than ambiguous. Caroline had recently married. With that restraint gone, Sophie Dupin's life had given matter for speculation.

She was still a fascinating woman. As middle age encroached upon her, she tried to prove to herself, like all women whose physical attractiveness has been their strongest asset, that she was not yet bankrupt in beauty. What nature destroyed, she supplied through art. She was constantly renewing her toilettes, altering hats and dresses, changing her coiffure. Not content with that, she supplied herself with a variety of wigs, even though she still had a mass of jet-black hair, and would wear them as caprice dictated, appearing now as a blonde, now as a towhead, now chestnut, now red-haired, not caring how she looked if only she might quell her restlessness with change.

She brought the same unrest to her behavior toward Aurore.

She was not happy except when experiencing violent emotion; thunder and lightning must be constant props in her daily drama. Irresistible in her good moods, she tolerated them only long enough for one to know that she was capable of them. Then thunder rolled again, and lightning struck from unexpected quarters. Yet, in her way, she loved Aurore, or, as the girl sometimes thought, she loved the remembrance of Maurice in her. ("I have loved only one man in my life," Sophie never tired of repeating.) Unfortunately, just as she saw her husband in her daughter, she also found in her the handiwork of Madame Dupin and the hated Deschartres.

She showed her resentment by forbidding Aurore to read the few books she had allowed her to bring from Nohant. "I've tried to read them myself and I can't make head or tail of them. I'm sure they can't be good for you. Besides, you have enough *originality* as it is," she flung at Aurore with profound mistrust. She carried that mistrust to everyone and everything Aurore loved, even to her dog, a descendant of Madame Dupin's Brillant. One day, without a word of explanation, she got rid of it.

Aurore wept bitterly. "It was the drop that made the cup brim over," she wrote in remembrance of the petty revenge. She suffered other losses through Sophie, most regrettable the friendship of René de Villeneuve. He had called, one day, to invite Aurore to dine with his family. "Your wife should have come in person to extend the invitation," said Sophie. No doubt she was right, but her tone was so sharp that Villeneuve forgot himself and retorted, "My wife will never set foot in this house!" With that he went out and never called again.

Aurore's health reflected the fluctuations of her mother's temper. She could not go to her books for comfort, nor could she communicate with Deschartres, who had been left in the dull grief of the undemonstrative, to look after Nohant. Uncle Beaumont was now the only member of the family who would receive them. But he had grown capricious and increasingly self-indulgent in his extreme age, and could not bear anyone about who did not amuse him. He was anxious to marry off Aurore, both to take her away from Sophie and to cure her of her cheerless looks and her apathy toward food. It hurt his gourmet's pride to see her return her plates untouched. She was getting thin. At that rate she would never attract a husband, even among those respectable retired oldsters who had come to him for her hand.

With life growing more intolerable for her now that Sophie persisted in seeing in her a secretly irreconcilable enemy, Aurore too turned her thoughts to marriage. So far she had rejected the superannuated suitors proposed by Uncle Beaumont, knowing she could hope for nothing from those quarters except a *mariage de convenance* in which her dowry was the chief attraction. She decided to marry for love, like Sophie.

For, she reflected, she had the blood of Sophie running through her veins, as well as the precious ichor of the great-great-grandson of the King of Poland; and if she was obliquely related to Louis XVIII from one quarter, she was no less a daughter of the people from the other. "And with no illegitimacy on that side," she mused. She had taken to heart her reading of Rousseau and the fervidly democratic writings of the accomplished Madame de Genlis, governess of the future Louis Philippe. Her novel, *Les Battuécas,* had recently awakened Aurore to a defiant pride in her humble blood. Of course, the reasoning of Madame de Genlis' hero, a noble savage who would have delighted Rousseau, was of a naïveté that sometimes brought a smile, but it was to him that Aurore owed the germ of her later socialist democratic principles and her love of the common man.

As the spring of 1822 progressed, Sophie's unpredictable moods were aggravated to the point of derangement. Everything irritated her, the weather, Aurore's unhappiness. "You're not looking at all well," she said one day, and without further warning she packed a few things and took Aurore to visit the Plessis family who had a large house and grounds in the vicinity of Melun. They were friends of long standing whom she had seen again recently at the house of one of Uncle Beaumont's relatives. The meeting had been enough to set her mind working.

The day after she had settled Aurore with the Plessis', Sophie prepared to leave for Paris. "The country air will do you good," she said to Aurore. "I'll come for you in a week." She left her there for five months. She had need of her freedom.

Aurore quickly adjusted herself to her new home. James Roettiers du Plessis, in his early forties, was a hearty man who still had about him the jauntiness of his captain of cavalry days. He had been an intimate friend of Maurice Dupin's and had done the campaigns with him under Napoleon. As a bachelor he used to visit Maurice's young family, and after his death often went to Nohant to cheer Sophie and Madame Dupin with reminiscence. Aurore had been too small to remember him, but she liked him when she met him again.

Angèle, his wife, a rich heiress, adored him. Theirs had been a love match. Even as a child Angèle had loved her dashing uncle in his handsome uniform, and finally married him against the objections of her family who had disapproved of his too gay life. Her marriage could not have been happier. She was now only twenty-seven, but her prematurely gray hair brought her nearer her husband's age while lending a piquant strangeness to her

59

looks. They had five children, all girls, the eldest of whom was being raised by James's brother. The other four romped about the park of Plessis-Picard, dressed as boys, perhaps to console the captain for the sons he had not had.

Aurore and Angèle became friends at once. James treated her like a daughter. Soon the relationship was so harmoniously established, that the servants in speaking to Aurore, would say, "Mademoiselle, your father would like to talk to you. . . . Your mother is waiting for you in the garden."

She joined the girls in their games. Little by little she recaptured the gaiety of her years and learned to laugh again. In the rambling park she could also be alone if she chose, pondering her future as she stared into a secluded, willow-bordered pool. Thoughts of love filled her solitude at this time, thoughts of a young officer.

Where had she met him? Who was he? She never told. Perhaps it had been in Paris while she was living with her mother, or, it may be, in Uncle Beaumont's house. Perhaps he was an army friend of James du Plessis. They may have stolen a meeting or two and exchanged an occasional note. The affair is surrounded by mystery except for a sentence in a letter he sent Aurore. "If you persist in looking upon the happiness I implore as criminal, God forbid that I should strive to obtain favors that you would reproach yourself for granting. Therefore, good-by. . . ." There is no ambiguity here. The young man had made an improper proposal and Aurore had rejected him. She had met her mother's test and won. Grandmother Dupin would have been proud.

Toward the close of the spring the Plessis' went to spend a few days in Paris and took Aurore with them so that Sophie might see how much good the country had been doing her. Aurore lodged with her mother, but her days were an endless round of gaiety with Angèle and James. Now they dined at the cabarets, now they walked along the boulevards. The Café de Paris and the Frères Provençaux, former haunts of James, the man-about-town, thrilled the two women. The opéra opened a new world for Aurore. She loved Paris. The tempo of its life quickened her blood, and she enjoyed all its pleasures indiscriminately, from the military shows at the Cirque which roused the warrior in James, to the majestic ritual of the classical theater.

They were having their ices one evening at Tortoni's after the play when Angèle cried, "Look, there's Casimir!"

She had scarcely spoken when a slight man of about thirty walked toward their table and, after an exchange of greetings, was invited to sit beside Angèle. Aurore studied him. She found him pleasant. She liked his military bearing and his ease of manner. She heard him report on the health of Colonel Dude-

MADAME DUPIN AND HER SON MAURICE

"Maurice was as much absorbed in her as she was in him."

Musée Carnavalet

vant, his father; then she saw him lean toward Angèle to whisper.
"She's my daughter," Angèle said aloud, laughing.
"Ah, then she's my wife?" Casimir queried. "You remember,
you promised me your eldest daughter."
Aurore turned away, embarrassed. In those words spoken so
lightly, she heard prophecy. Marriage, surely, must be better than
living with Sophie's temper. Besides, she could not expect her
friends to keep her till her majority.
Sophie had changed little. Now when she found that her scenes
had no effect upon Aurore's resignation, she taunted: "When
you've gone through as much as I have you'll stop being St.
Tranquilla."
At the end of the visit, as Sophie made no offer either to keep
her daughter or to accompany her, Aurore left, not without
relief, with her friends.
She was not surprised when, a few days later, Casimir Dudevant
came to Melun. Angèle greeted him with sly satisfaction. The
children seized upon him for their games. Aurore, too, was glad
to see him, and, having no coquetry, showed her pleasure. He
entered into the spirit of the hoydenish romps and played with
the children as if he had been their age. Aurore liked his boyish-
ness. Meanwhile Angèle furthered her own particular game,
calling Aurore her daughter and Casimir her son-in-law.
"Your daughter's a jolly good fellow," Casimir would say
falling into the sport.
Aurore laughed and answered in kind. Soon they were play-
fully referring to each other as *husband* and *wife,* so that by the
time Casimir left, Angèle knew she would be having interesting
news for Sophie before long.
Casimir could not stay away. In a few days he was back, this
time in so grave a mood that Aurore hardly knew what to expect
when he drew her aside and said: "This may not be strictly
according to rule, but I'd like your consent before I tell my
father to broach the subject to your mother."
A proposal! How unconventional of Casimir to consult her
first. And, if she could apply the word to this practical young
man, how romantic! She listened as he talked, reflecting on what
Angèle had told her of his steady habits, of his solid family.
Oddly enough, he said not a word about love. "To prove to you
that I am sure of my feelings," he continued, "I'll make a confession. Do you know what struck me the first time I saw you?
Your nice sensible looks. I didn't find you beautiful nor even
pretty—" What compliments from a lover! "I didn't even know
who you were. But when I said in fun to Angèle that you'd be
my wife, I had a sudden feeling that I'd be happy if it really
happened. Every day the thought has come to me more clearly."

61

Aurore heard him through, half amused yet sympathetically. She liked the camaraderie he offered. He said it was what had attracted him to her as they played and laughed together—"that feeling of being old friends."

In Aurore's present emotional state, shocked by the rejected officer's suggestion, yet impatient for expansion made impossible by her mother, any warmer approach would have frightened her. What she wanted was freedom, which she was ready to pay for with a pleasant comradeship, perhaps later with love. Casimir was not antipathetic to her, as perhaps many another suitor might have been. They could arrange to have a tolerable life together—he demanded so little. The only difficulty was to obtain Sophie's consent.

They discussed practical matters with Angèle who arranged to have Sophie meet Colonel Dudevant. Aurore herself knew nothing about Casimir except for what Angèle had told her. His baptismal name was François; Casimir remained unexplained. He had served two years in the army where he had risen to the rank of sub-lieutenant, and he had been licensed at law. His mother was said to be a certain Augustine Souls, "a dame exiled in Spain whose existence is not known," as a document put it.

In less euphemistic terms, Casimir was the natural son of Colonel Jean François Dudevant, baron of the Empire and member of the Legion of Honor. Besides possessing money of his own Baron Dudevant, who counted the notorious Scottish speculator Law among his kin, had also married a fortune in his wife, the present baronne. He had no issue but Casimir, who would eventually be his heir. On the whole it seemed a good match for the heiress of Nohant.

Sophie, to Aurore's relief, was impressed by the distinction and gentleness of the silver-haired baron of the Empire whose wife, he explained, would have joined him at the pleasant interview had she not been visiting relatives at Le Mans. The two discussed the marriage proposal privately and then came to join the company.

"I said *yes*," Sophie told Aurore, "but not in such a way that I couldn't change it to *no*. I'm not yet sure whether I like the son. He's far from good looking. I'd have liked a handsome son-in-law to take my arm."

The following day she left for Paris.

In justice to Sophie's taste, Casimir was insignificant enough. Heinrich Heine, who met him in later years, said he had the look of a grocer, though he seemed neither coarse nor brutal. At the time of Aurore's engagement, however, Casimir had not yet acquired, or perhaps he had skillfully concealed, "the tepid vulgarity, the banal nullity, the porcelain stare and the appearance of a Chinese pagoda" that irritated Heine. It is certain that he also kept from her a disorderly past and an abnormal attachment to money.

Sophie, who despite her irrationality, was devoted as well as shrewd, somehow divined both the fact and the tendency in her son-in-law-to-be, and descended like a bolt at Melun. "He's led a scandalous life," she screamed. "Why, he was even a waiter at a café. I can't let him marry my daughter."

The laughter which greeted her information—Sophie always obtained special information—infuriated her. It took all of Angèle's persuasions to keep her from declaring the agreement null and void. "Anyway, I don't like his nose," she objected, when James proved there was no truth to the waiter story, and that the irregularity had been neither more nor less than one might find in the life of any lusty young man who had taken his time about marrying.

Even after the Baronne Dudevant condescended to pay her respects to Sophie, the marriage continued to hang in the balance, now because Sophie detected snobbery in the Dudevants, now because of Casimir, and now out of concern for Aurore's happiness.

Finally, on the tenth of September, 1822, Aurore became the wife of Casimir, with "Dame Antoinette Sophie Victoire Delaborde Dupin present and consenting." Because of Sophie's perspicacity Aurore was married under the dotal régime which preserved for the young wife her personal fortune of five hundred thousand francs.

Aurore was always reticent about her marriage. In her biography she mentions it at the end of a chapter, and begins the next: "I spent the winter of 1822–1823 at Nohant, very ill, but absorbed by the sentiment of maternal love." Not a word about her feelings as a wife, no mention of any happiness.

There is a letter of hers, however, written in 1843, which speaks where elsewhere she is silent. It is addressed to Hippolyte on the eve of his daughter Léontine's marriage. "If you can, try to prevent your son-in-law from brutalizing your daughter on the wedding night. . . . There's nothing so frightful as the terror, the suffering and revulsion of a poor child, ignorant of the facts of life, who is subjected to violation by a brute."

Chapter VII: The Cold Hearth

IT was a long, rigorous winter, that of 1822–1823. The snow, fallen early in the season, hardened to ice. Frost clung to the branches till the birds, unable to find foothold, fell to the ground and froze to death. Aurore had been forbidden to leave her bed for six weeks.

Soon after her marriage she had begun to suffer from a strange debility, an utter lassitude which, together with her pregnancy, made Deschartres prescribe complete rest. She was not unhappy in her seclusion. Her bed, whose four corners had once been adorned with plumes, now held huge branches of spruce and fir. A wide green cloth was spread over the counterpane, and in the improvised bower Aurore, true grandchild of the bird fancier Delaborde, nursed back to life the little victims which had been picked up half dead in the snow. Robins, linnets and chaffinches fluttered about the room, and sparrows pecked for food at her hands. The little creatures had become so accustomed to their captivity that they would not fly out when the window was opened for them. The newcomers, so frozen that they barely breathed, Aurore restored to life against the warmth of her body. The birds eventually flew away except for an obstinate robin who would flutter on the window sill only to fly back into the room and the diet of almond paste on which he had grown fat. He did not leave until April. By then Aurore too was allowed to go out into the garden.

She could not explain her mysterious languor. Whatever it was, Casimir did not think it serious enough for him to give up any of his pleasures. So he disputed the management of Nohant with Deschartres and went hunting with Hippolyte. Casimir, as a matter of fact, was not given to overmuch concern about anyone but himself. If he had all the necessities and most of the luxuries he demanded, he was as happy as a well-fed stallion and about as aware of the needs of others. Aurore was ill. She was pregnant. Women were always more or less ailing, which was inconvenient but not irreparable. She would be well again in due course.

As sensitive as Casimir was callous, Aurore betrayed by her

illness some deep disillusionment, either in herself or in her husband, certainly in their marriage. She had entered into it willingly but without love, a usual state of affairs in most marriages of convenience. She and Casimir, moreover, had at least had something of a choice in the matter which, if it lent the union no mist of romance, set it apart from the mere money interest of most marital arrangements. There was not too much difference in their years, and they had been drawn to each other by mutual liking. However, it was also true that if Aurore had not chafed at her mother's domination, she would have given herself time to look beyond Casimir.

The differences, small though they were, between her lot and that of the majority of girls in her class, may have led Aurore to expect more than she found in the consummation of her marriage. Her head had been filled with Byronic passion; Chateaubriand had contributed his glowing pictures of love. Unfortunately, Casimir had brought to their union the experience of tavern amours and the prose of a man devoid of imagination. The violation, spiritual, if not physical, had exacted its toll of ill health, always in Aurore an index to psychic disturbance.

In his own deep wisdom Deschartres had unconsciously divined the true cause when he confined Aurore to her bed and so placed her out of reach of marital exactions. To the idealistic girl they had no doubt become so distasteful that the organism took refuge in physical illness to escape them.

Beyond the shock that might have affected the nervous system of any sensitive girl, there was in Aurore a self-confessed anomaly which for many years kept her from experiencing physical fulfillment. She is explicit in *Lélia*, wherein her fictional alter ego declared: "Desire in me was an ardor of the soul that rendered the senses incapable even before rousing them. It was a fine frenzy that possessed the mind with savage fury and concentrated there." Elsewhere the unhappy heroine admits that she had never known the supreme joy of the senses with any of her lovers. Was it frigidity or a late awakening in Aurore, an awakening retarded by the disillusionment of her wedding night?

Physical dyspathy is sufficient to mar the basic harmony of any marriage. Aurore soon discovered, however, that once the stimulation of other people was gone and she remained alone with Casimir, they had little to say to each other. As it was, she had never been given to talking. Even in the midst of a gathering, she would sit quietly with a far-off look and speak only when directly addressed, a habit she had formed under the dogmatism of Deschartres, and also from a desire for self-effacement necessitated in a family circle where she had often been the object of contention.

65

Casimir interpreted her silence as a sign of mental weakness. He was confirmed in his judgment, the longer he lived with Aurore. Like Sophie, he had a dread of originality, and certainly Aurore had been endowed with more than her share of it. Without apparent cause, she would veer from gay to grave, now romping like a tomboy, then suddenly spiraling inward to a secrecy that none could penetrate. Money, solidity, position meant little or nothing to her. He was amazed at how indifferently she had turned over her purse strings to him. On the other hand, a foolish trifle, like the twitter of a bird, would be enough to keep her happy for a day. He was always made uncomfortable by such childish delight before other people. "Don't be singular," he would chide her. His *épicier* nature did not like its dullness exhibited, even unintentionally.

Then a strange thing happened. As he gradually came to accept Aurore's self-effacement as idiocy and her nervous variability as eccentricity, he arrived, by contrast, at such a high valuation of his own powers that he was affronted each time Aurore dared to express an opinion. Inwardly he knew her superiority, just as he knew that even if they were to live together for a hundred years they would be no closer than they were now. There was no interpenetration of their characters; there never could be. They were two rocks which the deceptive green windings of a vine unite for a season. How long the season of their union, time alone would tell.

Meanwhile Aurore went from illness to dejection, in a mute unhappiness that only the shrewd eyes of Deschartres could fathom. The neighbors, on the whole, thought Casimir Dudevant a good master. He was always occupied with improvements in his determination to make Nohant pay. Everything began to change under his hand. The gardens yielded more, the servants stole less. The dead trees that had given the landscape the look of a Piranesi ruin were cut down for firewood. He killed the toothless mastiffs and sold the old horses, replacing them with fresh stock. He did not even spare the last of Madame Dupin's peacocks which used to peck at strawberries out of her hand. It was a matter of time before Deschartres too would have to go. There were irreconcilable differences of opinion between him and the new master. It wrung Aurore's heart whenever she heard the old man mutter in prescience of his dismissal: "I've lived all my life for others. It's time I began to live for myself."

Early in June, 1823, Aurore and Casimir left Nohant. After spending a few days with Angèle and James du Plessis, they took a furnished apartment in Paris at the Hôtel de Florence. The hotel, run by an ancient chef of Napoleon's, contained a small pavilion in the middle of a tree-shaded court. It was here that on the thirtieth of June, Aurore gave birth to her son, Maurice. "It was the most beautiful moment of my life," she wrote, "when I awoke from my sleep of exhaustion and found that little mite asleep on my pillow." Already maternity had given her more joys than she had found in marriage.

Deschartres, wearing his best habit for the occasion, set out for Paris to see Madame Dupin's great-grandchild. People in the big city turned to stare at the old man in his antiquated blue frock coat and gold buttons. Aurore welcomed him with a foreboding sadness and watched him as he picked up the child, unswaddled it, examined the tiny body without a word, and then held it gravely across his knees for a long interval. "It's time I began to live for myself," he muttered.

Casimir did not strongly dissuade him. When Aurore pleaded with Deschartres to stay on and take care of the young Maurice as he had cared for her father, he talked of grand schemes he had for making his fortune. He must think of himself now, he repeated. When he left Nohant, not long afterward, he made the tacit dismissal appear to be a voluntary departure. Miserably Aurore saw him go, like another part of her life.

The poor old tutor started out on his career with no great hopes and little money after more than thirty years of service to the Dupins. Aurore was married, however badly; she no longer needed him. Nohant had fallen into other hands which had dug up even the roots he had sunk there. Moreover, it was anguish for him to share with another the place he had seen grow from a ruin to a gracious domain, every inch of which was holy ground not only for its associations but for the unrealized ambitions buried there, Madame Dupin's in her son, Sophie Dupin's in her infant. There too were buried an old love and an unshaken fidelity.

At first Deschartres did not go too far from Nohant. He bought a small property, and with his alchemist's curiosity, abetted by the large promises of a speculator, embarked on a series of experiments which, he was sure, would enrich them both. Unfortunately his plantation of rape failed to yield the expected amount of oil, and the base clods obstinately refused to turn themselves into gold. Worse, the experiments devoured most of his small capital.

Like many a younger man in search of success, he then set out for the metropolis. Paris proved equally unlucky. But he never complained, never asked for help. Whenever Aurore went to see him, he entertained her with his vast plans. Alone, he would be filled with mortal weariness. The man who had lived for others could not make his own life. One day, in 1825, he was found dead in his apartment at the Porte Royale. Had he died a natural death? Had he killed himself? Aurore never knew, though she believed that the proud, broken man had preferred to die by his own hand rather than to depend upon the charity of others. Deschartres had really ceased to live after he left Nohant. For two years he had merely existed posthumously in an alien world.

The Dudevants returned home shortly after the birth of Maurice and passed there the autumn and winter. Casimir was beginning to be bored with the place. He went out hunting more often with Hippolyte who had recently married, and oftener still joined him in breaking countless bottles of *vin cru*.

Hippolyte worried Aurore. As a boy he had shown marked aptitude for study in spite of his wildness and later, even after the novelty of the uniform had worn off, he had distinguished himself in the Hussars. Somehow he did not possess the discipline of self to carry anything through. Now, although he had married a girl with a fair fortune, he showed no sign of settling down. A feverish activity sent him from La Châtre to Nohant, from Nohant to Paris on what invariably turned out to be sleeveless errands which succeeded only in reducing his wife's dowry. Then, in disappointment, he tried to forget his failures in drink.

Hippolyte's tragedy, which he did not understand and which Aurore, perhaps, avoided facing, had been plotted for him long since in the *petite maison* that had made him the son, yet not the heir, of Maurice Dupin. The illegitimate child, intelligent, high-spirited, had always been given second place, even though he was a boy and, therefore, a member of the ruling sex in a society that had tried to level every inequality but nature's, and had as much claim to his father's blood as his half sister. True, Madame Dupin had placed him, with Aurore, under Deschartres. But the boy was made to swallow the fact of his inferiority. He did not live in the big house. His name was Châtiron and not Dupin. He knew that when Madame Dupin died, if she had not made any provision for him in her will, he would have had no more claim on the inheritance than the remotest acquaintance.

As he and Aurore grew older, he had had to acknowledge his subservience to her, the legitimate heir. She could either recognize or ignore him as her position in society changed. Aurore not only recognized him, but in her genuine fondness for him, brought him into closer intimacy by having him live at Nohant. Nonetheless, the daily experience of the plenty that might have been his, of the social prestige he might have enjoyed but for the accident of his birth, must have had a destructive effect on a character that had not inherited strength as one of its attri-

68

butes. And so the tragedy of Hippolyte, begun with bastardy, was pointing toward its unhappy dénouement.

Aurore devoted herself to the care of her child. She nursed him herself and sewed his clothes. At night, while she watched over him in the apprehensive solicitude of one whose only happiness lay in that beribboned cradle, she amused herself by following the advice her cousin René had once given her. She was writing a novel. It was not good, and she knew it. Shapeless, inchoate, full of bizarre adventures and improbabilities, it pleased her nevertheless because thesis had given way to an interest in character. Besides, it offered refuge from boredom.[1]

Casimir, on his part, considered himself an impeccable husband. He was capable, strong, and solicitous for his wife's welfare. He had shown such wisdom in administering her fortune that Aurore of her own accord had turned over to him her personal allowance of three thousand francs a year. Aurore was sensible about money matters, at any rate, whatever singularity she exhibited in other respects. He loved her. Yes, he had learned to love her in spite of her many faults. She was young; she would improve. If they had another child she would not spend so many hours reading after dinner, till he was so bored that he fell asleep in his chair. She would not fritter away her time painting pictures or, what was intolerable to him, making that infernal noise at the harpsichord, when she played music without a tune that anyone could follow. Perhaps she would even be gay again. He liked gaiety. The sound of laughter substituted so pleasantly for the effort of thought.

Yet underneath his reasonableness there was a feeling of rancor. Aurore should dutifully try to amuse him instead of thinking of herself and her books. She knew they had no interest for him, that he could not even read a newspaper without dozing. Still she persisted, even though it was probably that constant application which was making her sick. She was so wan and listless that he was beginning to wonder what he had ever seen in her. If he did not love her as much as he did, he would be justified in seeking stronger pleasures than the wine he drank with Hippolyte.

One morning, while they were sitting together at breakfast Casimir, staring at her downcast looks with his uncomprehending china blue eyes, was startled by her suddenly breaking into a fit of hysterical crying. He had given her no provocation that he could see; they had hardly exchanged a word. "What's the matter? What are you crying about?" he asked.

Aurore shook her head in misery. What could she tell him? She herself did not know what trifle, the way he ate, his look

[1] *L'Histoire d'un Rêveur* was never published in her lifetime.

of brute complacency, or what overwhelming hopelessness, what sense of knowing herself alone yet indissolubly chained to that stranger at the other end of the table, had loosed her pent-up despair. "Nothing, it's nothing," she said when she could speak. "I've often felt this causeless dejection before. Perhaps there's something wrong with me. I may have a weak head—"

"I'm sure that must be it," Casimir agreed. "I've always told you so."

He also generously suggested, however, that she might still be feeling the death of her grandmother which the people of Nohant did not allow her to forget. Perhaps she needed change. As for himself, he would be grateful for it, too. He was getting tired of his duties as an administrator. She had no idea how many there were. Why not quit Nohant for a time?"

In an unconscious desire to recapture their short-lived joys, they arranged to stay with the Plessis. The house at Melun rang again with the games of the young people. Little Maurice gurgled happily, delighted with all the attention he was getting. Aurore was transformed. In the light and gaiety of the household she shed her melancholy like an imprisoning husk. She was again the playfellow, as free and frolicsome as the Plessis children.

Casimir, whose wounded vanity sharpened his perceptions, noted the change and resented it. Evidently Aurore needed other people to amuse her. He, the perfect husband, was not the center of her universe. With him she drooped, while here, after a few days with her friends, she lost that sick look and seemed almost pretty again. He could not forgive her that slight to his manhood, that ingratitude toward his dutiful husbandry.

He grew pettish, as if every burst of laughter mocked him. One evening, Angèle and James were having their after-dinner coffee on the terrace with Casimir while Aurore, in a fit of irrepressible gaity, was romping about with the children. During the sport someone threw a handful of gravel, and a few grains fell into James's cup. Casimir's temper smoldered.

"Stop that, Aurore!" he shouted.

In the heat of play Aurore did not heed him. This public defiance of his authority incensed him. Rising from the table, he strode toward her in a fury, shook her roughly and struck her across the face.

Aurore could not believe it, in her momentary daze from the violence of the blow, and the greater shock to her pride. Casimir had struck her. This man, whose bed she shared, whose child she had borne, had behaved toward her like a brute. Too wounded to speak, too humiliated to face her friends, she ran to the woods and spent half the night bemoaning the wreck of her life. She could do nothing about it. She was married and the marriage bonds could not be broken. In the future she must try to avoid storms by being the sort of wife Casimir wished her to be, bowing to his superiority, concealing her disillusionment in a false cheerfulness. There could be no more question of love. He had killed it with that blow.

In the autumn, instead of returning home, they rented a house at Ormesson, on the outskirts of Paris. Neither had any wish to resume the depressing intimacy they had fled from at Nohant. In her cottage Aurore received her neighbors and entertained her Aunt Lucie. Sometimes she joined the charades at Madame Richardot's. In a new desire for communion, she wrote innumerable letters to Hippolyte, to her mother, all about Maurice, "that love, that Cupid." She reached out for human companionship, as if to test the length of the chain that bound her to Casimir. Everything outside the sphere of her marriage assumed the proportions of great adventure. Casimir was often away on business in Paris. Aurore did not question him. Men had their interests outside the home; she had hers in her son whom she loved with an absorbing devotion.

As the winter approached, everyone left Ormesson. The Dudevants stayed on. In spite of the loneliness Aurore enjoyed the quiet of the place, whose English gardens and somber landscape made a harmonious background for her thoughts. It was like an engraving for a scene from *René*, even to a fountain and a tomb shaded by a grove of cypresses. The tomb was to reappear in the novel *Lélia*.

Finally, however, as bad weather kept her often indoors, and as Casimir had taken to spending most of his nights away from home, Aurore found the solitude so oppressive that not even the ingratiating common sense of Montaigne's *Essays* which she read from cover to cover, could dispel it. She felt her dejection threatening again. They decided to take a furnished apartment in Paris after Casimir quarreled with the gardener.

Aurore weaned her baby. She was weak from the long period of nursing. The depression which had merely threatened became a dread actuality, and she was almost convinced, like Casimir, that she was tainted by some mental weakness. On the advice of her old confessor, Abbé Prémord, she made a retreat at Les Anglaises. Casimir, who had no faith of any kind, sent her off gladly. Religion was good for a woman, he said. Besides, he had no objection to a little bachelor freedom.

Aurore found the nuns so far gone in holiness as to be bigoted. Only Sister Mary Alicia, still the favorite, seemed to have any understanding of what unspoken sorrow might be weighing upon this revenant from the outside world.

"You tell me you have a lovely boy," she said to Aurore. "What more does a woman need to be happy? Life is short."

What more indeed? In spite of her profound instinct for motherhood, Aurore knew that life held many things which it had yet to give her. Perhaps she would never have them. For the present, her dissatisfaction was like a promise.

She stayed out her period at Les Anglaises and toward the end was even permitted to have Maurice with her. "What! A young man here among us?" cried the housekeeper. "Well, if he's small enough to come in through the *tour,* we'll make an exception." And so Maurice was duly handed in through the revolving cylinder in the outside wall that served to receive packages.

"Bunnies! Bunnies!" shrieked the child excitedly when he saw the nuns.

Colonel and Madame Dudevant who were staying in Paris at the time, occasionally entertained Aurore and Casimir. Aurore was very fond of the colonel who admired his daughter-in-law and did not hesitate to show it. It was different with his wife. A chill, plangent rail of a woman, she had no love for anyone but herself. No longer young, she envied Aurore her youth. Too frigid ever to have borne a child, she took no pains to conceal her annoyance at Maurice's little mishaps on her rug. Aurore tried to like her but was forced by the woman's coldness to a barren civility. It did not keep her, however, from accepting the colonel's invitation to spend a few months with the baby at Guillery, the Dudevant place near Nérac in Gascony. It would be at least one distraction to look forward to the following year.

Chapter VIII: A Platonic Interlude

AURORE'S health took a turn for the worse. She had an obstinate cough; she was feverish; her heart beat too fast. She was haunted by the fear of consumption, and the neurotic dread affected her nerves. Nothing amused her any more, and she saw pass like a pageant in a dream the festival the villagers held on the thirtieth of June, Maurice's birthday, and on her own coming of age in July, 1825. Even Casimir was convinced that something had to be done. On the fifth of the month he took her, the baby and a servant for a change of air in the Pyrenees.

Aurore left Nohant certain that she would nevermore return. A Romantic, to the very malady that she believed consuming her, she had to express her sense of fatality in a tearful sensibility. All dying young poets want to scratch their names, even in sand. True to tradition, she took along a provision of notebooks. *A Voyage to the Pyrenees,* she titled the first, before starting off. "In ten minutes I shall have left Nohant," she recorded for the hypothetical reader. "I leave nothing that I shall miss, except, perhaps, my brother. But how cold our old affection has grown! . . . Ah, well, farewell, Nohant. Perhaps I shall never see you again."

"My servants were crying," she took up the journal at Chalus. "I could not control myself and I wept, too. In the coach I read some pages of Ossian. . . ." Tears and fictive emotionalism, with Ossian as the tutelary god. Aurore was ripe for whatever fate might bring.

At Cauterets fate brought her the friendship of Zoe Leroy, a young woman possessed of intellect as well as contempt for convention, and a meeting with Aurélien de Sèze, a lawyer whom she had seen once before at Bordeaux. Casimir frowned on both for he saw danger in both. The impudent Zoe did not hesitate to laugh in his face, and there was nothing Casimir dreaded more than public ridicule.

"Aurore, you're being singular," he would remind his wife at every step of the way to the Marborée caves.

"You're being singular," Zoe echoed, while Aurore broke into peals of laughter that rang out in a mocking chorus.

Casimir threw them furious looks. That bold young woman was encouraging his wife in her insubordination. He wondered what it was they talked about when they went off by themselves; his suspicion told him it was about him.

The young women, however, had quite other subjects to occupy their minds. They had both read much and lived hardly at all. Their intellectual curiosity had been as little appeased as their hunger for experience. They were adolescents with the yearning and desires of mature women—a dangerous unbalance, aggravated by their setting themselves apart from the rest of their sex. Love, religion, philosophy, marriage: they discussed them all, Aurore from the advantage of her matronly summit.

"Marriage is good for lovers and useful for saints," she pontificated. "Besides saints and lovers there is a generality of peaceful dull souls who know nothing of love and could never become saints. Marriage is the culmination of love. When love is no longer there, sacrifice remains, which is all very well for those who understand sacrifice. . . . Perhaps there is no happy medium between the strength of great souls which constitutes sanctity, and the comfortable dullness of little souls. Ah, but there is a medium: despair."

She savored that despair with the keenness induced by the romantic setting and the knowledge that she was herself for the first time in love, spiritually, platonically in love with a brother soul whose very name marked him the lover destined for her from the beginning of time. Aurélien, Aurore. Not Dante and Beatrice had heard fate speak so clearly, not Petrarch and Laura, nor all the celebrated lovers who have been beacon lights to humanity. She loved, and Aurélien de Sèze returned her love. She swung between bliss and despair. For there was Casimir.

She had not forgotten her husband, for she was a good woman who took seriously the duties she owed him. Faithfulness was one of them. Not that she had entertained the thought of infidelity, even for a moment. Nevertheless, she could not overcome an obstinate feeling of guilt. With the devil's advocacy of a woman in love she tried to shift the blame, at least in her journal, to Casimir.

"Monsieur hunts with passion," she noted before her disquisition on marriage. "He shoots chamois and eagles. He gets up at two in the morning and does not come back until late at night. His wife complains." Casimir was neglecting her, she convinced herself, adding on a note of sad wisdom, "He does not seem to foresee that there may come a time when she will rejoice."

An innate honesty, however, removed the scales from her moral vision. She loved Aurélien with her soul only, she told herself, and gave him nothing that Casimir would have missed. But was she not as guilty as if she had committed actual adultery? Who was to determine where innocence ended and crime began? "There are certain pure, discreet, mysterious relationships that do more to undermine a husband's peace of mind than outright infidelities," she wrote elsewhere at this time.

Who was this lover already painfully disturbing to Casimir's placidity? Aurélien de Sèze, who had his practice at Bordeaux, came of a family of distinguished advocates. His great-uncle had been the defender of Louis XVI and later won the dubious distinction of making Napoleon snort, "Lawyer de Sèze—idealogue!" Aurélien himself showed promise of a successful career. In 1823 he had been named substitute on the Bordeaux tribunal. It was axiomatic that with such an ancestry and with such beginnings he was bound to go far.

It was not worldly success, however, that counted with Aurore so much as the young man's obvious qualities. His charm of manner and delightful wit had already devastated the female population of Cauterets, like all watering places at the peak of susceptibility in the excitement of the season. Zoe, before Aurore arrived, had fallen victim, but she generously made way when she saw how eagerly Aurélien responded to the young woman's originality. He was the opposite of Casimir in looks, dark, vibrant from the electric charge of his intellect, and he was young, just twenty-six.

Casimir began to watch Aurore, and his jealousy, long dormant from taking her virtue for granted, knew no rest. He saw how the two were never at a loss for conversation, how De Sèze delighted in Aurore's music whenever she played in the hotel salon, how, even in their silences, they seemed to speak. In fact, he read more in their looks than Aurore and Aurélien were aware of. For, if one is to believe Aurore's later account, she was so taken aback at Aurélien's first declaration that she repulsed him.

Casimir, of course, knew nothing about it, although he had been lurking in the background of their innocent meetings on the expectation of surprising them in their guilt. For three days Aurore avoided Aurélien and wandered alone in desolation. She adored him—but she was Casimir's wife. She had given him up—but she could not live without him. She saw Aurélien as woebegone as herself. Touched by his unhappiness, she granted him a final interview that evening on the terrace that they might drink to the dregs the bittersweet sorrows of renunciation.

Aurélien spoke of his overpowering love. So great was its spiritual flame that the body and its needs had been consumed in it. He adored her as one adores a saint. What greater happiness than that their souls mingle in a love as imperishable as the divine essence itself? Aurore listened beatified, hardly conscious that Aurélien's corporal arm was sliding round her waist and that, even as he spoke, he was pressing her to his heart. She let him kiss her, on the cheek. So much another man's wife might accord her eternal beloved.

Casimir who had followed, and this time caught, them, in their embrace, was of quite another mind. He made a violent scene when he was alone with Aurore who, fresh from her uplifting spiritual surrender, and softened to pity for Casimir, confessed her love for Aurélien, explaining how nobly beautiful a thing it was. What a chapter the three of them might write in the story of the human heart if only Casimir would understand how far above an "affair" her love was! Affair? Why, she and Aurélien in their exalted passion and he, Casimir, in his sublime generosity, might set such an ennobling example that husbands and lovers in ages to come would be edified.

She was so transported by her vision that she convinced herself renunciation was sweeter than any fulfillment. She even succeeded in proving to Casimir's satisfaction the entire innocence of her relationship with her lover, and obtained his magnanimous consent that she continue to see Aurélien under his chaperoning tutelage, and to write to him, subject to uxorious censorship.

Toward the end of August the fogs drove the Dudevants from Cauterets. After a short stop at Bagnères they set off for Guillery where they spent the winter with Colonel Dudevant and his wife, Aurore enveloped in ecstatic reverie, Casimir bursting with good intentions which the life at his father's house did not permit him to carry out to the full.

Sublimely inspired, Aurélien fell in with Aurore's plan, not doubting in the least that it could be carried out to the glory of the three. He was a very correct young man; he had, besides, a highly developed legal mind. Aurore belonged to Casimir by the rights of a signed contract, he reasoned. It would take more than ordinary magnanimity on the part of a husband to share her—spiritually, of course—with another.

"Aurore," he wrote to her. "I leave it to you to express my gratitude and admiration for Casimir. Never was there a more delicate heart, a nobler soul. . . . Oh, how unjust we were to him! But we shall make it up to him. If it is possible for him to be happy, we must see to it that he is, by doing all we can toward that end. You must surround him with care and affection. You must, together, bring up Maurice. Teach him to be good, loving and tender, like his mother, noble and generous, like your husband. . . ."

Thus elevated to the level of the two noble lovers, Casimir endeavored to make himself worthy of his apotheosis. He had many heart-to-heart talks with Aurore during which he admitted his shortcomings and begged her to show him how to reach Aurélien's height of perfection. She supervised his reading and behavior, pointing out his faults with such tender sorrow that Casimir's porcelain blue eyes overflowed in repentance. Let him but try to love books a little more, and be patient with her, and he would have the most loving wife any man had ever possessed. "You have my heart," she wrote him from Guillery after he left for a short stay at Nohant. "Come back soon. Have faith in me. Sleep in peace."

Casimir responded to admiration. Since Aurore kept a journal and Aurélien, too, no doubt, he wrote her a letter in the form of a diary. At Nohant he had been filled with a desire to improve himself, he declared. "I have chosen *Les Pensées* of Pascal as you advised. I read the introduction and I thought it very beautiful. How I blame myself for my past idleness!" He was also studying English and always went to bed with a book to keep him company in his loneliness. He adored her, he assured her. And doubtless he did. There is no stronger stimulant to appreciation than the knowledge that another covets the neglected object.

Not to be outdone, certainly not by Casimir, Aurore took a supply of well-sharpened quills and composed a document for his return. It was a full confession, eighteen crowded pages, on the inception and growth of her love for Aurélien, together with a review of her life with Casimir. In it she beat her breast in blame with one hand, and pointed a monitory finger at Casimir with the other. "Casimir, my friend, my indulgent judge, at this point forget that you are my lord and master; be my father. Let me open my heart to you and pour out my tears and contrition upon your breast. Forget these futile prejudices, these false notions of honor that often turn a husband into a despicable tyrant. . . ."

Yes, she had sinned in allowing Aurélien to kiss her, even though it had been a blameless kiss. But not for an instant had she forgotten that she was bound to Casimir, who from now on must really be her true husband and understanding comrade. He must read aloud to her in the evening and listen without yawning whenever she played the pianoforte. He must go to Paris with her and study languages. He must . . . Roman numerals followed each other in legalistic array as Aurore specified her terms. It was not too great a price for her noble abnegation.

Casimir agreed to her conditions and lived up to as many of them as he could. He promised to show Aurore what a model he could be. He would engage in business. He would make a fortune for them.

Aurore was content and began in earnest her life of the heart symbolized by the mystic triangle, "God—he—and I." The masculine pronoun stood for Aurélien. God made a first appearance in her formulation of love which she elaborated as she gained in practical wisdom. "People say with a laugh," she wrote, "that there's nothing so easy as procreation: it takes only two. Not at all. It takes three: a man, a woman and the god within them."

From Guillery Aurore and Casimir went to Bordeaux, Aurélien's city, where they received the news of Colonel Dudevant's sudden death. By the provisions of the will, framed under his stepmother's supervision, if not at her dictation, Casimir found himself no richer than before. The baronne had a large fortune on her own account. Nevertheless she tied up Casimir's expectations, so that when she died many years later, she left this stepson whom she had never loved, only the riches she had not been able to take from him during her long and selfish life.

The reformed Casimir, spurred on by his ambition, set about proving that he was superior to his misfortune by entering big business: nothing less than shipbuilding. He had met a man at Bordeaux, a certain Desgranges, who talked of his shipping interests and of the profits to be made on even a moderate investment. There was this beauty—Desgranges showed Casimir the picture of a handsome ship. A small investment, say of twenty-five thousand francs, would yield enormous dividends. Casimir gave Desgranges the desired notes.

For two years he made frequent trips to Bordeaux while Aurore mildly complained that their life of the spirit had hardly begun before it was over. Casimir soothed her by making mysterious allusions to his affairs. To Aurore's dismay the affairs turned out to be singular and incarnate in Desgranges' mistress whom Casimir had taken for his own. The pursuit of the ideal had been too much for him.

Although her letters to Aurélien continued as spiritually impassioned as the outpourings of a medieval saint, the strain was becoming too much for Aurore as well, for by a tacit compact the bride of Aurélien, in Plato, had little by little almost ceased to be the wife of Casimir in the flesh, a lack which Casimir supplied in his own way. Aurélien alone kept the flame burning in its pristine purity, feeding it on the fervor of his love.

"Aurore, if I should *never* see you again. I shudder at the dreadful word," he wrote her in his longing. "If I knew that at some time I might see you, if only for a day, even ten years from now, I should be happy. The hope alone would sustain me."

As it was, chance proved less niggardly than he anticipated,

78

for one day early in September, 1828, he found himself at Nohant on unexpected business and called upon Aurore. She was putting away some baby clothes when he entered. Did he imagine a note of constraint in her voice when she greeted him?

"What is it you're doing?" he asked, himself suddenly shocked to realize that his spiritual bride was about to become a mother for the second time.

"Really! Can't you see?" she replied, turning her confusion to pleasantry. "I'm preparing in a hurry for someone who's arriving sooner than I expected."

Aurélien took his leave without comment. In that moment of realization the platonic edifice, so devoutly built for three years, tumbled to ruin. He returned to Bordeaux where the penetrating eyes of Zoe read his wretchedness and disillusionment. "He's no longer the same," she wrote Aurore who, on the fourteenth of September had given birth to a daughter, Solange. "I even fear for his mental state."

Not only Aurélien but Casimir also had been troubled by the arrival of Solange, Aurélien because he was torn with doubt as to whether the baby was Casimir's or the child of someone who had had fewer scruples than himself; Casimir because, in his irreligion, he was puzzled by that almost immaculate conception.

Stéphane de Grandsaigne had returned to Nohant the latter part of 1827. Early the following year Aurore announced her pregnancy, which sent Casimir on a course of dissipation such as he had never indulged in before. After the child's birth he was confirmed in drunkenness and brutality.

In her platonic lover and in her husband Lélia had claimed her first victims.[1]

[1] On January 6, 1900, *Le Moniteur* published an article by the eldest son of Stéphane de Grandsaigne, based on letters of George Sand to his father, in which the relationship of Aurore and Stéphane left no room for doubt. On January 10 of the same year, Ernest Gégoux wrote a similar article which appeared in the *Télégramme*. A lawsuit was instituted by Aurore's heirs. The court, on examining pertinent documents, gave them no redress.

Part Two

THE ROMANTIC AGONY

Chapter IX: Vive la Liberté

IN 1822 the members of the jury for the French Salon, sitting in judgment on the works submitted for their approval, had a panoramic view of the art of their country in the eclectic canvases that passed before their eyes. Here the descendants of the court painter David exhibited their soulless classicism, for many years on the wane but not yet eclipsed; there the imitators of Ingres showed immaculate nudes that failed, however, for lack of the master's purity of line. The grand style was still predominant. Now and then, like an interloper, a rebel canvas flaunted its unorthodoxy amid all that formalism, only to be hurried out of sight by the indignant jury. Before one such canvas, however, the gentlemen were compelled to pause.

The subject of the "Dante and Virgil" by an unknown Eugène Delacroix was as classical as could have been desired. But the treatment was a scandal. Guérin, the teacher of Delacroix, had already disclaimed responsibility for it. Color glowed from every inch of the canvas, enclosed in a frame that proclaimed the artist's poverty. The composition was a tumult of tortured action. Against the background of a city in flames, Dante and Virgil, not the complacent figures of the usual heroic pageant, but two living men moved by the passions surrounding them, sway in their frail boat, besieged by the lost souls of the river Styx. The waves boil into foam. Half emerging from the infernal waters, the naked bodies of the damned struggle to board the craft. Man fights with man. In the center, one clings to the brink of the boat, his foot on the body of a woman, the better to climb to safety. At the stern an anguished figure grapples to the bark with hands and teeth.

Here indeed was a work calculated to infuriate the Academicians. Three years earlier, however, they had felt a similar jolt when Théodore Géricault had entered his "Raft of the Medusa," a realistic subject, painted with power and imagination. It had been shown at the Salon, and for two years it enjoyed an enormous success in England. Too close to the subject, however, the Academicians did not identify it as the inaugural canvas of the Romantic movement in French painting. Perhaps here, in Dela-

81

croix, who had something of Géricault together with a great deal more of himself, the jury might discover a future genius. A violent debate broke out among the members. It was Gros, himself a rebel from the school of David, who put an end to the argument by having the disputed painting suitably framed at his own expense for exhibition at the Salon.

For the twenty-four-year-old Delacroix, the recognition of his first ambitious work ushered in a new era. He was an accepted painter, a man to be reckoned with. He must put off childish things and be an artist among artists. He must carry on the work of Géricault, his initiator.

"The Massacre at Scio" of 1824 confirmed Delacroix' position. Dithyrambic praise and violent attacks, both affirmations of his merit, paved his way to glory. The canvas was purchased for the state. Taking up the brush from Géricault's dead hand, he led the ranks of *la jeune peinture*. A stay in England the following year improved his technique through a close study of Constable, and widened his Romantic scope as he acquired a more intimate appreciation of Byron and Sir Walter Scott.

For three years private and official commissions had been pouring in. But alas, his vaulting romanticism o'erleapt itself in his daring "Death of Sardanapalus," exhibited in the Salon of 1827. Before the tumultuous canvas which surrounded death with orgiastic luxury as the somber Sardanapalus brooded among his dead and dying courtesans, followers and enemies of Romanticism stood alike dismayed. "When a foolhardy soldier," wrote the redoubtable Vitet of *Le Globe*, "shoots at his friends as well as his foes, he must be banished from the ranks." Worse, Vitet adjured the young school to break away from Delacroix' treacherous independence. The painter's commissions fell away. His struggles began anew.

"I am bored with the whole Salon," he complained to Raymond Soulier in a letter of March 11, 1828. "They'll end by convincing me that I've made a real fiasco. But I am not yet convinced. Some say that my fall is complete, and that the 'Death of Sardanapalus' is the death of the Romantics. . . . I say that they're all imbeciles. The canvas has both faults and virtues, and while I wish that some things in it might be better, there are plenty more which I'm proud to have achieved—would that they could do the same!"

Confident of his own powers, Delacroix continued to paint from the urgent impulses of his genius. Fashions change; art is eternal. He preferred the eternal. Now, in the current Salon of 1831, he was exhibiting a canvas that again drew the crowds, his "Liberty Leading the People."

Once more the subject of the prodigious painting dealt with violence and death. But like an angel of resurrection, the bare-breasted figure of Liberty, whose speed molds her gown to her mighty limbs, strides onward over the foreground paved with dead, toward the light of triumph. Her left arm, swung backward, holds a musket. Aloft in her right hand ripples the tricolor of the Republic, its broad, white central band one with the sky on which it is unfurled. Her face, which might have belonged to the Victory of Samothrace, is turned toward her followers with a look of fire. Students armed with guns, workmen with swords and sabers, carrying improvised standards torn from their shirts and smocks, members of the Old Guard, obey her summons. The wounded crawl toward her over the torn-up paving stones. On her left, a child of the Paris streets, perhaps the prototype of Hugo's Gavroche, marches forward, a pistol in each hand. He is posterity that has known the kiss of Liberty and will ever remember its intoxication. At her feet is one who has died for her. He is young and virginal, from the pure dead face to the naked loins, still heaving from the only ecstasy he has ever known. Another, beside him, lifts up his eyes to her before he dies. Already his countenance is touched with the final transfiguration.

The people paused before the painting and looked grave. Knuckles tensed, lips curled in bitter memory of the events of July, 1830, which it portrayed. Yes, Liberty had led the people. They had given everything for her sake . . . only to find Louis Philippe on the throne and the bankers behind him. They hardly knew how it had happened. But Thiers was a cunning statesman and Laffitte had the power of money.

On the death of Louis XVIII in September of 1824, his brother, the Comte d'Artois, succeeded him as Charles X. No sooner was he crowned in the Rheims Cathedral, than the people knew what to expect. First, the new monarch passed a measure appropriating a vast sum from the treasury to indemnify the Royalist emigrés whose lands had been confiscated during the Revolution. There followed immediately a decree on sacrilege, and another to restore the rights of primogeniture. These bills struck the keynote; the rest sounded an alarm to the Liberals. Reaction had set in. Even men like the Duc de Broglie were uneasy and spoke out their concern: "Your Majesty is bringing about another revolution to set at nought the Revolution that changed France nearly forty years ago."

But Charles X did not heed him. With the Royalists behind him and the seat of power solid beneath him, he forgot what Napoleon had discovered: that the throne is only a few wooden planks covered with velvet. He proceeded from one reactionary measure to another, until in 1830, he found his way blocked by the risen people.

Another would have taken warning from the ominous rumbling in February of that year, at the first performance of Hugo's *Hernani,* when the youth of the nation, with Gautier and Balzac in their ranks, staged a demonstration, as much in support of their leader as in protest against the royal muzzling of Hugo's earlier tragedy, *Marion Delorme,* for representing a monarch as other than divine. In March, the Liberals in the Chambers voted their mistrust of the government by a large majority, in spite of the king's attempt to forestall such a vote by increasing the Chamber of Peers to outbalance the deputies. Then Charles X resorted to the Napoleonic expedient of making a little conquest as a sop to public disaffection. Accordingly, taking as a pretext the incident that the Dey of Algiers had insulted France in the person of the French consul, Charles X sent Beaumont with an expedition to Algiers. By the early part of July Algiers had been seized. A few days later its annexation (and that of more than fifty millions of francs in spoils) was announced.

Drunk with victory, Charles X dissolved the unfriendly Chambers by an edict, signed on the twenty-fourth of July, after he had duly attended mass. His ministers added their names. The following day the Orders in Council were made public in *Le Moniteur.*

Immediately the anger of the people, too long restrained, broke out in just violence. Overnight the streets of Paris became a maze of barricades, six hundred of them, to block the advance of tyranny. Workers, burghers, soldiers, all joined in a common cause, led by the republican Cavaignac and François Raspail. The portal of Notre Dame was forced by a horde of students and the tricolor raised on its towers. The Tuileries and the Louvre were stormed as during the Revolution, and they too unfurled the red, white and blue of freedom. The National Guard brought out the banners of past glory and wore their tricolor cockades. Every house and public building became a fortress during what was to be known as the Great Week.

Through it all, Charles X, overconfident of the divinity that doth hedge a king, played whist at St. Cloud and waved away Marshal Marmont's exclamation: "Sire, it is no longer a riot but a revolution."

"Put Paris under a state of siege," ordered the king.

When the cannonading shook the palace, he asked in mild wonder: "Where do they get their powder?"

"From the soldiers," came the unexpected answer.

Still the king made no concession, disapproving such action

84

as weakness which would only strengthen the rebels. "I've no desire to ride like my brother on a cart," he said.

Meanwhile the people had captured the Hôtel de Ville and installed a municipal commission. When at last Charles X agreed to countermand his edict, it was too late. The people had deposed him and proclaimed a republic whose presidency they offered to Lafayette. But the general was old. Moreover, he was cognizant of the troubles he would have inherited. He suggested, and Thiers seconded him, Louis Philippe, Duc D'Orléans, son of Philippe Égalité, thus giving a double edge to the observation of the deposed king: "Lafayette and I are the only two who have not changed since 1789."

Like his father, Louis Philippe had a revolutionary past. At eighteen, as lieutenant general, he had fought side by side with Dumouriez in the victories of Valmy and Jemappes, a fact which he brought out with affected modesty at every opportunity. He had lived for a long time in America and in England under an assumed name, and in Switzerland he had taught foreign languages to support himself. In 1809 while at Palermo he married the daughter of Ferdinand IV, the Princess Maria Amelia. Thereafter he had kept a wakeful eye on the fortunes of Napoleon, then of Louis XVIII, and then of Charles X.

When destiny called him to the rôle of citizen king, he was prepared to the very appurtenances of a good bourgeois, the tubular trouser and the hard round hat. He also knew when to agree or disagree.

"You must know," Lafayette confided to him before the coronation, "that I consider the Constitution of the United States as the best ever framed."

"Do you think we should adopt it, conditions in France being what they are?" Louis Philippe asked tentatively.

"Not yet," said Lafayette. "The French people need a throne supported by republican institutions."

"That's exactly what I think," Louis Philippe cordially agreed. He gave a still heartier affirmation when Laffitte, escorting the newly made monarch, decorated by a tricolor scarf, to the Hôtel de Ville, remarked: "From now on the bankers will rule." It did not disturb him that Laffitte's words and Lafayette's exclamation, "You are our best republic!" as he handed him the tricolor of freedom, were mutually exclusive. Rather, he strove to fit them into his Procrustean "golden mean" of government which, realistically interpreted, meant the rule of the middle class according to the light of Louis Philippe, who now had a personal fortune of more than eight million pounds to protect.

The people put up with him but were not fooled. If the Great Week had succeeded in ridding them of the trunk of the

Bourbon tree only to foist upon them a lesser branch, it had nonetheless reawakened in them the spirit of Liberty.—Did not Delacroix portray her indomitably advancing?—From one extreme to the other the people vibrated to her electric charge. The Carlists, clinging to their castles and *prie-dieux,* hoped through power and the clergy to rid themselves of the citizen king. The citizens, on the other hand, plotted for the overthrow of the bankers' puppet. In the intervals of strikes and riots they found release in their satirical spirit, expressed in endless caricatures of their monarch, with his face of a pear, his little round hat and, inevitably, that newly invented bourgeois protection, an umbrella.

Among the masses the laughter ended in ominous thunder when they considered how craftily they were being deprived of the franchise because of insufficient income, and how they were excluded from the newly revived National Guard because they could not afford to buy their uniforms. They joined instead the flourishing secret societies of disaffected Republicans, and the meliorist organizations of Blanqui and the Saint-Simonists. The dues were within their means and their grievances made them eligible.

In protest to their outwardly correct king, the people plunged into a carnival of extravagance, led by the hotheaded Romantics, since 1830 in the fore as arbiters of life and letters. Not that they were as yet aware of the significance of the date. It was posterity that fixed 1830 as the beginning of a period which had been gestating since the close of the previous century, and giving intimations of prenatal vitality in the poetry of André Chénier, the avowed model of Victor Hugo, de Vigny and of Sainte-Beuve. It was a movement of youth, though Chateaubriand embraced it with grandfatherly pride, and the shade of Rousseau conferred post-mortem blessing; and like youth, it knew nothing of any golden mean unless it meant the color of a louis d'or or the shade of a waistcoat. Its leader, Hugo, was now only twenty-eight, and among his followers were boys like Alfred de Musset and Théophile Gautier, still in their teens who, like him, had lisped in numbers.

What they lacked in years they compensated for in extravagance. Already Gautier's crimson waistcoat and flowing locks had become notorious through imitation, while the burlesque dances of the romantic crew round the bust of the periwigged Racine were to result in the irreverent *can-can,* as much a manifestation of the era as the waltz had been of Waterloo. Romantics and *perruques, bousingots* and *grisâtres:* the literary aligned themselves into factions, the wild hair of the youths against the wigs of the classicists; the little round varnished leather caps of the emancipated hotheads versus the neutral gray hats of the die-hards.

Between the extremes stretched the rainbow-hued cohorts of elegant and dandy: anglophile, sport-loving, luxurious and literate, as ready to fight a duel over a sonnet as over a mistress. They were the fashionables (they used the English word) who sported their satin gilets at the Tuileries and the Boulevard de Gand; who attended first nights and dined at the Café de Paris on the Boulevard des Italiens; who would not be seen having their ices anywhere except at Tortoni's, and who made sure that the horses they rode through the Bois came from the best stables. Thoroughbred and spirited, as adjectives of admiration, Balzac noted, were beginning to replace the flowering Ossianics of a less sporting generation.

The Romantics were the ornaments of the salons and the rakes of the Jockey Club, the menace to the peace of every husband and the ambition of the supernumeraries of the opéra and the theater of the Porte-Saint-Martin. They were the idle sons of the rich and the more prosperous fringe of the writing craft; the seekers after experience from weariness of material surfeit, and the crashers of salon and club for the benefit of a hungry Pegasus. They were the *enfants du siècle,* weary and disillusioned from the cradle, incurably touched by the malady of the century, youths whose torpid blood and jaded imagination demanded the strongest kinds of stimuli to make them feel. For them the madness of the carnival knew no peak. For them the Porte-Saint-Martin brewed intellectual fare in poison plots and degeneracy, blood and sadism, murder and passion that would have exploded the cauldron of a witches' sabbath. Anything to escape the dullness of reality, they cried. And any land but theirs, always, of course, excepting the dandies' paradise of the boulevards, beyond which lay only *terra incognita.*

They did have a country of their choice, however. Spain, the Spain of the hidalgos and of passionate women, of poetry, chivalry, romance and song. Victor Hugo made it the setting of his best known tragedy, and to its rehearsal would come the most ardent of his devotees, showing a red card, like a conspirator's pass, with the one word *Hierro* [1] written upon it. Spanish dances and Spanish costumes drew crowds to the Porte-Saint-Martin, where an actress had only to wear a mantilla, or better, the body-molding costume of the Spanish cavalier, to become the toast of the boulevards. Spain was the dreamland of the poet, the Avalon of French Romanticism.

Alfred de Musset's *Contes d'Espagne et d'Italie,* his first volume of verse which burst upon the Paris of 1830, could not

[1] Spanish, Iron, in the sense of weapon.

have appeared more conspicuously or more appropriately. Even before the publication of his volume, late in 1829, he had been looked upon as the wonder child of Romanticism. Born on December 11, 1810, he counted among his ancestors Joan of Arc, Du Bellay, Ronsard's Cassandre, a troubadour, Colin Muset and, on the side of the sword, Alexandre de Musset, Chevalier de St. Louis, and companion-at-arms of Maurice de Saxe. There was also Guyot Desherbiers, a perfect Fantasio of the eighteenth century, who wrote a long poem on cats, whom he chose to celebrate as the humanitarians among living creatures, friends of the poor and singers at their hearths.

Victor Donatien de Musset, Alfred's father, had fought at Marengo and carried on the literary tradition, first in a number of imaginative works and later, retiring to the life of a government functionary, in erudite critical essays composed in the leisure of his office. He was fifty when Alfred, his second son, was born. The third child, a daughter, Herminie, came nine years later.

The two boys, Paul and Alfred, were brought up by a rigid aristocratic mother on small means and lofty thinking. For a time Alfred attended the Collège Henri IV, where his fellow students ranged from the sons of prosperous tradesmen to the heir of Louis Philippe. He also studied painting and English. Impatient for life, he exhausted every interest almost as soon as he acquired it, as if in the interval of reaching for the fruit it might crumble to ashes in his hand. Even as a child that fretful impatience had characterized him. He was a baby of three when, on awaking one morning, he was brought a pair of bright red shoes. Delighted with the color, he could not wait to put them on, and as his mother seemed to take longer than usual combing his hair, he stamped his feet and cried: "Hurry, hurry, Mamma, or my new shoes will be old."

Life was always his pair of red shoes. He must catch the future before it became the past. Restless, visionary from infancy, he had a taint of epilepsy which so frightened his parents that he was left to do more or less as he pleased, even when he broke mirrors, tore the window curtains to ribbons, and stuck sealing wax all over the walls. But he was also such a beautiful child, of such endearing charm, that they would have done out of bewitchment what they did from fear. His brother Paul, who was five years older, knew even then that Alfred was the master and accepted his inferior position.

Alfred was thirteen when he was introduced to the *cénacle* of Victor Hugo, who was already inclined to pontificate among his juniors, both because he had recently married his cousin Adèle Foucher and had therefore established himself as a man, and because his wreath of Master of Floral Games, while fading, had left with him the indelible assurance of his genius. Alfred de Vigny, Sainte-Beuve and Prosper Mérimée were to be found there, with other youths who had still to make their names. They would read aloud from their works, or, more often, listen to the master's latest poem. Alfred and his friend, Paul Foucher, Hugo's brother-in-law, sat by respectfully. Only once, the slight, girlish, long-haired Alfred stepped out of his obscurity to imitate a drunkard for Hugo's amusement. He gave such a realistic performance that Hugo remembered it longer than he was to recall that Musset, too, was a poet.

All that had been in the 1820's when the Romantics were still under the aura of medievalism and nature worship. At the master's behest, they would climb up to the towers of Notre Dame and while savoring their ices by moonlight, imagine they were beholding the Paris of the troubadours. They were enthusiasts of architecture and of scenery, seeing all civilization in a flying buttress, and man's primal innocence in a morning landscape. At that time, the irreverent Alfred laughed at their posturing, but he was to adopt so many of the trappings of Romanticism in his life, if not in his poetry, that he came to be looked upon as its exponent par excellence.

Meanwhile he began to write, at first in the manner of the *cénacle,* as the fledgling learns his song; but soon his impatient precocity sent him out into the world and rival salons, still under the guidance of Paul Foucher who, as the master's kin, had access to the literary coteries. Now the slim adolescent, with his face of a Renaissance page, was to be seen at Charles Nodier's Arsenal, where poetry vied with the dance, the graceful waltz that allowed the dandy to encircle the waist of some beautiful girl whom otherwise he would have had to gaze at from afar. More thrilling than the dance, however, was the sight of Lamartine, who sometimes adorned Nodier's salon, and sat aloof as if shaded by Apollo's laurel bough. The budding poet threw him looks of admiration. They never exchanged a word. But Lamartine noticed the youth, and left a portrait of him—"A beautiful boy with glossy hair floating over his shoulders, a brow abstracted, rather than pensive, and dreamy eyes. . . . His mouth, very delicate, hesitated between a smile and an expression of sadness. He had a tall, supple form, which even then seemed to bend under the weight, still so light, of his youth."

The older poet had seen what a less perspicacious vision had not yet discerned. Musset, in his abnormal sensibility, was having a difficult time crossing from adolescence to manhood. He tried to prepare himself for a career to please his father, went without conviction from law to medicine and even attempted a bureaucratic post, only to give up conforming forever. "I'll never amount to anything in a profession," he told his brother. "Man is a little enough thing as it is. I'll never resign myself to fitting into a particular pigeonhole."

He desired every woman he saw, yet mistrusted them all. He wanted love, yet feared it, warned perhaps by a subliminal knowledge that once he gave himself up to it he was lost. "I hate women in theory," wrote the seventeen-year-old to his friend Foucher. "But I struggle in vain; I shall be caught. Deceive me, yes, deceive me, wicked beauties—you'll have no glory in deceiving me! . . . Do you know what I'd like to be, what sort of character I aspire to?" he added in the same letter. "I'd like to be a man of easy conquests. Not for my happiness, but to torment women to death, to play on all the stops of my spirit without ever touching my soul. I'd love to be envied by men and adored by women."

So far the young misogynist differed little from other impressionable adolescents lured by the unknown. But a significant confession marked him exceptional. "With me poetry is akin to love. The one gives birth to the other, and they always arrive together." It was extraordinary self-knowledge for one so young, even if the letter closed with the naïve hope, "Just think, my dear fellow, maybe this winter I shall find a woman. You, too, perhaps . . . and then, what more could we want?"

He found his woman, one of those *bonnes fortunes* whose conquest he was anxious to make. His brother Paul guessed at Alfred's triumph when he saw him one day go out with his top hat perched rakishly over one ear and come back wearing it at an even more precarious angle.

The year 1828 was to mark a milestone for the young Romantic. Besides finding a mistress, he published his first poem —in an obscure Dijon sheet, it is true, and signed only with his initials—and embarked upon his double career of poet and dandy.

"I too write verses," he announced early one morning to Sainte-Beuve who was still in bed. Then and there he recited a long elegy on a priestess of Diana, and several ballads. Sainte-Beuve was instantly awake. As a discoverer of genius he kept his eyes and ears open for any manifestation of Apollo's votaries. This time there was no mistaking it. A few days later he was writing to the world, "There has recently come among us a child full of genius."

Chateaubriand had his Hugo, Sainte-Beuve his Musset.

Meanwhile the child full of genius plunged resolutely into fashionable life. One had to appear rich if one was not; therefore he consorted with wealthy young beaux. One had to gamble; he played at high stakes, losing a month's allowance in an hour.

He ordered his clothes from the best tailors and spent a fortune on hired horses. He danced, he dined, he turned night into day, he drank—and he wrote verses. "I must experience everything," he said to the reproachful Paul. "There are two persons in me, one who acts and another who looks on. If the first makes a mistake, the other profits by it."

Repentance, too, had its charms, especially if it could be accomplished in masquerade. Somewhere he had picked up an old yellow redingote with a six-tiered cape, ample enough to go round him twice. After dissipation, he would envelop himself in it and curl up on the rug in his room, humming a plaintive tune. "Leave me," he would cry in mock tearfulness to Paul. "Leave me, to my rags and my despair."

Paul doted on his wonderful brother and made notes for the future.

The garment of repentance was not worn often enough, however. "If I were at this moment in Paris," he once wrote Foucher, "I should quench what little of the noble is left in me in punch and beer, and I would feel relieved. They put a sick man to sleep with opium, even though they know that such sleep might prove fatal. I would act in the same fashion with my soul. . . ."

The adolescent of 1827 was father to the man of 1828, man not in years but in experience. With Alfred de Musset growth remained organic; it was merely an intensification of the traits that had already differentiated him from the rest. More than ever he demanded stronger stimuli, greater shocks to a system abnormally exacting because morbidly precocious. And he was in Paris, where he could gratify every desire.

Craving for drink was one of the strongest. Now, however, he demanded more powerful potions than beer or punch, perhaps more powerful stimulants than drink. He had attended for a time the classes in anatomy conducted by Bérard. In that medical environment he learned no doubt the properties of newly discovered drugs. At any rate, he was fascinated by them and could not forbear talking and writing about them. Hence his mention of opium was not without significance. More meaningful was his dedication of four concentrated weeks to translating De Quincey's *Confessions of an English Opium Eater*.

And what a translation! Taking De Quincey's classically correct narrative as a springboard, the bold Romantic vaulted so high that he very nearly lost sight of his original. The subject was made to order for the sensation-hungry youth. The true life story of an opium eater! He liked it so well that he retitled it baldly, *Opium-Eater*, and so it would have remained if the publisher, out of excessive consideration for his race, had not insisted on keeping the onus abroad by specifying that the opium eater was no Frenchman.

L'Anglais, Mangeur d'Opium came out without the translator's name. But anyone could have seen that it was the work of a youth, imaginative, perverse, ridden by a hundred bizarreries, but with a highly developed style, if still injudicious, taste. Musset made the pathetic Ann of Oxford Street a well-kept woman, like those he knew, and in a three-thousand word interpolation elevated her to Anna, Lady C. . . . He magnified everything in his boyish enthusiasm. The few pounds given to De Quincey in his straits became twenty-five thousand francs; fortunes rose to astronomical heights. Sensation, likewise, grew to sensationalism, at the expense of some of De Quincey's finest passages, mercilessly cut out to make room for adventures in the taste of the day, even to reminiscences of Musset's anatomy class. He might well have said as in the line he amusingly mistranslated: "It was the Apocalypse that I had inside of me."

By 1829 the Apocalypse within, while still untamed, had provided him with poetry enough for a volume. For to Alfred de Musset poetry signified experience made eternal. He could not write except from personal emotion recollected in an ecstasy of the imagination that was like a divine madness. Love remembered became a voluptuousness of the soul which, in such a soul, attained the delirium of a pagan who had seen Pan. Cries of desire, sighs of fulfillment, the very quivering of passion relived in remembrance intoxicated him to song; but while he sang, chaos gathered to order and made a primal music. Another voice had joined France's poets and, for an exception, the people listened.

Contes d'Espagne et d'Italie would have been remarkable in any age, transcending, as it did, styles and schools, though the Romantics claimed it for their own. Indeed, before the manuscript went to the printer, Alfred read it aloud, with effects that shook the chandelier, before a select group of the brotherhood who declared themselves enchanted, especially by the long "Mardoche." That poem had been composed almost as an afterthought because Urbain Canel, publisher of the Romantics, felt that the book needed five hundred lines more to make up a volume of the proper format and thickness. The manner of Childe Harold in "Mardoche" sometimes even his accent, revealed Musset's close discipleship to Byron. For the rest, the dramatic "Don Paez" the "Portia" and the long fragment on the willow, speak with his own voice. "Newspapers are so insipid, critics so shallow," he had complained at seventeen. "Build up your systems, my friends, establish your rules. You're only working on the cold monuments of the past. Just let a man of genius step

AURORE DUDEVANT (George Sand)

SELF-PORTRAIT, LATE 1830

"There was something sentimental yet pathetic in that child's face—she did not look her twenty-six years— clouded by such intensity of suffering."

forth and he will overthrow your scaffolding and laugh at your poetics."

Though not yet mature in his art, he tumbled more than one edifice and succeeded even in creating a scandal with his "Ballad to the Moon" for the novel comparison in its first and closing stanzas:

> *C'était dans la nuit brune,*
> *Sur le clocher jauni,*
> > *La lune*
> *Comme un point sur un* i.

No one had ever had the boldness to compare the moon over a steeple to the dot over an *i*. This bit of literary levity shocked not only the Classicists but the Romantics. They had not the advantage of time to know that in the imagery and music of the moon ballad, as of another lyric, "Venise," Musset had heralded Verlaine.

The poet also painted a portrait of himself, a youth whom love had betrayed and banished forever from security. The lines to "Madame B——" are explicit; so too the quotation from *Othello* which introduces "Don Paez":

> *I had been happy if the general camp,*
> *Pioneers and all, had tasted her sweet body*
> *So I had nothing known.*

One of those women whom in his adolescent mistrust of the unknown he had dreamed of tormenting, had made him suffer. The wound of the infidelity was never to close. "Love, scourge of the world, execrable folly!" he cursed with Don Paez.

But he had not yet really known either love or passion. Lélia, destroyer of men, had only begun to stir in her chrysalis.

Chapter X: The Colibri of the Savannahs

SIX months after that July of 1830 when Liberty had raised
her standard over the towers of Notre Dame, the diligence
was speeding Aurore Dudevant to Paris, alone and as free as
a mutual understanding between incompatible temperaments
could make her. The last two years of her life with Casimir had
clearly demonstrated the irreparable breach between them. Whatever the causes of their estrangement, whether Aurore's platonics
which had led to the unanticipated appearance of Solange, or
Casimir's attempt at reformation with its antidotes in Desgranges'
mistress and the maidservants of the countryside, the two ceased
all marital relations after 1828. Aurore gave as her reason that
she had overheard Casimir "in a criminal conversation" with a
woman of the household in the room adjoining her bedchamber
where she lay after her confinement. But Aurore had known as
much, and worse, of Casimir for a long time. As it was, his gross
amours contributed to the amusement of the neighbors who
tolerated everything except what they could not understand.

In the dislocation of her marriage Aurore had been thrown
still more upon herself, although externally the Dudevants led
a livelier social life than before. A group of friends from La
Châtre, sometimes with their wives, more often without, called
frequently at Nohant, to drink with Casimir and to talk with
Aurore. They were childhood acquaintances of Aurore's who had
made themselves careers. Charles Duvernet practiced law in Paris;
Alphonse Fleury dabbled in politics. Gustave Papet, who was
well to do, wrote for the newspapers; Alexis Dutheil had a keen
mind which sharpened hers and made her overlook his unpre-
possessing exterior, while Jules Néraud, nicknamed Malgache
because he had lived in Madagascar and never ceased talking
about it, gave her rare botanical specimens for her herbal collection and helped her discover strange plants in her familiar
countryside. Later there was also François Rollinat, a man of
subtle intelligence and warm sympathy toward whom Aurore
turned with instinctive confidence and whom she kept as her
confidant for many years.

Now at one house, now at another, the young people would

94

meet to read aloud, to discuss Hugo and the Romantics, to bewail the state of France and to build utopias of words. Aurore was stimulated by her friends. They had contact with the world of literature and politics. They went to museums, the theater and to art galleries. Although like her they lived in Berry, they were equally at home in Paris and in far-off lands, like Néraud who knew tropical islands as well as the Berrichon country, and would keep her entranced with descriptions of those exotic places in his talks and in long, well-written letters.

Then, in the summer of 1830, the circle also included Jules Sandeau, a friend of the Duvernets. A native of Berry like the rest, Jules was on vacation from his law courses in Paris. As a representative of *La Jeune France,* he was rebellious, enthusiastic, a liberal in politics, an intransigent Hugo worshiper in literature. For that matter, the whole Berry group swore by Victor Hugo. They gave one another the title Hugolâtre, and wore it like the cockade of their intellectual independence.

Aurore was touched by the young man's love of poetry, but more by his long fair hair and girlish face. He was slight and agile in his motions, and somewhat shy before the lady of Nohant. He was only nineteen. "When I met him," Aurore wrote to a friend, "I was in a state of disillusionment. I no longer believed that anything could make one happy. He warmed my chill heart."

After the birth of Solange, Aurélien's letters had brought her little comfort. He sounded tired, at times even cold. In the devious mode of reasoning which Aurore invariably adopted whenever she felt blameworthy in a relationship, she convinced herself that the impending rupture was a sacrifice brought about by her for the other's good. In Aurélien's case she pretended that the platonic pledge she had exacted was the source of his coolness. Assuming from there that the continued friendship had become an unbearable chain for Aurélien, she eased it by the simple expedient of not answering his letters. Once that tranquil divorce was accomplished, she had the courage to see him, for the last time. She found him "looking older and less attractive." How could Aurélien compare with the *cher enfant* who paid her daily visits and read Hugo aloud to her while Casimir snored in his chair?

There was a rustic bench in a little wood that formed part of the Nohant property. "It was there that our hearts and hands joined for the first time," Aurore told her confidant of the moment, with the urgency of King Midas' barber, who must whisper the overwhelming secret, if only to a clump of reeds. The triangle which had once held God, Aurore's platonic lover and her, expanded geometrically to a quadrangle, to include the inevitable sharer of her affairs of the heart. Throughout her life she had that need of a sympathetic ear into which to pour the joys and raptures she could not contain, the self-justification of her lovers' quarrels, the doubts and agonies of disillusionment, the aches that must be spoken or shatter the burdened heart.

As it was, Aurore's mind carried more than it could bear that autumn when, the summer holidays over, the coterie disbanded and Sandeau left for Paris. It was unendurable for her now to be alone with Casimir. His boorishness, his petty tyrannies to assert his superiority over his "idiot" wife, his annoyance with books and music she had sustained with the fortitude of one who knew security within herself. But the future looked dark indeed. How long, how much longer, would she have strength to continue yoked to this unequal mate? Why, of all men, had it had to be Casimir? She could not divorce him as she had tacitly cut off Aurélien. She was legally Casimir's chattel and the law provided no loophole for freedom, even with tangible proof of Casimir's adultery in the illegitimate child of Claire, one of the Nohant maids, who had publicly sued him for the baby's maintenance. There had been many other Claires. But even if the law had granted a divorce, the Church would not have allowed it.

How long? How long? The question kept pounding through her head as she escaped from Casimir's oppressive presence to the one room in the house which was cut off from the living quarters, her grandmother's tiny boudoir. The children slept in the adjacent bedroom. She could hear them breathe in the pauses of Casimir's rioting with his drinking partners, and it gave her the inner calm to write the stories that had been shaping themselves in her mind. She had finished one short novel, *Aimée,* written after breaking with Aurélien, and she was writing more; but always the themes were the same, Aurore and her woes. She saw herself as the heroine of a life of recurrent sacrifices, in a wilderness of misunderstanding, and she fed upon them like another St. John upon the locusts. Unhappily she was no saint, and she sickened on the diet.

She escaped from reality into her deepest self. For two days she lay unconscious from a cerebral congestion, and when she came to she wished that she had died. But the thought of her children gave her the strength to live. If she was an unhappy wife, she was fulfilled as a mother, at least in Maurice, whom she idolized. "If I were to lose Maurice nothing on earth would console me. . . . My Maurice, my naughty scamp, whom I love more than everything in the world." Solange from the first was not only relegated to second place, but was sometimes treated like a spiritual stepchild.

In a few weeks Aurore had recovered but her problems remained, immeasurably aggravated. The marital division was complete. Casimir's latent brutality came oftener to the surface; now he did not even try to conceal the resentment which, planted in the beginning of the Aurélien de Sèze affair, had grown to an unreasoning hate.

Aurore found relief in feverish activity. She played the piano, she painted, she sewed and embroidered, but most of all she wrote. If something should happen—she dared not think more specifically—she must be prepared to earn enough for herself and the children. For Casimir had made it clear that he thought her an extravagant manager, and doled out her allowance with a grudging churlishness. Everything was in his hands. If she wished to give a few pennies to a beggar she had to apply to Casimir. Somehow, she must be financially independent—if something should happen. And she set about painting snuffboxes and attempting portraits. She made a sketch of Caroline from memory and she also drew a self portrait in a tight-bodiced, puff-sleeved dress and a white Byronic collar from which her face, in its dark frame of curls, rose like the image of her frustration. There was something sentimental yet pathetic in that child's face—she did not look her twenty-six years—clouded by such intensity of suffering.

Her thoughts turned constantly to Paris and to the Berrichon group that lived and worked there. If only she were free to join them and live like them! She might be able to write for the papers, like Sandeau, who was abandoning the bar for journalism. Jules Boucoiran, a model young Deschartres whom she had engaged as a tutor for Maurice, might look after the children till she could send for them. Why should not a woman make her way as an equal among men? Dreams. She was Casimir's wife, rather, Casimir's prisoner. She contented herself with writing letters in a mock-Romantic strain to her friends from Berry.

"Oh, blond Charles," she apostrophized Duvernet, "sweet youth of pensive melancholy! And thou, gigantic Fleury! And thou, little Sandeau, lovable and fleet as the colibri of the balmy Savannahs! Graceful and sharp as the nettle that blows on the windswept towers of Châteaubrun! Since you no longer traverse the little square, swift as a chamois, the fair ladies rise only at sundown, like the bats and the screech-owls. Their curling irons lie useless on the spent embers."

While she wrote, a cricket that had found refuge, like her, in Madame Dupin's boudoir, hopped over her paper and dipped its legs in the wet ink. The little creature was so tame that it would sit contentedly on the table and eat her sealing wafers, which Aurore made sure to choose uncolored for fear of poisoning it. When it had had enough it would hop into a drawer and there it would sing, accompanying the scratching of her pen. Aurore was so used to the company of her *cricri* that she would look for it whenever she sat down to write. It seemed to her like the hearth spirit of her room, the symbol of a domestic peace which, alas, she could find only in this small corner of her large house.

One day she was rummaging for something in her husband's secretary, when she came upon a small package addressed to her. She picked it up, wondering what it could be, her curiosity rising as she read, *Not To Be Opened till after My Death.* In the precariousness of her own health, she might never know. Compelled, under the circumstances, by something stronger than propriety, she opened it.

"My God, what a testament!" she wrote of it to Jules Boucoiran on December 3, 1830. "Curses, and nothing more. He had assembled there all his anger and rancor against me, all his brooding on my perverseness, all his mistrust of my character. And he was leaving me all that as a pledge of his tenderness. . . . Without waiting another moment, feeble and ill as I was, I went to him and made my demands, defining my motives with such boldness and poise that he was dumbfounded."

She had not had to ponder on those demands. Too many nights and days had been consumed in dreaming about them. "I want an allowance. I want to go to Paris." And, after establishing herself there, she wanted her children. She outlined her plans to Boucoiran, the reliable Boucoiran who was away on business but would be back to look after Maurice and Solange. "He (Casimir) has treated me all along as if I were odious to him," she justified herself. "Today he is weeping for me—so much the worse for him. I'll show him that I won't be tolerated like a burden; but I shall be sought and sued like a free companion who will not live with him until he proves himself deserving. Don't think me unreasonable. Remember what humiliation I've suffered, and for eight years!"

Casimir's will could not have appeared more opportunely. In her hurt and discontent, Aurore took advantage of its revelations. Casimir could not oppose her decision. He had set down in black and white what he thought of his wife, and if those were indeed his sentiments, he should consider himself well rid of her. Faced with that diminutive fury, Casimir remonstrated and argued, implored and even shed tears. But Aurore remained unmoved. She had not received an omen from destiny in order to ignore it.

For a month, frail as she was, she made her preparations, writing to her mother, reasoning with Hippolyte who, while not actively taking Casimir's part, disapproved of her step. People would think her an immoral woman, he said. Casimir wasn't so bad, *un bon garçon* who had his shortcomings like everybody else. Seeing that she could not be dissuaded, Hippolyte tried a last expedient by telling Maurice that he would never see his mother again if he let her go. The boy clung to her, but even his sobs that hurt her cruelly, did not shake her determination.

She left for Paris on the fourth of January, a thin, beshawled figure, not much bigger than her son. Casimir had consented to her living six months in Paris to every three at Nohant, on an allowance of two-hundred and fifty francs a month during her stay in the city. The parting was not unfriendly. It was, rather, as if she were leaving a strict parent to try her wings in the world.

Boucoiran accompanied her a little of the way and suggested taking her as far as Nîmes, but she refused. Was it because she was afraid people might talk? The youth left her, disconcerted that a spirit so free, which had done so much to open his mind, should still be shackled by convention. No sooner did he reach Nohant, than he wrote her his sentiments.

The teacher must not be outdone by the pupil. "You misunderstood me," replied the emancipated Aurore. "Convention is the guiding rule of people devoid of soul and of virtue, and public opinion is a prostitute that sells herself to the highest bidder." That for the overzealous proselyte.

On the eighth of January, 1831, a bitter cold night, the diligence pulled up at the Paris coach yard on Rue Racine. Aurore had had plenty of time to reflect upon her step. She could still change her mind.

Shortly before her departure her cricket had disappeared, and when she found it at last, there was only its little brown body, dry as paper, crushed against the window ledge by a careless maid. Had that too been an omen? She took the cricket's death to mean the end of her life with Casimir. One can always interpret omens to one's satisfaction.

She had now come too far to turn back. Besides, she had only to think of Casimir to strengthen her resolve.

"Welcome to Bohemia!" cried a familiar voice as she came down the coach steps. It was Jules Sandeau, the dainty creature of the Savannahs, muffled in a great cocoon of an overcoat. With him had come Félix Pyat, another Berrichon, who was engaged in journalism. She was fatigued from the journey, so that night they escorted her to 31 Rue de Seine, Hippolyte's Paris apartment, which he had consented to let her have until she found one of her own. The two men arranged to call for her in the morning.

Despite the cold of Paris, in midwinter, Aurore, recently recovered from a serious illness and declared a consumptive by her doctor, throve like a plant restored to its natural soil. At last she was living the life for which she had been starved, living it among spirits as free as her own, in the excitement of a city in the midst of its winter season. The opening of *Freischütz* or *Wilhelm Tell* at the opéra saw her in the pit among the journalists and impecunious students, her small frame wrapped in a man's overcoat, her friends forming a protective barrier against the *claqueurs* and roughs, ever ready to start a disturbance, depending upon who paid them. She visited galleries and museums day after day, and stood before the same Tintorettos, Titians, Rubenses, admiring but not knowing why, and thrilling to color as she thrilled to music. No one explained to her what made a masterpiece, but as she contemplated each canvas, she told herself that in a great painting one obtained a true sense of life, represented in a splendid synthesis of form and color; it was a pageant of nature and humanity seen through the genius of the artist.

Still under the spell of art she would go to a pastry cook's and quietly munch a brioche, telling herself as she ate the ungarnished bun, that in spite of the leanness of the purse furnished her— from her own fortune—she had earned the right to go to a show. Was she not paying for it by doing without her dinner?

She roamed the streets at all hours, unobserved, in the man's costume she had adopted after a few disastrous ventures in trailing skirts and thin shoes along frozen pavements which she had navigated like a ship on ice. After all, masculine clothes were for her no novelty. She had put on her first pair of pantaloons at the age of four, and had practically lived in boys' suits in her adolescence. Besides, the male mode of the day lent itself to disguise, and many women who, like Aurore, chafed at restraint, went about in the newfangled square redingote *à la propriétaire* which Hippolyte said was modeled on a sentry box and thus suited a whole regiment. For that matter, as long ago as Plato's time, emancipated women like the two female disciples of the philosopher, assumed male attire to make themselves inconspicuous among men.

Aurore, therefore, had a sentry-box redingote cut to her measure, of a sturdy gray cloth to stand all weather. She ordered a pair of trousers and a waistcoat of the same material and topped the whole with a tall hat of furry nap that partly concealed her hair. A woolen muffler was wound high against the chin. So accoutered, she might have passed for a Sorbonne student in the first year. Her boots, reinforced with iron at the heel, were her delight. In them she walked with the comfort she had enjoyed when she had wandered through brush and bog in a pair of rustic sabots.

No one paid any more attention to her than to a young boy.

She had noticed that it is the look in one's eyes that magnetizes curiosity. As she had no coquetry, she learned to gaze unobtrusively on the ground, reserving her fascination for her friends.

Sandeau had long ago responded to the power of her glance. But at Nohant, on the little bench in the woods, the lovable and fleet colibri had been too much in awe of the châtelaine Dudevant to do more than flutter toward her hand and heart. Casimir's shadow, moreover, unlike the gentle dusk of their meetings, threatened with storm. They had been cautious, therefore, contenting themselves with the platonics of which Aurore had had so long an experience.

In the free air of Paris the colibri grew bolder. Before long he and Aurore had found a snug nest in the old Hôtel Jean Jacques Rousseau, at No. 4, Rue des Cordeliers. It was a cubicle of a room in a squalid quarter of Paris, but what had been good enough for the great Jean Jacques, for Condillac and Mably, seemed sublime to the literary tyros.

For, through Félix Pyat, who wrote for *Figaro,* Aurore and Jules had met its editor, Henri de Latouche, another Berrichon, who promptly gave Sandeau a place on his paper and so far relaxed his prejudice against women as to make room for the trousered Aurore. Latouche gave her no encouragement on her novel, *Aimée,* the virtue of whose heroine was so much milk and water to the absinthe taste of the day. But he offered to pay her seven francs a column, "counting the white spaces," for every article of hers published in *Figaro.*

Taking her place by the fire in the copy room, Aurore made the quills fly over the paper; but by the end of the day the sheets, slashed by Latouche's editorial pencil, served only to feed the fire. Her style rambled too far from the subject assigned. By the end of the first month she had earned exactly fifteen francs. However, she had collaborated with Jules on an article for the *Revue de Paris* which appeared under his name. "When we're far enough advanced to fly on our own wings," she wrote Duvernet, "I shall leave Jules all the honors of publication and share only in the profits."

Soon, however, Aurore was publishing stories in *La Mode,* and *L'Artiste,* which did not escape Latouche's eye. Perhaps, after all, Aurore had better turn to writing fiction, he advised. Aurore wanted nothing better. Her mind was bursting with ideas, inspired by the life of *La Jeune France,* at the Mazarin reading room and the sidewalk cafés, at the earnest meetings of the Saint-Simonists and the noisy gaiety of the backstage parties. She became as drunk on theories of reform as on the new and wonderful headiness of liberty.

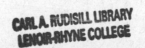

For the present, liberty superseded even love, for it was liberty that made possible love and everything else in her exhilarating life. Her letters to her mother, who disapproved, and to her friends, who understood, burned with the fervor of a liberator of her sex, while indirectly they answered the aspersions of the world. "It's not a material life, excitement, plays or fine clothes that I need, but liberty," she wrote to Sophie. "It is being alone in the street and saying to myself, 'I'll dine at four or at seven, according to my whim.' If I come across people who take my innocent caprices for concealed vices, I cannot take the trouble to disabuse them. I simply know that such people bore me, that they do not know me and that they do me an injustice. I say nothing in my own defense, and leave them flat. I seek neither vengeance nor redress. I bear no one ill will. I put everything out of my mind, though they say I am frivolous on that account."

With Duvernet she had no need for self-justification. Her letters to him sang paeans on her freedom. "If only I could convey to you this faculty of feeling alive, joyous and ardent, as it runs through my blood and bubbles in my breast. How wonderful it is to live, and how good!—in spite of troubles, husbands, annoyances, debts, relatives. . . . To live! It is delirium! To love, to be loved—it is happiness. It is heaven!"

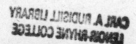

Chapter XI: Aurore Becomes George Sand

AURORE made no concealment of her liaison with Sandeau and her friends did not think the less of her for it. For years the Saint-Simonists had been preaching free love and practicing it openly, answering the Philistine's cry of "Scandalous!" with a louder, "Divine!" Their faith derived from Claude Saint-Simon's dictum that society should be founded on "the material, intellectual and moral improvement of the poorest and most numerous class." An idealistic but fuliginous intellect, Saint-Simon pronounced the Pope and Rome devoid of authority, urged society to fight against the despotism of convention, and preached hope in humanity and the coming social order of "the great industrialists," heralds of future economic power.

Saint-Simon, the prophet, died in 1825, but his cult of science and material welfare had its high priests and followers, branching to wild growth from the original root, and creating offshoots in the anticlerical socialism of Louis Auguste Blanqui, who summed up the people's aspirations in the maxim, "Neither God nor master."

Aurore gave ear to all and adopted as much as suited her peculiar wants. Even without her acceptance of free love she would have considered it within her right to live with Sandeau, since by leaving Casimir she had openly declared herself no longer his wife.

Émile Regnault, a friend of Sandeau's, found the pair an apartment under the roof of a large corner house on the Quai Saint-Michel. Aurore was in ecstasies when she saw it. Its three small rooms had windows opening out on a balcony from which she could look up and down the traffic of the Seine, its busy boats and fishermen, and the permanent fair of bookstalls along the tree-lined embankment. The gray mass of Notre Dame seemed hardly a stone's throw away. She could follow almost to the clouds the slim spire of the Sainte-Chapelle, that Gothic jewel set within its circle of buildings. The morgue was across the way. But one grew used to the near presence of death, so used indeed, that nursemaids had their rendezvous there, and workmen ate their bread and cheese on the near-by benches. From her height of five stories above the street, and with monuments of the Middle Ages for scenery, Aurore felt more than ever a Hugolâtre. This was Hugo's Paris, the gray, legendary city of the Romantics.

She wrote, therefore, in her mock-Gothic style a letter of thanks to Regnault, in which she described Sandeau's room, "the mysterious dark chamber, the hiding place of the ghost, the cave of the treasure. . . ." She also assumed financial responsibility for the apartment; *le cher enfant* was too poor for her to expect him to share expenses. Besides, the pattern of behavior had been traced long ago for the daughter of Sophie, who used to give Maurice Dupin spending money from the allowance of the general who kept her. Certainly it never entered Aurore's head that in such relationships the rôles were ordinarily reversed. The dainty colibri was her pet, her toy, her lover, her child. A hummingbird is not of the breed of Elijah's provident ravens. In order to meet the increase in rent, she exhibited a portrait of her *"Portière,"* in a café of the Quai Saint-Michel, but as she had not quite captured the likeness of the woman who was well known in the neighborhood, she failed to lure prospective sitters.

She wrote with feverish assiduity, sometimes with Sandeau's collaboration, oftener without it. The pot must be kept boiling and she had to provide the fuel. Latouche decided to risk the publication of Aurore's stories and articles. *"La Molinara,"* which appeared anonymously in the issue of the third of March, 1831, created such a stir, that the *Figaro* was kept busy answering inquiries about the author. Two days later both she and Jules were represented, Jules by an article and Aurore by a political medley, *"Bigarrure,"* which nearly sent Latouche to jail when the censor decided it contained subversive criticism of the government. Aurore reveled in that taste of notoriety and magnified her danger in her letters. It was exciting to be thought a political menace.

She must make money, however. Since she produced fiction so easily—she had published a novelette, *"Prima Donna"* in *La Revue de Paris* and another, *"La Fille d'Albano"* in *La Mode* almost simultaneously with her political pastiche—she planned a novel, to be written in collaboration with Sandeau. But what slant should they give it? "Literature is in the same chaos as politics," she wrote Boucoiran. "People want novelty, and in order to provide it, one manufactures horrors. Balzac is on a pinnacle for portraying the love of a soldier for a tigress, and the love of an artist for a *castrato*. What is it all about, good God! Monsters are in fashion. Let us make monsters."

She did not set out to make a monster with Jules, however. No writer ever does. There are always imponderables, among them the chance of creating a masterpiece. But they did try to satisfy the taste of the times by providing something for everyone.

Rose et Blanche, or The Actress and the Nun, flowed on, a contrapuntal narrative wherein Aurore's spiritual treble of the virtuous Blanche, ran against the base of Sandeau's adventurous Rose. As a collaboration, it betrayed too much the style of individual hands. But the trifling flaw did not discourage Monsieur Dupuy, the publisher, who was in as great a hurry to place the novel before the public as were the authors to receive the much needed cash. Dupuy was sure the book would sell. The heroes balanced the heroines in virtue and vice, and one, at least, Horace, was destined by his fascinating wickedness, to make the chambermaids enjoy a pleasurable shudder. For Aurore had long ago learned from her·grandmother's Julie to respect the taste of chambermaids, as she frankly admitted when she later explained the reasons for her success: "Knowing the passion of chambermaids for novels, I often bear them in mind when I write my own."

Her mother-in-law came to have a talk with Aurore as soon as rumors of the forthcoming book reached her ears. The Baronne Dudevant was very tender of the family reputation. Moreover, she thought it a scandal that Casimir should be biding at home while his wife gallivanted about Paris. "Why do you keep on living here without your husband?" she asked.

"My husband finds it convenient," replied Aurore.

"Is it really true, what I've been hearing?" the baronne went on. "Is it true that you intend to publish a book?"

"Yes, madame."

"What a ridiculous idea!"

"Yes, madame."

"I daresay it's all well and good. But I hope you won't be putting the name I bear on the covers of printed books."

"Certainly not, madame. You run no such danger."

They never saw each other again after the interview.

It was not only the baronne who showed concern over the unpleasant notoriety of having a writer in the family. Jules's father, too, did not wish his name taken in vain in such a connection. "Bah!" exclaimed the practical Latouche when Jules came to him with his problem. "Cut Sandeau in two and your own father won't know you."

Accordingly, in December of 1831, *Rose et Blanche* appeared under the pseudonym of Jules Sand.

Not only the chambermaids of Paris but the general reader devoured the novel despite its inchoate plot and divergent styles. Here and there a descriptive passage, a stroke of character, glowed like gold amid the muddy contents of the authors' sifted experience: Aurore's convent years utilized for Blanche, and Jules's nocturnal Paris exploits, which served to enliven Horace. Whatever gold the book contained was Aurore's as the publisher saw. Oddly, this first published novel by the woman who was to become the most widely read French Romantic writer of fiction, was remarkable for its realism.

The authors made two hundred francs each on the book. What was more important, Monsieur Dupuy demanded another novel. Aurore promptly submitted a manuscript, *Indiana,* which she had written during her stay at Nohant, earlier that year, and which she and Jules had almost forgotten in the agitation of their joint début. Monsieur Dupuy read the novel and cheered. He would publish it, and at once.

How had Aurore created *Indiana,* the first authentic Sand novel? She hardly knew, but there it was, in many well-filled pages that had poured out of her mind in the boudoir that she had shared with the *cricri.* All night long she had sat at her writing table, and when the window whitened in the dawn, she had lain down to snatch a few hours' sleep in the hammock which she had stretched across the room, too narrow to hold a bed. In the rest of the house life had not changed. Casimir was still the master and asserted his authority by showing his ill temper at her being there according to their agreement. The carousing lasted till dawn. The general decadence showed itself in the disorientation of the servants and in the flourishing weeds of the once model gardens.

Aurore and Casimir had never had much to say to each other. But now their silence was funereal in the wake of their dead marriage. After dinner they would sit at opposite sides of the hearth, watching the wood crumble to ashes, watching the hands of the clock on the mantel marking the leaden minutes.

It must have been after one such evening with Casimir that Aurore took refuge in her room and found the beginning for her novel. The truth of its opening is striking: the weariness, the dumb unhappiness of a man and a woman by their own fireside remaining strangers before the glowing warmth that can draw even savages together.

Once she began the book the words came faster than she could write them, in a fury of possession that made her the instrument of her own creation. Indiana and her husband, Colonel Delmare—were they Aurore and Casimir? The pure Sir Ralph— was he Aurélien de Sèze? Her characters came to life under her pen, and once alive led their own existences, true, however to their essential personalities.

Indiana, the dreamy Creole, afflicted like Aurore by romantic discontent pined, a tropical flower, beneath the shadow of her prosaic husband. Her passionate nature wilted under his cold dominance and, to aggravate her torment, she penetrated his respectable exterior and saw the man he was, brutal with impunity, tyrannical with self-righteousness. "Do you know what sort of person they call an honest man in the provinces? The man who does not encroach upon his neighbors' fields, who does not ask a cent more than is due him by his creditors . . . who does not violate girls on the broad highway. . . . He may beat his wife, abuse his servants, ruin his children—that is no one's concern. Such was Colonel Delmare's social code. A man devoid of wit, tact and breeding, he was skilful with sabre and sword. . . . Since he could never appreciate a joke, he was always obsessed by the fear that people were making fun of him. . . . His nature was the most antipathetic possible to that of his wife, his heart the least created to understand her, his mind the most incapable of appreciating her. . . ."

Aurore drew a faithful portrait of Casimir.

She was as clear-eyed about herself, and even more unsparing. "Indiana was rigid and haughty in her submissiveness. Her resignation was as the dignity of a king who submits to irons and a dungeon rather than relinquish his crown. . . . Deception, and not her passion, was the crime in her eyes, and twenty times a day she was on the verge of telling her husband that she loved Raymon. Fear alone of losing Raymon deterred her."

Who was Raymon de Ramière, the elegant, the seductive, the correct, to whom Indiana gave the treasures of heart and imagination and the passion her husband had never awakened? Like Sir Ralph, he was Aurélien de Sèze, but Aurélien as Aurore had seen him, through no veil of illusion, after the tacit divorce of their souls and the break of even their friendship when the punctilious advocate heard that she had left Casimir. He was the Aurélien who, after having loved her, could marry another woman—as he had recently done. Aurore is faithful to her original feelings in the relationship, however, although in the novel her love is fulfilled; for, inspired by the Saint-Simonist doctrine of woman's right to freedom of self-disposal, she has Indiana eschew platonics. Moreover, she makes Indiana fully cognizant of her behavior. "She would have thought herself far more to blame in evincing love for a husband toward whom she did not feel it, than in according it to her lover who inspired it in her."

The story has a simple structure. Indiana, adored by Sir Ralph and unhappily married to the retired Colonel Delmare, falls in love with Raymon de Ramière and leaves her husband to live her brave new life in the face of convention. Raymon, incapable of fidelity in his quality of ambitious man of the world, first betrays her with her waiting woman, Noun, then abandons her to make a rich marriage and follow a parliamentary career. The outcast Indiana, scorned by the society whose codes she had defied, turns away from a false civilization to the innocence of a primitive island, for which Malgache had provided local color in his talks and letters. There Indiana is joined by Sir Ralph, as faithful as he is pure. Both have had enough of the world and are resolved to quit it together by leaping from a cliff when— Aurore thought of the tender hearts of a million chambermaids and saved the two suffering spirits almost in mid-air.[1]

On the ninth of May, 1832, *Indiana* appeared as the work of George Sand, the Jules having been left to Sandeau as rightfully his own, and the George chosen for lack of a more euphonious name at the moment. Like Lord Byron, George Sand awoke one morning and found herself famous.

The novel could not have failed of popular success. It was a book patterned for the times, the portrait of a female René, as well as the story of a woman waking, in her subjection, to the knowledge that her heart and body were her own. "She is will battling against necessity," George Sand explained to *Indiana's* readers. "She is love beating its head against the barriers raised by civilization." Elsewhere she said more explicitly: "It is my protest against tyranny in general. If I personified this tyranny in a man, if I confined the struggle within a domestic frame, it is because I wished simply to write a *roman de moeurs*."

Aurore had not listened to the Saint-Simonist doctrines in vain. From the fire of the idealist prophet she took a smoldering brand and with it traced the message that physical joys are as legitimate as the joys of the spirit, and that beauty is as much to be worshiped as genius, for both derive from God. Saint-Simon had deified matter. George Sand sanctified the flesh. In a larger sense *Indiana* represented every man and every woman of that discontented generation. By their acclaim they paid the author the tribute of recognizing the likeness.

George Sand wrote as easily as she breathed, but the guarantee of a public, given her by Ernest Dupuy's eagerness to publish anything she might write, added impetus to her pen. She needed money to maintain her independence, since Casimir worried as little about the source of her daily bread as of the sparrow's in the field, and money, it was now clear, came to her only through her novels. She had no thought of creating masterpieces. Enough for her that Dupuy paid well, and that the critics used a flattering adjective or two in their estimate of her work, despite their perplexity in finding a suitable pigeonhole for the newly risen

[1] In the original and better version of *Indiana* Sir Ralph and the lovely Creole die.

novelist who combined with the vigor of a man an uncannily intimate knowledge of a woman's heart.

Soon after Dupuy had taken the manuscript of *Indiana,* George Sand, as we shall henceforth call her, had left Paris like a reluctant Persephone, to spend her three months at Nohant. In the interval between the acceptance of *Indiana* and its publication, she had completed *Valentine* and begun still another novel, *Lélia,* in a different strain. *Valentine,* a more objective study of woman than *Indiana,* had almost written itself. George had the Berry country to inspire her, and thoughts of her charming Sandeau whom she had left in Paris, with which to dress in convincing romanticism Valentine's lover, Benedict, who shared with the heroine an illicit passion. More than Raymon or Sir Ralph of the earlier novel, Benedict typified disillusioned, Romantic youth. It cost her a pang to have to kill Benedict as well as Valentine in the end, to satisfy the cry of the moralists for blood as the wages of sin. But she did it, and the novel was ready for the printer by the time she returned to Paris.

Lélia, on the other hand, began in an agony unlike anything she had ever known, and threatened to continue keeping her in torment. She had no plan for the book, nor did she write it consistently. Suddenly, while in the midst of other work, she would quake to an inner convulsion, as from her spirit in eruption, and ideas, speeches, characters, burning still from the internal seething, would shoot up to the surface of her mind. She wrote as the mood seized her, and the novel accreted, amorphous yet hot with life. She was the vessel of accumulated experiences and reflections, and like the vase of the genii, the narrow confines could not hold the illimitable imagination which overflowed and took shape upon contact with the world of reality.

After *Indiana* an extraordinary change had come over her creative expression. Her writing no longer rushed like the outpouring of a medium in a trance, although throughout her life she was to know a peculiar amnesia, also that of a medium, which erased from her mind all memory of her work, the moment it left her. *Indiana* had acted as the liberator of her psyche. Corambé and the semi-hallucinatory creatures which had crowded her adolescence vanished as at the stroke of a wand, and George Sand the novelist, was born. "I did not think myself cured of a mental malady," she wrote of the phenomenon, "but on the contrary I felt myself deprived of a faculty."

She never lost, however, that power of identification with nature which even as a child had enabled her, by her extreme sensitivity, to become the thing she saw. The faculty grew with her, so that at will she could merge herself in her surroundings with the ease of a chameleon. Everyone remarked upon her capacity for quiet in a noisy room, where her serenity held that almost eternal quality of a rock.

"There are times," she was to write in *Impressions and Souvenirs*, "when I escape from myself, when I live in a plant, when I feel myself to be the grass, a bird, the topmost branch of a tree, a cloud, the running water, the horizon's edge . . . times when I run or fly or swim, or drink the dew, or expand to the sun, when I sleep under the leaves, or skim the sky with the larks, when I crawl with the lizards or twinkle with the stars and the glowworms. . . . I am not at all dreaming when, before the spectacle of a vast edifice of rocks, I feel that these mighty bones of nature are my own, and that my spirit's calm partakes of their apparent death."

Chapter XII: The Carnival of Death

NOHANT always gave George Sand the reserves to draw upon during her six months in Paris; and hectic months they now became. She had left the city virtually unknown, to return as a public figure, discussed in the salons, mentioned curiously in the gossip paragraphs that had sprung into fashion in the frenzied gaiety with which Paris reacted to the stodginess of its bourgeois king. She had money to live on for a year or more—three thousand francs for the four volumes of *Indiana* and *Valentine,* enough for the colibri, enough for Solange whom she had taken to live with her while the nine-year-old Maurice was being prepared for admission to the Collège Henri IV by Casimir, much against George's wishes.

That year all classes joined in a huge carnival, madder than any Paris had ever seen. Masquerades and routs lasted far into the morning, began again at dusk, survived another night and day and started anew in a round that whirled more madly still when death led the dance as cholera broke out in the city.

The plague had started in the Polish and Prussian armies the previous year, had spread to England, and now was decimating Paris. The Left Bank, among the most congested quarters of the city, felt it most acutely. Story by story, it climbed almost as far as George's garret, and somehow stopped there, but not before claiming six victims on the way.

George lived in dread for Solange. The cholera seized its prey so quickly, so irrevocably. One felt the preliminary chill of its approach; the blood congealed, the face turned purple, and in the interval of waiting for the hospital cart, death had reached out its inescapable hand. In her anxiety George thought of returning with her child to the country, but the dangers of contagion on the journey were too great. She took whatever precautions she could, and remained in Paris. Besides, Maurice was still at Nohant. She must not carry the infection there. Every day, therefore, the group of Berry friends arranged to meet in the Luxembourg gardens at a definite hour, that they might at least check up on one another's safety. If any failed to keep the appointment, one of the party hastened to his house. Fortunately none of them succumbed.

From her windows George could observe the progress of the pestilence. At night, as she rested from her writings and looked out, she could see here and there the red points of light of the ambulance lanterns in the deserted streets. During the day, the *tapissières,* moving vans which had become the hearses of the poor, crossed the Saint-Michel Bridge in their frequent trips to the cemeteries. The corpses, heaped like so many bales, rose higher and higher, while the coachmen cracked their whips, urging on their horses to keep pace with death. No mourners followed; there was no time for funeral garlands. Death was too avid for the banquet to have the board set.

In the general terror, the workers grumbled and raised menacing fists, blaming the cholera, like everything else, upon the government. In a larger sense they were right. Inequalities bred wars; wars brought on pestilence. The Four Horsemen were more than a figure of speech as Paris knew when, between the end of March and the middle of June, 1832, it buried its twenty-thousand dead.

Restlessness increased and threatened to turn to anarchy, as it had been doing sporadically since the disappointing July revolution. Like another epidemic, dissatisfaction spread throughout the classes which changed sides overnight, the workers yearning for a Legitimist king, the Legitimists sighing after a republic, or even for the advent of another Bonaparte, although for some years the dazzle of the Empire had gone out of people's eyes and the myth of Napoleon had found breath only in nostalgic sighs. As the times grew out of joint aims were confused in the general dislocation. While the satirical journals staggered under a bumper crop of caricatures of the pear-faced parliamentary monarch, the party in power, alarmed at the unrest, tried to resort to an elementary thaumaturgy, by suggesting that the government bring back to France the ashes of Napoleon. The proposal went as far as the Chamber of Deputies. "True, Napoleon suppressed anarchy," protested Charles Lameth in a moment of clarity. "But why bring in his coffin to aggravate it now?" The Cabinet contented itself by replacing the emperor's statue on the column in the Place Vendôme, to exert whatever influence it could.

Alas, even that power had grown feeble. The people demanded an outlet for their exasperation and found it in the massacre of several men whom they had charged with poisoning the population by means of the cholera. The death of the Cabinet leader, Casimir Périer, by the same scourge restored quiet for a time. Then anarchy broke forth anew, in insurrection and conspiracy, as if, now that Périer's strong hand had slackened in death, the vials of the Apocalypse had been let loose over the land. A Royalist plot engineered by the Duchesse de Berry had hardly been quelled when another, and more violent, fermentation boiled up among the revolutionists who had not forgotten how close they had come to seizing power in 1830—a power which had eluded them, according to Guizot, "through that divine pity for France which has so often disarmed the enemies of her welfare at the very instant of their seeming triumph."

It was the death of General Lamarque that had created the pretext for the new uprising. A man of enlightened liberalism as well as a popular soldier who had won the love and confidence of the people, General Lamarque had died when he could least be spared. On the fifth of June, 1832, as his body was being conveyed to the cemetery on the outskirts of Paris, an immense crowd gathered to pay him homage. His victories, together with the perished glory that had once been France, remembered in heated speeches, ignited the ready passions of the people. Cries of "Long live the Republic!" drowned the funeral oratory. In a flash the red flag replaced the tricolor, and "Down with Louis Philippe! Down with the Bourbons!" rose from a thousand throats. Someone signaled the troops. But the people were in no mood to submit. Gunsmiths' shops and armories were pillaged, and once again the restless paving stones of Paris were ripped up to make barricades. Liberty was leading the people.

In the Luxembourg gardens George Sand, watching over Solange who was playing in a sand pile at the foot of a statue, was too much absorbed by her own thoughts to notice the hasty thinning out of the promenaders in the alleys. It was late in the afternoon, time to go home. Suddenly, she was startled by the roll of drums, as a cordon of troops marched in through one gate and made as if to traverse the park, by now empty except for her and the child. In a panic she picked her up and ran out into the street.

At the sound of shooting, terrified crowds huddled in doorways, stampeded madly and broke into other groups, to reunite in mobs that aggregated like their mounting fear.

"Go back! Go back! The troops are coming!" people shouted. "They're firing on everybody!"

The shopkeepers, weathercocks of law and order, hurriedly pulled down their iron shutters, careless of what heads were in the way. Solange shrieked at the cries and confusion of the demoralized crowds that filled even the side streets which George had taken for safety. Finally she reached her quay and dashed up the stairs with the child. George had never seen street fighting, but for the sake of Solange she thought it wiser to be out of it, although she was distraught with anxiety to know what new calamity had overtaken the people.

That night she did not light her lamp, and as Solange was

113

growing hysterical with terror, she tried to quiet her by pretending there was nothing to fear. "It's only people shooting bats," she said. "Like that time when your father and Uncle Hippolyte hunted them on the terrace at home." When Solange fell asleep George blocked the window of the child's room with a mattress, for fear of straying bullets, and spent the night on the balcony, endeavoring in the darkness to give meaning to those spurts of gunfire, to those horrible death cries that reached her. Even more dreadful was the hush that fell over the city at dawn.

The morning of the sixth of June, George learned that a group of insurgents, posted at the bridgehead near the Hôtel Dieu, had been surprised by a column of the National Guard, mercilessly slaughtered, and their dismembered bodies thrown into the Seine. The two who managed to run away were overtaken and slain. It was their death agony George had heard.

Other carnage had flooded the streets with blood that fatal day, as a minor riot had taken on the proportions of an organized uprising. The king, summoned from Neuilly to Paris, rode to the bivouacs which had been set up to crush the insurgents, and tried to re-evoke his courage of Jemappes. "I have an excellent armor," he said to those who cautioned him. "I have my five sons."

The fighting continued through the morning of the sixth with important positions falling "to the side of order." But a group of insurgents, a hundred strong, took their stand at the Cloister of St. Merry to defend their principles with their lives. The National Guard were sent out against them. "They performed their duty with a courage that amazed their military leaders," Guizot wrote, "perhaps because of the personal interests that were everywhere in danger." The insurgents, on the other hand, defended their invisible ideals. Surrounded and outnumbered, amid fire and ruin, they fought while there was breath left in them and died crying, "Long live the Republic!"

Order was restored. After the carnage, Paris looked like a dead city. The cowed people dreaded to venture out into the streets and when they did, it was under the watchful eyes of the troops, guarding crossing and bridgehead. Along the Seine embankment the soldiers' bayonets, gathered in bundles on the parapet, glistened in the sun. Even the birds seemed frightened. Little by little the swallows darted over the water, and the flocks of swifts returned again to their nests on the towers of Notre Dame. But the city long showed its wounds. For days the Cloister of St. Merry ran with blood, and dark stains covered the stones of the Quai Saint-Michel. Beyond, the windows of the morgue showed a gruesome fretwork of severed heads. Never before had it held so many bodies. It was choked with them and disgorged a red

114

stream that flowed sluggishly under the arches and stopped short at the river's edge. Everywhere was the smell of death.

But the summer storms washed away the stains and cleansed the air, and Paris revived. And with it revived the people's hopes. Once more they had risen only to fall. The time would come when victory would reward their sacrifice.

George returned to her writing. Every night, after putting Solange to bed, she lighted her lamp, replenished her stock of candles, and wrapping herself in a Balzacian dressing gown, covered page upon page with her fluent scrawl. The oil in the lamp gave out. She lighted her candles. They flickered palely in the dawn. She snuffed them out and went to bed. Jules had accommodated himself to her unconventional habits. But he was now taken so much for granted that he might have been an article of furniture. It was a union, more agreeable than the marriage with Casimir, but threatening, like it, to smother her in boredom.

Nevertheless when she left her garret for the larger and handsomer third floor of 26 Quai Malaquais, whose lease Latouche had turned over to her, she furnished a cosy nest for the colibri in one of its pleasantest rooms. The new apartment was a charming place to which she gave as much the air of Nohant as she could to a city dwelling. Her views of Paris she saw through the interlacing branches of tall trees. The rooms were spacious, and one of them gave out onto a balcony as large as a garden. On it roses and jasmine bloomed among orange trees in tubs, and a currant bush made a fine show with its clusters of ripening berries. A pair of green canaries hopped about in a cage, marveling as much as Solange at their newly hatched nestful. "So tiny, so wrinkled, so naked, weak and ugly that they look as if a breath would make an end of them," George told Maurice. It was home. Had her son been with her, what more could she have wanted for happiness? Perhaps a literary success for Jules. He had been looking singularly crestfallen since the enthusiastic reception of *Indiana*.

Indeed, the position was an awkward one for Sandeau. The shining light of a small town, he had begun to shed a glimmer in the metropolis when his mistress, an unknown provincial housewife, had not only dimmed his luster but threatened to extinguish it altogether. His vanity suffered. As a writer and as a male he felt his inadequacy. George who had begun by looking up to him, at least in the field of literature, had now, in spite of herself, assumed dominance. Jules had to accept his inferiority. George earned the money. George paid the bills. George planned a pleasure trip to Italy for them, and was even now preparing to finance it by the labor of her indefatigable pen. There was one way in which Jules could prove himself, one way in which he could assert himself as a man. He took it.

George, however, had her secret frustrations. Love, in her, was so closely allied to imagination, it was such a complex of aspiration and desire, that physical expression carried with it its own disillusionment. She expected so much from the act of love that no reality could ever have wholly satisfied her. From the moment her passion was roused, to the climax of the lover, she yearned for fulfillment and yearned in vain. Her gratification was never more than a reflex of her partner's ecstasy. She was troubled by her anomaly. Casimir, with his brutal directness, the colibri with his delicate arts, failed alike. She was only an instrument of pleasure for her lovers. Was she never, in her own body and soul, to feel the divine shock? In her solitary nights, while Sandeau slept, she explored herself through Lélia, passionate yet unappeased. Jules proved himself in vain.

Not only did he fail, but he succeeded in alarming her. She was worried by his passion. He was growing thin; his once fresh complexion had a livid look. She warned him against herself, but he did not understand her fears. Then she did what in her was always a sign of indecision. She sought a solution, and the responsibility of a solution, outside herself, by consulting Jules's friend Regnault.

Candor was always one of George's virtues. Here she exercised it almost to a fault. "Jules laughs at my fear as if I were a child, and when, during his transports, it comes over me and chills me, he says that it is thus that he would like to die. . . . I have seen him a hundred times fainting in my arms. I have sacrificed my will; but I am killing him, and the bliss I give him is purchased at the expense of his days."

If anything emerged from George's confession it was that she was tiring of Sandeau, although she would have been the last to admit it. Such an admission would have reflected upon the exemplary quality of their union, outwardly so harmonious and so productive of good works, that the Saint-Simonists might have pointed to it as a paragon of the free-love marriage. She still found Jules charming, and if his moulting plumage made no great éclat among the rare literary birds who had begun to seek her out, she still owed him the fidelity of her free election. Besides, he had become a habit.

With the appearance of *Valentine,* George Sand affirmed herself as more than a literary flash, a fear which Charles Augustin Sainte-Beuve, while admiring her *Indiana,* had expressed, not so much from the autobiographical tone of the first book, as from his theory that each man and woman is capable of one work, inspired by personal emotion, but that the test of the true novelist lies in the ability to find matter for creativeness outside the circle of individual experience. Had George Sand written herself out in *Indiana?* His reading of *Valentine* disproved it. In the new novel the self-conscious striving for effect was gone. There was a sureness of touch, an adroitness of style and composition, an objectivity, that marked a master in the art of fiction.

Valentine had come out in the middle of November, 1832. On the last day of the year Sainte-Beuve reviewed it for the *National.* In the hierarchy of criticism a favorable review by Sainte-Beuve was a nod from the Almighty. In his treatment of George Sand he not only nodded approval with his large cherubic head whose vastness combined the contours of infancy with the bosses of accumulated wisdom, but he also reached out his arms to welcome her among the elect. There could be no doubt about George Sand's merit. "It is the work of a true novelist," he wrote, "a painter of the heart and of life, a fecund person who has only to walk patiently to attain to the goal." Not content with such praise, he summed up: "The author has the key to the human heart, the creative gift. The name of George Sand conceals a master."

George thrilled to the generous recognition, and from such a source. She had the impulse to sit down and write the critic a letter of thanks. But how could the dead words on a page express her appreciation? She must see Sainte-Beuve. She must tell him how much his encouragement meant to her. But how could she go to him? A woman, however bohemian, cannot take the initiative in such a delicate matter. She consulted her friend, Gustave Planche, toward whom she had had no such scruple. Knowing his power as critic on the increasingly influential *Revue des Deux Mondes,* she had sought him out in his lodgings at the Jean Jacques Rousseau and introduced herself. A friendship began and Planche was soon presenting George to his friends, including François Buloz, editor and part owner of the *Revue* which, under his shrewd direction, had been luring subscribers by the hundreds from rival magazines.

Planche was exactly George's age. The son of the distinguished Hellenist, Joseph Planche, Gustave had carried into the field of criticism a sound scholarship and a respect for the word which made him approach each article with the reverence of an act of devotion, so that although he had not yet affirmed his talent in a work of large scope, he had managed to impress the public with his superiority. An eccentric among a group known for its deviation, he lived in disorderly poverty in a squalid quarter, yet had the haughty and disdainful airs of a mogul. He rushed into excess like a war horse into battle, keeping throughout a mind as sharp and unclouded as a diamond. There was nothing he could not treat with authority. Literature, art, science, politics, he chose as the core of articles which he wrought with the precision of a jeweler till every facet sent out its own particular spark and the whole gem dazzled in the combined brilliance of his allusions.

His life, on the other hand, had the untidiness of a rook's nest in his scorn of material detail, an untidiness further aggravated by actual want when, seized as he often was by paralyzing inactivity, he would shut himself up for days, his mind seething with ideas, his hands folded idle in a mood of black futility. Insecurity haunted him although he was assured of an income by Buloz who knew a good literary investment when he met one. But the insecurity worked from within, a canker not wholly malignant, for while it filled him with doubts and fears, it forced him out of passivity to active excess which, for a time, at least, relieved him of the oppressive burden of his intellect until the next creative surge.

George found stimulation in his brilliant conversation, and was always at home to him. There was something, moreover, pathetic about the youth who might have been attractive had he been less uncouth. A few, like Balzac, saw a Byronic kinship in Planche's biting satire and his scorn of opinion. But Planche was a Byron prematurely gone to seed, his green pod hoary with potentialities destined never to bear fruit.

Planche was flattered by George's friendship, and not a little grateful. He was no favorite with women whom he alienated by his lack of gallantry and, in the case of those in the public eye who courted him for favorable notices, by his intransigent frankness. Something about George, however, perhaps her smallness, her candor, and her innocence of approach, had overcome his mistrust of the sex. Perhaps, too, his infallible judgment told him that here was an individual who would set her mark upon the age.

However it was, after their first few meetings he became her devoted slave, considering no task too humble for his doing. Whenever Casimir came to Paris, it was Gustave who relieved George of her husband's ponderous presence by taking him to see the sights; it was Gustave who arranged for the delivery of the piano which Casimir, on a generous impulse, prompted no doubt by George's rising fame, provided for her new apartment. It was Gustave who called the doctor whenever Solange was sick, Gustave who ran the little errands for his female confrère, Gustave who delivered Maurice to the Henri IV academy, and who called for him on the free days when the boy came to stay with his mother. It was Gustave, too, who tried to comfort her when she sank into a taciturn despair at the sight of Maurice trying to keep back the tears at their leave-taking.

Planche accomplished everything with such respectful assiduity that the colibri, fluttering in the shadows, could not take it amiss. Besides, had not Jules made a special friend of Marie Dorval, the tragedienne? He accepted George's friends. With equal magnanimity George took on his.

If Planche's friendship was a source of comfort to George the woman, it was inestimable to the author. Already he had roused Buloz' interest in the still unfinished *Lélia,* and what is more, he had so praised *Indiana* and *Valentine,* whose commercial advantages the canny editor had seen for himself, that Buloz offered to sign up George on his magazine for the sum of four thousand francs a year. George, of course, accepted even though Latouche cried treason. Latouche had to admit, however, that his *Figaro* was no match for the *Revue des Deux Mondes.*

The little provincial lady had snapped her leading strings. There could be no doubt about it. As Sainte-Beuve had predicted, George Sand would attain her goal, and in the competitive world of men, such men as Hugo, De Vigny, the virile Mérimée, Dumas, Balzac, the astounding young Alfred de Musset, and Sainte-Beuve himself, all contributors or collaborators on Buloz' review. Latouche, half in love with George, could never forgive her for leaving him for the *Revue.* She was young, however, while he had reached "twice twenty-five," as he referred to his unwillingly borne middle age. In his regret at her going, he took more credit than he deserved and never tired of reiterating that he had given her her literary beginnings and guarded her against the pitfalls of imitation. Balzac and Planche he always held in abhorrence, the novelist because Latouche had suspected his influence on *Indiana,* and Planche for stealing George for the *Revue.*

Latouche's suspicion of the Balzacian overtone was not unfounded, but it had been wholly unconscious on George's part. She never set out with a theory on beginning a book. It is even doubtful that she had either plot or fixed characters. The story, like the personages in it, sprang from her inner reserves, and took on her experiences and development. It was such an effortless investiture, and so naturally accomplished, that George, whenever charged with placing herself and her friends in her books, invariably denied it. *Indiana* contained, if not the matter of Balzac, at least a hint of his manner, for she had read and admired him, in spite of her reproaching him for making monsters.

But with equal justice she might have been accused of imitating Chateaubriand, whom she loved, or the sensational

Kératry whom she dutifully read for the secret of his popularity but loathed for his perverse subjects. His *Dernier des Beaumanoir,* for example, had as its theme the rape of a woman, thought to be dead, by the priest in charge of burying her—a not untypical subject in the fiction for mass consumption in which even the most reputable writers sought to outdo one another with accounts of necrophilia, nymphomania, transvestitism, vampires, androgynes, bleeding ghosts—anything and everything in the literary cabinet of horrors wherewith to jolt the generation out of itself. The difference between a masterpiece like Balzac's fantastic *Peau de Chagrin* and the latest Kératry penny-dreadful lay solely in the art of the one and the mediocrity of the other. If George absorbed the influence of both it was to her credit that she distinguished between genius and nullity.

She had met both men in her early days in Paris. Kératry, to whom Latouche had sent her for advice, looked at the young woman from the height of his affluent old age and sighed with a hypocritical shake of the head, "Believe me, don't waste your time making books. Make children instead!" Balzac had had no such antifeminist prejudice. In the boundlessness of his generosity which almost equaled his unaffected self-esteem, he thought the field of literature large enough for anyone who would till his own plot. There was room in it for the woman who called herself George Sand as for the genius of the age, Honoré de Balzac. What competition could anyone oppose to his vigorous fecundity? And so he would carry his great bulk up the many flights to George's apartment, pick up the sheets lying about her writing table, read here and there with a nod or a word of praise, and immediately plunge, a joyful diver, into the ocean of his inexhaustible projects. Once immersed, he swam along, an energetic leviathan, splashing, bounding, shaking himself in the exhilaration of his potency. He had no trace of envy, nor fear that anyone would appropriate his ideas. In any audience, were they writers, artists or *épiciers,* he would tell the story he was writing in dramatic detail, enacting the characters, inventing situations then and there and, in endearing naïveté, turning to his listeners for advice. He had scarcely stopped to listen when he was again improvising on his themes, his work and himself.

George, though five years younger than Balzac, humored him like an elder sister. She was fond of the *bon enfant* and respectful of the writer in whom, earlier than most of her contemporaries, she had detected the master, whose greatness was only thrown into relief by his trifling faults. And they were trifling: his ingenuous self-absorption, and an overmastering love of the *bibelot.* George always remembered with tender amusement how, after selling his *Peau de Chagrin* for a good price in 1831, Balzac had hung his little entresol in silks and satins till it looked like the boudoir of a king's mistress, and invited his friends for ices. And that other time, when in his delight at his new dressing gown, Balzac insisted on wearing it, could not bear to take it off, and ended by accompanying George and her friends most of the way home, a lighted candlestick in his hand and the ample folds of the *robe de chambre* enveloping his ampler frame. "Aren't you afraid you might be murdered on the way back?" one of the party asked. "Certainly not," he said. "If I should meet with thieves they would either take me for a madman and be frightened, or for a prince, in which case they would be too respectful to molest me."

George's friendship with the author of the *Comédie Humaine* endured calm and uncomplicated. "Childlike and powerful, he was ever covetous of a *bibelot*, but never envious of another's glory . . . intemperate in his capacity for work and restrained in his other passions."

With Sainte-Beuve the relation was to become personal yet never close. His involved self-protectiveness saw to that. On the noon that Planche took him to see George, her very attractiveness gave Sainte-Beuve warning. The young woman's hypnotic eyes, fine brow and lustrous hair, her slight, rounded form in a simple long dress, were signal flares to his suspiciousness. Her absorbed quiet and infrequent speech reassured him, however. They became friends at once.

But it was a cautious letting down of bars on Sainte-Beuve's part. A man of twenty-nine at the time, he was so gravely vestured in his authority, that he might have been mistaken for a well preserved oldster. He was born old. The torpid blood of his parents who had begot him in middle age, was seldom to run in him tumultuous with passion. He was wary of violent emotions, and eschewed them. But, insatiably curious about them, like one of Boccaccio's monks whom he resembled in the plumpness of his chin and the tonsure-like thinness of his reddish-blond hair, he would place himself in situations to enjoy what he had not the courage to experience. Salacious curiosity took the place of desire in that meager body overweighted by its too large cranium, and he was never so gratified as when he could be the third party to a liaison, as pander or confidant it did not matter, provided he had his post in the wings of the alcove.

His friendships with women, therefore, partook more of the avuncular than of the lover, so that from Ondine Valmore with whom he translated Horace, to the titillating actress-bluestocking, Hortense Allart, none altogether succeeded in seducing him to an indiscretion. To make the likelihood impossible, he protected himself by a secret love for Adèle Foucher, which finally cost him the friendship of Victor Hugo.

Even without his elaborate defenses Sainte-Beuve's literary preoccupations would have kept him from the life of the zealous lover. Whenever he was not writing in the study of his secluded house, half convent, half library, which he shared with his aged mother, he was sitting knee-deep in manuscripts in the offices of the *Revue de Paris,* the *National,* or Buloz' magazine. Nevertheless he still found time to follow the amorous fortunes of the people about him. It was the riotously glamourous career of libertine, as much as his poetry, which made Sainte-Beuve blunder like a moth against Alfred de Musset's flame.

In the person of the tranquil woman before him, whose reputation surrounded her with an incongruous aura, he saw another object for his vicarious enjoyment through the permutations of human relationship. He was tempted to play mathematician.

Chapter XIII: The Triumph of Lélia

JULES SANDEAU was nothing if not human. The admixture of Adam in him had been put to the test beyond his endurance. George was famous; he was still only a journalistic hack. George was collecting a circle of friends who radiated from the center of influence to the general world of the outer rim; he was tolerated as the inevitable shadow to her light. Even the few people he introduced to the ménage ended by being more George's friends than his. He felt himself visibly diminishing and blamed George for the diminution. Work brought him neither satisfaction nor reward. Love itself had grown stale. When George left for the country early in 1833 he was almost relieved.

Resentment must find an outlet. Occasionally, without George's knowledge, he had looked for solace in other women. Marie Dorval, who later became his acknowledged mistress, was one. There had been others. It was as if by his infidelity he were paying back George for making him feel inferior. He knew she had no suspicion of his lapses and therefore could not be humiliated. For the time, however, his satisfaction sufficed his wounded vanity. Emboldened by George's absence, he worked out a systematic revenge in the person of the laundress.

George found them together on her return. The shock of the discovery had a disastrous effect upon her. True, Sandeau's insipid charm had begun to pall; but there is loyalty, there is the calm, even enjoyment of friendship in the ebb of passion. She had been undeviatingly his during their life together, and considered herself as much his wife as if the union had been sanctioned by ritual. Infidelity in a marriage where the two parties have been brought together by convenience she could understand. Infidelity in a tie contracted in love and mutual esteem was a sin against the ideal. Hence, although George had too often yawned in their joint intimacy, she had decked it in the romanticism of her imagination, converting dullness into the interval where

> *The heart must pause to breathe*
> *And love itself have rest.*

Sandeau's betrayal destroyed her faith in man.

As for Sandeau, he found that his revenge humiliated him

more than it did George, who felt that under the circumstances the better part of valor was a generous heaping up of coals upon his diminished head. They had planned a trip to Italy together. George sent him to enjoy it alone, at her expense. She offered to pay his rent in Paris until he found himself permanent lodgings and, without anger or recrimination, parted with him. The break was a clean one.

"I shall make a bundle of Jules's things that are still in the closets," she wrote Regnault on the fifteenth of June, 1833, "and I shall send them to you, for I do not wish to have any meeting, any word with him, on his return. . . . I have been too deeply hurt by the discoveries I have made about his conduct to have any feeling for him other than a rueful compassion. . . . Spare him the pain of knowing that he has lost everything, even my respect. He has probably lost his own."

The tenor of her complaint was noble, much too noble, not to betray the blow to her self-esteem; for it is one of the contradictions of human nature that no matter how misprized a partner in an emotional bond may become, one wants the initiative in bringing about the rupture. The end had come before George had prepared herself for it. Indeed, it is hardly likely that she wanted it. Surprising her as it did, like the climax to a third-rate farce, it cheapened all that had gone before. The great experiment in the freedom of the heart turned out to be only a sordid affair.

At a less crucial period in George's life the blow would hardly have grazed her vulnerability. In the transitional stage of her heart and her career, it was almost fatal to her personality. Flimsy reed though he was, George had leaned on Sandeau, hoping through him to achieve full growth. As a writer she had made rapid progress. As a woman she was beginning to realize herself, at least in losing her mistrust of the male, when the gentlest, the most delicate of them all, behaved as abominably as any Delmare. She pitied herself, and, in the chronically susceptible state of her emotional nature, dramatized her disillusionment. What woman had ever been more unjustly betrayed? Was love possible in the world? She was not yet thirty, and yet her heart was sick, her body weary, her soul disenchanted, her whole being desirous of nothing so much as oblivion. At times the suicidal moods she had known in adolescence took such hold, that she could not be near the river without struggling against temptation. She heard the voice of her own Valentine crying out to her, "You may not love, yet you cannot live without it."

In her dejection she turned to Marie Dorval, the least likely mentor to lead her toward moderation. "I saw beside me a woman without restraint, and I found her sublime," she confided to

SAINTE-BEUVE

*"Sainte-Beuve . . . with his large cherubic head whose vastness com-
bined the contours of infancy with the bosses of accumulated wisdom."*

Sainte-Beuve. "In contrast I looked at myself, austere, almost callow, and I thought myself hideous in my egotism and isolation. I tried to overcome my nature." Marie Dorval helped her.

The actress had been introduced to George's intimacy when George impulsively invited her to her house after one of Marie Dorval's performances. Marie arrived, rather, she floated into the room, a creature as airy as the plume upon her hat, and with a cry of "Here I am!" flung her arms about George. Jules, who already knew her, was pleased to have her on a footing of friendship with George, though he was soon jealous to find himself superseded.

When the two women met, Marie Dorval was at the height of her career. Her performances in *Marion Delorme* used to end in riots of enthusiasm. A long line of dandies escorted her carriage; women copied her dress and adopted her coiffure. She was not strictly beautiful, but she had the attributes of beauty —charm and spontaneity. Her slender body reminded George of a reed swayed and shaken by some mysterious breath. The accents of her somewhat husky voice vibrated from a deep chord of passion. The woman's intensity communicated itself even across the footlights. George felt herself drawn to the actress by an instinctive affinity.

Everything was the keenest drama with Marie—art, friendship, devotion, anger. She knew no curb. Living in the moment, she gave herself to life as to an inconstant lover whom she tried to keep by her headlong surrender. Her days hardly had hours enough for her crowded experiences. She must have everything. She must feel and know all with every avid sense. On the boards she exerted something of the contagion of fire. With the first spark the whole audience was aflame. She was as amoral as an elemental force, and as irresistible. Also, as destructive.

People remarked the growing intimacy between the actress and the novelist after George's rupture with Sandeau, and disapproved. No good could come to George from the influence of a woman who went from lover to lover, who knew nothing of constancy and would as easily betray a friend as an enemy. George's faithful warned her, telling her that even while she was giving herself so devotedly to her friendship, Marie was playing her false. "Let me love her!" George cried out in desperation. "I know what she is and what she is worth. Yes, I know her faults, her vices, even. . . . You say she has betrayed me. I know it.—But you, my good friends, what man is there among you who has not betrayed me?" The accent was not a little theatrical, but the pain was real.

"You can only cure love with love," the bacchante whispered meanwhile in her ear.

If only she could be like Marie. Or if she could find a man capable of dominating her, who could match strength with strength, conquer and make her a woman at last. In the midst of her dejection some ironic fate responded to her wish. She met Prosper Mérimée, an aggressively masculine man, suave, phlegmatic, who took a woman as he would have taken an after-dinner brandy. Their liaison lasted a week, leaving George humiliated and broken. "I slept with Mérimée last night," she told Marie. "He is less than nothing." Her scorn was no revenge for Mérimée's cold brutality.

She had to unburden herself to one who would understand. Sainte-Beuve was waiting. "In one of my periods of ennui and despair, I met a man stanch in his beliefs, calm and full of strength, who understood nothing of my nature and laughed at my distress. I was fascinated by his force of character. . . . I thought he had found the secret to a happy life, that he could teach it to me. . . . Even now I cannot decide whether he was strong because of his greatness or of his worthlessness. . . . He had the art of rousing my desire, and made me believe there could be a kind of love which would appease the senses and exalt the soul. Well, I behaved at the age of thirty as a fifteen-year-old girl would not have. . . . It is not a pleasant story. The whole thing was a failure. I wept with disgust and hopelessness."

She omitted to tell Sainte-Beuve what Victorien Sardou, who had it from Mérimée himself, bruited about all Paris long after the event: the phlegmatic lover had left a five-franc piece on her mantel, following a mutually disenchanting night.

"If Prosper Mérimée had understood me perhaps he would have loved me," George wrote sadly to her confessor. "Had he loved me, he might have dominated me. If I could have submitted to a man I might have been saved, for my independence is a canker that is killing me."

"She is a coldly debauched woman," Mérimée complained in turn, "more out of curiosity than by temperament."

The affair shed no glory upon either. Throughout her life George carried the humiliation of it, together with an unconquerable suspicion of the strong male. Mérimée went on in his imperturbable career, which he had initiated by two literary hoaxes and enlarged by political benefices obtained through wooing the right people at the right time. His style, deliberately controlled, reflected the man. As he progressed from success to success it assumed a lapidary coldness like the chill of his petrifying soul.

Sainte-Beuve listened to George's laments and extended canonical comfort. From the first, an odd sympathy had subsisted between the two, temperamentally so dissimilar. Most feminine of women, George competed with men on their own terms. Indeed, in the dangerous stream of contemporary Paris, she swam more boldly than the rest, in the recklessness of her hard-won freedom. Sainte-Beuve, on the other hand, preferred watching the race from the safe perspective of his domestic prebend.

Nevertheless, like St. Anthony, he was goaded by his erotic imagination that found an outlet in the verses which, as if apologizing for them, he published under the pseudonym of Joseph Delorme. The first volume had appeared in 1829, a year after the publication of his *Tableau Historique et Critique de la Poésie Française du XVI⁰ Siècle.* The book of essays established him as a critic. Joseph Delorme's verses had the distinction of being noticed by Guizot who described the author as a hybrid Werther and Jacobin. The public turned an indifferent shoulder on Delorme and seemed only slightly more interested in his second poetic effort, *Consolations,* which was to remain Sainte-Beuve's literary Benjamin, in that illogic of the heart which makes a parent dote on the weakest offspring. At the time he met George Sand the critic was working on a novel that blazoned the title, *Volupté.*

"I have my faults," he was to admit. "They are like King Solomon's which disenchanted him with everything and filled him with disgust of life. At times I may have regretted that I was thus quenching my fire. But I have never perverted my heart."

In 1833 his fire emitted disturbing sparks in the presence of that brooding incarnate energy that was George Sand. Absorbed as much as Goethe in elective affinities, Sainte-Beuve was tempted by a combination, and the name of Alfred de Musset occasionally entered the conversation. "I must bring him here to meet you some day," he said.

George turned away, her silence eloquent. She did not want another man. Like her own Lélia she cursed God for making woman pay the burden of original sin.

Sainte-Beuve misconstrued her indifference to that young exquisite, to whom, as Joseph Delorme, he had addressed verses inspired by his grace in waltzing. If George Sand could resist Musset it must be because she had designs on the author of *Consolations.* Forestalling possible consequences, he gave her an unflattering account of himself. On her assuring him that henceforth she wanted nothing but friendship from men the critic breathed more freely. So great is the power of words that they made him impervious to her magnetic eyes.

Not for a moment, however, did he relax his wariness. "By all means be Lélia," he advised, "but only in the prose of real life. . . . You must regain a more just and tolerant view of the world and men. I know that you can fulfill yourself in a noble and fairly peaceful life."

Then, as if to bring that nobility and that peace within her reach, he wrote to her slyly that for her distraction he was going to introduce her to the admirable philosopher, Théodore Jouffroy, "one of the best men you could possibly meet, good, clever, a fine psychologist, calm and disinterested, and the most devoted of friends. . . . What is more," he added with telling subtlety, "he admires you for the right reason—because there is *soul* in your works, and not because you have wit and talent."

"My friend, I shall receive Jouffroy at your hands," she humbly acquiesced.

On further reflection, and with the memory of another calm, disinterested man still too fresh, she changed her mind. She no longer had faith in paragons who were too good to be true.

"Then what about Alfred de Musset?" Sainte-Beuve returned to the charge. He was more than ever curious about the results of the meeting between Lélia and the beautiful boy, Mademoiselle Byron, the golden Apollo, as he was variously called.

Again instinct warned her. "I don't want you to bring Alfred de Musset," she wrote. "He is far too much of a dandy. We'd never get along. I should be drawn more by curiosity than by interest. . . . Why don't you bring Dumas instead, in whose art I have found *soul?*"

Was the request her retort to Sainte-Beuve for offering Jouffroy? However it was, the solemn confessor arranged a luncheon for the meeting, but the inglorious Alexandre never appeared.

From the first Sainte-Beuve had followed the growth of *Lélia* with the perplexed admiration of a hen that finds a bird of strange plumage amid its undistinguished brood. Even among the highly colored products of Romanticism *Lélia* was a flamingo. As she wrote, George herself was dismayed by the power of her own creation, so dismayed, that unlike her usual reticent self which made her friends quip, "George Sand is the only man of letters who never says a word about her work," she begged Sainte-Beuve to listen to a reading of it a few weeks after their meeting.

Sainte-Beuve was honored. Sitting uneasily in George's small salon, he followed her exposition of the theme as far as she, who was never happy in talking about her work, could project it. She spoke rapidly in her embarrassment, but as she warmed to her subject, she shot him sudden lambencies from her eyes, interrogating his expression. Then she began to read from her manuscript:

"Who are you? Why does your love give one such anguish? You must hold within yourself some dreadful secret unknown to men. Surely you are not like one of us, not made of the same clay and animated by the same life. You must be an angel or devil; you are no human creature. If you are from God, speak and we shall adore you. If you derive from hell— You, from hell? You are so beautiful and pure! Have evil spirits so divine a look, a voice of such harmony, words that exalt the soul and bear it up toward God?

"And yet, Lélia, there is about you something of hell. Your bitter smile belies the heavenly promise of your look. Sometimes your words are as desolating as a denial of God. . . . Why, Lélia, why are you so? What of your faith? What of your soul, if you reject love? . . . Lélia, I am frightened of you. The more I see you, the less can I fathom you."

A cry from the depths of his passion, the young poet Sténio's exhortation to Lélia opened the book, instantly communicating his own bewildered questing into the nature of that mysterious being. Who was she? What was she that she filled men with such spiritual disquiet?

Sainte-Beuve sat up, listening to those fragments without plan or preliminary, which rolled like boulders in a chaos of the soul—Sténio's, Lélia's, the very century's—as the perspicacious Gustave Planche divined when, summing up *Lélia* in his review, he wrote: "She is the thought of the age upon itself, the cry of a society in its death throes."

As the novel progressed the tumult resolved itself into order. But it was such order as dream commands in its domain uncircumscribed by reality, and furnished by the Byronic paraphernalia of heights and solitudes, ruins, specters, tragedy and death. Just as Indiana was a female René, Lélia was another Manfred. Both Lélia and Byron's hero were fathered by Faust. But since Lélia belonged to French Romanticism, she travailed in the Spanish setting selected as their spiritual home by Louis Philippe's discontented poets, instead of in Manfred's Alpine fastnesses.

More than a novel *Lélia* is a poetic allegory and should be read as such to make credible its gallery of animated abstractions that enact their scenes and say their say—this superbly—amid a *décor* that would have suggested a painting to Salvator Rosa on every page. Trenmor, the convict who had committed murder and through penance and meditation was striving to regenerate his soul—what is he but imperfect man seeking spiritual perfection? Magnus, the monk who desires Lélia for her beauty yet hates her as an incarnation of Satan for her ascendency over his senses—is he not the degenerate Church against which Grandmother Dupin used to inveigh with eighteenth century logic? Pulchérie, the prostitute, is she not the body, avid for pleasure, to Lélia's soul, "tormented always by things divine"—like George Sand herself in her duality?

Sainte-Beuve penetrated the secret and wrote George about it the following day in a letter that was a testimonial to friendship and a tribute to the artist. "Most of all I admire the Lélia in yourself, in your soul's essence. . . . Indeed, madame, you are a rare and powerful soul. If, in your book, thought and emotion occasionally betray bitterness it is only because the wine in the goblet has shown itself corrosive. The goblet itself, of purest metal, remains intact, unspoiled."

It was a penetrating comment on the part of the bachelor who, as he listened, outwardly so composed, was wondering what defects that demonically clever woman was discovering in himself. He had expected a lady of facile morals. He found, instead, an earnest woman, almost too earnest who, like her own Lélia would face misunderstanding, even persecution, to impose her truth upon a recalcitrant society. The very people who most enjoyed her novels branded her with immorality. The few understood. "George Sand immoral?" Henry James heard one of her admirers exclaim long after she was dead. "The only fault I find with her is that she is insufferably virtuous."

The wine was still corrosive, however, though the vessel remained untouched, and here was not the least of Lélia's lures. How had that slight body contained all that ferment and not been destroyed? "Even without considering Lélia as a literary feat, but approaching it only as a revelation of its creator," Sainte-Beuve wrote, "I doubt that I can make you understand how I marveled at the sureness of touch, the continuity of concept, and the sustained power with which you transport us across regions so vast and deep that at every step we are frightened and dismayed. To be a woman . . . and yet to bear a burden of wisdom that would have turned a man's hair white—that is what I admire in you."

That admiration was not all he felt he admitted only long afterward when, the danger over, he confided in Les Poisons: "For a long time I found myself beside the author of Lélia as if beside an abyss whose brink was concealed by a magnificent, smiling vegetation and, lying in the tall grass, I marveled. But one day, at last, I leaned over and I saw. O quanta Charybdis!"

It was probably after that view that the determined bachelor grew so trepidant over his safety that he kept away from George almost a month and did not even write.

"Do you know you're a rather queer bird?" she reproved him, irritated. "Are you annoyed with me or are you just lazy? . . . If you don't like me, come out with it. It couldn't possibly hurt me as I am hardly vulnerable in that respect."

Such directness had to be met in kind. Very well, Sainte-Beuve would tell her the truth in a way she would not misinterpret.

"There is one side of you (permit me to say it)—the side that made Sténio say to Lélia *I am frightened of you*—which has made me say the same thing. . . . But on knowing you better, I have been able to appreciate all the rest, your man's loyalty with your woman's grace." No woman could be complimented more than that.

The flattery worked. Pursuing his advantage, Sainte-Beuve turned from confessor to confider. He loved another woman, he told her. He had loved her without hope for years. She reciprocated his love but they could never marry. George was edified by such virtuous renunciation. "You give me back the courage that has so often failed me," she said, grateful for his confidence. "You love, you are beloved . . . thank God for that."

On this note of piety they resumed their friendship. George described it retrospectively as "a completely candid relationship with no *arrière-pensée*."

Sainte-Beuve was not alone in his amazement after he read the completed *Lélia*. George's old friend Malgache sent her a note about it in which astonishment mingled with admiration. "What the devil is it? Where did you get it all? Why did you write this book? Where does it come from, whither does it go? . . . They're making fun of me at home because I love the novel as much as I do. Perhaps I am wrong to love it, but it has seized hold of me and deprives me of sleep. God bless you for shaking and agitating me like that. But who is the author of *Lélia*? Is it you? No. This fellow is imaginary. He does not resemble you in the least—not you, that gay person who dances the *bourrée*, who appreciates lepidoptera, who is not above a pun, who sews not too badly, and who is an excellent hand at preserves. It may very well be that we did not know you at all. . . . But is it possible that you could have reflected on so many things, pondered so many questions, and swallowed so many philosophic pills without anybody's suspecting anything at all?"

Like the influential critic and the good Malgache, the whole generation received *Lélia* with wonder and perplexity when the novel appeared on the tenth of August, 1833. George, who had been reluctant to publish it, hardly expected the pyrotechnics it kindled. The journals coruscated in columns of praise and adverse criticism, most of the reviewers approving the novelty of the form but attacking with asperity what they called the immoral font of the book. The public snatched up the volumes as rapidly as they poured from the press. Everyone talked *Lélia*. The women modeled themselves after the heroine, the men desired her. Writers, emulous of the book's success, sharpened their quills to make a stab at little *Lélias*. Envious novelists, turned critics, damned it volubly, but found they were voices in the wilderness. *Lélia* had come, *Lélia* had conquered, and there was nothing anyone could do about it.

Not anyone, at any rate, except a certain Capo de Feuillide whose name cheated oblivion only because George Sand's was briefly connected with it. He edited a small magazine, *Europe Littéraire*. The day before *Lélia*'s publication, he published a denunciatory article about the book and its author. Not satisfied that he had done enough, he followed it with a still more virulent attack on the twenty-second of the month. George Sand could not be a woman, he said among other things, for no woman would so far have forgotten her modesty as to perpetrate such obscenity as *Lélia*.

George, as a representative and champion of her sisters in bondage, felt aggrieved. What was wrong with Sainte-Beuve that he kept silent? Why had he not yet reviewed *Lélia* in the *National?* "Why do you not defend me?" she asked him.

After a long silence he answered, "Of course I'll do for *Lélia* what I should have done long ago," and on the twenty-ninth of September his critique appeared, warm but a little disappointing. "*Lélia* is at bottom the incapacity to love and to believe," he summarized. "It is the premature sterility of a heart that has worn itself out in disillusionment and dreams."

That was hardly a retort to Capo de Feuillide.

But her knight arose, eventually, none other than Gustave Planche who, seeing his lady in such distress, challenged the offender to a duel. Planche's friends warned him not to be quixotic. The many enemies he had made through his criticism laughed aloud. Advice and mockery fell alike on deaf ears, and Planche, who had never held anything more lethal than a pen, engaged to meet Capo de Feuillide with pistols. As it turned out neither of the two was injured, but the story made the rounds of the salons, gaining in fantasy as it circulated.

"Was either of them hurt?"

"No."

"No? What a shame!"

"But Planche's bullet hit a cow and killed it."

"Ha! Ha! A cow!"

"And damages had to be paid."

"By Planche? But he hasn't a sou."

"By Buloz, of course."

Everybody laughed. Louder than any laughed Alfred de Musset.

Chapter XIV: The Vessel and the Wine

GEORGE SAND and Alfred de Musset had met on the twentieth of June, 1833 at a dinner given by François Buloz to his contributors at the Frères Provençaux. The *Revue des Deux Mondes* was prospering beyond his hopes, and the shrewd editor knew the wisdom of coddling his literary geese for the resplendent results in golden eggs.

It was a distinguished dinner and an elegant one. Sainte-Beuve was there, together with a group of the finest minds of the day. George Sand had come, escorted by Planche. The only woman present, George was at her most feminine in a toilette that carried out an original motif *à l'orientale,* in protest against the constricted waist and exaggerated necklines of the mode of the moment. Her brown silk dress had the simple line she affected, but the simplicity was not without its cunning, bringing into relief, as it did, the girlishness of her figure. A bolero in braided gold pursued the oriental theme, further advanced by a turban-like headdress that partly concealed her hair. The small jeweled dagger at the waist might, to the fastidious, have seemed superfluous.

On her left, Alfred de Musset adhered as much to fashion as she rebelled against it. He was the dandy type—had she not condemned him for it to Sainte-Beuve?—and from the tight fitting jacket with its velvet revers to the polished boots made by the *bottier* most in vogue, he looked the model of the young exquisite. George noted his long, fair hair, not entirely innocent of the curling iron. She surprised his exploring observation when he thought she was not looking; and she listened appreciatively to his brilliant participation in the general conversation. Had she not been vaguely disturbed by the curiosity he aroused in her, in spite of her Lélian cold heart, she might have seen a conspiratory guilt in Sainte-Beuve and a jealous concentration in Gustave Planche.

As the wine flowed, Musset addressed himself to her. He became bolder. The awe in which he had begun by holding the author relaxed, and from profound observations on the respective merits of Humboldt and Galileo, he descended to roguish looks and still more roguish jests on the jeweled safeguard at her waist. Lélia smiled indulgently. Charming Sténio. . . . But he could not know her heart was dead.

Planche took George home.

Alfred de Musset, stimulated by the wine, rounded out the night in his habitual fashion. George Sand, that quiet woman of the slow and infrequent speech, was the author of *Indiana*. He had never read it, nor had he read anything else of hers; but he had been impressed by critical acclaim. George Sand. He did not know what sort of writing amazon he had expected, but he was wholly unprepared for that slim body, those devouring eyes which in the light had a strange amber glow. He had half anticipated seeing her in the masculine suit that people talked about. He met, instead, a pasha's houri. At what moment during dinner had she deftly removed her ornamental dagger? For he had noticed with pleasure that she was no longer wearing it when the party broke up. She did not interest him as a conquest, however. She was not fashionable and he must have women of fashion. She was not beautiful. He was twenty-two. She must be nearly thirty. She did not interest him.

Nevertheless, he went to a book shop at the first opportunity and bought a copy of *Indiana*. He read it critically, pencil in hand, to make up for his blind acceptance of the critics' praise. By the time he finished the novel he had curtailed it considerably as he rigorously struck out phrases and adjectives—to prove to himself, at least, his faultless taste. Still, he had to admit that the book had power, and not only power, but a fascination which carried one along and created that sense of identification with the characters and their conflicts that is the test of successful art.

He was driven to emulation. He must communicate to George Sand the spell which, in spite of himself, *Indiana* had worked upon him. He was curious about the woman behind the author. How much of the novel had she actually lived? How much was pure imagination?

He chose as his text the scene during which Raymon, betraying Indiana with Noun, seeks to find in the handmaid the body of his mistress. "Sand," he addressed the author in the first of six stanzas,

> . . . *Quand tu l'écrivais, où donc l'avais-tu vue*
> *Cette scène terrible où Noun à demi nue*
> *Sur le lit d'Indiana s'enivre avec Raymond?*
> *Qui donc te la dictait cette page brûlante* . . .

Had George beheld such a scene? What power had dictated that burning page? "Was it one of your own experiences?" he went on, emboldened, using in his address the second person singular which, while carrying reverence when employed to God and king bears, nonetheless, a touch of intimacy toward beings less exalted. "O George!" he concluded, "is not the true Ideal that celestial bride whose lover is the angel of desire? . . . Ah, woe to him who seeks in the body of one the phantom of another!"

He sent her the verses on the twenty-fourth of June with a sly note. He had been inspired to write them upon *rereading Indiana,* he wrote. "They're of so little worth that I would hesitate to offer them did they not give me the opportunity of expressing the sincere and profound admiration that prompted them."

George accepted the tribute to her art, wondering perhaps why he wrote Raymond for Raymon after having read the novel for the second time, and judiciously ignored the intimate implications. "Would Alfred de Musset lend her his manuscript *Rolla?*" She tactfully returned the compliment without in any way committing herself. Alfred sent it promptly, begging her not to share her "caprice of curiosity" with anyone—was he referring to Planche?—and shortly afterward followed his poem in person.

Lélia was smitten—and disturbed. As a *femme fatale* whose love brought havoc into men's lives she had no wish to harm this sensitive youth, abnormally vulnerable under the exaggerated sophistication of the man of the world. She caught that sensitivity in his dandyism carried to extremes—in his redingote whose velvet revers came down to the waist, in the vivid sky blue of his pantaloons, in the curled beard and floating hair, too long even for a prince in that world of *flâneurs* and Jockey Club enthusiasts of which the reckless, tubercular Duc Ludovic de Gramont-Caderousse was king, and d'Alton-Shée, Alfred Tattet, Guttinguer, Prince Belgioioso and another select half dozen formed the peers, or *cocodès,* as the duke called his intimates. Their mistresses, the *cocodettes,* added another word to the language.

George was further troubled on discovering that among the ashes of Lélia's spent hearth smoldered a stubborn ember that threatened to start another conflagration, at the very time when she had thought to find peace in the undemanding friendship of Gustave Planche. She was done with men as lovers, she told herself. And yet, she could not live without her pain, as she confessed to Sainte-Beuve. She must have that excitant to her jaded nerves, that incentive to curse and yet to struggle, in a turmoil of body and soul which for her was the very pulse of life. Lélia could not know that in her love of suffering she was romantic sister to Musset, whose cry was to echo for a century in the ears of French youth: "I love and I would pale, I love and I would suffer!" Musset, too, was ripe for his greatest pain.

As much in self-defense as for his protection, she gave him warning. She was sick at heart. She could no longer love. Love had been for her a cruel ill that had nearly dispatched her to the other world.

How did the irresistible child respond? "Your sickness is no laughing matter. . . . Unfortunately we have as yet discovered no plaster to place upon an ailing heart. Don't look too much at the moon, I pray you, and don't die before we've carried out our wonderful project of traveling together, which we have already discussed. You see how selfish I am. You tell me you nearly went to the other world. I hardly know what I am doing in this. *Tout à vous de coeur*," he subscribed himself.

How could one withstand his charm? A few weeks earlier, on the fifteenth of May, the *Revue* had published his comedy, *Les Caprices de Marianne*. George had read the sparkling piece, so artfully mingling grotesque and high comedy tones in a brilliance of dialogue new and startling in French drama. What had struck her more than its originality was the intimate characterization of the two heroes, Octave and Coelio. Criticism was already attaching its labels to them: Octave was the man of the world, Coelio the man of feeling. To George, as she learned to know Alfred de Musset, they became the two sides of his character, painted to the life: Octave, debauched, lazy, skeptical, lover of wine and stronger stimulants that gyrated pleasantly in his head, proof against everything but intoxication; Coelio, melancholy, sentimental, scorning the vulgar triumphs of the libertine, in love with love yet without the will to realize his dream. "Which is Musset, Octave or Coelio?" someone asked her in the early days of her acquaintance with the poet. "Both," she answered, taking no warning from her penetration.

As it was, Musset had far too much pride to thrust himself upon anyone. A woman had hurt that pride with betrayal; hence he mistrusted all womankind. The public had wounded it more deeply still when his *Nuit Vénitienne* was hissed off the stage; hence he abhorred society. He had hoped much from the play. But the Classicists had opposed it for one reason, the Romantic group for another. An unfortunate accident killed the performance in a howl of laughter when Mademoiselle Béranger in white satin, leaned against a freshly painted trellis and, turning about to deliver a poetic speech, revealed her rondures stenciled in green squares. Musset never recovered from the humiliation. "Do you still deliver yourself up to the beasts at night?" Prosper Chalas asked him. "No, I've said good-by to the menagerie," he answered, "and for a long time." By that interval the progress of the French theater was retarded.

In his poetry he chose to walk alone. Let the Classicists have their cohorts and Victor Hugo his *cénacle*. He reserved for himself the freedom to create, to think and to speak as he chose—

136

to retort, when Hugo boasted, "I have twenty thousand verses before me," with the impudent, "I should prefer to have them behind me."

He belonged to that class of men whose intellect and ambitions, superior to the mediocrity they see about them, unfit them to cope with the meanness of daily living and the scramble for fame. But the standard of life, unfortunately, is set by the very mediocrity they abhor, and unless their genius has the force to break that mediocrity and impose itself upon it, it remains a virtue cut off and doomed to sterility. For even the highest art must be fed by the currents of the commonplace.

Musset struggled against those currents in his way. His life was a daily protest. Whenever he wrote, fitfully and only when the conception clamored for birth, he removed himself to a room glaring with lights and curtained off from the outside world, and isolating himself still more with the fumes of alcohol, wooed his muse.

"I am, alas, travailing over my latest monster," he wrote to De Vigny in the summer of 1832 when he was composing *La Coupe et les Lèvres,* "a monster which the naturalists are free to classify as they please. Instead of putting it into a bocal of alcohol, I am drawing it out painfully by the legs from a bottle of *eau de vie.*"

He needed the illusion that intoxication afforded, and the poem grew. After a satisfactory passage he would come out of his room and, rubbing his hands, congratulate himself before his brother Paul. "Well, I'm not a soldier yet," for in his morbidity at what he thought his failures, he had thought of joining the Hussars of Chartres.

Nevertheless he had already asserted himself with a body of exceptional verse and prose. Besides his first volume and his play, *Nuit Vénitienne,* he had adapted a tableau from Walter Scott, *La Quittance du Diable,* whose production was interrupted by the July revolution. In 1831 he published his *Poésies Diverses* which marked him as the adherent of one school, his own. A drama followed, *Les Caprices de Marianne,* after his volume, *Un Spectacle dans un Fauteuil,* disappointed him by its luke-warm reception. His Wertherian poem, *Rolla,* in the *Revue* for August 15, 1833, again brought him fame, rather, the manifestations of fame. Heads would turn as he walked along the boulevards. At Tortoni's, where he entered by the back door reserved for dandy and *cocodès* so that the elect might not be contaminated by the Philistine members of the Bourse who invaded the front porch, a loud whispering would arise on his appearance. On one occasion he knew he was somebody and he delightedly recounted the incident to Paul. He had just thrown away the butt of his cigar on entering the opéra when a youth who had recognized him, ran for the trophy, wrapped it carefully in a bit of paper and put it away. At such moments mediocrity had its merits, though he could never reconcile himself to it.

What attracted him to George was her defiance of the commonplace. She had given him the two volumes of her *Lélia,* one inscribed "To my *gamin,* Alfred," the other "To Monsieur le Vicomte Alfred de Musset, with the respectful homage of his devoted servant." They were signed *George* and *George Sand* to suit the intimate roguery of the inscriptions. Alfred's reading of the novel, without a pencil, this time, proved her as exceptional in her way as he was in his. He wrote her his admiration in their frequent exchange of notes. "There are some twenty pages in *Lélia* that go straight to the heart, frank, forceful pages as beautiful as any in *René* and *Lara.* They set you apart as George Sand and not as a mere Madame So-and-So who writes books."

Twenty pages out of two volumes—a grudging paucity. Nonetheless George was pleased. The wonderful boy was very hard to please.

Meanwhile he consented to abide by the simple friendship to which she restricted him and even went so far as to set down the agreement in writing. "The ridiculous words 'Will you' or 'Won't you' will never cross my lips," he assured her. There was the whole Baltic Sea between them in that respect. "You could give me only platonic love, which I could not give to any woman." Such being the case, he would be a sort of comrade who could have no claims upon her and therefore could feel no jealousy, "Someone who would smoke your tobacco, rip your dressing gowns and catch cold in the head discussing philosophy with you under the horse-chestnut trees." —An impeccable comrade but for the ripping of her dressing gowns.

Now and then he confused comradely feelings with those of a lover, as when he confessed he had been so haunted all night by her "beautiful black eyes" that he had had to get up to make a sketch of her. But whenever they were together, whether on the towers of Notre-Dame, still the resort of the Romantics, or promenading the Luxembourg gardens, his behavior continued irreproachable.

The day after they had taken one such walk, George received a letter which did not come altogether as a surprise. "My dear George, I have something foolish and ridiculous to tell you . . . You'll laugh in my face and accuse me of phrasemongering in my relations with you. You'll show me the door and you'll think I am lying. I am in love with you. I have loved you from the first day I came to see you."

George did not show him the door, but she made one feeble

138

attempt to keep her freedom. Alfred, though so young, was cynical and embittered. "What a prison wall you are!" she said to him. "Everything would destroy itself against you."

"George, you should learn to know me better," he defended himself. "You must not make me greater than I am, nor minimize me, either. . . . I have loved you not while I was with you, close to you, but here in the solitude of my room, where I am now. It is here that I said to you what I have never said to any other being. Have pity on my nature which has had to get used to living in a sealed coffin, hating those who forced it there. 'What a prison wall,' you said to me yesterday . . . Yes, George, a prison wall. But you forget one thing. Behind that wall there is a prisoner."

It might have been a letter from René. It might have been the voice of all unhappy youth crying out to her for love. In the state of her heart George might have withstood even that despair. One word she could not resist. "You should love those who know how to love. I know only how to suffer. . . . Good-by, George. I love you like a child."

To the child George could deny nothing.

She invited him to come to see her at midnight, the predilected hour of romanticism. For a long time they remained on the balcony, gazing silently at the midnight arras of Paris hung out before them. Then they went in. When Alfred took leave of her in the morning, he wrote a date in his private notebook: "July 29, 1833."

"Perhaps I have blasphemed against God in *Lélia*," Sainte-Beuve read in the letter George sent him. "God, who has other things to do besides taking vengeance, has sealed my lips by restoring the youth of my heart and compelling me to admit that He has bestowed upon all the capacity for supreme joy."

Thus the affair reached its logical conclusion, facilitated as usual by divine intervention. Perhaps George was also heeding the voice of the philosopher, Jean Lerminier, who exhorted in a review: "Pursue, O Lélia, thy triumphantly dolorous march. . . . Sing and weep not. Let not the divine fire lodged in thy flanks consume thee. Release it rather upon the world!"

"I am happy, very happy, my friend," read Sainte-Beuve who continued to receive her grateful avowals of a joy so intense that it had to be communicated. "Every day I am drawn closer to him. Every day I see his little unpleasantnesses, which used to make me suffer, disappear. Every day I see new virtues rise and shine. . . ."

Among Alfred's little unpleasantnesses was a carping jealousy in which he persisted with the stubbornness of a spoiled child. Gustave Planche became its object. Alfred loathed the familiarity

139

of the critic who used to come in and out as he chose—for that matter most of George's friends seldom troubled to announce themselves—assuming toward George a proprietary air which, she remonstrated in vain, was only the prerogative of the purest friendship. However, that friendship sometimes overstepped its bounds, as when, in a puerility irreconcilable with his sober mind, Planche had fed the poet chocolate-covered purgative pills, in revenge for some real or fancied slight. George must dismiss the critic, and quickly, Musset insisted. People were talking.

And George dismissed the faithful Planche with a lame explanation and a warm handshake. She informed Sainte-Beuve at once of this latest step. "Many impudent persons have been saying that Planche was my lover. It doesn't matter, for *he never was*. But I cannot have any implication that I would share my love with two men. It's not in the nature of any one of us three. People will say that I am fickle and fantastic, that I go from Planche to Musset, while waiting to pass from Musset to another. I care little, provided they don't say that my bed receives two men on the same day."

A delicate scruple. Sainte-Beuve carefully dated and annotated the letter and put it away in a special pigeonhole with the rest of the Sand correspondence. The relationship in which he had been the power behind the scenes was proving more titillating than he had hoped. Meanwhile, he must not allow himself to be too much involved in it. Napoleonic, he must wait and let everything come to him.

Alfred's brother and the gay *cocodès* perceived Alfred's absorption in Madame Sand and were filled with concern, particularly Paul to whom Alfred represented the bold champion of that electric life which he, Paul, dared not conquer for himself and which, at best, he could enjoy only at second hand. He had noted Alfred's visits at the Quai Malaquais, first at weekly intervals and then every few days, the tall hat at the required angle, then suddenly at the tilt of conquest. From that point on Alfred's room had remained untenanted and the family table waited in vain for him to appear at dinner. He had settled at the Quai Malaquais and nothing could budge him. Madame de Musset raised her brows but no word violated discretion for fear of bringing out matters unsuited to her young daughter's ears.

After domesticity had been established, Paul visited at Madame Sand's. He found a cheerful apartment, furnished after a bohemian taste tinged with the current orientalism, and a humming gaiety in which everyone talked and laughed and painted and made music. He had never seen Alfred so lighthearted. The burden of the century had fallen from him. He was as young as his years, adoring George, sketching her, extemporizing verses about her, calling her *Savante* in mischievous raillery for her wisdom in so many matters, and protesting himself her foolishly devoted "Mussaillon."

Paul did not like it. This was no simple affair. It went far below the surface. The two personalities, while dissimilar in many respects, nevertheless absorbed and penetrated each other. Paul dreaded the consequences for Alfred. His extreme sensibility reacted too strongly to pleasure or pain.—"A lute forgotten on a chair," Alfred had said of himself, "vibrating to the least breath." Now the lute was responding to a whirlwind.

Like Paul, Alfred's most intimate friend, Alfred Tattet, had his fears about the liaison. Partial to his boon companion, he was willing to believe the worst of George and warned Alfred against her. But Alfred was the knight held captive by *la belle dame sans merci*. He knew only that her eyes were the wells of his enchantment wherein he willingly sought death.

Tattet waited. A rich young man and a leader among the *cocodès*, he knew that Alfred would come back to the open house he kept on the Rue Grange-Batelière. Their friendship was too close to be broken by a mere affair of the heart. Alfred had had too many amours before it; he would have as many again when George Sand was forgotten. The man whose "Mardoche" had thrilled every fiber in him, as Tattet never tired of repeating, whose other works were for him the miracles of the century, must not become the victim of a woman, even a George Sand.

Alfred Tattet had much of the fanatic in his contradictory make-up. Everything was for him either divine or execrable. In 1830 he, the rich man, had found the revolutionists divine and had fought beside them on the barricades in an enthusiasm that cooled as quickly as it had ignited. From the first, Musset too, he decided, was divine. As the poet's charm outlasted the flare of a revolution, Tattet remained constant to his worship. Anyone else necessarily suffered by comparison, since Tattet was strictly monotheistic in his friendship. He and Paul de Musset, therefore, had a common concern. Often the name of George Sand appeared in their conversation, and not in blessing.

In George's apartment, meanwhile, the lovers tried to keep their happiness unmarred by interested interference and curiosity. George, however, was too well known. Since her first public success her privacy had been invaded by every would-be author with a masterpiece under his arm for her to read and launch. Indigent artists, actors out of a job, widows and orphans, climbed up the three flights to her door to tell their tale of woe, the empty hand outstretched for whatever she might put into it. The more she gave, the more the horde of the needy grew, till she discovered to her dismay that Paris had an organized band of mendicants who passed about the name of the charitable dupe, and fastened upon their victim like tropical ants till there was no more to be had.

Little by little the procession of beggars dwindled, but nothing could discourage the unpublished novelist and poet. Each day brought some new aspirant who assured her that his manuscript had the combined excellence of *Indiana* and *Lélia* and that if she would only find a publisher, the author would give her half the profits. Young girls, bitten by the Romantic germ, came to offer their services as chambermaids for the privilege of living in her proximity. Painters and musicians asked for her patronage, that her name might silence the cabals which mediocrity had raised against them. Even small shopkeepers of the neighborhood applied to her for money. "It's such a trifle for you. Surely you can't refuse."

No wonder Alfred wrote:

> *George est dans sa chambrette*
> *Entre deux pots de fleurs,*
> *Fumant sa cigarette,*
> *Les yeux baignés de pleurs.*

Even her flower pots and her cigarette could not check her tears of vexation.

Alfred's little word pictures were delightful, almost as delightful as the many sketches he made of her, drawing, smoking, writing; in a décolleté gown and a fan in her hand; in her morning robe (unripped); in poses so natural and so deftly caught that Delacroix, who never liked Musset's poetry, regretted that Alfred had not chosen painting instead.

Musset and George had gay, prankish parties among chosen friends when the world left them alone. On one occasion, wishing to take down the grave Lerminier from his intellectual heights, they arranged with the mime Debureau to impersonate a visiting British diplomat, and seated him at table next to the ponderous critic. Throughout the dinner the haughty diplomat did not deign to open his mouth except to eat, in contrast to the vivacious new Breton maid who interrupted the conversation, poured wine indiscriminately into glasses and over the guests, and finally took the empty chair on Lerminier's left.

The visiting Englishman did not twitch a brow. Finally, after someone introduced the subject of the political situation in Europe, the diplomat took up his plate and began to juggle with it, keeping up at the same time a running commentary on the balance of power among the nations, to the amazement of the company who expected the demonstration to end in a crash of china. At the close of the dinner it was difficult to tell what had created the greater surprise, the disclosure of Debureau as the diplomat or of Musset as the maid.

But alas, the summer was hardly over when Musset began to show signs of that inner turbulence which he had thus far managed to keep in check, to an extent that had made George tempt destiny by her boast of happiness. The first rumble of the storm had come when Alfred, jealous of Gustave Planche, insisted on George's dismissing him. But that sacrifice of friendship, far from propitiating Alfred's exigent possessiveness, made him demand more victims. It was not enough that George prove that she was absolutely his; she must, through confession, purge her soul of the taint of past loves.

"I am not tender—I am excessive," he boasted.

His excessiveness he used as the whip that mortified his victim and excited him to that "evil drunkenness" which alone procured him the gratification he sought, a gratification beyond physical appeasement, like a violation of the soul.

Love had hardly brought the two together before it became a goad toward mutual torture, as if only through that suffering which they both required as the very sustenance of their beings, could they fulfill themselves. Avidly he received it at her hands, in every admission of past satisfactions wrung from her, and from the galling cup he drank not only moral anguish, but an exquisite physical pain. In George he had at last found the supreme source of intoxication, the proof of the verses:

> Aimer est le grand point, qu'importe la maîtresse,
> Qu'importe le flacon, pourvu qu'on ait l'ivresse.

Yes, to love was the important thing. It was the ecstasy, not the vessel that gave it, which mattered. Now, however, the vessel itself could not be ignored. To the jaded youth one woman had been like another and the intoxication the same—until he met George and found not only desire met with desire, but his complexity dovetailed to the least excess and void. The instrument of pleasure held more than pleasure. It was in itself wonderful. Like the perverse child he was ever to remain, Alfred must know the delight surpassing all others. He must break the vessel.

He set about it with the awful deliberateness of a madman. The spoiled darling of his day, arrogantly devil-may-care toward everyone else, he was exacting only with her. "Savante!" he hurled at her, no longer in banter, but to humiliate her before those who thought her great. Not that he disagreed with the general opinion. He would allude to her as "a divine being." But by chipping off a little of the idol, one brought it nearer to human imperfection. Also, one asserted one's ascendency thereby.

George, who had cried out her despair at not finding the man to dominate, and so save, her, yielded to the tyranny of the child. Her yielding urged him on. "Was Gustave Planche ever your lover?"

"No, never!"

"You're keeping it from me."

"I swear he never was."

"You never gave yourself to him?"

"I swear it."

The inquisition of the night he pursued on their awakening. George, angered, withdrew into disdainful silence. Her resistance incited him even more than her submission. His imagination, pursuing the guilt she would not admit, tortured itself with lustful images, flung at her with taunts and maledictions. She was destroying him by keeping him in doubt. He must know what men had been her lovers, that he might avoid them, that in the presence of the many who came to see her, he might be free of agony and suspicion.

"I must know! I must know!"

George defended in vain her prerogative as a free woman. He laughed and called her a Saint-Simonist. She pleaded for her rights as an individual to pursue her happiness. He sneered at her, and by his tantrums during which he stamped his feet and burst into sobs, he overthrew the libertarian edifice so bravely constructed by the sacrifices of Indiana and Lélia and Valentine.

"I must know! I must know!"

In the early autumn the Quai Malaquais apartment was abandoned to Boucoirain and Solange and the lovers secluded themselves in the forest of Fontainebleau. Perhaps without Paul de Musset's solicitous hovering over his brother, and the importunities of Alfred Tattet, with no visitors to rouse Alfred's jealousy and with the sanative influence of nature to soothe him, he might be restored to the lover he had been in the first weeks of their union.

They lodged in the house of a gamekeeper and lived the simple life. Once more George put on the blue woolen blouse and the trousers she had worn when she went riding with her old tutor. Alfred loved horses. They hired two handsome animals and together they roamed the wide stretches of woods, meeting no one on the way to bring back the agitations they had left behind in Paris. Alfred carried his sketchbook. George mused on the new novel she had promised to Buloz. In the evening they read aloud to each other by the fireside.

For the first few days it was as if the cure had been accomplished, Alfred was so tender and repentant. Almost, the veil-lidded Angel of Love in the verses he had written her on the

144

second of August, seemed once again to have embodied itself in her:

> *Jamais amant aimé mourant sur sa maîtresse*
> *N'a dans deux yeux plus noirs bu la céleste ivresse,*
> *Nul sur un plus beau front ne t'a jamais baisé.*

But alas, that brow and those eyes from which he had drunk celestial rapture too soon reminded him of other lovers who had there found intoxication before him. It was futile for him to seek to be other than himself. No matter how he strove to control his obsession, "the thought would always roar in the brazen bull." Once more the inquisition and the torture began, and continued with no respite now that they were alone. It was madness.

George, who had never seen him so overwrought, even at his worst, took a final desperate step. She went with him one day to a rocky ledge, a shrine of Romanticism, at Fontainebleau. Crouched at his feet, her head leaning against a rock, she made a full confession of her past life, concealing nothing, justifying nothing.

Alfred drank in every word in a concentration of desire, and when she had no more to say, lifted her up "in a paroxysm of exaltation." He possessed her at last. His sharpest senses had attained the ultimate in satisfaction—his sight at the view of her face in humiliation and tears, his hearing, the acutest of all, at the sound of that voice, now softened to a whisper, now broken with sobs. He saw her not as she was, but with that intenser vividness of his imagination, which could summon up images more living than life. With that peculiarity of his hearing, Alfred, who sustained that sound had color—that *fa* was yellow, *sol* red, that a soprano had a golden quality and a contralto a somber hue [1]— he made a sensual music of her words. For a day he lived in a rapture of the senses.

But once the spring of his abnormal organization was released, it let loose a whole Pandora's box of fantasy. What had been his past? What would be his future? He who felt himself live, love and suffer with a hot intensity and yet would watch and analyze himself, as everyone else, like the coolest scientist, searched within himself.

"Alfred de Musset," Delacroix once criticized, "is a poet without color. He uses his pen like a burin. With it he cuts into the heart of man and kills him with the corrosive of his poisoned soul." Alfred now practiced that method on his own heart, cutting deep and wide.

Soon after her confession George found him roaming the

[1] In his color-hearing Alfred de Musset foreshadowed Rimbaud. See Rimbaud's sonnet on the vowels.

forest in a state of hallucination, his eyes wild, the muscles of his face rigid with terror. Fearful of the worst, she kissed him and soothed him as if he were a child. For a long time he could not speak; then finally he told her the cause of his distress. He had lain down at the foot of a ravine when suddenly he heard an echo start up of itself and sing. It was an obscene song. Raising himself on his hands, he looked about and there in the heath he saw a man running. His face had the lividness of death. His clothes were in tatters. "I saw him so clearly that I was sure he must be some poor fellow who had been attacked by thieves and was trying to get away. But as I was about to pick up my cane to help him he came close. And I saw that he was drunk. . . . As he passed he threw me a hideous, besotted look and made a grimace full of contempt and loathing. Then I was terrified and threw myself upon the ground and hid my face. For that man —that man was myself!"

George was alarmed by the effects of his vision. For two days Alfred lay in a delirium of fever through which she nursed him. Then, as soon as she could, she returned with him to Paris. They took with them Alfred's sketchbook full of souvenirs of their stay. The last sketch commemorated the scene of the hallucination. "Honeymoon in a Cemetery," he had labeled it, adding under the picture of George, "with her heart as torn as her dress."

Alfred must have a change of scene. They had often talked of going to Italy together. They planned to take the trip before the end of the year.

Chapter XV: The Fatal Journey

IT was December before the lovers were ready to leave Paris. There had been preparations to make, difficulties to overcome. George settled her affairs with businesslike expedition. She left the apartment in charge of Boucoiran who, besides the offices of manager, secretary and treasurer to the novelist, held the humbler positions of housekeeper, male nursemaid and tutor to Solange. She arranged with Buloz for regular advances, to be sent her on the novel which she promised to have ready for him by June of the following year. She furnished Casimir a plausible excuse for the voyage, and gently prepared her son for the news which she would not break to him until the last minute—the boy was still so little resigned to being away from her.

Her financial position gave no cause for worry; her literary reputation kept flourishing with her fertile output, whose latest burgeon, the novelette *Metella,* published in the *Revue* in October, had lifted Sainte-Beuve out of his temporary apathy long enough to pen a note in which he called it the best thing she had ever done. It held him by its spell, he wrote. "As I read it I had a conscious pride in being your friend and in holding a place, however small, in the affection of a person of such rare and delightful genius." George returned the compliment by admiring *Volupté.*

Yes, all was well. Even Alfred showed signs of improvement after the chastening nightmare of Fontainebleau. If only people would not meddle. She knew Paul was opposed to the Italian voyage; she suspected Tattet of trying to prevent it. She did not know, and Alfred was too much the gentleman to tell her, how far they went in their dissuasions. Between Paul and Tattet it was a constant exchange of premonitory fears about the poor boy, the unfortunate child in the toils of the fateful Lélia, who, not content to lure him from the bosom of his family, was carrying him off to a strange land.

"You cannot go, you must not go!" Tattet pleaded.

"But you went there with an actress, didn't you?" Alfred reminded him.

"Oh, but that was quite different. I am not a poet, and an

actress is not a novelist." What sinister threat lay in the *novelist* Tattet did not explain, but the word planted itself in Alfred's mind.

The most serious objection came from an unexpected quarter. Madame de Musset, a cold, wry-faced woman whose rectitude was patent in the unbending line of her frail person, had always spoiled her younger son. Although she had been scandalized by his liaison with "a notorious person" she had closed an eye upon it while waiting for passion to cool and the prodigal to return. To her horror, instead of coming home, Alfred was threatening to leave Paris, a calamity which Paul painted in the dark colors of his interested prejudice. When, therefore, on the eve of his departure, Alfred went to his mother for her blessing, he met unprecedented resistance.

"Never! I will never give my consent!" she cried. "I know that all my objections will be futile and that you will go. But it will be against my wishes and without my permission."

She wept, she wrung her hands, reiterating her gloomiest forebodings. "It will be a dangerous, a fatal undertaking. I will never consent!"

He bowed before her grief. "Very well, I shall not go," he said. "If anyone must weep, it won't be you."

And out he went, as Paul thought, to countermand the order for the departure.

Somewhat later that evening, while Madame de Musset and her daughter were sitting by the fire, a servant announced that a strange lady was waiting below on the Rue de Grenelle and that she wished to speak to Madame. Mother and daughter exchanged looks, but Madame de Musset followed the servant down. A hired coach was standing not far from the house and from its open door a woman whom she knew at once to be George Sand, invited her in. The interview was confined to the privacy of the carriage, but when Madame de Musset returned to her daughter she cried, "That siren has wrung my consent from me!" As she said it, she wept.

On the twelfth of December Paul, who had no choice but to escort the two voyagers to the starting station of the Messageries Lafitte et Caillard, observed them closely. George wore for the occasion a black velvet spencer, pearl gray trousers and Russia leather boots. Her hair was covered by a small visored velvet cap that shaded her eyes. In one hand she was carrying a sack containing a meat pasty against their hunger, in the other a bottle of champagne against their thirst. Alfred was in high spirits. His mother, besides the permission forced from her, had given him a modest purse to supplement the four thousand francs providently furnished by Buloz for George's *Jacques,* to be written in Italy. (Incredible woman! No doubt she would have it ready, too, in despite of love and adventure!)

"Look, our coach is the thirteenth on the line," remarked Alfred, too much the child of Romanticism to miss an omen. Paul stored the little fact for later reference.

As it was, a considerate destiny was doing its best to give warning of things to come with a persistence that would have opened the eyes of two less hypnotized by their dream. The diligence had hardly started when it struck a post and knocked down a water carrier. George and Alfred saw, commented, and pursued their way with the obstinacy of the predestined.

What did they seek that they had not found in Paris? From what were they escaping? Doubtless they had ready answers in their moments of rationalization. They were still to learn that whatever they did, wherever they went, they remained the prisoners of their personalities, their efforts to escape from themselves only the frantic bluster of squirrels in a wheel. But the activity had its excitement, at least while it lasted, and when it was over, the reward of a deadening sleep. Meanwhile they enjoyed the moment as they watched the familiar receding, and adventure inviting ahead. "At last I have you all to myself," Alfred exclaimed again and again.

At Lyons they left the coach for the Rhone River boat which was to take them to Avignon, whence another stage would go on toward Marseilles and the Genoa packet.

They had hardly embarked when they saw a bustling, pot-bellied little man in furred boots pushing his way toward them. It was Henri Beyle—Stendhal, as literary fame preferred. George, immediate in her instinctive reactions, was puzzled by Stendhal's sharp-tongued wit and by the spiteful smile that looked as if it had been painted on. She laughed at his quips, and his fleshy face in its frame of curling hair which art kept youthful, flushed with pleasure and self-gratulation. His short, thick neck disappeared like a turtle's as the shoulders rose and shook in mirth at his own cleverness. He became more daring and outspoken, and the prominent underlip thrust out still farther as if he would miss nothing of his own salacity.

George confessed to Alfred that she was not sure whether she liked the great man. Perhaps she was *bête,* she admitted. Balzac had actually called her stupid and prudish not so long ago when, on his insisting on pointing out particularly savory passages in his *Contes Drolatiques,* she had thrown the book at his impenitent head. "*Gros indécent!*" she had paid back for his "*Bête!*" But they had remained as good friends as ever despite their differences, and would go on accepting each other for what they were, without greater intimacy and with no diminution of affection. As for Balzac's droll stories, he had a ready answer for those who asked why he had written them. "To make money, and to increase the population of France."

Intimacy, to say nothing of an emotion as human as affection, could hardly be thought of in connection with Stendhal, who felt no farther than his own concerns. He was imprisoned in the circle of his personality; but, embittered by frustration, he had turned to self-love engendered by self-pity, and had nothing but scorn left for anything outside his protective periphery.

George was revolted by him at Avignon, when he took her and Alfred to visit the cathedral, where, at a side chapel, he stopped to point out an antique, life-size Christ carved in wood. The wounds on hands, feet and side oozed with blood in the crude realism of primitive art. Death and the horror of man's cruelty stressed their lesson with naïve directness. Suddenly Stendhal burst into a tirade on the hideousness of that Christ, damned the faithful who required such pain and repulsive nudity, and ended by saying he could hardly refrain from falling upon the image and belaboring it with his fists. George, who recalled similar shrines at Les Anglaises which had first awakened her religious emotion (it was never more than that) was offended by Stendhal's cynicism and was glad, when they were about to take the boat from Marseilles to Genoa, that he chose to go by land to his consulship at Cività-Vecchia. "If he had taken to the sea I would have taken to the mountains," she said in her intense dislike.

Before leaving Marseilles George took the opportunity to write a few letters. Boucoiran needed instructions; Casimir, to whom she still communicated her comings and goings, had to be kept posted; and she must try to make Maurice understand certain things. The boy had come to depend so much upon her, unlike Solange who was beginning to assert a precociously rebellious nature, that absence brought on alarming crises of nerves. "I am just about to sail on the sea for Italy," she wrote her son. "But don't worry, I shall not be gone long. I am obliged by my poor health to spend some time in a warm climate. . . . How I wish I could have you with me!" she exclaimed sincerely after her falsehood. "But your sister is not old enough to travel, and as for you, you must finish your education."

Far from suffering from ill health George enjoyed a robustness during the sea voyage that irritated the delicate Alfred who was unsettled by the motion of the boat. He watched her on deck smoking her cigarette, and improvised a jingle, not without its little acrid note:

George est sur le tillac
Fumant sa cigarette;
Musset comme une bête
A mal à l'estomac.

Amazing woman! Even in that she proved the better man, he brooded in the misery of seasickness. He was beginning to resent her Spartan virtues.

However, they had no sooner reached Genoa than George began to feel ill, as if in punishment for her lie to Maurice. She attributed her fever to the severe cold they had suffered on the Rhone River boat and, counting on the Italian climate to cure her, she joined Alfred in visiting monuments and museums, as if nothing were the matter. Alfred gladly put her sickness out of his mind. In his loathing of physical ills he preferred to have her pretend to health, even if she ran the risk of aggravating her malady, than that she disenchant him in the unbecoming rôle of invalid. The poet, so sensitive that he felt all suffering to the point of personal pain, could be coldly indifferent to those he loved if, for one moment, they left the niche in which he adored them among the flowers and votive offerings of his fancy, and came down to earth in human weakness.

They had been almost exclusively in each other's company for nearly three weeks. By degrees, however, Alfred ceased expressing his delight at having her all to himself. The poetry of Italy filled him with restlessness, like its wine. He admired its women to whom, as they passed, he gave those long, possessive, insinuating looks out of his lashless eyes that had made him the terror of the Paris salons.

George noticed but was not jealous. How could she be jealous when they had come to each other freely? Her serenity irritated him, all the more because she could not be out of his sight a moment without his imagining her in the arms of another. A perverse conflict began within him. He wanted the freedom of Italy for himself, yet he wasted it in jealous fears. George's confession at Fontainebleau, far from allaying his suspicion, had raised ghosts with features and names to haunt him. Worse, it had shaken his confidence in his hold on her fidelity. What had been might be again, he argued.

Other divergences of character asserted themselves daily. Slight in themselves, the differences came like the crack, finer than a spider's thread, which finally shatters the vase. The first irritation occurred in Genoa. They had been visiting the churches, and after a walk to the Villa Pallavicini, they stopped to look at paintings. Alfred would select a detail in a picture— the agony of a face, a gesture, any stirring moment of human emotion caught on canvas—and describe its effect upon him in words more vivid than the painting. George, on the other hand, had to perceive some grand philosophical concept, or at least a moral communicable to all, before she responded to the artist's labor. Alfred sought the individual at the height of pleasure or pain, George the whole of humanity in a moment of collective exaltation.

"My little boy," she would say somewhat patronizingly.

"Omniscient one," he retorted.

It was the same, whether they went to the museums or merely walked through the streets. He would always select the person; she lost herself in the crowd. At the opera he would delight in the aria; she thrilled to the choral song. He sought the shock of contact of an individual with another; she was happiest when she could feel herself swept away in a merging of souls. "Even in our happiest hours I never felt she belonged entirely to me," Alfred was to say in unforgotten bitterness to Louise Colet. "She never knew jealousy and possessiveness . . . I was never the center of her emotions."

This quality of George he was now beginning to see in its every manifestation, and each brought its annoyance. In Paris he had objected to George's bohemian circle. Now that it was far behind them, he realized it had merely been a proof of her inclusiveness. Her ability to write through the distractions of a child wanting constant attention, of visitors coming in and out, of household duties to oversee, had filled with awe the sybarite of the ivory tower. Now that, even in the novelty of their *solitude à deux* and the unexplored beauty of a poetic country, she was resuming her routine of work, he was overwhelmed and reproachful. He too had promised Buloz stories and poems for the *Revue*, but he had not even begun to think about them. It would have been a sin against the god of Romance, an insult to his mistress. George's matter-of-factness in their unusual situation confounded him. How little in reality did she resemble the heroines of her novels! In the want of the Romantic element, as Alfred understood it, in that calm, almost complacent, spirit, she might have been any provincial housewife. The trousers *à l'orientale*, the narghile she smoked, were only the appurtenances of an unconvincing fancy dress. George in real life was no Lélia, and he, alas, was all the heroes of romance incorporated in that slight, almost girlish, frame.

He was all the heroes of romance, and all their ills. At twenty-three he had already reached the chronic state of the *grand malade*, the morbid child of the age, ardent of soul, uncontrolled in emotion, sensitive, insatiable, excessive, and so far gone in his malady that the ordinary passions of youth had to be vices for his satisfaction: a mere pleasure, an orgy; a stimulant, a delirium; a drinking party, a bacchanal; a night out, a debauch. He was only a boy when he had begun to cure himself of boredom through excess. The cure was beginning to kill, for the disease was incurable and pervasive, claiming more victims even than the cholera.

A current anecdote illustrated the spread of the malady of the century. A gloomy man suffering from depression, entered the office of a well-known doctor. He found no pleasure in anything, he said, and was in such a state of disillusionment that he could not bear to go on living. The doctor advised distraction. "Go to the Funambules," he suggested, "where the great Debureau performs. He will cure you."

"I am Debureau," retorted the man.

Like the comedian, Alfred might have said to one who would have healed him through himself, "I am Musset." He was himself his own sickness.

In obedience to their fatality, George and Alfred followed their itinerary. George's health, in spite of the climate, did not improve. At Pisa they visited the famous Campo Santo and saw the solemn triumph of the Dance of Death, painted with the directness of prophecy, and did not heed it. For that matter, George had become so weak that she no longer cared what they did or where they went.

"Rome or Venice?" they asked each other. Neither could decide.

They took a coin and questioned fate. Ten times they tossed the coin. Each time fate answered, "Venice." Why did they have to consult destiny so often before they accepted the answer? Was it fate they feared, or Venice, or themselves?

However it was, they set out for Venice via Florence. There George's fever broke out anew, but still she did not give in to it. Cellini's Perseus, Michelangelo's allegories on the tombs of the Medici chapel, reminded her only that her body was as inert as bronze or marble. In sleep the sights of the morning would return as nightmares. She was a statue. Or she saw herself as a mosaic and counted the pieces until she fell into a stupor.

Alfred tired of her illness and went out by himself. He had discovered the subject for a Shakespearean drama in Varchi's *Chronicles of Florence*. He found it in the history of that disappointed poet and accomplished murderer, Lorenzino de Medici, who assassinated his kinsman, Duke Alessandro out of cold brutality, and justified it by a literary masterpiece. *Lorenzaccio*. That would be the title of the tragedy. Meanwhile Alfred began his research in the dives of Florence.

"Don't drink, *mon enfant*," George would call after him. "Be careful, dear boy." To keep his mind on his work she wrote out a scenario of *Lorenzaccio* for him.

Alone, she gave herself over to gloom. Now, unhappily, she had no Sainte-Beuve at hand in whom to confide, and Boucoiran was too busy taking care of her affairs to be burdened with her melancholy. Besides, even if a confessor had been there, she could not have told him how quickly the Romantic novel of their life was turning to depressing realism. It would have been too humiliating to admit. She turned, of all people, to Casimir. Of course she could not write him the true causes of her despondency, although she knew Casimir must be as well informed as anybody in Paris of the reasons for her trip; she put the blame on Italy. The country did not interest her. Its charms, overrated by generations of tourists, left her entirely unmoved. She felt relief in writing. If only she could have unburdened the weight in her heart that her Coelio was so soon proving himself Octave!

Alfred tired of Florence after a few days, and they went on toward Venice. A brief passage through Ferrara and Bologna, and then the Po, winding through endless plains, as silent and desolate as death. The mood communicated itself to the travelers. At Mestre they left the stagecoach and crawled into a gondola as if it were a coffin. Behind the black curtains, drawn to make a deeper darkness of the night, they dozed in the rhythmic gliding till, jolted awake when the gondolier pulled the boat to, they looked out upon a scene as unreal as a mirage: St. Mark's and its lights redoubled in the water and, dark against the circle of the rising moon, the bizarre tracery of the Byzantine towers. George's apathy left her at the sight. Venice had always been her city of dreams. She knew with her first glimpse that it would always keep something of her.

It was the beginning of January. They had hardly settled in their suite at the ancient Hotel Danieli overlooking the Grand Canal, when George had to take to her bed. She had pushed herself beyond her strength and, what was more, she had succumbed to dysentery. Alfred raged and blamed her for being ill. He had started out on a glorious tour with the woman he loved and he found himself shackled to an invalid. He would not be cheated of his holiday. Leaving George in the care of the hotel attendants, he went out, as in Florence, by himself. George put on her solemn face and gave him last minute advice from the bed where, in spite of her sickness, she had arranged her paper and quills for a few hours' work during his absence. The sight of the industrious invalid enraged him the more, and he would bang the door on her motherly counsels.

He felt maltreated and took his revenge by doing the very things she had warned him against. What had he, the poet who

154

at twenty had sung the supreme joy of caressing "the gleaming breasts of a tempestuous mistress,"—what had he to do with an ailing woman who, instead of the headlong passion he demanded, gave him the reproachful words and looks of a monitor? He cursed fate, he cursed himself, he cursed love which, so far, had been the only god he worshiped.

Even then, he worshiped it solely in the aspect of Eros, the beautiful but wanton boy who knew nothing of spirituality or self-sacrifice and who had found his special votaries in those eras that had overthrown faith and spread doubt of everything, including self. Musset was no isolated phenomenon. One had only to walk the boulevards, to enter the favorite meeting places of the young men of his circle, to find his likes, the heirs to that disabused century which had learned doubt and blasphemy from Voltaire's mocking lips, and borne a generation of children with May upon their cheeks and winter in their hearts.

Alfred de Musset differed from his fellows only because his nervous organization made of him an acutely keyed emotional being. May in his face had the innocent charm of a Renaissance page, as in the portrait Achille Devéria drew of him when Alfred had begun to frequent the salons; but the winter in his heart was of the iciest, requiring the most ardent emotions to melt it. He had sought those emotions in female devotees of the pagan god, in passions quickly suscitated and as quickly spent, in false illusions that led him on in a never-ending quest of the true, and, most of all, in a hunger for sensation and more sensation. The Renaissance page gave way to the libertine, and the libertine to the pose of the lost man who would be regenerated only by the devotion of a noble woman.

The plea had been the theme of his seductions and invariably it had worked, for no woman is ever more accessible than when she is approached as a redeemer. He had employed it in overcoming the resistance of Lélia, also with success. The trouble began, however, when the humorless George took her mission too seriously and Alfred found himself undergoing a daily baptism of purification, in the process of being converted from a libertine to a noble spirit, and from a naughty child to a man. Graver still, Alfred discovered that he had no vocation for redemption. He knew his faults and he cherished them. He would no more have been Alfred de Musset without them than a storm would have been a storm without its lightning and thunder. Indeed, Alfred's whole character partook of the tempest, in contrast to George's exasperating serenity. But it is the nature of the storm to shatter calm.

George bore with her "naughty boy." She could not blame him for being himself. Besides, it was still too early for reformation.

She could, however, set him an example of productiveness and fortitude. Her perfection only aggravated his remissness. Where he had previously stayed out late, he did not return until morning, much the worse for the Cyprus wine he had discovered in Venice, and *Lorenzaccio*, planned with such enthusiasm in Florence, was not given a thought.

He grew sarcastic whenever he found her at work. "Ah, poets," he sighed. "We are the lilies of literature, spinning without effort only when we please."

The implication was obvious. But Buloz had provided the cash which was financing their trip, and Buloz expected returns in enough manuscript to make a novel, before the excursion was over. George could not afford to be a lily of literature. On the contrary, she had to force herself to write, in spite of sickness, in spite of the violent headaches that had set in. If only it were true, as Alfred taunted, that she had only to release a spring in her head to make imagination flow!

The headaches became so severe that she had to send for a doctor. He came, a florid young man with reddish-brown hair and an awkward shyness before the woman whose crimson kerchief, tied like a turban round her head, gave an odd oriental look to her face. He thought she seemed very frail as she lay on the divan. The fair youth who was standing beside her suggested bloodletting. Dr. Pietro Pagello examined the patient, performed the slight operation and, when she felt relieved, left her.

Two days later he came again to see her. She was up, and greeted him affably. Reassured that she was doing well, he went away, wondering what she was to the young man, or what he was to her.

George had no sooner recovered than she tried to make up to Alfred for the days she had had to spend in bed. They went out together, and, in the gaiety of Venetian life, recaptured something of their early zest. They visited the Armenian monastery where Alfred, always a lover of costumes, was so entranced by the cowled cassock of the monks, like Byron before him, that he had it duplicated for himself. George humored him by getting herself up as a Doge's lady. They enjoyed their fancy dress and in the laughter forgot their differences.

But work had to be done and George's conscience plagued her. The dear boy must understand. He tried, but as he lay in bed waiting for her to finish her work for the night, he chafed and fumed and finally, in exhaustion, fell asleep. He could not forgive her that rigorous application, any more than Prosper Mérimée had understood or forgiven when, during his brief period with George, he had awakened in the middle of the night to see her crouched shivering on the hearth, her dressing

GEORGE SAND AT THIRTY
PAINTED BY EUGENE DELACROIX
*"Her face, wide-eyed and wistful, gazes far away
with heavy lids, toward the cause of her obsession."*

gown wrapped round her and a candle flickering beside her, kindling the fire that she might sit down to her task while her lover slept on.

Alfred took to going out again alone. He had had enough of goodness. Let George spin out her novels by the yard. He was young and life, Venetian life, with its Byronic legend, seduced him. In the charmed corruption, the lily of literature bloomed.

> *At Saint Blaise, at La Zuecca,*
> *Oh, to gather the vervain in flowering meadows,—*
> *At Saint Blaise, at La Zuecca,*
> *Oh, there to live and die!*

But the vervain Alfred gathered blossomed in the night, and the flowering meadows were more often than not the gambling dens and brothels to which the gondoliers led him. He would return to the Danieli in the morning and, as George slept late, they would sometimes not meet till dinner. The poet's pallor, his eyes red-rimmed from dissipation, brought on the usual admonitions from George whose long face, after the gaiety of his companions of the night, excited in him a ruthless exasperation. "I am talking to you like a mother. . . ."

"Mother, indeed!" he taunted.

She was becoming too much the mother and he strained after liberty. Her homilies had only the effect of irritants. He felt trapped, and his keeper was a woman who tried by words to ennoble his imprisonment. But he knew it for what it was. Paul and Tattet were right. He had made a mistake. He must free himself from the dominion of this too virtuous woman. (And he had thought her a spirit as liberated as himself—this person who carried on her industry, spinning her romances like a spider in the night!)

"George," he said coldly one day at dinner. "You are an annoying prude. You're boredom personified."

She looked at him and her eyes widened.

"I am sorry, George," he went on with the same chill. "I have made a mistake. I no longer love you."

She rose with quiet dignity. "We no longer love each other," she said. Then, haughtily, as she walked toward the exit of the dining hall, "We have never loved each other," she added.

That night the door was bolted between their rooms. It was the eighteenth of January, another date for George to mark on the calendar of her disillusionment. All was over. Their great adventure which the world had been following as eagerly as the installments of a *feuilleton* had ended abruptly in bitter words. There would be no more but for the word *Finis* as the ultimate irony on its inconclusion.

She thought of packing her things and going home. But she could not abandon Alfred to his temptations. If they were no longer lovers, surely they could still be friends. They were too civilized to make an end of everything with their physical divorce —alas, too civilized also to remember, in their present hurt, that love is as much of the body as it is of the spirit.

Alfred went on a wild debauch that lasted nearly two weeks. He was sparing neither of Cyprus wine nor of sarcasm; for they still talked to each other and had their meals, whenever possible, together, in the frigid civility which their new relationship imposed.

"Have a good time," she would say as he left her for his nocturnal excursions.

"You may be sure I will," he flung back.

She could not blame him for his behavior; she could not complain. The words they had uttered had separated them even more effectively than the bolt which she drew every night between their rooms. They were heart-free again, at least theoretically, and owed each other no fidelity. At any rate George tried to console herself by such reasoning for the wreck of the Italian idyl. She was no longer Alfred's mistress. Very well. She could still be his sister and friend.

"Really, George!" he scoffed whenever she approached him on the new footing. "It's all too absurd. Yesterday you were my mother, today you're my sister!"

George swallowed the insults, pitying herself in her unhappiness but pitying him more. He had spoken words which had made her feel like a discarded harlot. By that wound to her woman's pride he had lost her. She worked harder than ever, to forget her misery. By the end of the month she had written a good part of a novel. Buloz, at least, would not be disappointed.

The release of tension brought about by satisfaction with her work, relieved the strain between them and they made up their quarrel. Again they were seen together on the Piazza San Marco and, of a late afternoon, on the balcony of the Hotel Danieli, George in her red turban smoking cigarettes, Alfred beside her looking out upon the bustle of the canal. The Venetians wondered about the two foreigners and their relationship, among them Dr. Pagello who often saw them on his rounds to the hospitals.

Early in February, a few days after the reconciliation, the same Dr. Pagello received a note brought by a messenger from the Hotel Danieli, which served to enlighten him. It was written in faulty Italian, but between the beginning and the signature, *George Sand*, he was left in no doubt as to the state of affairs. The fair-haired young man he had met at the bedside of his former patient was very ill, in a delirium, and he, Pagello, was

158

requested to call with a fellow doctor for consultation as soon as possible. The sick man, the writer explained, was a famous poet, but more than that, a person whom she loved more than anyone in the world.

Dr. Pagello left immediately, picked up his colleague, Dr. Juannini at the hospital with which they were both connected, and left with him for the Danieli. They found Alfred de Musset in a high fever and a state of insane excitation. He sang, he roared, he screamed, and went into such convulsions that the two doctors were alarmed. Dr. Pagello noticed that Madame Sand's divan had been moved into the patient's bedroom.

They diagnosed Musset's sickness politely as typhoid fever, complicated by alcoholic frenzy. It was *delirium tremens*. The nights during which Alfred had paid off George for shutting the door against him had told upon his hypersensitive constitution.

George dismissed the consulting physician and kept Dr. Pagello. There was a simple dependability about him, an air of quiet efficiency which did her as much good as it seemed to do the patient. Alfred's improvement, however, was extremely slow. During one of his seizures he became so uncontrolled that in spite of the efforts of two men to hold him, he raced about the room naked and grasping George by the collar of her dress drew it so tight that, had help not been there, he might have strangled her.

Dr. Pagello became concerned for the safety of Madame Sand and offered to watch with her over Musset in the long nights. She accepted gratefully. She was helpless, in a foreign country, and the young doctor inspired confidence.

They talked together during their vigils, in poor French and worse Italian, but they understood each other in that language of sympathy more communicative than any verbalism. George felt secure with him. He was quiet, he was good, he was selfless, a man who, by his very profession, had dedicated himself to the service of humanity. And he was handsome. His large, powerful body had the solidity of a Gibraltar. In the light of the lamp his auburn hair had glints of gold, and his eyes glowed softly. He was the very opposite of Alfred.

But it was Alfred she loved, in spite of his cruelty, his possessiveness, his jealousy, his wanton boy's lust to break her for the pleasure of seeing what made her the woman she was. She loved him for the very turbulence of his nature, even though it had humbled her and made her suffer in her human dignity.

The hurt to her pride still rankled. Would Pagello have wounded the woman he loved, or any woman, for that matter, as Alfred had wounded and humbled her? The doctor was a good man, simple, kind and honest. She was indebted to him for saving Alfred; for after the twelfth day of their joint nursing she knew he would be saved.

She wrote to Boucoiran, begging him not to breathe a word of Alfred's illness. She wrote to Buloz, who clamored for copy, begging him to send a thousand francs, as they were reduced to their last sixty. She wrote to Madame de Musset, who was frantic at not having heard from Alfred, and told her that her son had been gravely ill but that, thanks to an excellent doctor, their "child" was now out of danger and would be returning home as soon as he could travel.

For seventeen days George did not leave Alfred's bedside. She had witnessed his paroxysms, heard his shrieks, "I am going mad! I am losing my mind!" She had calmed him in his delirium and reassured him by her constant presence. Whenever he slept she stole an hour's rest on the divan. Sometimes she forced herself to stay awake with cup after cup of strong black coffee and tried to write the copy Buloz demanded. How long would it take for the money to reach her? (Alfred had lost so much of their common funds, gambling with an Englishman.) A letter took ten days. How could she pay the doctors, the hotel, the pharmacist? She implored Boucoiran to prod Buloz to some activity.

Dr. Pagello became the friend in need. She must not worry about paying him, he said. He continued as faithful and respectful as ever. When Alfred was sufficiently recovered to be shifted, Dr. Pagello suggested that they move from the expensive Danieli to an apartment in the adjoining building. George took his advice.

She became so used to the doctor's presence that she sometimes worked on her novel while he was there. Occasionally she raised her eyes and gazed at him in enigmatic concentration. He flushed like a girl at the insistence of that look.

Chapter XVI: Love in Venice

ONE night, during Alfred's convalescence, while George and the doctor were watching as usual at his bedside, the patient grew restless and told them to leave him. The two withdrew to the fireplace, George sitting at the small table where she did her writing. They conversed in whispers about literature, about the poets and artists of Italy, and when Pagello's attention wandered, George would interrupt herself to ask: "What are you thinking about, Doctor?" Pagello would blush and stammer an answer.

The fire crackled cozily. The lamp shed an intimate glow. Pagello found himself intercepting one after another of George's long looks.

"Do you think, madame," he said to overcome his embarrassment. "Do you think you will some day write a novel on our beautiful Venice?"

She gazed at him abstracted, her face expressionless. "Perhaps," she answered.

Then she took a sheet of paper and after glancing toward Alfred's bed and again at the doctor, she began to write rapidly, almost automatically. Pagello observed her for a while. Was she starting on her night's work, or would she be stopping soon? He waited respectfully, and as the pen continued racing over the sheet, he took up a volume of Hugo and began to read.

Alfred was asleep. There was no sound but the scratching of George's quill. Occasionally the fire sputtered. Now and then Pagello quietly turned a page. For nearly an hour George kept on writing. Then she laid down her pen. Without a word, without a look at the doctor, she took her head between her hands, and, resting her elbows on the table, stared into space. The doctor studied her close, set face, and awed by such intensity of concentration, scarcely dared to breathe for fear of disturbing her.

All of a sudden she started awake and folding the sheet, handed it to Pagello. He turned it about, not knowing what to do with it.

"For whom is it?" he asked.

She snatched it from his hand and in large characters scrawled upon it, "For stupid Pagello." The look with which she returned it to him was a dismissal and a promise.

Pagello did not unfold the sheet until he was in his room at home, and after reading it, he had to begin all over again. Was it possible? Had the young Frenchman's devoted nurse who had not taken off her clothes for a week in her vigil by his bedside—had she written that letter to him, Pagello? The woman who had confessed to loving Alfred de Musset more than anyone in the world—could she mean that ardent declaration for him, her lover's doctor? But there were the words, before his eyes. He had seen her soft, plump little boneless hands tracing them on the paper. Perhaps it was the beginning of the novel on Venice that she said she might write. Those two words at the top of the page, *"En Morée,"* perhaps were the title.

But no, the real meaning was unmistakable. ". . . The generous sun that has bronzed your brow—what passions has it infused in you? I have learned how to love and suffer. And you, how do you love? Your burning looks, the rude strength of your arms, the boldness of your desire lure and yet frighten me. . . . I can neither struggle against your passion nor share it. In France men do not love as you love. . . . I gaze upon you dismayed, wondering, yearning. . . . I cannot tell whether you really love me. I shall never know. . . . My frail nature and your ardent temperament will engender quite different thoughts. . . . You would laugh at the things that make me weep. . . .

"What will you be to me, my support or my master? And I, what shall I be to you, your companion or your slave? Do you merely desire me or do you love me? Do you know what I am? . . . Am I something mysterious that makes you dream and seek, or do you see in me only a woman, like those that grow fat in harems? . . . Do you know that soul's desire which time cannot tame, which human caresses can neither appease nor weary? When your mistress falls asleep in your arms, do you lie awake gazing at her, praying to God and weeping? Do the pleasures of love leave you panting and sottish, or do they rouse you to a divine ecstasy?

"Perhaps what I have sought vainly in others I shall not find in you. But I can always believe that you possess it. Love's looks and endearments have always lied to me. You will permit me to translate them as I please without the aid of deceiving words. . . . Shroud your soul from me, that I may always believe it beautiful."

Such passages and others from George's letter left Pagello bewildered. Had he read *Lélia* he would have recognized the same poetic prose in the effusion, but unacquainted with George's writings, in fact, knowing nothing about her except what his simple mind had been able to apprehend in the close familiarity of the sickroom, he deliberated whether to fly to her as to a

162

divine being and throw himself at her feet, or to despise her as the lowest of her kind. He turned, as always under moral stress, to his mother's portrait. If only she had been there to guide him! Then he looked at the time. It was very late. Even if he had decided to fall at Madame Sand's feet, it was not a respectable hour in which to do it. He went to bed and to sleep.

The following morning, at the usual time, he left to call upon his patient. The agitations, quieted by sleep, assailed him full force in the light of day. As a doctor he was responsible for Alfred de Musset; his first duty was to the poet. But he was also fascinated by Madame Sand. In fact, even before she had summoned him for her headaches, he had felt her spell in his glimpses of her on the balcony.

But he had problems, serious problems. To begin with, there was his old father who would be scandalized if he, an honorable physician, entered into an affair with one of those light foreign women. Not that Madame Sand was light. He had seen with what devotion she had tended her lover. But she was foreign and therefore to be looked upon with suspicion. Then there was his brother, who would wonder why he was complicating his life still further.

For the life of Pietro Pagello, so simple, so honest and such a good fellow, had somehow or other become involved to an extraordinary degree, both because of his good looks and for the reason that at thirty he was still unmarried. First, there was Arpalice Manin, a Titian-haired Venetian Juno of twenty-three who adored her Pietro and would have felt no hesitation in using a stiletto on any serious rival. Besides, she had two brothers, powerful lawyers, who would have come to their sister's help with legal briefs, if not more direct means, should Pietro wrong her. But even without Arpalice, he had Giulia Puppati to think about, though Giulia, partly related to him, was no serious menace. Still, women will take umbrage at the most unexpected trifles and Giulia, who sang like an angel, might use her voice in quite another way if her suspicions were aroused. Then, he had also to consider Antonia Segato, a virtuous young woman. How would she take his unideal attachment to a French lady? For it was obvious from Madame Sand's letter that she expected him to be more than a *cavalier sirvente*. Last, but perhaps most important of all, he must think of his sainted mother. Last night her portrait had seemed to speak, warning him against falling into the pit of temptation.

Nevertheless, by the time he reached Madame Sand's house, he was so full of her that he had a keen pang of disappointment when, on going into Alfred's room, he did not find her there. His patient was lucid and in good spirits. They chatted pleasantly for a while, but the doctor glanced so often at the door that Alfred's jealousy was instantly alert. But he must not, he must not have such thoughts, he told himself. That way madness lay. George and Pagello had saved his life. They had no common interest except for his welfare.

Soon the door opened. Pagello saw a small, white-gloved hand rest upon the jamb, and then Madame Sand entered. But what a transformation. The turban had been thrown aside for a stylish beaver hat decked with a swaying ostrich plume. A cashmere shawl in a Persian design half covered her nut-brown satin dress. She was carrying a purse. As she came toward the doctor with carefree grace, she went through the feminine motions of smoothing her gloves. Dr. Pagello stood up to meet her, gaping before such elegance.

"I have a little shopping to do, Dr. Pagello," she said. "If it's not too much trouble, would you go with me?"

The shopping began and ended at the Piazza San Marco, where for more than three hours they walked and sat and talked and walked again, in that agitation of body and mind before its resolution into decisive action. George, as a gallant free spirit, put her past before Pagello and dwelt specifically upon Alfred. They had been lovers; Alfred had wronged her; she was determined not to return to Paris with him. She had loved him, she still loved him, as a sister, but she considered herself free. She had been free from the moment he told her that he no longer loved her.

Pagello listened, gazed into the dangerous depths and, less wise than Sainte-Beuve, floundered. "I then saw my fate," he recorded. "I felt neither pleasure nor pain, but plunged into the gulf, my eyes closed."

In the third week of February, 1834, however, and for many months to come, it was no gulf in which he found himself, but a living novel, more perilous and exciting than any natural prodigy. For the winds of hell that carried him and the other two characters to the final shore, much the worse for the experience and yet by it singled out for fame, were the creations of two phenomenal imaginations, powerful in good and ill. In the particular circle of that inferno of passion, jealousy and impossible idealism, Pietro Pagello, most inert of human beings, remained the passive element, but he was essential to the Romantic fulfillment of George Sand and Alfred de Musset.

George and Pagello became lovers. The exigence of her nature could no longer be denied, even though she tried to explain away her act as the revenge of her wounded pride, and her choice of Pagello as a yearning to identify herself with Italy through one of its representative sons. The latter had been implicit in her epistle to "Stupid Pagello." The irony of it was, however, that in racial heritage Pagello owed more to Austria than to Italy.

Musset, floating in the midland of consciousness during his slow convalescence lived his intervals of lucidity with acutely sharpened senses. His jealousy, abnormally awake in health, became an Argus of awareness. George and Pagello were lovers. The thought, at first merely a suspicion, became an obsession. He spied upon them with half-shut eyes when they thought he was asleep. He caught, or thought he caught, looks, kisses, caresses. One night—he could never be sure whether it was reality or hallucination—he saw, beyond the curtains that screened his bed, a woman sitting on a man's knee. Her head was thrown back, her lips parted. Then a man's head leaned down toward her and his mouth clung to hers. Alfred wanted to scream but uttered only a feeble cry. At the sound Pagello came to him, felt his pulse, and said to George, "He is better."

Then there was the scene of the teacup. Alfred had just awakened and saw near the hearth a tea table all set. There was only one teacup upon it.

"Did you have tea last night?" he asked George.

"Yes, I had tea with the doctor."

"Then why is it there is only one cup?"

"They've probably taken away the other."

"They have not taken it away," he contradicted in a cold fury. "You've drunk out of the same cup."

"Even if it were so, you no longer have the right to be concerned about such things."

"Oh, but I do, since I still pass for your lover."

Words, quarrels, sordidness. Whether the scene had really occurred, or whether he had imagined it, Musset made it a crucial one in *La Confession d'un Enfant du Siècle,* and in 1852, in the fog of his darkened intellect, he dictated it to Paul, among other memories of the Venetian period. Paul was to use the damaging material in his answer to George Sand's *Elle et Lui, her* confession. But even then the final word was not said, for Louise Colet, one of Alfred's last mistresses, drew from the same source in her *Lui* which followed Paul de Musset's *Lui et Elle.* Both novels carried rancor to the limits of bad taste; both novels pleaded for "the poor child" against the malefactions of Lélia.

Even if Alfred had imagined the incidents, his torment was real enough, and so enduring that toward the end of his life he could narrate to his brother as fact a phantasmagory of such macabre grotesqueness that it would have been excessive in a tale of Gérard de Nerval's. Alfred, it appears, surprised George in bed, writing a letter to the doctor and flew into a rage. She denied she was writing to Pagello but would not let him see the paper. "She became a fury," Paul recorded, ostensibly from Alfred's dictation, "and ,threatened that if I continued in my present behavior, I'd never leave Venice. I asked her how she could prevent it. 'By having you shut up in a madhouse.' . . . I admit I was terrified." Alfred thereupon went back to his room and from there he heard her opening her window. She must be throwing out the letter she had torn up. With that suspicion in mind, he got up at dawn and slipped out into the street in his robe. He found her there before him, bending over to pick up the scraps of her letter. She fled from his maniac face. He pursued in the wintry cold. She leapt into a gondola; he jumped in after her. "When we got out at the Lido she began to run again, leaping from grave to grave in the Jewish cemetery there. I followed her and leapt across the tombs like her. Finally she sat down exhausted on one of the gravestones and burst into tears of rage and vexation. 'In your place,' I said to her, 'I would give up. . . . You'll never succeed in shutting me up with the insane. Why don't you admit you're a whore!' 'Yes, yes,' she replied. 'A wretched whore,' I added.—And so I led her back subjugated to the house." Paul made capital of the scene in *Elle et Lui,* omitting no element of the improbable or the ludicrous.

At the height of the Venetian tempest, enter Paul Tattet, himself on pleasure bent. He found his friend recovered, though much the worse for his sickness, and George Sand in a too cordial entente with Alfred's doctor. Tattet was shrewd; Tattet was loyal; Tattet had an invincible mistrust of writing women in general and of this *homme-de-lettres* and Saint-Simonist Joan of Arc in particular. He questioned her. She answered his questions with candor so absolute that he was nonplused. She and Alfred were lovers no longer. They had ceased being lovers a month since. (She narrated the circumstances.) She admired and loved Pietro Pagello, and when Alfred returned to France she would remain in Italy to create a new, useful and productive life for herself. Alfred, she said, was unfit for love; he must renounce it if he would live. As she spoke Lélia wept softly for Alfred, for herself, for the unhappy world.

Tattet commiserated Lélia and gave his blessing to Pagello with whom he struck up one of those unequal fellowships wherein extreme worldliness is pleased to dally with simplicity. He did not forget, however, that he was primarily Alfred's friend. As gently as he could he intimated a state of affairs to him which Alfred already knew too well. His good deed done, Tattet left Venice after a handclasp from Lélia and a kiss on both cheeks from Pagello who swore eternal friendship to the spoiled, rich sophisticate.

Tattet's brief passage brought matters to a head. Alfred verged

166

upon a new fit of insanity as a result of the poison distilled in his ear. George and Pagello, finding their secret too difficult to keep, decided to reveal it, whether it killed or cured. Certainly Alfred could not be worse than he was; he might perhaps be better for the knowledge.

One day the two enacted a prearranged scene.

"Do you think, Doctor, that Alfred is strong enough to bear a serious shock?" asked George with a look of motherly tenderness toward the poet.

"You mean?—" Pagello prompted.

"Very well, I shall speak out," continued George. "Dearest Alfred, I am no longer your mistress. From now on I can only be your friend. I love Dr. Pagello."

The mystified poet looked from one to the other, not because of what he heard, but out of incredulity at its having been uttered. In an impulse of blind fury he made for George as if to strike her. "You're a whore! A whore!" he shouted.

Pagello threw himself between them. Lélia wept. What good was candor, O great Rousseau?

Shocking as they had been to hear, George's words had the effect of cold water upon Alfred's heated emotions. He was being called upon to play a superhuman part. The hand lifted to strike fell to his side. When he raised it again, it was to join Lélia's to her Pietro's. "You love each other and yet you love me too," he said, tremulous with emotion. "You have redeemed me, body and soul."

In the stress of that sublime renunciation the three wept together.

As if by magic the mystical Sandesque quadrangle flew into shape, its four points being held respectively by God, by George, by her fortunate lover and by the sad but ennobled victim. God extended benison and the three outdid one another in love and self-sacrifice.

Musset, extreme in his renunciatory elevation, as in everything else, behaved like the angel he looked. Pagello was his friend whom he loved better than himself. George, once mistress, then mother, then sister, arrived at another degree of relationship and became his brother. Not a day passed but Musset devised some expiatory act for his past sins as a pledge of his reformation. How beautiful the example they set before mankind! How great was George in her triumphant daring! How lofty Pagello to take to his bosom the loved one's former lover! How heroic that lover to immolate himself on the altar of their happiness! Behind the scenes farce cackled at the antics of the human puppets.

The pattern, however, had a familiar look. It was Aurore,

Aurélien and Casimir all over again, with Musset in the part of the husband and Pagello in Aurélien's rôle. But now the design had been achieved to perfection in the sacrifice of the husband for the fulfillment of an ideal love.

That the likeness did not escape George is apparent in the novel, *Jacques,* written, as it were, from life, during the very months of the Venetian quadrangle. In it the husband, Casimir-Musset-Jacques, braver than Indiana and Sir Ralph, leaps to his death in an Alpine crevasse so that the lovers may be free to be united.

However, Musset's part became increasingly difficult, once the original fervor cooled and he saw Pagello in possession of the joys that had once been his. Never had George's deep black eyes shone with such fascination for the victim who saw them turned tenderly toward Pagello, in meanings intended to uplift Musset's soul, but which succeeded only in making him realize the greatness of his loss. He loved George. He had never loved her as much as now that she was lost to him. But he invoked God to bless his sacrifice and in the divine comfort Musset endeavored to find the strength to persevere.

It was too much for him. He decided to go home. "I'll bring you back a broken body," he wrote to his family, "a soul laid low, and a bleeding heart."

He fixed on the twenty-ninth of March as the day of his departure. On the twenty-eighth he reported his intention to the Venetian police. George stuffed his luggage with a thousand little surprises to cheer him on his journey. Pagello showered him with affectionate attentions. One might have thought him a beloved son leaving reluctant parents. The morning of the twenty-ninth Alfred obtained a visa for his passport. George gave him as a final gift half of the money which Buloz had sent, and begged Antonio, a hairdresser whom Alfred was taking along as his valet to guard his master with his very life.

George accompanied Alfred in the gondola as far as Mestre. Out of delicacy Pagello waited for her return on the steps of the Piazzetta.

That night George, with Pagello beside her watching her pen fly as on another memorable occasion, began writing the first of her *Lettres d'un Voyageur,* in which, more of an improvisatrice than in her novels, she set down her heart's dictation in a prose which for emotional force came close to poetry. It was dedicated "To a Poet" and when it appeared in print no one was left in the least doubt of his identity.

She had just left her poet to rejoin the man who was waiting for her. "I felt that my soul was going away with you (Musset)" she wrote. " 'Have courage,' said the other (Pagello) to me. 'Yes,

yes,' I replied. 'It was the very thing you said to me the night he lay dying in our arms. . . . Now he is saved, he is traveling, he will return to his country, to his mother, to his friends and his pleasures. It is well that it should be so. And yet, think what you will, I yearn for that dreadful night when his head leaned against your shoulder and his cold hand lay in mine. He was there between us, and he is here no more. You are weeping, too. . . . You see, your tears know no reason, any more than mine do. He is gone, and we willed it. He is no longer with us and we are desolate."

Pagello, as much under the dominion of Lélia as Musset, and equally lost in the emotional maze, saw nothing to rouse his jealousy in that letter. George was a superior woman; he and Musset were superior men. Theirs was a combination to astound the ages. But he was nevertheless worried about George. She was completely prostrated after "the dear boy's" departure. Again, as in her periods of nervous strain, she suffered from reversed vision during which the visible world, like her inner life, turned upside down. Pagello suggested a walking trip through the Venetian Alps. It was spring and the fair weather tempted. George put on her trousers and blouse, took a knotted stick, and followed her Pierre, as she had taken to calling him.

Another went with them all the way, another who, as they paused to admire a waterfall, cast his shadow on the water, although his body, aching with love of George, was being borne toward France. "You bade me leave and I have left," he was even then writing to George. "You bade me live and I live. . . . . Oh, write to me at Milan, dearest brother, George my beloved!"

On the fifth of April, from Geneva, Musset wrote her again in the anguish of his discovery: "I still love you as a lover, George!" Yet he must assume a tranquillity he did not feel. He told her of roaming the streets in Geneva, of looking into shop-windows. "I saw my reflection in a pane, and I knew again the boy I had been. . . . That was the man you wished to love! . . . Poor George, my poor love! You were deceived. You thought you were my mistress but you were only my mother. Heaven had made us for each other. Our minds, in their elevated sphere, met in recognition like two mountain birds; they flew toward each other, but the embrace was too close; we committed incest. . . . Oh, my only friend, I have nearly been your executioner."

Almost simultaneously George was composing the rest of her *Lettre d'un Voyageur*. Everything reminded her of Alfred and of his suffering. "The murmuring of the Brenta, the last sighing of the wind in the dense foliage of the olive trees, the raindrops that left the branches and fell upon the rocks with a little sound like that of a kiss—I know not what ineffable mood of sorrow and tenderness permeated the air and breathed through the plants. I thought of Christ's vigil in the Garden of Olives, and I remembered how once you and I spent a whole evening talking about this canto in the divine poem. It was a sad evening, that, one of those somber nights when we have drunk together the bitter cup. You too have suffered an inexorable martyrdom; you too have been stretched upon a cross. Had you then some great sin to expiate, thus to be offered up as a victim on the altar of pain? What had you done so to be doomed, to be chastened so? Can one be culpable at your age? Can one distinguish between good and evil? You felt youth within you. You believed that life and joy should form but one delight. You wore yourself out in pleasure. . . . You little knew your greatness, and so you flung your life to the passions for them to do with as they pleased, and they used it and consumed it. . . . You forgot that you were one of those who do not belong to themselves. You wished to live your life and left your glory to kill itself in scorn of all things human. You cast pell-mell into the abyss the precious stones of the crown that God placed upon your brow—power and beauty and genius, and even the innocence of your young years which you trampled underfoot, O arrogant child!"

This and more George wrote, and when her excursion with Pierre was over and they returned to Venice, she finished the letter and sent it on to Alfred, telling him he might keep it, burn it, or give it to Buloz for publication.

The words were so much fuel to Alfred's resuscitated ardor. "My George, you have never written anything so beautiful, so sublime. . . . It is to me, it is to me that you write thus!" he answered her. "And the woman who penned those pages I have held in my arms! . . . The noblest sympathies, all the harmonies of the world drew us to each other, and yet an eternal abyss divides us! . . ."

Such was their doom. Together they destroyed each other in the intensity of their love. Apart, they perished of longing and regret. Between them Pagello held the place of a wooden idol, which he resembled in muteness and immobility, thanked by George for affording the tranquillity she sought even though it bordered on ennui, and praised by Musset for granting something he had never been able to give her. "I love this good fellow almost as much as you do," wrote Alfred generously. "Figure it out as best you can. He is the cause of my losing all the riches of my life, yet I love him as if, on the contrary, he had bestowed them upon me. I should never want to see you together, yet I am happy that you are with him. . . . Good-by, my brother, my angel, my dove, my beloved darling," he concluded. "Do you still sing our old Spanish songs?"

George's Venetian life very quickly turned to prose, and she had been too close to poetry in its sublimity and its anguish to learn to live without it. Even the platitudinous domesticity with Pierre had all too short a lease. Within a fortnight the Titian-haired Arpalice burst into George's study demanding back her lover. Not long afterward Arpalice was followed by the other two neglected women, each claiming priority. "Monsieur Pagello is a sentimental Don Juan," George communicated wryly to Alfred, "who suddenly finds himself encumbered by four women. Each day brings some new comedy or tragedy on the part of his mistresses."

The quiet which above all she had sought with Pagello was only the first of the blessings to leave. The rest, like migrant birds at the flight of the leader, followed after. In her dismay, George made much of the little things that remained. There was the starling, Pierre's gift, which used to perch on the stem of her long pipe and steal the tobacco from its bowl. There were the posies of mountain flowers which Pierre used to walk miles to pick for her; and there remained his considerateness, his devotion, his very prose. "He is a mute who would have his head cut off for my sake," George praised him. "I hardly express a wish that he does not anticipate."

Nevertheless George soon had too much even of his virtues. Quietly she left the common household with its disturbing irruptions of screaming women, and rented herself a first floor apartment on a side street leading to the Barcaroli Bridge. Pagello made his rounds of visits and came to call upon her toward dusk. After dinner he would stretch out on the sofa and doze over his pipe. It brought back Nohant, Casimir and his heavy after-dinner sleep. But this was Venice, this was an Italian lover.

George forgot herself in her work, wrote at the rate of twelve hours a day, and went for distraction to a neighboring café where she drank innumerable cups of black coffee. Alfred, Alfred, was it for this? . . .

The separate apartments were not enough to give her the privacy she sought. She dreamed of going to Constantinople, and the better to hold herself to it, she began to inform her friends in Paris of her intention. "You tell me that you're thinking of going to Constantinople, *mon enfant*," Alfred wrote with a novel note of protectiveness. "What will you live on? How will you succeed in doing so, unless you give up your children? Even if you managed to get along for a while, aren't you much too proud to get into debt? Explain yourself on that score, if the peace of your poor Mussaillon means anything to you."

Poor Mussaillon, sacrificed to the dumb wooden idol. Mussaillon, *enfant superbe*, scattering the jewels of his crown into the abyss. How could she make comparisons? She might as well liken the artless barcaroles which Pagello sang for her in the gondola to Alfred's glowing verses. "Send me," she begged Musset, "send me in your next letter all the poems you've written to me, from first to last. You will find the early ones in a volume of mine, bound in Russia leather. If you don't trust yourself to go to the apartment, let Boucoiran get them."

Alfred did her errand, as he had done others, such as delivering her manuscripts to Buloz, buying her gloves "of glacé kid, six pairs in yellow, six in white," and purchasing a supply of patchouli, "at Leblanc's, on the Rue Saint-Anne, opposite No. 50. And don't let him cheat you, because the stuff is worth only two francs the quarter. Marquis sells it at six francs. . . ." He had been saddened on revisiting the rooms where he had spent so many hours with her. The covers on the furniture were like shrouds on the dead. The whole place looked as mournful as death. Alfred found the poems and lingered in the familiar corners, yielding to an ineffable melancholy. "I came across some cigarettes you had made just before we went away and which you left in a saucer. I smoked them sadly and yet with a strange happiness. I also stole a little broken comb of yours from your dressing table and I carry it about with me in my pocket."

He still loved her. Now, more than ever, he loved her. "Be proud of yourself, my great and wonderful George," he said in the same letter. "You have made a man out of a boy . . . I have only you. I have denied everything, I have blasphemed everything, I mistrust everything and everyone but you. You do not lie, that is why I love you. . . . If there is any worth-while thing in me, if ever I create anything great with my hands or with my pen, tell yourself that you know whence it springs. . . . I shall make a novel about it. I should like to write our story. I would build you an altar, were it only with my bones."

George's heart went out to him. Since she could not reach him, she shut herself up in her study and thought of a hero, captivating and amoral like Alfred, a man for whose love any woman would have considered the world well lost. She would call him Léone Léoni, a king among men in fascination and daring; it would also be the title of her novel. She would set the scene in Venice, beautiful city of corruption. It might perhaps tell something of their story.

She finished the novel in less than a month, as if in the gushing forth of her spontaneous expression, she feared she might lose inspiration in pausing for breath. The plot, as usual, held enough excitement to accelerate the heartbeat of the susceptible. Every woman, however, was to see herself in the beautiful and infatuated Juliette, confronted by Léone who, with the wiles of the seducer, held the persuasive charm of Satan. Léone was weak, Léone was faithless and ignoble, Léone destroyed himself and all who came in contact with him. But he was the one Juliette loved. For that love she surrendered position, tranquillity, the respect of her fellow creatures. Better misery and dishonor with Léone than all the world's gifts with another.

Did Juliette's abnegation anticipate George's desire? George knew only that Alfred's accents, as she heard them in his letters, summoned her as irresistibly as Léone's voice.

When it appeared in 1835, *Léone Léoni* was an immediate success. As a work of art it sinned in redundance and structural looseness because of the haste in which it had been written. But it won every reader by its drive, before which emotion was fanned to flame and infused with a sense of self-identification. It was George Sand's defense of deeds done and her prophecy of deeds to do. To this novel, more than to any which had preceded, applies Henry James's criticism: "There is something very liberal and universal in George Sand's genius, as well as very masculine; but our final impression of her always is that she is a woman, and a Frenchwoman. . . . Women, we are told, do not value the truth for its own sake, but only for some personal use they may make of it. . . . The effect is that of a witness who is eager to tell more than is asked of him, the worth of whose testimony is impaired by its importunity." She exalted Juliette too much for objectivity. She was George Sand's apologia for George Sand, to the very device of Juliette's telling her own story.

The book was to serve as devil's advocate to young Franz Liszt and to the Countess Marie d'Agoult, at the height of their romantic attachment. More, even, than the young musician, the countess, susceptible as a chameleon, colored to the book. She saw herself as the heroine, a nobler Juliette, for besides position she would have to sacrifice husband and children for love of her Léone. At the time, the two lovers read merely, and made analogies.

In the middle of June, George received a letter from Musset which cried out in Léone's voice. "O my Georgeot, may God protect me! Sometimes I kneel and cry, May God protect me! For I give up! . . . Am I to be lost or saved? Pray God for me, my love, whatever happens. . . . I met you a year too soon. I believed too long in my luck, in a sort of star that watched over me. A fulminant spark of this trembling orb fell upon my head. I have been purified by this celestial fire, even though it has almost consumed me. If ever you revisit the Danieli, look upon the bed where I agonized. There you will find my corpse, for the man who rose up from that bed is not the man who lay down in it. . . . I go to the boulevards, to the Bois, to the opéra, to the *quai,* to the Champs-Elysées. How sweet yet how strange—is it not?—to walk, so young, through a dead life!"

173

Chapter XVII: The Ideal Triangle

GEORGE forgot Constantinople and decided to return to France. She was worried about Alfred and homesick for Paris. She longed for Maurice and Solange, for Maurice most of all. School would be out by the time she arrived. She could take the children with her to Nohant and make it up to them for the months she had been away. Boucoiran sent her letters about them which made her absence an exile. Alfred, too, tried to set her mind at rest by writing of his visits to Maurice at the academy. God, God, why had she ever left them? What was she doing here, hundreds of miles away, among strangers? Maurice, Solange, how often had she thought of them during her quarrels with Alfred and reproached herself for allowing him to tear her away from her children, her friends, her duties, her work, almost. "My children, my children," she repeated, now that the vision of a splendid Venetian life with Pagello had turned to a drab family drama, crowded, much too crowded, with supernumeraries.

She made her plans. First of all she sent the manuscript of *Jacques* to Alfred.—"You'll do me the favor of reading it and cutting out foolishness."—He was then to deliver it to Buloz who would, in turn, send her a thousand francs for the return journey.

Everything proceeded as she had hoped. It remained only to include Pagello in those plans.

The poor doctor had himself been floundering for a solution. His attempt at a peaceful domesticity with one woman had loosed pandemonium over his head. The establishment of La Sand, as he referred to George, in her own apartment had had the effect of making him feel more like a visitor than a husband or a lover. As the relationship now stood, he might as well have been living the life of one of those monks in the Armenian monastery. La Sand did not seem to want anything but friendship from him or, for that matter, from Alfred, in spite of the poor mad boy's impassioned letters. It was all a mystery which would have further perplexed Pagello had he read in George's letter to the poet, early in June: "He loves me peacefully and he is happy at no expense to me in suffering. . . . But alas, I must suffer for someone. I must nurture this maternal solicitude of mine, accustomed to watch over a weak and weary being. Oh, why could I not live with you both, and make both of you happy, without belonging to one or the other?"

This friendship *à trois* was exactly what George would have wanted. She was sick of love and spent with passion. But would Pagello come with her to Paris? Alfred had written him that he must not, under any circumstances, permit George to make the trip of three hundred leagues alone. "She'll tell you that she's as strong as a Turk," he had argued in his charming Fantasio vein. "But I'll whisper something in your ear. . . . The smallest Turk is stronger than the strongest European woman. I'm no Turk, but I assure you it's true."

Pagello watched George make her preparations, but still neither of them mentioned the subject uppermost in their minds. George broached it at last. Pagello agreed to go with her but, he said with Italian scrupulosity, not on her money. He was as good as his pride. Within a day he had sold his silver and disposed of his engravings. Then, after packing the portrait of his mother for moral support, and four paintings of Zuccarelli's to raise funds in France should his money give out, he was ready to accompany La Sand. He made it explicit beforehand, however, that he was not accompanying her to Nohant, but would live by himself in Paris, to visit the hospitals and pursue his medical studies.

George said quietly, "My dear, you will do as you think best." They had understood each other.

From Paris Musset was writing: "What joy it will be for me to see you again! . . . How I love you, Georgeot! How blissful is this tranquil and exalted friendship between us, like the perfume of our love."

How blissful, echoed George, prepared to build a temple of friendship from the ruins of that love.

Pagello, harassed by his own concerns, not the least of which was an aged father who from the first had prophesied calamity from his connection with a Frenchwoman who smoked and wrote and called herself by a man's name, sent the old man a last minute reassurance, the better to reconcile him to the impending departure. "I have reached the last stage of my folly, and I must go through with it as through the others, with my eyes closed. Tomorrow I leave for Paris, where I shall quit La Sand and come back to fall upon your neck, and be worthy of you once more. . . ." This was one letter George never saw.

They arrived in Paris on the fourteenth of August. George went to her apartment, made ready for her by the dependable Boucoiran, and Pagello established himself at the Hôtel d'Orléans, on the Rue des Petits Augustins, not too far away.

175

He took a room on the third floor, at one franc fifty a day. But then, it was understood that he could be at George's whenever he wished.

Buloz, delighted at the return of the prodigal novelist, celebrated the event by giving her a dinner. Out of delicacy Musset was not invited. Everyone was curious about the Italian—doctor, archaeologist, they did not know which—and the attendance was large. Pagello emerged from his silence in his effort to shine in that bright gathering, but he would have fared better had he remained his taciturn self. George looked at him as he uttered vapid remarks in abominable French and her eyes were not gentle. They darkened perceptibly when, with what was meant to be ingratiating humility, Pagello took her hand and, kissing it, turned to the company, saying, "I am among you only the *cavalier sirvente* of the illustrious signora."

Knowing George to be in Paris, Alfred struggled in vain against the predestined attraction of the moth to the flame. No sooner had he left Venice behind him, than his life had become a ritual to his lost love. For days he would remain shut up in his room, leaving it only when he heard his sister playing a favorite composition of Hummel's. A word, the least allusion to Venice, sent him back to his solitude, shared occasionally with his valet Antonio, so that he might hear from the boy's lips the soft Venetian dialect. The sounds only fed his grief and made Antonio so homesick that he had to be sent away.

Finally Alfred's door opened to Paul and Tattet. Then the room itself became unbearable. He burned his engravings and changed the books on his shelves, as if by ridding himself of externalities he would cure himself of memory. Nothing availed. He thought of the final remedy. But he dared not trust himself with women. "Not even with a *fille*," he confessed to George. "I think that at the crisis I might strangle her like a howling maniac." He suffered, it is true, but he cherished his torment and, like a goldsmith, made it the touchstone of his every experience.

He begged George for an interview. She gave it, the third day of her arrival, and also invited Pagello. It was a sultry afternoon, and the windows of George's little salon were open. She greeted Alfred with constraint. Pagello, large-hearted in his assured incumbency, welcomed him like a brother. Alfred looked at George, and in that look the resolve of four agonized months crumbled. They exchanged banalities—What else could they do in the presence of a third party?—And again, before that third person, George affirmed, not too convincingly, that she was happy. Pagello hovered about her, solicitous and possessive, refusing to leave her side while Alfred remained. Then, on the heavy August air came the strains of a waltz which George and Alfred, in the universal fashion of lovers down to Proust's Odette and Swann, had made part of their intimacy. Alfred turned to George. Under his look her eyes filled with tears but her face remained impassive. The past was dead. They must be friends and no more.

Alfred left her with Pagello and went home, determined that if he could not have her he was done with life. He must obtain a last meeting with her alone and then he would go away to Spain, to Germany, anywhere out of the world they knew, until he left it forever. "George," he supplicated in a letter. "The time I left Venice you gave me a whole day. Now I am leaving forever, alone, without a friend, with not even a dog to keep me company. I ask of you one hour only, and a last kiss. . . . You must see me alone, if you are brave. . . . Why should you fear to listen to the solemn voice of destiny calling aloud to us? Did you not weep yesterday when you heard it murmuring to us through the window, in the sad music of my poor waltz? . . . Take me to your heart. Let us not talk of the past, nor of the present, nor of the future. Let us be two souls that have suffered, two ailing minds, two wounded eagles that meet on the heights and exchange a cry of agony before they part for all eternity. . . . It will be the last memory you will carry away of one who will no longer be."

George steeled herself against her yearning and refused. In a few days she would be in the country, in the peace of simple things with her children and—alas—Casimir. She would work. She would be cured forever of that madness which, whenever she and Alfred were together, goaded them on to brutality and abasement. She was done with love. She had her children. She must think of her children.

"Listen, listen to me, George," the voice of Léone pleaded through her determination. "Let us meet once more, at your house, at mine, in the Jardin de Plantes, at the cemetery by my father's tomb. It is there that I had wished to say good-by. . . . Remember that I am going away forever. Let us not shut so lightly such eternal doors."

She saw him alone, in the familiar salon, a little shabby and dismal in the rain. She was in poor health and looked it. Her pallor only intensified her desire. She was the incarnation of pain, and pain for the Romanticist was the supreme ecstasy. George, made strong by memory of past hurt, withstood him, although for two hours they talked with gentle regret of what might have been. As they parted she kissed him chastely on the brow and on each cheek. "You were destined to be my life or my death," he said. "You have made the right choice. All is over for me."

She did not call him back.

Within a few days of each other they took their separate ways, Alfred for Baden, George for Nohant. Pagello remained in Paris where he renewed acquaintance with, of all inappropriate cronies, George's archenemy, Alfred Tattet. The doctor had need of a friend. He felt lost in the bewildering capital without George's anchorage and her protective hospitality. Besides, his money was giving out and he would sooner have begged than applied to her for it. He stayed on, therefore, in his cheap lodging, attended classes at the clinic of Velpeau, and ate his unadorned loaf to the accompaniment of gloomy reflections. George and he had parted under a cloud. He, the magnanimous, had made jealous scenes on account of Alfred, and had gone so far as to break the seal of a letter which George had addressed to her former lover. It would have been a reprehensible act by all standards; it was unforgivable in the ideal quality of the triple relationship.

Nevertheless George felt guilty about him. After all, she had brought him there; she was responsible for him. "He's probably in need of money," she wrote Boucoiran, "but he'd never accept it from a woman, even as a loan." Boucoiran would have to overcome such masculine resistance, with George's cash.

The more she thought of Pagello, the more she felt with him in his situation, little knowing that while she shed tears over "Poor Pierre," he was lending a willing ear to the calumnies of Tattet. He ended by feeling himself the victim of Lélia like Alfred, like Sandeau, like—Tattet had no scruple about making a list as long as Leporello's of this female Don Giovanni's conquests. George was therefore surprised when, on inviting Pagello to spend a week at Nohant, "with the consent of Monsieur Dudevant," he refused on a note of injured dignity which was quite out of character and implied a clear break.

Meanwhile from Baden came Alfred's burning missives which scorched the very paper. Far from committing suicide, he had awakened, a more flamboyant phoenix, from the ashes of his love, and stopped at nothing in his exigence, even though he still played on the muted strings of death. "Oh, my flesh and blood! I die of love. . . . No, I shall never be cured, nor shall I try to live. Death for love of you is dearer by far than life. . . . They tell me you have another lover. It kills me, but I love you, love you, love you. . . . I love my suffering better than life. Oh, my beloved, let your heart go out to me, weep for me. Send me a letter wherein you write of nothing but your love. Tell me you give me your lips . . . your hair, everything, all that head of yours. . . . Ah, it is terrible to die, terrible to love as I love. . . . Oh, George! My first, my last love!"

George received this letter when she was herself in a suicidal mood. Casimir, who always took her visits as an intrusion, proved more difficult than ever, now that gossip gave fuel to his rages. For, although since January, 1831, they had been virtually divorced and Casimir held Nohant only through George's generosity, he felt injured in his pre-eminence as lord of the domain and fumed at having the sign of the cuckold attached so patently to his door. He was sick of his position and sick of Nohant, he shouted in front of the servants and before the children who were terrified at the altercations and, in Maurice's case, moved to angry tears. George tried to placate Casimir, but to everything she suggested he made objections for the sake of objecting. She had only to say she would take over Nohant for him to be ready to fight for it; and to release him of all obligation for Casimir to insist on his rights by virtue of the marriage contract.

Casimir, Pagello, Alfred—Paul de Musset, Tattet: the whole world of men was in a conspiracy against her peace, whether they loved or hated her. She knew the accusations good people everywhere leveled against her. From the point of view of society no doubt they were justified. But she had always lived by her own principles, established between herself and her God, and when the noise of gossip came to her, she thought of herself as a young girl in the chapel of Les Anglaises when the market wagons of La Halle used to rattle by. In the peace of the sanctuary the oaths and blasphemies, the foul words of the carters had distracted her from her prayers for a moment. But neither her ears nor her heart had really heard them, and she would return to her worship unsullied. Later she had made another sanctuary of love, and had withdrawn into it as much as the world allowed. When, as now, the rumors from without came to her, she thought of those other blasphemies and told herself, "It's only the carters passing by." They had been passing by too often of late, however, and she found herself unable to keep her inner peace inviolate.

It was during one such period of discouragement that she went to the woods to answer Alfred's letter—the woods where she used to find refuge as a girl, and to which instinctively she resorted now. She was exhausted. She was—once again—disillusioned in the capacity of man to give her the reciprocity she sought. Alfred's letter, emotionally so uncontrolled, demanding a return to what had been a spiritual hell, caught her when she was experiencing the keenest tortures of the mind. Was she never to know tranquillity, even in friendship? When she had given Alfred those parting kisses, had he not understood that they were those of a mother?

"This is passion, not friendship," she reproved him. And she did not want passion either from him or from Pagello, who

179

toward the end, had become equally unreasonable. Could they not realize that she had much more than their selfish sensibilities to worry her? She was unhappy. She was in bad health, and her problems were complicated by the demands they both made upon her. There was Pagello—"He suffers and I must endeavor to solace him. You will help me, will you not? I feel we must part, the three of us, without rancor, without violence. You must not love me any more, do you understand? . . . My heart is ice. I tell you this because if we are to meet again in Paris you are not to entertain any idea of a resumption of intimacy with me. We must part, do you understand? . . . Farewell to the beautiful poem of our ideal friendship. . . . It was only a dream which I alone believed in, poor fool that I am. Now, with my eyes open, I see that one desires me, and the other forsakes and slights me. . . . How right are those who scoff at everything! Were it not for my children I would gladly throw myself into the river."

She wrote stiffly, like a schoolmistress who by the verbal knuckle rapping of her "do you understand?" tried to impress her lesson upon a stubborn schoolboy. Alfred answered like one. Very well, if she would not have him, he had only to take the trouble to dress and go out to win any pretty woman in Baden! As for his helping her to comfort Pagello—let that Venetian suffer! Alfred would only be paying him in his own coin. "I am telling you this so that if you hear I am back, you're not to have any idea of a resumption of intimacy with me." One could almost hear him talking back in the teacher's own words.

George swallowed his petulance. She had taken much worse from that half angel, half demon. Almost mechanically, she plunged into a new novel. Money helped to solve so many problems. When she received her royalties she thought at once of Pagello. If he had money he would be able to return to Venice. She suggested a plan to Boucoiran. Immediately Boucoiran informed Pagello that Madame Sand had found a purchaser at Berry for his four Zuccarellis: the price, fifteen hundred francs. Pagello, delighted with the deal, closed it at once, received his money, and consigned the paintings to Tattet, at Boucoiran's suggestion, little knowing that George had taken that means of financing his departure.

Buloz' money also enabled George to leave Nohant. She arrived in Paris early in October with the children, arranged for their schooling, and waited for whatever destiny might bring, prodding it a little, however, through talks with Sainte-Beuve whom she met at the Collège Henri IV on her visits to Maurice. Sainte-Beuve was wary. He loved emotional titillations, but he loved quiet more. The Sand-Musset tempests, while blowing epistolary windfalls into his pigeonholes, also disturbed his calm.

Nevertheless he promised George to do what he could to bring Alfred to his senses.

George turned her attention to Pagello who, even more nervously than she, awaited Alfred's arrival and, unknown to her, was practicing with pistols in preparation for the duel which everyone was assuring him he would be compelled to fight with Musset. He was anxious to leave. George was still more anxious to see him go, and gave him an additional five hundred francs to pay for a new set of surgical instruments. Constraint froze them, Pagello because of his intimacy with Tattet; George because now that reality had unsealed her eyes, she wondered what she had ever seen in this dull, unimaginative man who for a moment had been made to soar, only to plump down stunned and injured, on the solid earth that was his element.

Musset arrived toward the middle of October, 1834. There was no duel. On the twenty-third Pagello left Paris. George, Boucoiran and the children saw him off. George and he parted without a word. He pressed her hand, unable even to look into her face. He then kissed Maurice and Solange, and took the arm of Boucoiran who accompanied him part of the way.

It was with a sense of a lesson learned that Pagello returned to his father and his mistresses. As time passed he became so objective about the affair that he gave to Antonia Segato the incandescent letter to "Stupid Pagello." More reverent than George's lover, his mistress kept the relic in her album where it was found long afterward. Long afterward, too—in the 1860's —a breath of the Venetian love affair came with its poignant memories to George when someone discovered another album in her Nohant attic, an herbarium in which she pressed and classified Pagello's rustic posies, gathered for her in the early Venetian dawns. Still other mementos of the Italian doctor's remained for a long time stored in a garret of Tattet's house— the four Zuccarellis which George never claimed and which turned up after Tattet's death.

No sooner had Pagello gone than George, as if his removal had lifted a barrier to her loving Alfred, forgot the resolutions so bravely, if prematurely, made, and again went to her confidant for advice. She had repulsed Alfred; Alfred was standing on his pride—and she wanted him. Sainte-Beuve's counsel at this point is not recorded. There is a letter of Alfred's to George, however, which reveals him chastened and as much in love with her as ever. "Once we meet again you will see how completely I am yours, body and soul. Trust yourself to me, George. God knows I shall never do you harm." As evidence of his amendment he quoted to her from the Bible, "Whither thou goest, I will go."

Again they became lovers, meeting with the mingled fire of

two flames but, alas, like that fire, destroying themselves and each other. The scene on the rocks of Fontainebleau was re-enacted after every satisfaction of Alfred's desire, as if with the possession of that body came madness at the thought of those who had enjoyed it before him. His own libertinism he took for granted as a man's prerogative. George was a woman. She had no right to usurp a man's privileges. If the ghosts of George's lovers had haunted him in the past, they faded to insignificance before the concreteness of Pagello for whom she had betrayed him when he, Musset, was dying.

Once more came the scenes of jealousy and recrimination, the self-torturing questions on how and when, and where George had given herself to Pagello. It had been while Musset lay half conscious on the bed at the Danieli—had it not? The kiss he had seen—it had not been exchanged by phantoms of his hallucination. She had thrown her head back for Pagello; it was Pagello who had clung to her mouth. The single cup on the tea table—he had not imagined that either. The letter she had been writing in bed—it was to arrange an assignation with Pagello. Again he shouted the foul word that had escaped him in Venice.

George denied and wept and loved him for his very tyranny. His jealousy devoured her like a fire from within, leaving nothing but an ashen shell.

But sometimes, remembering she was George Sand, she rose up and defended herself. "What do you want of me now? What do you ask of me? Questions, suspicions, reproaches! . . . Why do you speak to me of Pierre when I forbade you ever to mention him? Besides, by what right do you interrogate me about Venice? Did I belong to you in Venice? . . . Pierre used to come to see me and take care of me. You did not dream at all of being jealous then, and certainly I never thought of loving him. But even if I had loved him, even if I had given myself to him at that time, tell me what obligations I had toward you who called me bore-dom personified, a dreamer, a fool, a bigot? . . . You may believe anything you wish. I have but one answer: since I no longer belonged to you I was free to give myself to him. . . . I want no more of love. I have suffered too much. You wish me to lie to you, to tell you I did not love Pierre, that I never gave myself to him. . . . You are in a torment because I have been truthful with you. We cannot go on loving each other under these cir-cumstances. . . . What have we left of a bond that was once so beautiful? Oh, God, neither love nor friendship!"

Chapter XVIII: The Romantic Agony

YET, even as she wrote, "I want no more of love," George knew she had never been so much enslaved by it as she was then. Alfred, with all his cruelty, perhaps because of his cruelty, had the upper hand, and by that dominance asserted himself her master. She struggled to free herself and yet she could not break away. A word from him, a letter of repentance like the one he wrote after one of his inquisitions, pulled her back as powerfully as the magnet of his suffering. "I have just left you, and a dreadful idea has taken hold of me. My love, my love, how much I am to blame in my behavior toward you! How I tortured you tonight! . . . You drop a word that hurts me and I cannot be still, I cannot let it pass with a smile. I should be lying at your feet day and night, gazing mutely at you, waiting for a tear to fall from your wonderful eyes, that I may drink it, and revering all that there is of sorrow in your heart."

He fell ill from his emotional excess. She nursed him. "Ah, you pardon, you love me!" he cried in gratitude. "I am young. . . . Why am I young? That I may pour out my life, if only you might drain it from my lips. . . . Come, that I may fall upon my knees and beg you to live, to love, to forgive."

And George forgave, and went on forgiving, loving her agony with him more than happiness with any other. She knew that he betrayed her to Paul and Tattet, her enemies, as well as to her friends. She knew that if he followed evil counsel it was because the words had been whispered into the ear of Octave when Coelio, the god, had turned away. At times, however, she was so broken that she willed for a power beyond herself to release her. "Send me away," she cried to him. "Say but the word. . . ."

But when he said it and turned from her because, as in Venice, she was sick and spent, she became another Phèdre in her all-absorbing desire. Tattet, seeing Alfred apparently cured, rejoiced like a surgeon after a successful operation. Sainte-Beuve oscillated from one to the other, commiserating George, soothing Alfred.

In her unsatisfied ardor George for the first time awakened

as a woman and, since she could not speak her anguish to Alfred, she began a journal on the twenty-fifth of November, 1834. "You do not love me," she wrote. "You no longer love me. . . . Sensually you love me more than ever, and I you. Never until now have I loved anyone, not even you, with my senses. . . . Alas! it is all over between us!"

Vain now was Lélia's boast: "Desire in me was an ardor of the soul . . . a fine frenzy of the mind." It was her body that cried for satisfaction—*Vénus toute entière,* and no prey to cling to.

Sainte-Beuve whom Alfred now called Madame Pernelle on account of his "plaguy prying" advised distraction. George went to the Italian opera with Buloz for company. He slept through most of *Ernani,* waking up only long enough to cry, "Good Lord!" every time someone stepped on his feet. People stared at George. "She really looks decent enough in spite of everything," an old dowager commented audibly. "How very pretty she is," a gentleman in a vivid waistcoat appraised, peering at her through his lorgnon. A week ago the compliment would have pleased her. But now, what difference did it make? Alfred no longer loved her. Alfred refused even to see her.

As a final desperate move to win him back she cut off her hair and sent it to him, remembering his cry from Baden: "Give me your lips . . . your hair . . . all that head of yours!" He wept; he was ready to fly to her. Tattet, the surgeon, held him back.

Shorn of her hair, she went to pose for Delacroix, who had been commissioned to do a portrait of her for the *Revue.* They talked of Alfred. "He might have been a great painter, had he chosen," said Delacroix, who astonished her by asking to copy some of the sketches in Alfred's album. She opened her heart to him and spoke of her suffering. She could talk of nothing else. He listened sympathetically and gave her the advice she wanted. *Not* to be brave.

"Let yourself go," he said. "Whenever I'm in that state I have no pride at all. I wasn't born a Roman—I give myself up to despair. It grips me, gets the better of me and gnaws at my vitals. After it has had enough it is tired out and leaves me in peace."

When would despair have enough of her? It was not peace she wished for, but for the anguish that was Alfred's love.

Delacroix finished the portrait and made still other sketches. In one of his best portrayals he painted, rather, suggested her, for the whole canvas has an appealing spontaneity, in a wide, upswept, amazonian hat, under which her face, wide-eyed and wistful, gazes far away with heavy lids toward the cause of her obsession. The mouth turning up at the corners has an inexpressible sadness. The pupils, black and immense, burn with an inner fire. Delacroix also painted a portrait of her in her masculine redingote, slack cravat and top hat; her short wavy hair frames her face. Her eyes, under their bold brows, look out thoughtful and sad. The whole face has, nonetheless, a strange force as from a contained intellectual power.

The painter and the novelist struck up a friendship, sealed by the gift of a bronze serpent from George to Delacroix. She had received the paperweight from Marie Dorval, but in her impulsive generosity George could not resist the painter's admiration of the toy.

She lived in suspense. At every ring of the doorbell she started to her feet, thinking Alfred had succeeded in eluding his guardians and come to her. She looked for him everywhere and talked of him to everyone. Young Liszt whom Alfred had introduced to her, tried to lift the distraught woman from man to God, assuring her in his mystical sublimation, so soon to be brought to earth by Countess Marie d'Agoult, that only God deserved to be loved. "It may be true," said George, "but if one has loved a man it is very hard to love God."

"Earthly love will never get possession of me," boasted the young man.

"Very lucky, the good little Christian," George sneered in her diary.

Yet Liszt could be penetrating about her, as he saw her in *Lélia*. "Somber as Lara, despairing as Manfred, rebellious as Cain, you have ranged through all the depths of solitude. But you are more inconsolable . . . for you have never found a lover's heart womanly enough to love you as they were loved."

Still, she preferred Sainte-Beuve who, when she asked him for the meaning of her torment, answered simply, "Love means tears. If you weep, you love."

There was truth, too, in what Heinrich Heine, who had recently joined her circle, contributed on the subject, although she did not wholly agree with him. "We love with the mind and the senses. The heart counts for very little in love." Why, then, did the doctor find that her heart was affected?

Her friends rallied round her with touching loyalty. Gustave Papet, thinking perhaps to demonstrate by a concrete example that no suffering, however deep, is eternal, contrived to have her visit at his house while Jules Sandeau was there. Papet put a foot warmer in front of her, provided her with cigarettes and let her and Sandeau talk out their past grievances. There was nothing left of their old passion, but Jules was anxious to justify his behavior after the break. He had never indulged in recrimination, he said, never uttered a word against her. It had all been gossip.

George did not quite believe him. Although he looked sincerity itself, she detected a certain guardedness. "Ah, dear God," she exclaimed in her journal over such cold ashes, "why does emotion change and possess the soul with the same divine ardor for a new object?" Compared to her present love it was as if the other had never been.

Perhaps Jules, too, felt something of the same disappointment. If he did, he concealed it. As an old man, however, while looking through a photograph album at Buloz', he gazed at a picture of George Sand and murmured, "A cemetery . . . a cemetery." But before that he had cursed God and died in the person of the hero of his novel, *Marianne*. Revolving about the platonic romance of Aurore and Aurélien, it culminated with Aurore's affair with him, Sandeau. Marianne, the heroine, is a portrait of Aurore as she was when Sandeau had fallen in love with her. "Young, beautiful, she was one of those spirits which owe nothing to a world that cannot fathom them. . . . She was easy of approach; but her proud chastity and her instinctive nobility of character gave her . . . an odd admixture of the virginal and the regal which contrasted strangely with her scorn of convention and her unworldliness. . . . Her clear, pure brow acknowledged that the storms of passion had not yet growled over that noble head, but the expression of her eyes, burning, weary, sickly almost, spoke of inner struggles, unceasing and unavowed."

Now, however, George wore her heart's mourning openly and did not care who saw it. Buloz reported to her that Alfred, who boasted of a new mistress, suspected George of having an affair with Liszt. "Does he believe it?" she questioned in her diary. "Ah, my love, if you could really be jealous of me, how gladly would I send all those people away! But Liszt loves only God and the Holy Virgin who does not resemble me in the least." Buloz advised her, nevertheless, not to see Liszt for the present. People were talking. "Excellent young man! . . . But how could I manage it? What pretext could I give?"

In the hopelessness of her grief, George's mind was affected. How else could one interpret her irrational behavior? She hung a picture of the Magdalen in her room and saw herself in her. "I am Magdalen shorn of her hair, but carrying her cross and her death's-head." She was more like Samson robbed of strength.

She bought herself a skull, stuffed into it Alfred's last letter, and indulged in a worship so extreme that it verged on impiety. "Oh, give me back my lover!" she addressed an image of Christ. "Give me back my lover and I shall be devout. I shall wear out the church slabs with my knees!"

She fled to Nohant to escape her torment but it followed her there. She returned to Paris in a few weeks. Tattet must be rejoicing, she reflected. Yes, it was Tattet who was keeping Alfred from her. If Alfred were to come back to her Tattet would say in that superior way of his, "Heavens, what weakness!" That same Tattet who in his drunkenness used to sob in the lap of Mademoiselle Déjazet.

"The hour of my death approaches." But she did not die. She went for forgetfulness to the friend who had once before brought her consolation—the impulsive, amoral Marie Dorval.

"And you, poet, lovely flower, I wished to drink your dew. But it intoxicated me, it poisoned me, and then one day in anger I sought a counterpoison that killed me. . . . Oh, why, when I was about to die did I know embraces more ardent than those of men? What fury impels you against me that with your foot you push me into my coffin while your mouth slakes itself upon my body, upon my flesh? . . . Angel of Death, O fatal love, O darksome destiny in the shape of a fair and fragile child! Oh, my assassin, how much I love you still!"

Again George fled to the country and almost immediately, on the second of January, was recalled to Paris. While at Nohant she had received a lock of Alfred's hair; in return she had sent him a leaf from her garden. She had hardly arrived at the Quai Malaquais when Alfred appeared. They flew into each other's arms. Once more George had won.

In her triumph she sent a note to Tattet, remarkable for its cool irony. "Sir, there are highly skillful operations that do honor to the surgeon's ability but which, nonetheless, fail to prevent a recurrence of the disease. Such being the case, Alfred has once again become my lover. . . . I should like you to come and dine with us at my house at your earliest convenience." Tattet never answered her invitation. But then, George had not expected an answer.

The lovers had reached the final stage of their martyrdom. From now on they trudged painfully to the death of their love —or rather, desire, which was all that remained. Alfred's trust had been killed in Venice. Without it they were doomed. "What you did yesterday you will do tomorrow," Alfred repeated.

To demonstrate her fidelity George reluctantly dismissed Liszt. Alfred accepted the sacrifice with a sneer. Sneering, too, he would interrupt George, in the midst of her extolling the virtues of chastity and friendship before an admirer, with: "Madame, there is arsenic in your tea."

For two months they twisted in the death throes like wrestlers, clasping, parting, their strength ebbing, their struggle embittered. And as they both dealt in words, they left little unsaid in their last agony. George, abased in frustration, abdicated her will in fulfillment. Finally, she could bear the anguish no longer.

"Good-by, good-by, I cannot let you go yet I cannot take you back," she cried. "I want nothing, nothing. My knees are on the ground; my back is broken. . . . I want to kiss the earth and die. I no longer love you, yet I adore you. I no longer want you, yet I cannot do without you. . . . My only love, my life, my vitals, my brother, blood of my veins—go, but kill me before you go."

Unconsciously, even while tearing herself from him, she fell into the idiom of his farewell notes to her: "Good-by, O my George! Is it then true? I love you still. Good-by, good-by, my life, my only good. Good-by, my lips, my heart, my love. I love you so, oh God! Good-by."

To the end he believed in the fatality of their meeting. "I have had dreadful dreams and so have you. But your *Lélia* is no dream. You were mistaken only in its close. Your Sténio—he is not sleeping under the reeds of the lake. He is beside you. He is present in all your woes. His tear-filled eyes watch over your silent nights. Look about you. Does not his mournful, anguished shade rise up in your life's last dream? Yes, it is I! It is I! You foresaw me. When his pale face appeared before you in the quiet of the night, when for the first time you wrote his name upon your opening page, it was I drawing toward you. An invisible hand led me to you. Your Angel of Sorrows had placed within my hand a crown of thorns and a white shroud, saying, 'Tell her that these are the gifts I send her.' And I, I thought I was bearing a wreath of flowers and the veil of my betrothed. And so I came to you, and gave them to you."

George's last letter had no poetry in it and spoke a deadly weariness. "No, no, it is enough! Unhappy man, I loved you as a son. It was a mother's love I gave you. . . . I pity you, I forgive you, but we must part. . . . I cannot struggle. God has made me weak yet proud. But my pride is now broken and nothing remains of my love but compassion. . . . My God, to what a life I am condemning you! Drunkenness, wine, women, again and forever! Yet the more you have forfeited the right to jealousy, the more jealous you have become. It is like God's punishment upon your poor head. But my own children! Ah, my children, my children! Good-by, unhappy wretch! My children! My children!"

With the desperate awakening of her maternal love she could bear to leave him forever. On the sixth of March, 1835, she took refuge at Nohant. He did not hold her back. Boucoiran's report to her several days later that Alfred was well "and did not seem at all grieved" gave her the energy to get over her own illness.

Before leaving Paris, however, in the reckless generosity of her renunciation she had sent Alfred the intimate journal of her

ALFRED DE MUSSET IN THE COSTUME OF A PAGE

DRAWING BY ACHILLE DEVÉRIA

"He was all the heroes of romance, and all their ills."

love sickness. He promptly showed it to Paul who made full use of it later in his *Lui et Elle*. Then just as Pagello had given George's letter to Antonia, Alfred consigned the manuscript pages, written by George during her midnight anguish, to Madame Maxime Jaubert, d'Alton-Shée's sister, with whom, almost on the morrow of his parting from his "first and only love" he had initiated "a sentiment without a name," conveniently camouflaged in his calling her his "Godmother." To Madame Jaubert also he gave George's letters. In 1836 George asked to have them returned, as well as the *Journal Intime,* but her request was not heeded. Again in 1840 she demanded them back. Before returning the originals to Musset, Madame Jaubert, her daughter and a maid, stayed up most of the night making copies of the pages which George had written, if not in blood, at least in madness and tears.

In November, 1896, when George's letters to Alfred de Musset were published in the *Revue des Deux Mondes,* Henry James, shocked by their lack of reticence and knowing only half the story, since Alfred's part of the correspondence had not yet been made public, wrote of the revelation: "When we meet on the broad highway the rueful denuded figure we need some presence of mind to decide whether to cut it dead or to lead it gently home. . . ." James being James, he led it home and rehabilitated it in several articles.

But it is necessary for an understanding of George Sand as of Alfred de Musset to experience the shock of seeing them not only as naked as their letters reveal them, but also anatomized, as in the works engendered by their contact—whether their own novels and poems or those of friends and enemies alike. For good and ill their interval together was momentous in the unfolding of their personalities and, more important, for the translation of their experience into art.

Notwithstanding "Godmother" Jaubert, Musset, as good as his word, built George an altar in *La Confession d'un Enfant du Siècle.* "I shall end your story with a hymn of love," he had promised. The novel had its hymn. It had also its portrait of Alfred as a tragic child of the century, and of a colorless, long-suffering George whose martyrdom, to the level eyes of the present, appears not a little ridiculous. The era, pedestal of Bonaparte, came off best in the masterly opening of the novel, and it is for those incandescent pages that it will continue to hold its place in literature.

The true hymns to George Musset composed in his four *"Nuits,"* and in *"Souvenir,"* however loudly Paul tried to deny her the glory of their tribute. The internal evidence is there, in the lambent words, visible to all but one blinded by hate. Alfred

189

wrote the first, *"La Nuit de Mai"* two months after the parting. He had plunged into dissipation to cure himself of his wound and forget in laughter the tears of the past. The wound, cauterized by suffering, debauch deadened but never healed. The tears, remembered, fertilized his soul. One May evening, as he was walking through the reborn spring, his Muse called to him:

> *Poète, prends ton luth et me donne un baiser.*

He obeyed, took his lute, and once more broke into song, song in which sobs made music and his sorrows, rising from his heart, spoke to the hearts of all who have loved and, loving, suffered. In this, his dialogue with his Muse, he began a spiritual catharsis and learned the wisdom treasured by the true Romantic to whom the voluptuousness of pain is greater than that of love:

> *Rien ne nous rend si grands qu'une grande douleur,*
> *Les plus désespérés sont les chants les plus beaux,*
> *Et j'en sais d'immortels qui sont de purs sanglots.*

Sorrow, if not love, had ennobled him.

Through the other three *"Nuits,"* even in *"La Nuit d'Octobre,"* of the following year in which he chanted his love for his new mistress, Aimée d'Alton, the shade of "the woman of the somber eyes" haunted him. But then, who was little Aimée with her shaven head under her peruke, and her porcelain doll's face, to exorcise the mighty George?

Neither Aimée, Rachel, Madame Allan-Dépreaux, Louise Colet nor any of the other mistresses, ever succeeded. Everything evoked George's fateful presence. When he came face to face with her one night in 1840, in the lobby of Les Italiens, at a time when his mind had been filled with thoughts of Fontainebleau lately revisited, it was as if his wound reopened, and in the poignancy of memory he wrote *"Souvenir."* Yes, the wound bled afresh before the heart's murderer. But he had seen worse: he had seen her, forever dearest, become herself a whited sepulcher, a living tomb in the dust of their love. But sorrow had brought its resignation.

> *Je me dis seulement: "A cette heure, en ce lieu,*
> *Un jour je fus aimé, j'aimais, elle était belle.*
> *J'enfouis ce trésor dans mon âme immortelle,*
> *Et je l'emporte à Dieu.*

"Souvenir" was the poet's swan song. From 1840 to 1857 the lute his Muse reached out to him was silent. He listened, most often, to the voice of his memories, and now and then the people who saw him smoking his cigarettes and drinking his wine during

the last years of his posthumous life, would catch the word *Elle* breaking like a bubble from the depths.

But now it was still 1835. He had his "Godmother" to distract him. As for George, she was writing to Sainte-Beuve on the fourteenth of April, "I have met Michel de Bourges who promises to have me guillotined at the first opportunity."

Part Three

FROM SELF TO HUMANITY

Chapter XIX: From Self to Humanity

S INCE the July revolution liberty had intermittently led the populace against the repressions of Louis Philippe who, in spite of the courtesy that had proclaimed him King of the French *by the will of the people,* had consistently ignored his obligation by aligning himself with the forces of reaction. The domestic disturbances did not shake his security. His troops were strong and armed, and the largest mob, however well organized, has no chance against bayonets and guns.

But he was reckoning without the power of revolutionary ideas, which leaders like Mazzini and the ancient Carbonaro, Buonarroti, once associated with the martyred Babeuf, were disseminating with the patience of the sower who knows that though the time be inclement and the soil unready, the harvest will come. The newly risen industrial centers, with their agglomeration of men and women working for miserable wages under incredible conditions, were their fields. The crops of revolution, cut down by tyranny, sent up new shoots, stronger, more deeply rooted.

On the fifth of April, 1834, the workingmen of Lyons, indoctrinated by their leaders, rose up in a labor strike thousands strong. The troops marched to meet them. They found barricades in the streets, and behind them the workers, poorly armed but mighty in their anger. Blood flowed in the gutters as troops and workingmen engaged in hand to hand fighting. Marseilles, in the south, struck in support of Lyons. Paris joined the struggle. The people lost under the savage butchery of General Bougeaud, but Liberty marched unwavering over the corpses of her heroes.

Not satisfied with the slaughter, the government, the following April, brought to trial before the Court of Peers the conspirators who had been implicated in the Lyons strikes, hoping by the example, to quash further uprisings. The *procès monstre,* as it was called, was held in Paris. Twenty-two members of the Republican party were indicted for fomenting insurrection and four times as many workingmen for the crime of belonging to revolutionary societies and participating in the strikes.

It became a nationwide cause. The press, sympathetic to the

liberals, was promptly restricted, if not suppressed. But the Republicans, united under Armand Carrel, had their own organs besides the moral support of thousands of sympathizers, and able advocates in Michel de Bourges, the golden-tongued orator, and Pierre Dupont, the workingman's poet. Even if they lost—and they were ready to fight to the death for victory—the case would bring their socialist ideals before the people.

The trial lasted nine months. While it was in progress, a number of the accused made a melodramatic escape through an underground tunnel which they had dug with their own hands. Political societies everywhere gave it their support, punctuated by terrorist acts. On the twenty-eighth of July, the attempt of the Corsican, Fieschi, on Louis Philippe, struck down Broglie, the Duc d'Orléans, a marshal, a general and a captain; the explosion of the infernal machine left the king unscathed. Fieschi and his aides were put to death. The burghers and the king breathed freely again.

George Sand, so recently wrapped up in her personal gloom, unexpectedly found herself in the glare of the monster trial and in close contact with the principals of the defense. Michel de Bourges not only established himself near the Quai Malaquais to be near her, but when the court sessions were over, he would take his weak legs up the long flights of stairs to her apartment. Fleury, Planet, Emmanuel Arago, son of the more famous Dominique, radicals and revolutionaries of all shades and intensity followed, and soon George's walls echoed to Michel's voice, prophesying doom to the oppressor, while the chorus thundered, "Yea!"

What had happened to George's intention to seclude herself in Berry, and in asceticism and meditation forget the hurts inflicted by love? What of her allegory, *Myrza,* published that spring, in which she had her heroine retreat to the desert, like another wounded self? Did it express an intention, or was Myrza her substitute who, like the Egyptian figurines of the dead, worked out her expiation for her?

However it was, George that year was very much alive and active, whether at Nohant, Paris, Bourges or La Châtre. She wrote, she attended the trial, she helped frame articles for the defense, and even found time to study phrenology with the help of a Spurzheim skull (quite distinct from the repository of Alfred's last letter) whose sections were charted like a globe and the areas labeled with the barbarous names of aptitudes like philoprogenitiveness, amativeness, adhesiveness and a score of others. It served, otherwise, to terrify the gardener's wife at Nohant, who complained that "Madame had such an ugly head that it was enough to give her a miscarriage from fright."

194

George was also occupied with settling her marital difficulties. It had been primarily on this personal errand that she had started out with her friends Fleury and Planet, the second week in April, for Bourges where Michel lived. As a celebrated lawyer he could give the equally celebrated novelist the advice she sought.

George was inordinately impressed with Michel when Planet, who knew him well, conducted him to the inn to meet her, toward seven o'clock on the evening of their arrival. First of all, the amateur phrenologist gasped at the vastness and breadth of the great man's skull. "It looked," she noted, "as if there were two skulls welded together. The signs of the loftiest spiritual faculties were as prominent on the prow of this powerful ship as were those of the most generous instincts at the stern." Intelligence, veneration, subtlety and largeness of soul, she reflected with a nod to the ghost of Spurzheim must, in Michel, mingle with tender domesticity and physical courage. He did not look strong, however. That powerful ship was anchored to the frailest of bodies. How old was he? Impossible to tell. He might be thirty-five, he might be sixty, his cranium exposed so unashamedly his phrenological virtues. It must be premature baldness, George conjectured. The face, though lined with care and uncertain health, was that of a young man.

It was Michel's frailness, the absence, almost, of the physical in his make-up that made its appeal to George. He looked so much like something precious that should be kept in cotton wool—an impression further augmented by the layers of rough, warm, homespun clothes in which he was wrapped. But Michel was a purist in etiquette, despite the external habiliments of his peasant origin and the seven-league boots in which he trudged the Paris boulevards as democratically as his native fields. His shirts were always of the finest linen and white gloves, his tribute to elegance, completed his toilette, although the fashionables of the Jockey Club might have lifted their brows in horror. He also respected the observances of polite behavior, such as removing his hat when indoors or in the presence of a lady. But since his prematurely denuded head reacted adversely to drafts, he would ask permission of his hostess to protect his skull and, drawing a series of colored handkerchiefs from his pocket, he would knot them together and arrange them like the headgear of a *giaour*. In the vehemence of argument the improvised turban would slide to rakish angles, but nothing could render his eloquence ridiculous.

He was as much impressed with George as she had been with him. He had recently read *Lélia* and had been struck by the masculine power in it, and although he knew vaguely that George

Sand was the pseudonym of a woman, he betrayed astonishment when he came face to face with her. What an intellect! What emotional power! If the two could be harnessed to the cause of Republicanism what a gain for the party!

He complimented her on her work, listened with an inattentive ear to her matrimonial troubles, waved them aside, and then plunged into such speech as George had never heard. It flowed about her and enveloped her and carried her away. It kindled and burned and stung. It taunted to life a heart that had allowed itself to be deadened by the love of one, when it should have given itself to all. It was not too late. Humanity, Republicanism, the socialist cause waited for the heart of Lélia to pour out its vivifying warmth.

From seven until midnight Michel talked and kept on talking, while the three walked him home through the streets of Bourges. At the door of his house he swung round and they retraced their steps. From the inn they started back with him once more, for Michel had hardly tapped the reservoir of his arguments. The sleeping streets echoed to their heels. Windows opened to the unaccustomed oratory. It was four in the morning before Michel consented to be left at his door and the exhausted Berrichons went to sleep at their inn.

Next morning Fleury rushed George off before Michel could revisit them at the inn. They had both had the same terrifying dream, suggested by Michel's anarchic lust for the destruction of the old order in his zeal for the new. Fleury reckoned, however, without Michel's pertinacity. He wanted George for the cause and would not be put off by the distance of a few leagues. Besides, one's words could be given wings.

George had hardly wakened the following day when she received a bulky package from Bourges. She could not decipher Michel's scrawl at first, it was so feverish and tortured, as if exasperated by that physical medium of expression. But soon she learned to read it easily for Michel, goodness knows, did not stint her the opportunity of mastering her new accomplishment. The text of his letters was always the same. She must turn from self to society and devote her God-given powers to the good of mankind, beginning with all stanch Republicans. He never waited for an answer to his letters. He struck the iron while it was hot and kept on hammering, kindling sparks when the heat died down. "I know," he would say, "that your troubled mind comes from some secret heartache. Love is a selfish passion. Give this ardor, this devotion, to our suffering humanity, for you'll never receive as much as you give in this world. Enough agony over one individual! No man alive deserves it, but all humanity demands it as a law of creation!"

196

George could not resist such arguments. Under Michel's blows the soul of the lover of humanity broke through the mask of Lélia. In her salon where once Musset had played the piano and sketched every pose of her head, revolutionaries discussed the day's doings at the trial and enlisted the aid of her pen. "My son, you are too moderate, too moderate!" Michel reproved his newest disciple who, as much to please him as to enjoy the freedom of going about unremarked, the only woman among men, had resumed her male attire. Her short hair made the disguise easier. It did not, however, deceive a guard at the Chamber who, as she was about to make her way to the courtroom one day presented his musket and admonished her with Gallic nicety, "Sir, ladies are not admitted here."

She was smuggled in nevertheless by Emmanuel Arago who, as she put it, used to hide her in one of the huge pockets of his redingote and then deliver her safely home on top of the piano. "Next time," Arago would say, "we'll have to tuck our little brother into a paper cone so that he won't rumple his hair."

It was a tense, exciting life which for a time kept her from wholly fulfilling her obligations to Buloz. But how the blood boiled in her veins, and how alive she felt in an agitated France.

Societies for social reform were springing up everywhere. The Saint-Simonists, resurgent under Father Barthélemy Enfantin, gained membership by the thousands. Since 1832 when Enfantin's associate, Saint-Amand Bazard, had been struck down by apoplexy in the midst of a discussion of the society's policy, Father Enfantin had ruled it unopposed. Bazard, like Enfantin, schooled in the reformism of the *Carbonari* which both had joined at different periods of their career, had stressed, unlike the Father, the necessity for political regeneration. Enfantin maintained that social and moral change was more important, since perfected man would bring about the ideal society. With Bazard gone to a better world, Enfantin pursued his preaching against the tyranny of marriage, advocated the "priest-couple" united in a love as free as the soul, and, looking upon himself as the chosen of God, an election made visible by the badge labeled *Père* which he wore upon his breast, he sent out scouts to find a woman deserving to be "Mother" to his "Father."

So far no female messiah had been discovered, and the perfectionist colony at Ménilmontant, near Paris, yearned in vain for the accomplishment of the divine union. One day Adolphe Guéroult, a disciple and editor of *L'Opinion Nationale,* suggested a name. Some time later he presented himself at the Quai Malaquais and proposed to George Sand, in the name of his "Supreme Father" that she become the Mother of the Saint-Simonists.

George was astounded by the offer, and not a little complimented, for it is not given to every woman to be chosen as the mate of a neo-Christian Pope. She declined, however, and became a simple member, in recognition of similar views on women which she had long been advancing in her novels. The society appreciated her adherence and thereafter showed it in substantial New Year's gifts, most of them the handiwork of the faithful at Ménilmontant. In 1836 her garret was filled with an assortment which included a corset, water colors, a translation, a desk, an apron, a song, a bracelet, a foot (?), a thermometer, a waistcoat, a pair of trousers and a pair of earrings, the latter gifts probably in recognition of her exemplifying the best in male and female. A few years later she attended a Saint-Simonist meeting at the house of a certain Dr. Curie, accompanied by, of all inappropriate escorts, Alfred de Musset. By that time Father Enfantin had been discredited, after a number of trials in which women were implicated, and a prison term. By 1845 he exchanged his sacerdotal honors for the less august but more remunerative post of director of the Paris and Lyons Railway, leaving behind him, however, a brood of Ménilmontants scattered over Europe.

Liszt, with whom George had resumed her friendship, preached a higher Christian socialism than Enfantin's, and the name of Lamennais recurred in his conversations. George must meet him, he said.

Like everyone else, the author of *Essai sur l'Indifférence en Matière de Religion* whose effect, when the first volume appeared in 1817, created a renaissance of faith throughout the Continent, came to sit on one of the low chairs in George's salon. Liszt, his pagan god's face radiant with spirituality, could not take his eyes off the wonderful man. Beside him, Hermann Cohen, or Puzzi, a Jewish boy of unusual musical gifts who was his protégé and companion, looked from Abbé Lamennais to the trousered woman, and rested worshipfully on his master, the pianist of the century.

George listened to Lamennais, and had she not already declared herself Michel's disciple, would have joined him with her whole heart. Only the other day, however, she had written to Michel who, from mentor had scaled down the degrees to lover: "You are the only man I have loved in the phantoms in whom I thought for an instant to find you and possess you. (Alas, poor Alfred's ghost!) No man ever exercised a moral influence over me. My spirit, always free and untamed, never suffered guidance from anyone. . . . Then you came and enlightened me."

Enlightenment she could accept from Lamennais also, with no betrayal of Michel. But the Christian philosopher and fierce believer, whose recent *Paroles d'un Croyant* had made Pope Gregory XVI burst out in his encyclical, "A small book but immense in its perversity," was of a far different order from the Republican whose white gloves, clashing with his homespun, were like a visible index to worldly ambition in the midst of humanitarian dedication.

Lamennais was as intransigent in his beliefs as the early Christians. His wasted body, too delicate for the flame within, seemed to have shed all materiality. He lived only by the power of the spirit. Will and ardor gave character to his face, in the straight lines between his eyes and in the lightning of his looks, flashing as if behind that craggy brow his thoughts had struck fire. At fifty-three he had the appearance of a boy, and a boy's delight in a prank, provided it hurt no one. His heavy blue stockings and homely clothes which had supplanted the churchman's gown, reverted to a Breton simplicity, though his shipowner father had been rewarded for his services with a title by Louis XVI. Hugues Félicité Robert de La Mennais preferred to drop the *de* of nobility and be known simply as Lamennais in his merging with the people whose apostle be became, acting upon the promise of his *Paroles d'un Croyant*.

That book of prophecy, poetry and aphorism, marked his transition from the fanatical exponent of ecclesiastical authority based on revelation, to the Christian socialist who, shaking the dust of Rome from his feet after Gregory's excoriation, devoted himself to obtaining for all the expectations held in the Revolution's credo of liberty, fraternity and equality. The scourge of the rationalists became the missionary of the people under the standard of "God and Freedom."

At La Chênaie he had his paraclete. Among his friends he counted Chateaubriand and Sainte-Beuve who had made it possible for him to publish his *Paroles,* and among his followers Montalembert, Lacordaire, Maurice de Guérin and other pilgrims of liberty. Sainte-Beuve held the standard with his usual caution, admiring the leader and following his march, yet always with a careful step, as ready to withdraw as to advance. While Lamennais had remained in the realm of theory, Sainte-Beuve had given him courageous support. The swerve toward political action worried him. When he heard that George Sand adhered to Lamennais' principles, he warned her against becoming publicly involved with him and, even more, with dangerous Republicans.

"What could such an ill assorted company have had to talk about?" he asked irritably on learning that she had gone to a dinner party at Liszt's in the company of Lamennais, the mystic

Pierre Simon Ballanche, and Nourrit the singer. "I don't know," she said gently, "Lamennais talked to Ballanche, Liszt to Nourrit and I to the cat of the house."

Sainte-Beuve's letters, begun in banter, turned to criticism and ended by scolding. At the height of George's friendship with Michel de Bourges he became ill tempered and accusatory and then ceased writing to her altogether.

"I don't know what ails Sainte-Beuve," George confided to Liszt. "I've loved him like a brother, but he has spent his life in vexing me with his growling and carping and suspicion, so that I've sent him to the devil once for all. He was angry with me and, from what I can gather, there's been some sort of misunderstanding. I doubt that he knows what friendship is, but on the other hand he has a profound understanding of love—of self, not to say of *himself alone*."

It was unjust criticism of the patient confessor. But now that George had begun burning her bridges, she was as conscienceless as Michel about the casualties resulting from the debacle. Sainte-Beuve, more conservative, was also more observant of the duties of the friendship which George accused him of not understanding. When she was attacked in the *Quarterly Review* in 1836, he rose to her defense in the *Revue,* and four years later wrote in a survey of a decade of literature: "The most manifest, original and glorious newcomer was assuredly George Sand."

She had no time for a confidant in the daily excitement of her new activities. Perhaps, as he followed them from a distance, Sainte-Beuve might have been dazed by the marvelous recuperative powers of the woman who, not so long ago, in cursing the books and authors that had betrayed her with sophistries, sighed after the common-sense teachings of Benjamin Franklin, "whose picture, hanging over my bed, always makes me want to cry, as if it were that of a friend whom I had betrayed. I shall never return to Franklin . . . nor to my first platonic love. . . ." But that same voice, hardly a week later, had also said: "Ah, if I could be sure virtue is that ideal I believed it to be, how quickly would I return to it! I feel so much energy that I don't know what to do with it. But where can one find again that yearning, that faith, that hope?"

Michel and Lamennais provided the answer. For the present she collaborated with Michel and gave Lamennais pledges of future support. Her correspondence with Michel, necessitated by his, and her, frequent shifting of locale, resulted in *Lettres à Everard,* which, written with an eye to publication, quickly went from him to Buloz and from Buloz to the *Revue.* A public figure cannot afford private utterances. Besides, in the pseudonym of

Éverard the wise could see the symbol of her return to the world, rather, to humanity.

Through the summer and autumn the monster trial dragged on, although every day the Republicans expected not only triumph, but the crumbling of the rotten governmental system. Michel continued indulging his Apocalyptic fantasy, predicting from the overthrow of the impure Jerusalem the return of the terrestrial paradise, where the lion would lie down with the lamb, and everyone would have an equal share of the world's goods. The châtelaine of Nohant, every time the social question was discussed—and it was discussed a dozen times a day—gave assent but made her reservations. She was not entirely convinced of the evil of owning a parcel of private property. She thought of the time when, as a child, she had been given her own tiny plot of ground, like Hippolyte, and of how eagerly she had tended it. "The sense of property is so deeply ingrained in the human being," she argued, "that the child needs only four square feet of soil to learn to love the land he tills. . . . One has to recognize private property. . . . The land a man works with his own hands is as personal to him as the clothes he wears."

Despite George's adulation of her great Michel, she did not always see eye to eye with him, and told him so. There had been the matter of the open letter to the peers, intended by the Republicans to lift the failing spirits of the accused. George had drawn an eloquent draft, but Michel bristled at once at its moderation.

"You can't bolster up discouragement with homilies," he exclaimed. "Only righteous indignation can do it."

He wrote his own version, an admirable example of tactless oratory, which was seconded by an equally unyielding Republican, Dr. Trélat.

"Nobody will sign it," George cautioned. "The party members who would have put their names to mine will balk at yours."

"They'll have to sign," Michel retorted. "If they don't—well, we'll know how to do without them."

It turned out as George had predicted. Many Republicans who were wholeheartedly for the cause, hesitated to take needless risks. However, the letter was published with many signatures in two radical papers, with disastrous consequences. Besides bringing confusion into the party by creating dissidence, it eventuated in the trial of Michel and Trélat when the peers discovered that the major part of the signatures had been falsified.

The foremost Republicans attended the trial within the trial, among them Louis Blanc, then a youth of twenty-five. When he wrote of the event in his *Histoire de Dix Ans* he described Trélat's proud defiance of the peers and then said of Michel:

"Everyone knew his bold oratory and waited in solemn silence for him to speak . . . However, Michel was neither as bold nor as powerful as Trélat. He defended himself, which Trélat had not deigned to do, and the attacks which he launched against the peers were not entirely free of consideration. . . ."

The difference of approach on the part of the defendants told upon the judgments. Trélat, the martyr of the day, was heavily fined and sent to prison for three years. Michel got off with a month's sentence which, because he was suffering from bronchitis, he was permitted to postpone serving until November. Many of his fellow members turned against him. His pride suffered under hostile criticism but more because of the disparity in the sentences. He envied Trélat his three years' advantage. By its clemency to him, Michel, the court had too clearly demonstrated that he had been no hero.

While he was serving his sentence at Bourges after the trial, George came to consult him about her own affairs. Living under the same roof with Casimir was now a danger to herself and the children. Recently, during dinner, he had flown into one of his rages when Maurice accidentally overturned a pitcher of cream, and on George's protecting the boy, Casimir had threatened her with a gun. It was only one among similar scenes which he now seemed to relish performing in public, as if to assert his lordship over the woman who was daily growing in stature.

George, on her part, was passing through a period of acute discouragement. The April trial which was to have advanced the liberal cause had turned to a fiasco. The government, seizing upon the Fieschi attempt as a pretext, arrested Republican leaders like Armand Carrel. The people remained apathetic. George's personal life held little solace. Michel who had come to enlighten her on large issues was proving disappointingly illuminating about himself. The idol had clay feet. As she saw him more objectively she found that he had little of his own to offer. He was always under the dominion of some personality or of some book which filled him for a time, then left him blank till the next enthusiasm. Moreover, he was as jealously possessive of George's mind as Musset had been of her body. She resented the tyranny. For the present, however, she was still far from exclaiming, "I've had more than enough of great men. . . . I'd like to see them all in Plutarch. Let them be cut in marble or cast in bronze. May God protect us!"

She was also unhappy in her work. Too many made demands upon her time, and she must write or forfeit her independence. The writing itself had become a drain upon her. She had to produce without respite, drawing her novels out of herself to provide for the education of her children, for Solange's dowry, eventually. As it was, after the disastrous Musset affair, she had bound herself to deliver the story of her life to Buloz, so that Solange would not be left unprovided for in case of her mother's death. It was a debt that George had still to discharge, but there was work and yet more work to do.

During the summer she had taken refuge for a few weeks in an empty apartment on the ground floor of the Quai Malaquais house and there, using the carpenter's bench as a desk, and blissfully free of intrusion except for the mice, and the blackbirds from the garden that came to whistle inquisitively on the sill, she finished a novel, *Simon*. The hero was a fictional portrait of Michel, not as he was but as he filled her republican dream. The Buonarroti pamphlets which her fellow Republicans used to bring her to read, she used to good purpose. She included also the more spectacular elements of Michel's rise from a peasant origin to a position of political influence.

Since even the most salutary lesson must be sweetened for the reader, George introduced one of her typical emotional conflicts. Simon is made to marry a countess, (an aristocratic—bar-sinister—Aurore?) whom he adored as a woman, but whom he hated as the representative of the ruling class. And so the novel reached a conclusion that gave Buloz many a sleepless night.

George Sand was becoming revolutionary and mystical, he complained. The goose that had laid such golden eggs was fancying herself a chanticleer of the revolution—an estimable bird, no doubt, but for the purposes of popular fiction, unprofitable.

For the next two years George allayed his fears with charming short novels, *L'Orco, L'Uscoque, La Dernière Aldini,* all colorful and romantic and all set in the beautiful and wicked city where, like Musset, she had left her heart. For despite her protestations in her letters to Éverard—and to the world—humanitarianism, more than love, was involved in her alliance with Michel.

Buloz notwithstanding, George spent the better part of 1836 writing another novel, *Engelwald,* with Michel again as the hero. The setting, the Tyrol, was cold enough, but the three volumes, to judge by George's account, were more inflammatory than ever and made explicit the subversive calls to action which *Simon* had intimated.

Buloz boiled, but not from political idealism. Now George Sand was not only palming off in the guise of romances the ideas of Buonarroti, Michel, Lamennais, Leroux and other dangerous incendiaries, but she withheld her work from publication for fear of prejudicing the judges against her in the separation suit which Michel had finally consented to file for her in the court of Bourges. Strange caution for a fire-eater who could write to him, Buloz, a letter of caustic indignation because he, like any respectable editor, had congratulated Louis Philippe in the *Revue* for once again escaping an attempt upon his life when, in June, 1836, Louis Alibaud had discharged a pistol against him.

"It's a fact that should be judged from a moral, philosophical and psychological point of view," George wrote him on the third of July. "Alibaud is a hero. His name will shine in history side by side with Frédéric Stab's. You profess to abhor political assassination. You declare that Brutus and Cassius saw no farther than their noses. You treat them like *bousingots*. I say nothing to that, for everyone is entitled to his own convictions. . . . But what is the meaning of this shock of horror, this epilepsy of virtue, whenever you mention the *infamous* assassin? And what is this dainty little shrine that you set up for the *good King* who *walks about like a good citizen in the midst of his city?* In printing those words, my dear Buloz, you printed trashy non-sense."

Buloz could not help wishing that George possessed the political sanity of his other author, Musset, who, under similar circumstances, had addressed a sonnet of felicitation to Louis Philippe. Buloz did not know the sequel however. Far from being pleased on reading Musset's sonnet, Louis Philippe, the good citizen, had taken offense at the familiar *thou* employed by the poet. After all, there was a difference of level between a king and a poet.

George wrote her Venetian novels, yet her *Engelwald* she kept stubbornly from Buloz, to his great irritation. They quarreled. The novel never appeared. A quarter of a century later, George's friend Manceau burned it at her request, together with other documents.

By that time even the memory of the bald tribune was cold. Soon after the monster trial in which he had played both a glorious and an inglorious rôle, Michel, as if to meet a material-istic society on its own terms, retired to private practice and the accumulation of capital, so that in 1848 his name, which should have been among the first suggested for the provisional government, was absent from the rolls. The turn of political events during the *coup d'état* of 1851 brought him also his *coup de grâce*. For two years, from an embittered, neurotic retirement he watched his star paling till it was altogether extinguished. The publication of *Engelwald* after his death would have been too ironic a monument.

Chapter XX: The Fellows and the Piffoëls

ON the twenty-eighth of August George Sand, as if in celebration of her newly won freedom, set out for Switzerland on the insistent invitation of Liszt and the Countess d'Agoult. She took Maurice and Solange with her, and also Ursule, her maid.

For a month George had been enjoying the undisputed possession of Nohant after the royal court of Bourges had pronounced, for the fourth time, more or less in her favor in the separation suit. The jury still differed over details and a new trial was announced for the future, but the outcome appeared so clear that Casimir, convinced that he had prejudiced his case by overplaying his part, agreed on a division of George's fortune. The legal red tape, after the case was finally settled out of court, took still another year to disentangle, but Casimir's hate of the woman who had proved herself the better man never diminished.

It had been an unnecessarily unpleasant trial. Casimir who had at first accepted the terms of the separation, felt, on George's winning the judgment, that he was the loser in the settlement, although the gains, owing to George's innate generosity, were demonstrably on his side. Fearing he was relinquishing all in giving up his wife, he brought countersuit, pleading in extenuation the unreasonableness of a husband tormented by love and jealousy, and extended his arms in magnanimous forgiveness toward the mate he would first prove sinful. Fearful of losing her children in the unpredictable justice of a provincial jury, George converted as much of her capital as she could to cash, so that if Casimir won, she might escape to America with Maurice and Solange.

She fulminated against the barbarity of a social code that forbade divorce even between two such irreconcilable temperaments as hers and Casimir's and could not find words strong enough in condemnation of the perverted ethics that permitted a husband to drag the mother of his children through public ignominy and, after defamation and shame, to take her back, as if a family that had known such outrage could ever live in decency again.

Casimir, however, found a lawyer willing to handle his case.

But even his lawyer refused to introduce into court Casimir's list of defamatory accusations, one of which, suggested surely by the trial of Marie Antoinette, charged the woman and mother with the physical corruption of her son. Before the close of the trial the never too limpid course of their marital life was stirred up and muddied. Aurore's letters about Aurélien de Sèze were read before the jury, and finally her ingenuous self-accusing "confession" to her husband, written during the platonic episode, had its day in court when several paragraphs, chosen to furnish damaging evidence, were presented out of context by Casimir's lawyer.

Michel, at this point, was magnificent in his indignation. He tore the document out of the lawyer's hands and, gaining permission from the court, read the long letter, from first to last to the jury. The court burst into applause after this performance and some of the jurors wept. George won her case and the custody of her children. No one retained the least doubt but that the attractive woman who had come to the trial in a white dress, a flowered shawl, with feminine lace about her throat and a veil over her eyes, had been well rid of her husband. They were satisfied too, however, that her release had not come too easily. It might have suggested a similar procedure to other discontented wives who, as it was, borrowed freely from Madame Sand's novels to make life difficult for their poor husbands.

True to his nature, Casimir saw to it that he obtained everything to which he felt entitled, not omitting in his claims fifteen jars of preserves and an old cast-iron skillet worth, at the utmost, one franc fifty. The real estate too was divided, Casimir consenting to surrender claim to the Hôtel de Narbonne, George's Paris house inherited from her grandmother, for the trifle of forty thousand francs.

Relinquishment of Maurice was included in the bargain. Casimir stipulated further for an annual visit from his children at Guillery, provided, of course, that George paid half their traveling expenses. Before he was satisfied, however, he indulged in the bravado of kidnaping Solange and carrying her off to Guillery, where George recovered her only after bewildering communications to the local police via the newfangled invention called the telegraph, whose use had been especially granted her by the government.

"Why did you take Solange?" George reproached Casimir. "I thought you did not want her."

"No, I don't want her," he said. "I only did it to hurt you."

The year of the final settlement George also won a case against her publisher. "I've won two suits," she moaned, "and here I am, ruined."

In the midst of her many irritations George welcomed a change of scene. She was tired, but what was of considerably more importance to her, Maurice, whose heart had been affected by the domestic turmoil, needed rest. He had always been a high-strung child, unlike Solange who was like a tough little weed, and as he grew older his health gave her cause for alarm. "The boy actually breathes through you," Dr. Gaubert used to tell George when he noted Maurice's dependence upon his mother. Solange, now old enough to sense favoritism, showed her jealousy in screaming tantrums although George did her best to be fair to both her children. People talked, raking up old suspicions. *On dit,* the gossips repeated during the trial when Casimir made an attempt to gain control of the girl.—"*They say* Madame Dudevant cannot understand why he should want her, since she's no child of his." The fact that Solange looked like neither George nor Casimir lent support to the rumors. For many reasons it was important to remove the children from their immediate surroundings, if only to accustom them to the changed domestic situation.

George faced the responsibility of her position as the sole support of the family from now on. (But when had she not been?) She had to be both father and mother to her children; she had also to build up her resources, depleted by the rapacity of Casimir who, after inheriting a substantial estate on the death of his father's widow, grew in miserliness. Because of the dependent position of women in society, Solange worried her. She drew up a will and consulted Michel about it. "I leave my son to the care of my friends, and my daughter to their wives and sisters."

If her marriage had not been doomed by the clash of personalities she might have lived a peaceful life, like other women. She would have brought up her children and been ambitious for her husband. She would have lived and died happy as Madame So-and-So and never become George Sand.

Yet her work was a blessing. In it she forgot her troubles, and from the day it became an austere duty she loved it and thanked God for it. What if she had to be content with only four hours of sleep? What if headaches blinded her? Her duty was there. It had to be done for she had chosen it rather than continue a union that had become prejudicial to all of them. "Once the conjugal tie has been severed in the heart, it cannot be joined again by the hand of man. . . . The bond is broken the moment it has become odious to either wife or husband."

Still, George made no plea for easy divorce. "Marriage should be made as binding as possible," she wrote after obtaining her freedom. "For to guide so frail a bark as the security of a family through the stormy waves of our society takes as much as a man

207

and a woman, a father and mother, can do, by sharing the task according to their capacities. Indissoluble marriage is possible only when it is voluntary, and to make it voluntary it must be made possible. If, to come out of this vicious circle, you have something better to offer than a faith in the equal rights of the sexes, you have indeed made a wonderful discovery."

George and her little party arrived at Geneva only to find Liszt gone to Chamonix. On her intuition she went to the Hôtel de l'Union, and describing the musician and the Countess d'Agoult to the innkeeper, she was told, "Why, yes, monsieur. Such a party has just arrived. The lady seemed very tired, but the young girl was cheerful enough."

George was perplexed at the information, but a look at the hotel register convinced her that the "Mr. Fellows" who had just signed in could be none other than Liszt. He had filled out the descriptive blank to suit his fancy yet with regard to essential fact:

> *Occupation:* Musician-philosopher
> *Home:* Parnassus
> *Arrived:* From doubt
> *Destination:* Truth

George fell into the mood. She registered as "Piffoël and family," concocting the name from the colloquial *pif*, meaning a long nose, which both she and Maurice possessed, and then proceeded:

> *Home:* Nature
> *Arrived:* From God
> *Destination:* Heaven
> *Delivered by:* Public opinion

Like all imitation it lacked spontaneity, but her description, too, was basically correct.

The innkeeper looked at Piffoël and family and shrugged. All sorts of foreign oddities registered at his hotel, and it was foolishness to meddle provided they filled out the police questionnaire and paid their bills. He could not tell whether Monsieur Piffoël were male or female. Certainly the wavy hair that fell over the shoulders looked like a woman's. But then, like Mr. Fellows, Piffoël might be a musician. The dark blue blouse and black cravat were certainly masculine, and so was the red *gilet* with the gold filigree buttons. Still, there was something—but maybe not. No woman would have smoked a cigar with such gusto. He threw a look at the two boys—Solange was dressed like her brother—and at Ursule. At least he could tell what they were.

"You'll find your friends at Number 13," he called out after them.

George knocked and was let in by the "young girl," none other than Liszt's Puzzi. The boy's hair was longer than her own. He was dressed in a linen smock caught so tight at the waist that George readily understood the innkeeper's mistake. Liszt and the countess hugged her effusively, while Puzzi and the children sent up such shrieks of delight that the chambermaid dropped her candle and fled to spread the news that the hotel had been invaded by a tribe of savages.

There was still another member of the party who appeared later, a gaunt, atrabiliar Swiss, Major Adolphe Pictet, who fancied himself a philosopher and an author, and had nothing but contempt for inferior woman unless, like the Countess d'Agoult, she was redeemed by a title of nobility. From the first he was critical of George, chiefly for usurping man's place by her accomplishment. He accused her of levity for yawning at his Germanic pedantry and his eternal search for the Absolute which, he maintained, was identical with itself. Because she would not be drawn into such speculation for any length of time, he charged her with lacking the philosophic temper, with substituting intuition for intelligence and, finally, with having no intelligence. On the other hand he cast worshipful eyes upon the blond countess, discovering genius even in her banality.

For Marie d'Agoult had that quality of physical beauty which blinds one to grave faults, and by its marmoreal impassiveness gives the illusion of soul where often there is nothing but vacuity or, at best, mediocrity. The wide blue eyes that seemed so dreamy were in reality retentive mirrors, registering impressions, gestures, looks which were later reproduced as Marie's own. Her mind had the same speculative tendency. Seizing upon the originality of others, it assimilated the salient phrase, the seminal thought. Then, with marvelous effrontery, it flashed it back, unchanged but effective because uttered by such classically chiseled lips.

Tall, slim, fair, she was a type rarely met with in France. Her Teutonic beauty, mingled with Gallic irony acquired with her French education, puzzled and attracted. She was a woman of a thousand poses. She became Thaïs, Aspasia, as occasion demanded. She was a Charlotte to her many Werthers. She was Graziella. She had seen herself as a Sand heroine in the first book of George's which she had read. "There is a character in *Indiana*," she wrote to Madame de Flavigny, her mother, "a woman for whom people think I must surely have stood as model." She was always identifying herself with glamorous portraits. But most of all she thought of herself as that highest expression of womanhood, the inspirer, Beatrice.

Her career of Muse was already long when at thirty she had

met the twenty-four-year old Franz Liszt, crowned by his continental laurels, austere as a Dante in his mystical-religious aspirations. A card reader had predicted to Marie, wife of the Count d'Agoult, that she would soon meet a great man. Liszt's angelic face whose burning eyes nevertheless bespoke passion, told her, *Ecce homo.* There was the man and there, opportunely, was the book, *Léone Léoni,* to point the way.

Marie d'Agoult prevailed upon her all too human Dante, and then finding herself pregnant, abandoned her middle-aged husband and her two little girls, relinquished her position as a leader of the Paris salons and went with Liszt to Geneva to await her confinement of his child, Blandine. She was to bear him another daughter, Cosima, and a son, Daniel.

Too much absorbed in her hallowed mission, Marie had less concern for her offspring than a cat for her litter. Her children by her husband she left in the care of Madame de Flavigny, while the count, wiser, in his stolidness, than his wife, waited for the ultimate homecoming of the wayworn Beatrice. Liszt's children were brought up by his mother. In a letter sent by the countess to Madame Marliani from Italy, she wrote in a postscript, after many paragraphs on hats and dresses: "I forgot to tell you, by the way, that I was confined last month at Rome—a boy. I left him there. Madame Allart did likewise."

But the infatuated Liszt of Geneva was quite remote from the clear-eyed man of fifty who told Marie that her book of memoirs should have been called, *Poses et Mensonges*—poses and lies. He was still too much enwrapped in the incense of churches to behold reality without a haze. "You belong to art, not to religion," his father had cried angrily on seeing the youthful mystic spending hours on his knees when he should have been practicing the piano. Marie became another form of worship, the divinity of a sinful Mariolatry. She looked like a goddess and that was sufficient.

George, whose friends were predominantly male, had been smitten by a schoolgirl adulation when Liszt for the first time brought the countess to meet her. The two women began a busy correspondence. George's letters, of a falsetto gallantry, are absurd in their flattery. At the time, she was at her most anti-aristocratic, yet she found herself, against her proletarian judgment, admiring a countess. How reconcile her heart with her principles? "You appear to me to be the only beautiful, noble and worthy object ever to shine in the patrician orbit. You must be mighty indeed to make me so far forget that you are a countess. At present, however, you appear to me as the perfect type of the fairytale princess, loving, artistic, noble in manner and speech, like the daughters of kings of legendary times. That is how I see you, and I want to love you as you are and for what you are."

George's dedication of *Simon* to "Madame la comtesse de —"
is almost a poetic echo of her letter:

"Mysterious friend, deign to be the patron of this humble
tale.
Patrician, forgive the prejudices of the rustic narrator.
Madame, reveal to no one that you are his sister.
Thrice noble heart, bow down to him and make him proud.
Countess, may you be pardoned.
Veiled star, know yourself in these litanies.

Marie, for her part, began to reflect George from her many
facets. George wrote. She must write too. George kept a journal.
She started one at Chamonix. George said penetrating things
about music that made Liszt listen in admiration. Marie remembered, and echoed them at the opportune moment. She knew
other musicians. Frédéric Chopin was among those who used
to come to her salon in Paris. Marie needed flattery and admirers,
and greedy of both, she could not tolerate any sharing of them in
her proximity.

She was jealous of George. Before setting out, Lélia had spoken
of Marie and Liszt as the two noble palms in whose shade she
would refresh her tired spirit in the desert of life. Obviously
Liszt's palm gave more grateful rest. George and he could be
together for hours and feel no boredom. Franz enjoyed playing
the piano for her as she sat, still as a sleeping moth, in the em-
brasure of the window, betraying her presence only by the
smoke of her cigarette. One night he executed a rondo which he
had just composed on a Spanish song, *El Contrabandista*. George
was up all of that night, writing, and the following day she read
her lyric tale, *"Le Contrebandier,"* a theme in romantic variations, like the rondo. Neither of the compositions was worthy of
its author, the countess was glad to note, but it cost her a pang
to see the rondo dedicated "To Monsieur George Sand." Beatrice
should reign alone.

"George is an urchin always up to some prank," she condemned
from her altitude.

A woman should have a noble aloofness like a mountaintop
covered with snow, like herself slow to thaw. It had pleased her
to receive George's letters, gallant yet troubled like those of a
shy young man. It gave her a gratifying sense of power to find her
fascination effective on women as well as men. She saw herself
as George's inspiration, too, at first, and maintained herself
firmly on her height, avoiding the familiarity that breeds contempt. She did not forget for an instant, however, to exercise
her allurements. Whenever they were in a room together Marie,

"Without knowing the French language, you have style," Balzac told her further. Henry James, from a more objective perspective, was more generous. "Her language had to the end the odor of the hawthorn and the wild honeysuckle. . . . She appears to have begun at a stage of the journey at which most talents arrive when their time is up."

However, George Sand could not have written had she not first lived some phase of her romances and known in the flesh the models of her art. The transmutation from reality to fiction occurred, as it often does, unconsciously, so that it was in absolute good faith that she denied self-portraiture in *Indiana, Valentine, Lélia,* the princess in *Le Secrétaire Intime,* and in other female characters, and painting from life in Delmare, Simon, and the too recognizable Karol in *Lucrezia Floriani,* the novel which was to unfold the last phase of her emotional life.

More harshly than Balzac because more involved with the complexity of George Sand, Liszt, who had observed her naturalistic dilettantism at Nohant, found in it a figure for his satire, after the publication of *Lucrezia Floriani* in 1846: "George captures her butterfly and domesticates it by feeding it flowers and honey. This is the love period. When it begins to struggle, she sticks her pin into it. That is the dismissal, in which she takes the initiative. Then she dissects it, preserves it and adds it to her collection of heroes for novels." Although not strictly true as criticism of her liaisons and ruptures, the process of conversion from reality to art was valid.

The method was even more conspicuous in the utilization of experience. Without her unhappy marriage there would have been none of her early novels; without her sexual disillusionments, the world would have lost some of her finest works; without the influence of Michel, Lamennais, Leroux and the people's poets who since 1835 had been frequenting her studio, she would not have written her religious and philosophical *Spiridion,* nor her social-reformist *Horace* and *Le Compagnon du Tour de France* which, when it appeared in America, released the poetic urge of Walt Whitman and suggested to him the personality of the poet of democracy.[1]

Nevertheless, (peace, Balzac!) George was always at her best in works wherein her imagination was not too closely bound by matter of fact. In her tales of mystery and adventure she had the verve of a Byron and the fantasy of an E. T. A. Hoffmann, together with a spiritual refinement that lifted those works far above their medium. *Consuelo* and its sequel, *La Comtesse de Rudolstadt,* have an inventiveness out-Dumasing Alexandre, and

[1] See Esther Shephard's *Walt Whitman's Pose.* Harcourt, Brace and Company, 1938.

there were few contemporary works of fiction that could rival, for storytelling mastery, her unpretentious *La Dernière Aldini*, *Tévérino*, *L'Homme de Neige*, *Le Piccinino*, *Le Beau Laurence* and *Pierre qui Roule*, *La Filleule*, *Cadio*, *Antonia*, *La Famille de Germandre* and half a dozen other examples from her inexhaustible pen. Her prodigious fecundity continued through the half century of her creative life. She never tapped the source of her imagination in vain for her romances, her social novels, or the pastoral, and perhaps the best realized, works of her final period. In her more than eighty novels there may be diffuseness, there is redundancy, but boredom never. She had, besides, enough creative energy left for playwriting, for her series of *Lettres d'un Voyageur;* for a story of her life; for *Lettres à Marcie,* contributed without pay to Lamennais' journal *Le Monde,* only to have the great man who had impelled her forward in intellectual daring, retreat in fear when the pupil outdistanced the master; for political pamphleteering; for articles on social reform; for journals and journalism and for the work of her friends. In spite of general recognition (for a time the era was known as the Age of George Sand), she made no pretensions to being an *homme de lettres*. "Like me," commented Balzac, "she makes light of her fame." Light enough to lend her name to Balzac himself when, on his finding himself financially embarrassed, she signed his *"Voyage d'un Moineau de Paris"* so that Hetzel, who did not want it, would include it in his *Scènes de la Vie Privée des Animaux,* and so bring its author the much needed cash.

Work itself, however, was another matter. It was a means toward many ends. First of all, in freeing her from self-absorption, it made her reach out toward humanity in a sympathy acquired through her own suffering, "For such anguish is a common ill; it is the pain of the entire race." From the time she had read Madame de Genlis she had awakened to man's responsibility to man; but it was only after espousing an active socialism that she felt herself one with the human race. "As we are all bound together in humanity, there can be no isolated fact," she wrote with the austere nobility of a Donne without having read him. "There is never any crime without someone to cause it or abet it. And it is impossible to accuse oneself without accusing one's neighbor—not only the enemy who denounces us, but sometimes even the friend who defends us." The men who had taught her that wisdom may have proved false prophets. The wisdom had its own shining validity.

Her responsiveness was what Renan must have had in mind when he called George Sand "the aeolian harp of our times." "Genius plays with error," he wrote in his *Feuilles Détachées,* "as a child plays with serpents. He is not harmed by them.

Madame Sand experienced every dream. She smiled upon all; she believed for a moment in all. Her practical judgment might occasionally have gone astray. But as an artist she was never mistaken."

Good or bad, her work also gave her material freedom and with it the power to aid others. It had helped purchase her liberty through the courts. Before that it had provided not only for her but for her lovers in turn. It enabled her to finance Lamennais' journal and help the wild schemes of Pierre Leroux, from the manufacture of his pianotype, a sort of primitive typewriter, to the guano factory he established while in exile in Jersey. Coincidentally she came to the relief of thirty hungry mouths in Leroux' immediate family, and of the hundreds of male and female Christian-Socialists who at various periods threw in their lot and their poverty with him in a perfectionist society. She gave large sums to the families of striking workers and paid for the publication of proletarian poetry in which she had an engaging faith. She even drew up a delightful plan for a handbook of verses—Charles Poncy might write them or Perdiguier—to be called "Songs of all Trades" for, as she said, "Birds sing their love and happiness, and in that they are in harmony with nature. But man must do more—poets must move people and make them think." Besides encouraging the proletarian Muse, as long as she lived, she also supported her son and daughter, her daughter-in-law and son-in-law and her grandchildren, her brother Hippolyte and other members of the family and, until 1837, her willful, capricious, irresponsible mother.

Sophie's death came after a long and malignant illness. Before the end, mother and daughter, estranged by the memory of Madame Dupin, were once again drawn together. In her way Sophie took pride in George's work, although she reviled her after every adverse review and called her a genius with every laudatory article. As her cancer spread, Sophie's beauty faded. She looked a hundred, but her eyes, the eyes her daughter had inherited, remained young.

She responded to George's vibrancy. "Ah, I am not going to die," she cried when she saw her. "You bring me life." But the disease was stronger than her will to live, stronger than George's vitality.

"Don't bring any priests here," Sophie said to George when she knew there was no hope. "After all, why should I fear to face God? I've always loved Him. He can accuse me of all kinds of things," she added, "but of not loving Him—I defy Him!"

"Comb my hair," she said one day to her sister who had been nursing her.

Lucie brought her a hand mirror and dressed the hair which

had not grown old. Sophie gazed at her reflection, smiled, and the mirror dropped from her hand.

"You'll find me cured," she had told George on her last visit.

"Yes, cured," reflected George. "Cured of the awful weariness of life."

Chapter XXI: Music's Child

NOW, however, in 1838, life was taking on a new and graver significance for George. For nearly a year she had been finding compensation for the demands of the bald tribune in the docile affection of Félicien Mallefille, Maurice's tutor, a young man with literary leanings and a prosperous beard. "Decidedly Mallefille reigns," Buloz noted in his journal, adding irritably, "She suggests that I publish Mallefille, her children's tutor and her lover. She also suggests Abbé Rochet whose revolt against his superiors she encourages. She flatters me so that I'll be prevailed upon to publish."

George made no secret of the new alliance and with typical expansiveness announced it to Frédéric Girerd, a colleague of Michel's, whose ear she wished to reach. "I think I have at last succeeded in *overthrowing the dragon.* That tenacious passion, so ruinous to all my faculties, has at last been cured by another love, gentler, less exhilarating but also less bitter, and, I hope, more lasting."

She was fond of Mallefille. His shy devotion, not unlike that of a boy for a favorite teacher, gave her what she wanted. He copied her manuscripts for the hungry monthly press, taught her children, and also found time to be a lover. Neither passion nor imagination played any part in the affair; consequently, in spite of George's hope for its longevity, it was doomed to an early death. "Her kind of male is rare," Balzac had pronounced, judging the relationship under his microscopic eye. His formidable beard notwithstanding, Mallefille was not that male.

Always self-hypnotized, George acted as if he were and was grateful for his attentions. She read his novel, *Le Dernier Sauvage,* though she never found time to reread her own, and approached the mistrustful Buloz about it. The book was no worse than the popular successes that made history for a season. Nevertheless the manuscript returned to roost like any homing pigeon after each excursion to the publishers. Mallefille needed money and every rejection threw him into a depression. At last he asked George to do him a great favor. She obliged. That spring *Le Dernier Sauvage* appeared with her name and immediately gave signs of selling well.

But even while the book throve, the sentiment which had inspired George's generosity was definitely on the wane. A letter to the Polish count, Albert Grzymala, later that spring, marked the coming end of Mallefille's reign as inevitably as fate. For George was in the process of setting up the powerful quadrangle of her emotional pattern, this time with God, George Sand, Frédéric Chopin and Albert Grzymala holding their respective corners, the last, Chopin's close friend, assuming the function of the confidant.

"Let us clearly state the question once for all," George began. "Upon your answer thereto depends my future procedure." She had not been Michel's disciple in vain, for never had a woman, even when she adopted the forthrightness of a gentleman, laid her brief upon the table with such forensic acumen. One might have thought from such a beginning that George's lengthy document—it had as many pages as a short story—contained a proposal for some momentous social reform. It dealt instead with the ethical problem of whether or not, given the complexities of her life and Chopin's, she should yield to him as his mistress. There were many defects of character that puzzled her in the young composer, prejudices, a certain snobbishness, a puritanical narrowness about the freedom of the passions. Moreover, he was obviously still suffering under a recent unhappy love. Considering the circumstances, what was she to do?

Long after the events, legend, colored according to whether it was a partisan of Chopin's or a friend of George's who made it, gave varying versions of their first interview. According to one, Chopin, who had unusual premonitory powers, had had a powerful foreboding of evil the day he was introduced to George Sand. Another, exercising a poetic imagination, set the stage in a salon where Chopin was playing, and there he had him, like a fascinated bird, succumb to the spell of George's magnetic eyes. Still another spoke of a shadow brushing past Chopin on the stairs, while a fourth, no admirer of Sand's, had the musician exclaim after meeting her, "What a repugnant woman, that Sand! Is she really a woman? I have my doubts."

The meeting, a matter of record, held neither premonition nor drama. Liszt had called upon Chopin early in December and was invited to an evening of music for the thirteenth of the month when Chopin intended to play some of his new compositions for a group of friends. Liszt suggested bringing Madame Sand, a suggestion which Chopin obviously welcomed, for he listed her as an added attraction in his invitation to Joseph Brzowski: "I am receiving a few people today, Madame Sand among others. . . . Liszt will play and Nourrit will sing."

Liszt may have planned the meeting. It may be, however, that he had no choice but to invite George, since she had recently given up her apartment on the Quai Malaquais and was occupying a suite at the Hôtel de France where she shared a common salon with Marie, bolstered up by the support of the formidable bluestocking, Princess Belgioioso and the influential Charlotte Marliani, wife of the Spanish consul and mistress of Monsieur de Bonnechose.

Whether planned or fortuitous, the meeting had happy results. George yielded to Chopin's music and he responded to her absorbed silence as she sat deep in an armchair, one elbow on a side table, her eyes fixed upon him. Chopin returned her call at the Hôtel de France and soon visited there again. Marie watched the friendship growing and her wit took on a sharp edge.

George left for the country and from there she sent repeated invitations to Chopin. Each time, however, he was prevented from accepting because of the music lessons which kept him in Paris. In 1837 Liszt and Marie d'Agoult were frequent visitors at Nohant. In one of her invitations to Liszt in March George wrote: "Tell Chopin that I beg him to come along with you, that Marie cannot live without him and that I—I adore him. I shall write to Grzymala to persuade him, if possible, to come to see us. I'd like to surround Marie with all her friends."

Again Chopin did not come. He went instead to London where he played, as "Monsieur Fritz" for James Broadwood on one of the famous Broadwood pianos; but he was lionized, nevertheless, by the ladies, who recognized the unmistakable Chopin touch. He disappointed their expectations, however, by a morbid reticence. He accepted no invitations. He saw no one. He went nowhere except to concerts and then disappeared as mysteriously as he had arrived.

He was dejected and tormented. He had not been well. Always delicate, he caught cold easily. He called his throat affections "bronchitis" and never allowed the word consumption to pass his lips. It was in the family. One of his sisters had died of it. But his physical illness was nothing to the ache from another source.

He had very little tangible to connect with it: a few letters from the Countess Wodzinska, friendly and warm; a few letters from her daughter Marie, sprightly and coquettish, then formal to coldness. There was also a rose. Marie had given it to him at Dresden in September of 1835 when she thought herself in love with him, her brother Anton's friend. He had, before that, presented her with the manuscript of a waltz, dedicated "To Mademoiselle Marie." [1] There had been nothing more except looks and pressures of the hand and hours at the piano when he had

[1] Posthumously published. Opus 69, No. 1.

222

GEORGE SAND IN MALE ATTIRE
PORTRAIT BY EUGENE DELACROIX
*"Shorn of her hair, she went to pose for Delacroix,
commissioned to do a portrait of her for the* Revue.*"*

improvised what he dared not put into words. He had considered himself engaged after a twilight walk with Marie in the garden, when he told her he loved her and she had repeated his words. Marie was pretty, not yet twenty, courted by men and fond of admiration. A strain of Italian blood from the Sforza family lent warmth to her eyes and a deceptive exuberance to her nature. She was weak and submissive. She was also socially ambitious. When the count, her father, discouraged her attachment to the young composer who brought no asset but his genius, Marie obediently made the conversion from beloved to sister. The countess, with gentleness born of love for Chopin, softened the inevitable blow in the letters she sent him.

The break had not been overt, which made it all the harder for Chopin to bear. Had he not been simple Frédéric Chopin, son of a Polish mother and a French father who tutored in the household of the Countess Skarbek, Count Wodzinski would have consented to the marriage. Perhaps it was a similar regret that Marie expressed in the letter wherein, like another Juliet, she wished he had been born Chopinski and not Chopin—so that the French could not claim him for their own, she added with charming flattery.

By the summer of 1837, when Chopin received a final communication from the Countess Wodzinska, he knew there was no more to be hoped. Yet like an incurable who still clings to the illusion of health, he refused to believe that all was over. Marie had been his first real love, after a trial amourette here and there, which came to nothing even before it began. He was reticent with women. Very feminine himself, he could not pursue, and drew away in prudery when pursued. Friendship, with him, had the intensity he had not learned to transfer to love. Not even to Marie could he have written such declarations as he made at the age of twenty to his friend Tytus Wojciechowski: "My dearest life! Never have I missed you as I do now. . . . None but you shall have my portrait. There's only another person to whom I would offer it . . . but you are the dearest. . . . I always carry your letters about with me. . . . You are the only person I love. . . . No, you do not know how much I love you. I can't show it to you in any way. . . . Kiss me, dearest love." He closes one letter: "I know you're still fond of me, but I'm always afraid of you. . . . Lord knows, you're the only one who has any power over me."

Freudian psychology could interpret such letters and adduce evidence enough for a convincing theory. But without more tangible proof theory must remain theory. The virile Delacroix, who later became an intimate friend of Chopin's, had written similarly effusive letters to his comrades in his youth. Such demonstrativeness, while it undoubtedly had its roots in the psyche, was also stimulated by the Romantic literary style and the current exaltation of what the phrenologists called adhesiveness, the friendship of man for man, examples of which history and legend afforded. "With him friendship had the semblance of love," wrote the editor of Delacroix's *Correspondance,* André Joubin. "If he adored painting like a mistress, the fervor inspired by some of his friends seems often to overstep the bounds of simple friendship. Let us read nothing into it but the ardor, too long contained, of a passionate soul."

In Delacroix the ardor finally had its outlet in work and in life. In Chopin, while it found creative sublimation in his music, it continued to consume itself within him in frustration and insecurity, although no pianist, not even Liszt, was more petted and spoiled by his admirers. At a time when connoisseurs were endeavoring to determine the supremacy of Liszt or his rival, Sigismund Thalberg, a wit settled the question with the one word, "Chopin." Nevertheless, Chopin was so uncertain of himself, so uneasy at having to face an audience of strangers, that he ultimately discontinued concert engagements, contenting himself with playing in well-known salons before adoring ladies and his few, very few, Polish friends.

He was a Pole to the core. The years he lived in France did nothing to rouse in him the least desire for identification with his father's country. Yet he was so incapable of facing any disruption in the social order, that although he could have returned to Poland after its tragic dismemberment, he chose to live in virtual exile rather than see his native land in her anguish. His most intimate friends were Poles, like him refugees: Jean Matuszinski who practiced medicine and with whom for a time Chopin shared an apartment; the poet Adam Mickiewicz, and Count Grzymala.

Chopin was guided by his prejudices even in the choice of his acquaintances, and surrounded himself with people who afforded the only milieu in which he felt at home. Jews, except in business relations, were excluded unless the Semitic name were preceded by a title—for even as a schoolboy editing an amateur journal, Chopin had betrayed that unfortunate bias for which Poland was notorious. He was a favorite with women whose company he preferred to the competitive society of men. But even they had to be of a certain class. His engagement books sparkled with names of princesses, baronesses, countesses. His rooms were a clutter of doilies, embroidered cushions, needlepoint footstools and water colors made by their aristocratic hands. In return he flattered them with dedications on the compositions he published and played for them in their salons. Jealous of his favor, they became bacchantes disputing Orpheus. But through it all Chopin kept his head, for his vanity never went beyond an adolescent infatuation with his own person.

He could not have been better framed to awaken the idolatry of women. Without Liszt's beauty, he had a fragility that immediately made its appeal to their protectiveness. Slight, of medium height, he carried himself with a grace like his own music. His brown eyes gave an effective contrast to the transparency of his skin and the ash blond of his hair. His nose had an aristocratic curve and the thin nostrils of a consumptive. He wore his hair long, meticulously curled but always with a touch of artistic disarray. He usually dressed in gray, and he was careful to choose the same tone for his wallpaper. It harmonized with his personality and formed a gentle background for the flowers that always filled his rooms. He seldom bought them, for he had many ladies visiting him in the course of the day, each with her floral offering. In his manner he observed an impeccable courtliness which complimented them without compromising him. It was enough for them if he touched their fingertips with his slim, delicate hand, of a beauty always associated with the musician's but so seldom met with in life.

Although his was a highly spiritual nature, he was far from being preoccupied with philosophical questing like Liszt or, for that matter, George Sand who, after finishing her novel on a happy marriage, *Mauprat,* and *Les Maîtres Mosaïstes,* written for Maurice's instruction, began her daring *Spiridion,* a search into religion, embodying the teachings of Lamennais. Chopin remained as unaffected by the winds of doctrine in his uncompromising Catholicism as if he had lived in a medieval cell. He had a keen distaste for all forms of propaganda, whether religious or social, loathed any kind of "ism" and shrank from contact with the Father Enfantins and the Lerouxs of the day. Music held idealism enough for him, while Catholicism sufficed the needs of his soul.

In the face of such disparity between George Sand and Chopin, it is remarkable that they should have been even superficially attracted to each other. Still, there were many points of contact. Though not a countess, George Sand might have had justifiable claim to Polish royal blood. As the queen of French novelists she held undisputed title, and Chopin, with his obsessive perfectionism in his own work, respected achievement in others. He was drawn to her also by her capacity for silence, her complete receptivity to his music which she seemed to absorb through her whole being, focused in looks of unfathomable depth. Unlike the members of his female circle, she showed no effusiveness after his playing, yet her stillness held greater praise than their chorus of "Ohs" and "Ahs," sung out with uplifted eyes. Chopin himself was undemonstrative and talked hardly at all.

As for George, Chopin possessed all the necessary prerequisite to engage her emotionally. He was young, weak, suffering and a genius. (Mallefille had only his youth to recommend him.) Following her break with Michel, she experienced a sudden revulsion against the masterly male and, as always when her emotions were spent, she turned to nature. Often she would rise before daybreak and mounting a horse, gallop wildly across the country. Or she would tramp for miles alone, "herborizing," her specimen knapsack slung across her shoulders and a net in her hand. In the hot noons she would plunge fully dressed into the river and then lie on the grass till the sun had dried her. At home she communed with her alter ego, Dr. Piffoël, endeavoring in her journal to make order out of confusion.

In summing up her life in the autumn of 1837, she questioned Piffoël on inconsistencies of behavior. "Do you remember your gloom of three months ago? Meanwhile you've revisited the rocks of Franchard (at Fountainebleau) —and with whom? You've looked again on the peak of Marbore—under what circumstances? Now you've come home again. . . . Whom will you love? Whom will you hate? Next month, next year, tomorrow?" She had seen the places associated with Musset and Aurélien in the company of Mallefille. Musset was nothing but a shadow, Aurélien a figment of her memory. Yet how intensely she had loved them, in their time. What was this inconstancy in her? How could she allow herself again and again to be so self-deceived? "Anyone looking superficially on my life might think me either a fool or a hypocrite. But whoever examines it below the surface must see me as I really am—easily moved, carried away by love and beauty, eager for truth, mistaken in judgment, often preposterous, but always sincere."

She omitted one thing in her evaluation, the overpowering attraction she felt for the weak. Recently George had picked up a fledgling that had fallen out of its nest, and nursed it till it was ready to fly. The Piffoël journal received the story of the bird's trust in its human benefactor, and of her love for the helpless, ugly mite. "The love of weakness for strength is a sacred law of nature, but holier still is the love of strength for weakness," she commented, going on: "So woman cherishes her young and so man should cherish his woman. . . . What woman fulfilled in her love life would want an intellectual career?"

Her love of the weak was a projection of her strongest instinct, the maternal. It was called forth more strongly than ever when Chopin entered upon the scene.

Knowing her tendency, she had fought against the attraction

at first. Chopin was suffering over his love for someone else. Yet the fact that he suffered was in itself an allurement. When, later, she saw that Chopin was drawn to her and called on her often when she was in Paris early in 1838, she did not encourage his growing dependence on her company. Chopin was lonely, and men seek out substitute mothers in their loneliness. Or perhaps he was trying the time-honored expedient of forgetting an old love in a new.

He played for her alone, his own music, of which he seemed the perfect embodiment in delicacy and melancholy. He summoned moods of poetic revery which moved them both to the depths. One day he kissed her.

On the twenty-third of May, 1838, George wrote to Madame Marliani from the country, excusing herself for being such a lax correspondent: "You know how the weather changes in the season of love. . . . Often one says in the morning, *How intolerable,* only to say in the evening, *Truly, this is the height of happiness.*" George, who could not live in indecision, determined to settle the barometer with the help of Grzymala.

It was then that she wrote to him, man to man, and manfully the count read a declaration more astounding than the epistle to Pagello. George went directly to the point after her legalistic preamble, and throughout showed solicitude only for "our child, our little one."

"This person whom he wishes, ought, or believes he ought to love, is she capable of making him happy, or will she only aggravate his pains and sorrows? I don't ask whether he loves her, whether she loves him in return, whether that love is greater or less than mine. I know approximately, by what I am experiencing, what he too must feel. What I want to know is which of *us two* he must forget or give up for his peace of mind, for his happiness, for his very life . . . I would not dispute him at all from the friend of his childhood if she were a pure and beautiful Alice. . . . I don't want to play the part of a bad angel. . . . Had I known that there was an engagement in the life of our child . . . I should never have leaned over to inhale an incense intended for another altar. He, too, I am sure, would have drawn back from our first kiss if he had known that I was as good as married. . . . As for me, I have no wish to surrender myself to passion, although at times there smolders in the depths of my heart a still menacing potentiality. My children, however, would give me strength to destroy anything that would separate me from them. . . .

"There is, besides, an excellent being, perfect in heart and honor, from whom I shall never part because he is the only man who, during almost a year that he has been with me, has not caused me *a single moment's pain* through any fault of his. He is moreover the only man who has given himself absolutely and entirely to me. . . . He is malleable wax on which I have set my seal, and should I ever wish to change the imprint I would be able to do so, with care and patience. But for the present that would not be possible. His happiness is sacred to me. . . . Chained as I am, perhaps for years, I could not wish that our little one should snap his bonds."

What then did the amazing woman intend to do? She could not expect to have both her present lover and Chopin—Chopin, as much of a purist in his relationships as he was in his music. Ah, but here it was, the solution, with authority from on high to bless it: "I think our love can be lasting only under the conditions that gave it birth. From time to time . . . whenever a good wind brings us together, we shall wander for a while among the stars and then part, to walk the earth again alone, for we are children of earth, and God has not decreed that we accomplish our pilgrimage side by side. It is in heaven that we shall meet. . . . My duty, therefore, is laid down."

She gave the alternative to heavenly consummation: she must either keep away from Chopin and take care not to find herself alone with him, or she might share with him his quiet hours and "press him chastely to her heart," provided it did not compromise Mallefille's security.

She would adopt the procedure of avoiding Chopin if Grzymala assured her that Marie Wodzinska was the woman to make their "child" happy. "I have no wish to steal anyone from anyone else—unless it be captives from their jailers, victims from their executioners, and Poland from Russia," she declared with unintentional humor but genuine feeling. If, on the other hand, Grzymala decided in her favor, George would deign to inhale Chopin's proffered incense. "If his heart could be capable of two loves, like my heart, two loves different in nature, one, so to say of the *body* of life and the other of the *soul,* that would be best."

There was still, however, the very grave consideration of exclusive possession. Human beings were peculiar in demanding it where a loved one was concerned. For herself, George had no clear opinions, although she had written much about it and intended to write more. On the whole, she had been all for fidelity. "I have preached it, I have practiced it, I have demanded it. People did not always live up to it and neither did I. And yet I never felt any remorse, because in my very infidelities I have always submitted to a kind of fatality, an instinct for the ideal, which impelled me to leave the imperfect for what appeared to be nearer perfection. . . . My being entered into different phases, like the sun in the signs of the zodiac, Sainte-Beuve used to say. . . . It is not in my nature to govern myself through reason when love takes possession. . . . There is no love without fidelity. . . . But alas, I did not feel the same affection for Mallefille when I saw him again."

Assertions, contradictions, followed each other in the same paragraph, in the same sentence, as George, striving from the imperfect toward perfection, placed Mallefille and Chopin in their respective categories. In one passage George had even contemplated a possible pentagon with Mallefille occupying the fifth point. But his tenure did not survive the engendering thought. It was clear, through George's protestations, that she had fixed on Chopin, of the same age as Musset and of equal, if not greater talent, in another field.

There was about Chopin a prudery, however, which offended her sense of the holiness of sex. George knew that Chopin desired her, yet he contained himself, possibly through timidity, or respect for her, or even out of faithfulness to the other, as she thought. What was her shock when, as he was leaving her one evening, he said as if to quiet an unworthy urge, that "certain acts" might ruin everything.

"I have always been repelled by this attitude toward the ultimate embrace of love," George protested to Grzymala. "If it is not as sacred, as pure, as consecrated an act as the rest, there is no virtue in abstaining. The word *physical* which people use to describe something which has no name except in a higher region, displeases and *shocks* me. . . . Was there ever love without a kiss, or a kiss of love without desire? . . . Tell me—what he said was stupid, was it not? And he did not mean it. Who could be the wretched woman who has left him with such feelings about physical love? . . . Poor angel!"

She closed the document with an invitation to the country. "As for the little one, he may come if he wishes. But in that case I'd like some advance notice, for then I shall send Mallefille to Paris or perhaps Geneva."

Chopin accepted. He was in love and, for perhaps the first time, completely. More important for the rejected suitor of Marie Wodzinska, George returned his love. "She loves me!" Chopin exclaimed in his private notebook. "Aurore, what a charming name!" For him it was not George Sand the novelist, the comrade of revolutionists who loved him, but the woman, Aurore.

Although George received ample warning of Chopin's arrival, Mallefille was at Nohant. So were Maurice and Solange and, for a time, according to some authorities, Liszt and the countess. The days passed pleasantly enough on the surface. The tensions were all internal. Maurice, now nearly sixteen, looked suspiciously on the new intimate. Solange, a hoyden of ten, took notice of Chopin and, half innocently, half in precocious rivalry, disputed his attention with the ladies. Mallefille's "malleable wax," much to George's surprise, seemed to have undergone a stubborn hardening in the proximity of Chopin, which made her wonder whether she had not overestimated her power when she had assured Grzymala that she could change the imprint at will. She hoped Mallefille would not prove too difficult when the time came—for she knew it would soon come. Only Liszt with whom her friendship remained friendship, seemed content with the status George accorded him.

Marie came out openly in her disapproval, although she gave the wrong reasons for it. Her fastidiousness could not countenance the simultaneous presence of Mallefille and Chopin in George's house. *In petto,* the true causes brooded. Chopin was fickle. There was nothing constant about him except his cough, as she heartlessly put it. Only a year ago he had been an assiduous admirer. He had even paid her the tribute of dedicating his first group of *Études* to her. The queen bee could not forgive his defection for the sake of a woman who had not half her beauty, in whom she saw no beauty, if the truth were told. When she and George parted that July, before Marie left for Italy with Liszt, both knew that their friendship, never solidly founded, had toppled. George, always sentimental, tried to keep alive at least the illusion of it. Marie, on the contrary, shot off her barbs. "Chopin," she sneered, "that oyster dredged in sugar!"

She said her final word on George, too, modeled on Liszt's "butterfly" criticism. "Her lovers are like a piece of chalk to her. She scratches with them on the blackboard. When she has done, she crushes the chalk underfoot and nothing is left but the dust, which quickly blows away."

Chopin alone found what he wanted, the peaceful routine of family life with its simple joys and privacy for work, work which to him meant more pain than delight. He looked at Maurice, sensitive, sickly, George's spoiled darling, and wished himself in the boy's place. Why should he not have a home at last? He could do so much in a congenial household where the need for solitude was understood and respected.

He had already published more than thirty works, among them his two *Concertos,* the *E Minor* and the *F Minor;* his *Ballade in G Minor;* the two *Polonaises in C Sharp Minor* and *E Flat Minor* and a number of waltzes, mazurkas, nocturnes, variations; a *Grande Fantaisie on Polish Airs* with orchestral accompaniment, the first series of *Études,* and other compositions. Europe had detected the new idiom in his works and reacted with praise and criticism. All, however, agreed that it was music and it was

Chopin. He looked as much his music as his music expressed the man. Whenever he sat down at the candlelit piano, it was as if his compositions had taken physical form; when he played one would have thought he was melting away into music. Ernest Legouvé called him a harmonious trinity in the unity of the man, his music and the Romantic melancholy that pervaded them.

The summer over, Chopin returned to Paris. His stay in the country had done him good. He had played, he had worked, he had satisfied himself that he was happy in the society of George Sand. George too had only agreeable memories of their association, although she feared a problem in Maurice's jealous attachment to her. Mallefille also worried her. When she went to Paris late in August, she made sure to send Maurice and his tutor on a vacation to Le Havre, and saw Chopin alone. She had no doubt that they could live together in a productive domesticity.

Mauprat, recently published, revealed a change of heart in the creator of *Lélia.* She no longer cursed marriage as the legalized enslavement of woman, and went so far as to discern moral beauty in its principles. Her heroine, Edmée, far from suffering the martyrdom of an Indiana, becomes a female Pygmalion who succeeds in converting her husband, Bernard, from a clod to a spiritual being. After such a stride forward George's progress was marked on the road to a higher life. *Spiridion,* which she had been writing during Chopin's visit, was both a name and a symbol. In *Mauprat* she had purged marriage of its evil. In *Spiridion* she would effect the same catharsis for religion. Buloz, informed of the theme of the new novel, tore out his hair in exasperation. When, oh when, would George return to romance?

By the middle of October George and Chopin had agreed to join their lives in "the poem" of their free election. Chopin made a bundle of Marie Wodzinska's letters, pressed the crumbling rose among them and tied them about with ribbon. *"Moja Bieda"*[2] he wrote on the wrapper, tracing beneath the words a symbolic cross. He put the packet away among his records of the past and the handful of Polish soil which he had taken with him on his voluntary exile.

[2] Polish, "My Sorrow."

Chapter XXII: At the Charterhouse of Valdemosa

GEORGE had decided to take her family, augmented by Chopin and a *bonne*, to Majorca for the winter. Maurice had to have a warm climate for his rheumatism, Chopin's doctor advised change for his health, while George needed novel surroundings to refresh her creative springs as well as to facilitate her transit from Mallefille to his successor. The indocile tutor had finally been brought to reason by the uncouth Pierre Leroux, whom George insisted on regarding as a combination of Christ and Plato, in spite of proofs to the contrary strangely patent to less partial eyes. A few months' absence would also help to effect Mallefille's cure.

Accordingly George, the children and the *bonne* left Paris on the eighteenth of October. Chopin, to save appearances, arranged to meet them at Perpignan, from where they would proceed together. The fastidious Chopin, however, was given leeway to conciliate the guardians of morality should he decide to change his mind at the last moment. At any rate, they agreed that if he did not appear at Perpignan by the end of October, George and her party would go on without him.

Chopin arrived, however, "fresh as a rose and rosy as a turnip," as George announced to Madame Marliani, whose Spanish friends had suggested Majorca for the lovers' hibernal Eden. For a sick man he had borne nobly the four days and nights by coach, which strengthened George's confidence in the doctor's assurance that Chopin's lungs were not affected. If she had any forebodings on Chopin's account, they were based on his hate of change, even in his slightest habits, and this was a major revolution, involving the absence of his Polish friends and the temporary privation of his piano. But a piano would arrive as soon as they were settled, and the friends had promised to write. George knew, too, that Chopin had financial worries. He had had to borrow from the banker, August Leo. But which of her lovers, for that matter, which of her friends, had ever been solvent? In Chopin's case, lack of money resulted from no lack of industry. However, he had relinquished the most remunerative source of income from his loathing of public performances. His lessons brought him little besides an entrée into aristocratic circles, while his music was still too daring in its innovation to return adequate royalties.[1]

From Perpignan the party sailed on the *Phénicien* via Port-Vendres to Barcelona, where they took the larger *El Mallorquin* which landed them, uneventfully except for Solange's *mal-de-mer*, at Palma, Majorca's capital. The weather was everything George could have desired for her two invalids, but what was her dismay when the chief city of the Balearic Eden turned out to be as unprovided with hotels as the garden of Adam and Eve. Could Madame Marliani's friends have spoken from experience in their unqualified recommendation? George began to have her doubts.

For a week she allocated her group as best she could in two rooms of a boardinghouse while she went hunting for larger and more suitable quarters. Chopin was beginning to fret. The small villa which George found outside the city raised his spirits; at least he would not have to eat the greasy boardinghouse food. More important still, he would have a room of his own. "Go to Pleyel," he begged his friend Jules Fontana, a fellow pupil under his old teacher, Joseph Elsner. "The piano has not come as yet. How did they ship it?" He was working on some *préludes* and he needed his instrument.

The *Son Vent*, or the House of the Winds, had more disadvantages than met the eye in spite of its view of turquoise skies, lapis lazuli water, emerald hills and other gemlike enchantments described by Chopin, as if to demonstrate that he too could wield a colorful pen. The furnishings were of the most elementary and there was no way of heating the house except by open braziers which filled the rooms with smoke. During the beginning of their stay they were happy and comfortable enough. The weather resembled a Paris June, while the landscape was a Luxembourg garden where pomegranate and almond grew wild and cypress and palm introduced an exotic note, in keeping with the Moorish architecture of the houses below.

"Everything turns toward Africa, like the town," said Chopin. Everything except the season, alas, as they discovered when the rains set in and the villa offered no more protection than a rook's nest. The moisture seeped in through the cracks in the walls; the windows, blank in the sheets of rain, blotted out the landscape. The house hugged their shoulders like a mantle of ice. Chopin coughed in the fumes of the braziers and shivered in the inexorable cold. Then he began to spit blood. The doctors were sent for from Palma.

"One examined what I spat," Chopin wrote Fontana with a

[1] William Murdoch in his *Chopin: His Life* says, "He cannot have earned more than 25,000 francs during his whole life."

macabre humor that he often indulged in. "The second knocked where I spat from. The third . . . listened. One pronounced me dead, the second dying, while the third said I would surely die." All agreed that they must bleed him, which Chopin and George prevented with difficulty.

Far from helping, their visit resulted indirectly in mischief by arousing the suspicion of Señor Gomez, the landlord, and the people of Palma. The foreigner coughed. He had consumption, and consumption according to the Majorcans, was more to be dreaded than a visitation of the devil. For, half a century before the isolation of the tubercle bacillus, they had discovered the contagiousness of the disease, so that whenever they found it in their midst, they treated it as a menace to the whole community.

George looked at her poor invalid, frailer and paler than ever, and her heart was wrung. His whole life seemed turning gray like the world in the incessant rain. If only he had not insisted on accompanying her and the children on the three-mile walk to a ruined hermitage! When she wrote of that excursion in *Un Hiver à Majorque,* she attributed to Chopin's severe exhaustion, during the wind and the rainstorm, the first serious onslaught of his phthisis.

The hostility of the Majorcans was not long in manifesting itself. The male servant George had engaged turned sullen and threatened to leave. "He is a brute, bigoted, lazy and voracious, a real son of a monk—as I believe they all are," she complained, forgetting in her indignation the loftiness of her *Spiridion,* the first part of which was already appearing in the *Revue.* If she could have some relief from nursing, cooking, tutoring and house cleaning, she might finish the novel in its proper setting, at the charterhouse of Valdemosa where, she learned, a small block of cells might soon be available. Chopin received the idea with delight. Any change would be welcome.

A few days after the doctors' consultation George had a letter from the landlord, who would not risk a personal visit, requesting their immediate removal. He did not tolerate consumptives in his house. Furthermore, he demanded to have the rooms replastered, and the walls whitewashed. He also insisted on their paying for the linen they had used.

George was incensed at such brutality for its effect upon Chopin. She knew his dread of the family disease, a dread so haunting that he never allowed himself to speak of it. The pointed antagonism of the Majorcans embittered her for the mental anguish which it added to Chopin's physical pain. The shopkeepers refused to sell to them. In the streets of the town they were shunned like so many lepers.

She waited as anxiously as Chopin for the piano to arrive. He had been working on the *Préludes* and on a new *Ballade, in F Major,* that began like his own heartbeats set to music. If he had his instrument he might forget to brood upon his sickness and upon the effect news of it might have upon his publisher, Pleyel, who had advanced him money. He might not fret about Fontana's reliability in posting Chopin's letters from Paris, so that they would bear a Paris postmark and his relatives in Warsaw would have no suspicion that he was at Majorca with Madame Sand in an illicit intimacy. He worried about so many things in his morbidity.

Most of all he suffered from his incapacity to work. "I hope soon to be sending you my *Préludes* and a *Ballade,*" he promised in his letters to Fontana. "I heard that the piano was shipped on the 1st of December," he wrote again, and noting that the letter had taken a fortnight to arrive, predicted gloomily that the piano would be spending the winter on the dock. "In the meantime my manuscripts sleep and I cannot."

But he had good news, also. "Tomorrow I move to the ravishing monastery of Valdemosa, to live, dream and write in the cell of some ancient monk who had more fire in his soul, perhaps, than I . . . and who smothered and quenched it because he had it in vain. . . ." The letter was dated December 14.

Within a few days they were all settled in their new home, a group of cells in one of the more recent cloisters of the half-ruined monastery of Valdemosa. Two years earlier, the charter-house on the crest of the Valdemosa Mountains, had been threatened with destruction when the government of Mendizabal decreed the demolition of all monasteries occupied by fewer than a dozen monks. Valdemosa housed thirteen friars at the time, and so was spared. It was discontinued, however, as a monastery, and for several seasons its cells had been rented out to tourists during the spring.

For haunting beauty George and Chopin could have wanted no better setting. The massive buildings, with their masonry obliterated by century-old creepers, appeared all of an age in the mellowing of time. The three cloisters, the oldest dating from before the fifteenth century, were encircled by a gallery upon which opened the monastic cells. Pillars and arched windows, cypresses and ivy-grown ruins, thick oaken doors, tree-lined alleys, all might have been evoked from a Gothic romance and materialized in the solitude between sea and sky of a mountain height. "We have one of the most poetic cemeteries imaginable," wrote Chopin, as much in love as George with the melancholy of death. "It's only my piano that's missing."

They occupied three vast rooms which had recently been

vacated by a tourist and his family who sold George the furnishings for a thousand francs.

In his present despondency Chopin gave way to macabre imaginings. His vaulted cell became a huge coffin standing on end. The cypresses outside his window added to the funereal atmosphere. His door, solid as the slab of a tomb, shut him in as irrevocably. Even George and the children could not be heard in their many activities indoors and out. "The works of Bach, my rough drafts and manuscripts not my own, these are my furnishings," he wrote, alluding to the edition of Bach which he was editing for publication. "Silence—one could scream and there would still be silence," he burst out in the same letter as if the stillness were more than he could bear.

If he left his room, he stepped out upon the somber cloisters enclosing the cemetery like a motto in a moralistic sampler. A great cross, of bleached wood, flung out its ghostly arms within its circle of cypresses. But the little Hispano-Arab church, all carved wood and colored tile, with a font in every chapel, had an air of cheerful faith that dispelled gloom, like the blossoming of the winter roses in the snow of the surrounding gardens.

They were not alone in their monastery. Maria Antonia, whom George might have qualified as "a daughter of a monk," so much did the woman resemble the male servant of *Son Vent,* was a self-appointed maid of all work who insisted on being employed by the Sand ménage, as she was by the other two inhabitants, the apothecary and the sacristan. She was prying, dishonest and a general nuisance, but there was no avoiding her. She was as much part of the place as the hungry eagles that came to prey upon the sparrows on the very window ledges, as the winter drove them down from their rocky eyries.

George's novel languished. After a day devoted to tutoring her children, to cooking for Chopin who could eat no food but hers, to marketing in Palma and, for the amusement of Maurice and Solange, to endless explorations of the monastery grounds, she was too tired to write. As Chopin's morbidity deepened, she went out only to make purchases in town, and spent most of the day with her invalid. He was a trying patient. His nerves, sensitive as the strings of an instrument, responded to every breath. Although he bore his sickness with the fortitude of a martyr, he became maniacal over trifles. He never complained but brooded, leaving George to guess at the cause of his moods. Sometimes, when she returned after some necessary errand, she would find him, pale and staring, his hair on end, before specters summoned by his imagination. For the psychic powers which his friends attributed to him worked overtime at Valdemosa, to plague him with their terrors.

234

The piano arrived at last and with it a miraculous life. It was put into Chopin's room and soon "the vaults rejoiced at the wonderful sounds." Chopin's health, if not his spirits, improved with the best medicine that could have been prescribed. He worked again, and his active imagination, dispelling specters, spent itself on the *Ballade,* on a scherzo, two impromptus, the *Sonata in B Flat Minor* and new polonaises and mazurkas. They were not to be published till two years later, but they were conceived, and some of them completed, at Valdemosa. George too was able to work again. *Spiridion* was finished and she plunged immediately into the revision of *Lélia* which she had begun while waiting for her suit to go through its many hearings.

"Maurice and Solange study with me six hours a day," she wrote Madame Marliani. "They are very industrious, and Solange has been almost constantly charming since her seasickness. Maurice insists that she got rid of all her spitefulness. At night I write *Lélia,* which will be quite different from what it was."

Different, but unfortunately, not better.

Like Musset in Venice, Chopin, dependent upon George, counted every hour she spent away from him, whether she wrote or devoted the time to her children. Maurice resented Chopin and showed it. The boy was no longer the infant of the earlier affairs. He was precociously aware, and so jealously bound to George that he even tried to dispossess Solange from his mother's affection. In Chopin he saw a serious rival, sickly like him, and like him exacting to the point of tyranny. It was the most powerful tyranny of all, of the weak over the strong, and one that George could never resist.

As the winter increased in severity, they spent most of the time indoors. Snow covered pomegranate and palm, and the cypresses stood like great white tapers in the gardens. Mists shrouded the mountaintops. The screams of the eagles, disputing their prey with the vultures among the branches of the pomegranates just outside the windows, filled Chopin with irrepressible horror. He was obsessed with the thought of death and George, receptive to his moods, lived in daily expectation of calamity. One night, as they were all gathered together, reading and working, they were frozen by a weird howling. It was not the wind, for with its ceaseless wail they were too familiar. As they listened it came closer and closer, the sound punctuated by a clicking like bones knocked together. Chopin's face was a mask of terror when, as they peered out, they saw a procession of moving lights. As the red and white flares approached they could make out a company of devils in a wild dance. Chopin looked from them to George and the children. They would believe him now when he told them of the apparitions that haunted him.

But the fearful devils turned out to be Majorcans in masquerade, in their traditional celebration of the Mardi Gras, and the howling nothing more sinister than their singing of an eerie cantilena to the accompaniment of castanets.

Chopin, however, was not rid of his visionary fears. He still saw the phantoms of the long-dead monks gliding past him in the corridors. He still heard their ghostly voices in the wind. Death, death everywhere. It was almost as if Chopin had prepared his prothalamion in the funeral march which he had recently introduced into the *B Minor Sonata*. George, turned superstitious in her love, reflected him like another self. "Death seemed to hover overhead, ready to swoop upon one of us, and we were alone to dispute him his prey." To the overwrought Chopin sometimes it seemed as if death had succeeded, he became so much the victim of his hallucinations.

One day George had to go to Palma for supplies and took Maurice with her. They started out on a clear afternoon, leaving Chopin in spirits as fair as the weather. Suddenly the clouds burst and the two found themselves miles from home and with no means of returning except a rickety coach which its owner at first refused to risk on the rough roads. Lured by the money he ventured on the uphill drive.

The streams, swelled in the downpour, had overflowed. The coachman was terrified, and dumping his passengers on the road, drove back to town. George and Maurice who, fortunately, knew their way, groped ahead on foot in the darkness. They had only three miles to go, but it took them six hours to walk them in the tearing rain, along roads that had become river beds jagged with loosened stones. Their shoes were ripped off and left somewhere on the way. When they reached Valdemosa in the middle of the night, they might have been two ghosts, returned to the world by swimming across Lethe.

They heard Chopin's piano and followed a solemn, unearthly music to his room. A ghost was sitting at the keys, his face frozen to resigned despair as the tears flowed down his cheeks. The instant he saw them he started up with a shriek. "Ah, I knew it!" he cried in a strange daze. "I knew that you were dead."

It took some time before George could convince him that they were safe and then he sickened with anxiety at the dangers they had passed. When he could talk he reconstructed his hallucination. He had been almost insane with worry as he waited for them to come home after the outbreak of the storm and sat down at the piano to quiet his fears. He grew tranquil as he played, and then drowsy. And then it seemed as if he himself had died, drowned in the bottom of a lake. Chill, heavy drops seemed to fall rhythmically upon his chest. When George and Maurice appeared, streaming and spent, he knew they were all meeting in another world.

"There are your chill, heavy drops," said George, bidding him listen to the measured thud of the rain on the tiles. It was the rhythm, she implied, which he had translated into the music he had been playing when they entered. "It is imitative harmony," she added.

Chopin came out of his trance at the words. There was no imitation, even of nature's harmonies in his music, he retorted sharply. Such imitation was beneath him in its puerility. The music he made was no repetition of what he heard; it came from within, in harmonies audible only to his imagination. "The composition of that night," George wrote in her *Histoire de Ma Vie,* "was indeed full of the raindrops that resounded on the echoing tiles of the monastery, but they had been transmuted by his imagination." It became one of the *Twenty-Four Préludes* which Chopin published in 1839.

Finally, in the face of their many discomforts, the forlorn group had no choice but to leave their hostile paradise. But alas, it was sooner planned than done. Majorca did a thriving commerce in pigs, which it exported to the Continent. The robust looking creatures were poor travelers, however, and for the sake of their sensitive stomachs, as well as to preserve their sales value during the crossing, the Majorcans sailed only in weather most favorable to their cargo. It took a fortnight before the same *El Mallorquin* which had deposited George's party on the shores of Majorca was ready to take them (and the pigs) to Barcelona.

Chopin had never felt worse. The short drive from the monastery to Palma had brought on a hemorrhage. On the boat George did not leave his side, fearing for his life when she saw his acute suffering in the pestilential atmosphere of a hundred pigs. Knowing him, she was almost certain he would not make that crossing, but a farther one to the borderlands he had so often touched in his morbid imaginings. Everything that happened, which would merely annoy another, caused him a minor death. "That was his sickness," George diagnosed. "His soul was flayed to the quick. The wrinkle of a rose petal, the shadow of a fly, would make him bleed."

Somehow, in the middle of February, they arrived at Barcelona. On the twenty-ninth of the month they reached Marseilles, and almost at once Chopin began to improve. "Another month, and Chopin and I would have given up the ghost in Spain," George wrote, "Chopin of melancholia and I of anger and indignation. The Spaniards have struck at my sensitive spot. They

237

have tormented a suffering being with pinpricks before my very eyes. I shall never forgive them that, and if ever I write of them, it will be with gall. . . . Chopin no longer spits blood, he rests well, coughs little and, best of all, he is in France. He can sleep in a bed which won't be burned because he has lain in it. He won't see anyone recoil when he holds out his hand."

They were so happy to be on friendly soil again that they decided to spend the spring at Marseilles. They put up at the Hôtel de Beauvau. Dr. Cauvières, a friend of George's, gave such a favorable report upon examing Chopin that death, which had hung so close, ceased haunting them. They set to work immediately, Chopin on his music, George on an article. To keep tongues from wagging, Chopin asked his friends to write him at the Beauvau, while George received her mail at Dr. Cauvières'.

The Marseilles musical and literary bohemia, however, lost no time in ferreting out the famous visitors, and soon both George and Chopin were besieged by unpublished poets seeking prefaces; by unheard musical geniuses, their scores under their arms, anxious to give Chopin the privilege of discovering them; by beggars and thrill seekers, in fact, by the harbor city's equivalent of the Paris horde that clamored at George's door on the appearance of every new novel. George tried to protect herself and Chopin as best she could, and wrote amusingly to Madame Marliani: "Don't be alarmed if news reaches you from here that I am dying. . . . As for Chopin, at the moment I've given out that he's already dead, and if this sort of thing continues, we're going to send abroad letters inviting people to attend our joint funeral, so that they'll mourn us and leave us in peace."

Chopin, now tied to George by his dependence, looked upon the "poem of their marriage" as permanent, and so far abandoned his customary reticence as to inform Grzymala on the twenty-seventh of March that "My lady" had just finished writing a magnificent article on Goethe, Byron and Adam Mickiewicz, the Polish poet who had already inspired a number of Chopin's compositions. Mickiewicz's association with two giants of Romanticism contained George's subtle compliment to her "little one's" love of everything Polish. Besides, the article might help Mickiewicz whom she knew and admired, for George never hesitated to use her influence for a fellow writer.

"My angel is finishing a new novel, *Gabriel*," Chopin wrote still more intimately to the count. "Today she is writing in bed. . . . You would love her even more if you knew her as I now know her."

The letter was dated the twelfth of April, 1839. Earlier in the month, perhaps to escape their plague of locusts, George, Chopin and the children had made a brief excursion to Genoa. The

238

Italian city, which delighted Frédéric, suscitated in George memories of an earlier visit with another whom she had loved as she did not love Chopin, as she could never love again. It was in Genoa that she had been ill. Here it was that Musset, despotic in his jealousy and rebellion, had begun their joint martyrdom. What psychological factors had worked against them and their love? Why had that love not blossomed into the example of human devotion they had dreamed, when they compared themselves to the famous lovers of history? They had loved and yet they had almost destroyed each other. Why? Whose fault? Now she was tied to another being whom she cherished like a son. How long would this love last? What faults in him, in her, would bring it to a disastrous conclusion? Of what crimes would he accuse her before the end?

She put herself through a rigid self-analysis, and in the complicated processes of the creative brain, the germ of *Gabriel-Gabrielle* was conceived. George may have begun to write the novel in Genoa in her impatience to give it birth. The very compulsion to rid herself of it as quickly as possible had the urgency of a confession. The story, in the style of the "armchair dramas" which Musset so skillfully handled, had its source in George's adolescent years, and Gabrielle is none other than Aurore Dupin dressed in boys' clothes and brought up by Deschartres to mistrust her femininity.

Apart from the exigencies of the plot, the novel makes its appeal chiefly through the vitality of Gabrielle and the dissolute Astolphe and the authenticity of their love and conflict. Most significant are the psychological implications which Balzac was quick to detect when he praised George for *Gabrielle* as he had never praised her before. At thirty-five George had acquired the painful knowledge that woman cannot usurp with impunity the prerogatives of man. Her own character had been shaped by external forces too strong for her to cope with; they had nevertheless found the material responsive. Perhaps without her being aware of it, George had externalized in *Gabriel-Gabrielle* a latent apprehension of her way of life. The fact is that from 1839 on, she exercised her masculine will toward a more feminine life in a responsible domesticity shared by a man whom she loved, for the first time literally, with maternal tenderness.

Alfred de Musset had been much on her mind. Cruel words addressed to her in his *Nuit de Décembre* had wounded her by reawakening the old pain. Tales of his dissipation, moreover, had been coming to her through Pauline Garcia, Malibran's sister, who was making an almost equally brilliant career for herself as a singer. George was fond of the young girl who was soon to marry Louis Viardot, director of the Opéra Comique and associate of Pierre Leroux. She was shocked by accounts of Musset's libertinism, as if she had forgotten her own experience, and in her present access of virtue, found his drunkenness unforgivable. Alfred seemed to have lost all semblance of decency. He stalked women as if they were his prey and thought nothing of pursuing Pauline, Pauline's mother and the seventeen-year-old tragedienne, Rachel, at the same time.

Pauline had at first succumbed to the charm of the poet, though she had been warned by the bold stare of his red-rimmed eyes. She had been complimented, too, by the six-page article which he had devoted to her in the *Revue des Deux Mondes.* But she was revolted when she overheard him calculating aloud which of the two should fall to him first, Pauline or Rachel.

Doubtless the influence of similar talk stirred up the residue of bitterness in George's heart. At any rate, she let emotion dominate reason. In her re-writing of *Lélia,* remembering how Alfred had seen himself in her Sténio, she unloosed her scorn for his printed insult and for the graver insult of his debauched life, after what should have been the ennobling experience of his pain.

"Behold there below a dread phantom, howling in a tavern," she apostrophizes, harking back to the apparition of Fontainebleau. "What do they call him now? O thou specter, lift up thy trembling arm. . . . Drink as a challenge to the health of Lélia. . . . Go, go, Sténio will soon be no more than a wine sack fit to contain the fifty-seven vintages of the Archipelago. Lélia is not struck down because a man has cursed her. . . . Her heart still holds the apprehension of God. . . . Since when does one lose sight of the sun because an atom, which its rays have lighted, recoils again into the shadow?"

Musset was not slow to grasp the allusion although he did not retort until two years later, in his satirical *"Histoire d'un Merle Blanc."* He chose to take his revenge on George's prodigious torrent, his own poetic spring, alas, having now run dry. In the thinly veiled allegory of the white blackbird who falls in love with a little white female blackbird, a *merlette littéraire,* he taunts George for the crime he had resented more than her infidelity—her neglect of him, Alfred, for her work.

The satire had its barbs. "While I was composing my poems, she covered a ream of paper with her scribbling," complains the Merle Blanc. "I would recite my verses aloud to her, but that did not interfere with her writing in the least. . . . She hatched her novels with marvelous facility . . . choosing always the most dramatic subjects . . . taking care, incidentally, to attack the government and to preach the emancipation of all little female blackbirds. . . . She never had to scratch out a line, never to draw up a plan before she sat down to work. She was the model of the little literary blackbird."

From Marseilles, George requested Leroux, in Paris, to correct the proofs of *Lélia*. More and more she thought of home and a settled life. "I no longer love travel. Rather, I'm no longer in a position to enjoy it. I'm not a bachelor any more."

They left Marseilles on the twenty-second of May and returned to Nohant. On the left side of the casement window of her room George wrote in pencil, opposite the "Fading Sun" elegy she had scratched there as a young girl, the date: June 19, 1839.

George Sand had become Madame Sand.

Chapter XXIII: The Story of Fanchette

*S*PIRIDION, *Gabriel-Gabrielle, Un Hiver à Majorque, Pauline, Le Compagnon du Tour de France, Horace, Les Sept Cordes de la Lyre, Cosima,* a play, articles: George was writing at a terrific rate which, while it meant peace, also implied financial pressure. Her "poem" with Chopin had brought with it added responsibilities. Frédéric must be free to compose, and freedom meant relief from material worries. He too had been working as never before in a surge of energy which between 1839 and 1841 resulted in the publication of sixteen major compositions, among them the *Sonata in B Flat Minor,* the *Ballade in F Major* and the sunlit *A Flat Major,* three *Polonaises,* the *Fantaisie in F Minor,* besides the *Scherzo in C Sharp Minor,* an impromptu, nocturnes and waltzes. Always poetic, his music found depth and power which, implicit in the trial flights of his precocious imagination, now attained to the full wingspread of his eagle genius.

George's work, like her life, took on seriousness and stability. No longer goaded by the urgencies of her youth, she forsook subjective problems to consider the greater ills of humanity. Her *Pauline* was an exception. In the sober output of her maturity, this tale of a country girl who is taken to Paris, seduced, and then married by a man who threw riches into her lap, looks like a lurid exotic. It had been begun and abandoned immediately after *Indiana,* in 1832. When *Spiridion* appeared and George threatened to follow it with the still more unorthodox *Les Sept Cordes de la Lyre,* Buloz howled loud enough to be heard at Marseilles, from where George had written her literary factotum: "See to it that *Cordes de la Lyre* is published in the *Revue.* . . . Our friend Buloz demurs and recoils because it contains five or six bold phrases which the dear man is afraid will embroil him with his precious government. . . . Let him groan, let him weep hot tears at what he calls my *mysticism.* . . . The readers of the *Revue* must be educated to be a little less stupid, since I'm growing less stupid too, on my part . . ."

Buloz, however, resorted to the old expedient of withholding cash, and so George exhumed the half of *Pauline* which she had already written, composed the other half as quickly as if she had waved a wand, and threw the novel as a sop to her timid publisher, who was happy at last to have a book equally pleasing "to beautiful ladies as to their chambermaids"—a formula that had done much toward fattening his moneybags.

In the writing of the years between 1839 and 1843 which saw George's apogee in the literary sensation of *Consuelo,* she was gradually outgrowing Romanticism through novels of social import until, in 1844, with the publication of *Jeanne,* she sought eternal verities in her tales of simple folk. For the present, in *Spiridion, Les Sept Cordes de la Lyre, Le Compagnon du Tour de France, Horace,* and to a certain extent in the play *Cosima,* she acted as the inspired mouthpiece for the ideas of social betterment which men of good will were promulgating.

Spiridion, in which Pierre Leroux collaborated and which, more than any of George's novels alarmed her publisher, who expected both the government and the Church to close his shop, is George's quest, in the person of the young monk Alexis, of a true faith under the guidance of Lamennais who, in the novel, appears as the ghostly mentor, Spiridion. The book is a synthesis of the two men's teachings, Leroux providing the thesis of the continuity of progress, and Lamennais of the struggle of man toward spiritual perfection. In terms of poetic allegory, George traces her evolution from the near anarchy of her girlhood, through exalted Christian mysticism, to faith in the divinity of man, whose religion of brotherhood on earth was soon to be given the name of "Communism." The novel is written in a rapture of mysticism, as if Lélia, returned to earth as the monk Alexis, had learned the tongue of men and of angels. It is also a remarkable feat in that the characters are all male and that love, which everyone had learned to expect in a George Sand novel, appeared only in its highest manifestation, the divine.

Les Sept Cordes de la Lyre which no doubt influenced Ruskin's *Seven Lamps of Architecture,* published in 1849, is another exposition of Lamennais' religious doctrines crossed with Leroux' social theories, although the original impulse for writing it was given George by Michel as early as 1835. There is among her notes the drawing of a lyre, its strings bearing the names of Peace, War, Sorrows, Joys, Evocations, Love, God, with their translations into terms of daily living. George attributes the lyre symbol to Michel. Man's aspiration, according to George's thesis, is like a lyre and will attain to harmony with God only after his spirit has learned to vibrate in all its strings to the divine music.

Buloz turned thumbs down upon such symbolism, although rather than lose his author, he put the book through the press. He was obdurate, however, in his refusal of the novel, *Le Com-*

pagnon du Tour de France for serialization in the *Revue*. It was too revolutionary, too outspoken, too dangerous, too socialistic, in fact too much everything that Buloz associated with contemporary radicalism. George, disconcerted, took back her manuscript. It meant financial loss. More than that, it deprived her of the large body of magazine readers whom she wished to arouse to the importance of her message.

The novel came out as a volume only, and her relations with Buloz cooled perceptibly. It was certainly not the sort of book with which Buloz wished to be associated. For that matter, he was in accord with Chopin who knew the original of the novel's hero, Agricol Perdiguier, and suffered him as reluctantly as Boswell suffered Dr. Johnson's cat. Nohant and the Paris apartment at 16 Rue Pigalle saw too much of George's proletarian friends, a far cry from the princesses of Chopin's circle.

Somehow every awakened son of the people came, fiery-eyed, to sit at George's hearth, smoke her tobacco and fill the room with boisterous oratory. Chopin, whose studio was vis-à-vis George's in the Rue Pigalle pavilion, was sufficiently far removed to compose and give his lessons in peace. But it annoyed him that George should give up so much of her time to men and activities alien to his nature. A free Poland was his constant dream. He gave voice to it in his polonaises, in the ballades infused with the spirit of Mickiewicz' poetry. The brotherhood of man left him cold, and practical revolutionaries, like the poets of the people, Perdiguier and Poncy, social philosophers like the slovenly Leroux and his nondescript following, filled him with loathing.

Solange, who in the domestic camp aligned herself with Chopin against her mother and Maurice, shared his dislike. Both of them preferred it when the salon, decorated in tones of brown and buff, whose Chinese vases overflowed with flowers, with its Delacroix paintings and its genteel green furniture, with its candlelit rosewood piano and curio cabinet glinting with treasures, susurrated to the refined conversation of Chopin's friends to whom revolution was an abstraction and revolutionists were the troublemakers, kept in their place by the soldiers of Louis Philippe.

Agricol Perdiguier, a true son of the people, was a man in his early thirties who had started out as a journeyman-joiner, later acquired a knowledge of draftsmanship and art and who, when George met him, had opened a class in architectural design for Paris workmen. He had a natural poetic gift, like the people's poet Charles Poncy, and a revolutionary vision as broad as Leroux'. He placed his faith in brotherhoods or unions, as the practical means toward achieving the true republic, and he had

244

even written a book about them which he naïvely quoted as the gospel of the coming society. George had been struck by his life, one humble man's application of the Commandment, "Love thy neighbor as thyself," and, through Pierre Huguenin, the hero of her novel, she told his story.

Pierre, an idealistic young carpenter, while working with his father, enlarges his vision through books and, in his daily living, practices devotion and selflessness. He sees the workingman betrayed by his leaders and taught violence by ambitious zealots. He sees him victimized by a society which gives him the lowest place in its organization, and further alienates him from his fellows by trade union rivalries and dissensions. The vision of an indissoluble brotherhood held together by faith and love possesses him, and to its promulgation he dedicates his life.

The conservative press, of course, detected the cloven hoof of socialism under the laborer's smock of Pierre Huguenin, and raised its hue and cry. The foreword, by Mazzini, maker of revolutions, to *Le Compagnon,* wherein he hailed George Sand for tearing off the mask of a corrupt society, increased the alarm. But if the timid Bulozes and the *vieilles comtesses* shook nervously at the prospect of a world united by fraternal love, the workingmen, by far the largest class, rejoiced, and took the name of George Sand as the password to the future Republic.

When George Sand brought Buloz her *Horace,* a year after *Le Compagnon,* he refused to have anything to do with it, either as publisher or as editor of the *Revue.* Its proletarian-philosophic hero, Paul Arsène was, if possible, more dangerously radical than Huguenin and, worse, George saw fit to introduce actual history into the novel in the massacre at the Cloister St. Merry, whose horrors she had heard from her garret, and whose gruesome results she had seen in the severed heads lining the windows of the morgue. Moreover, George had now eschewed the semi-mystical style of Pierre Huguenin's preaching and come out boldly, calling to the proletariat to unite, for only through union could man fulfill the holy duties of his destiny. As if to dissociate himself publicly from George's radicalism, Buloz published in his review a denunciation of the principles implied in the upstart word, Communism. He must reassure his bourgeois readers that he stood on their side of the fence.

With *Horace* thrown back into her lap, George wrote Leroux for advice. "It is my moral opinion," he replied in his typical style, "that it is absurd and deplorable that Buloz' *Revue* should be the arbiter of your publications." Had she seen, he inquired, the diatribe in that same *Revue* against ideas which he and she were responsible for promulgating? "For, though you may not know it, dear friend, you are a Communist and I am a Communist." Only Lamennais, he regretted, did not wish to be connected with Communism, in which Leroux thought the philosopher mistaken. "It's the people, and certain writers of the people, who invented the word Communism, which is analogous in France to the Chartist movement in England . . . and means a republic based on equality." As for practical advice on the manuscript, he suggested its publication in the *Revue Indépendante*, a journal he had recently started in association with Louis Viardot—with George's financial help.

There *Horace* was published, with no modification of its message, and there also were to appear others of George's writings too daring for a commercial press. The *Revue Indépendante*, under Leroux' improvident management, meant a constant drain on George's resources, for she paid greatly for the support of the great man "according to whose gospel I bring up my son Maurice."

One of her social novels, *Le Péché de Monsieur Antoine* which fell into the transitional period between the Communist and the pastoral, was found too uncomfortable even for the radical journals. By an ironic fluke it was accepted by the obdurately conservative *Époque* which was willing to risk prosecution—hardly likely, considering its reputation—for the privilege of publishing a work by Madame Sand, who had meanwhile soared to unprecedented popularity with her *Consuelo* and *La Comtesse de Rudolstadt,* novels in which George's magician-like genius for weaving a romantic spell, had been exerted to further the revolutionary cause. *Le Péché de Monsieur Antoine* must have proved disappointing to many of its readers who expected Antoine's *péché* to uncover a sin of deepest dye, especially after the sensational publicity whereby the *Époque* had titillated public curiosity, only to find themselves absorbing a sociological treatise made exciting, however, by Madame Sand's verve and inventiveness.

Read today, there is nothing terrifying in the story of the conflict between Cardonnet, a forward-looking industrialist who brought "progress" to the rural district of Gargilesse, and his son Émile, who, far from seeing in the family mills the prosperity of the town, and in his father's wealth the legitimate rewards of enterprise, interprets them as the exploitation of the many for the profit of the individual. He refused to associate himself with his father's business, so as not to perpetuate social injustice, married the daughter of a carpenter—there is always a carpenter in George's social novels—and like Deucalion and Pyrrha, the two devoted themselves to the regeneration of humanity which is bound to come after the destruction of the present imperfect order.

In 1845 the humanitarian and social aspirations of George Sand's heroes hacked at the very root of Louis Philippe's power, the more so since the working class of France, educated to active protest by such books as Louis Blanc's *Organization of Labor* and Proudhon's *What is Property?*—a question which Proudhon answered with his defiant, "If this is property, then it is theft"—was becoming troublesome in its capably led, and effective, demonstrations. George Sand's novels, by the realistic presentation of existing conditions, and by the exhortative impact of her eloquence, fanned the revolutionary spark which despite the failure of the monster trial, leaders like Louis Blanc and Arago had been keeping alive.

Not in France alone did George's words reach the people, for throughout Europe they were heard and pondered. In Russia Dostoevski, as a boy of sixteen, had first read them in her novel *L'Uscoque* and spent a whole night in sleepless excitement. "It was George Sand," he wrote in his journal, "who was at the head of this evolution (toward an egalitarian society) . . . She was one of the noblest and finest of women—a name destined never to be forgotten. She was," he summed up, "the most consistent adept of Christ's teachings." Turgenev, too, was so much impressed by that same messianic quality, that he wrote to George Souvarine: "Believe me, George Sand is one of your saints. . . . In her presence one felt oneself before a profoundly generous and benevolent being in whom all egotism had long since been consumed by the inextinguishable fire of her faith in the ideal."

In translation her words carried their message across the Atlantic. A copy of *Le Compagnon du Tour de France,* or *The Journeyman-Joiner,* arrived at the office of the Brooklyn *Daily Eagle* for review, and on the twenty-seventh of September, 1847, Walt Whitman commented on it and upon its author whose reputation had preceded her book: "That Madame Sand's works are looked upon by a portion of the public, and of critics, with a feeling of great repugnance, there is no denying. But the talented Frenchwoman is nevertheless one of a class much needed in the world—needed lest the world stagnate in wrongs merely from precedent. We are fully of the belief that 'free discussion' upon any subject of general and profound interest is not only allowable, but in most cases desirable . . . *The Journeyman-Joiner* is a work of very great interest as a story. Indeed we know of few that are more so."

Whitman was noncommittal about the book, but then, he may have had his secret reasons.[1]

[1] See Esther Shephard's tracing of Walt Whitman's personality as the poet of humanity and the carpenter-comrade to *The Journeyman-Joiner* in her *Walt Whitman's Pose.*

After reading *Gabriel-Gabrielle*, Balzac suggested to George that she make a play of it. But she did not enjoy reworking old material. Besides, the limitations of the subject could not have borne the injection of the antiorthodox ideas which she now felt obliged to advance. She wrote the drama *Cosima* instead, an adroit exposition of her newly espoused gospel in terms sufficiently subtle to woo the audience by amusing it. She needed money, now more than ever, "with three persons to clothe," as she wrote Hippolyte. "Whether I stay in the country or live in the city, I must spin twenty-thousand francs a year out of my head." Marie Dorval, moreover, had been languishing for a leading rôle, what with the rise of younger actresses and the fickleness of the public.

Cosima opened on the twenty-ninth of April, 1840. George, with friends like Heine posted about ready to applaud, watched from her box the audience of the Théâtre Français. (There is no word of whether Chopin attended.) The curtain had hardly risen when the temper of the spectators revealed itself.

In his *Paris Letter* of April 30, Heine was certain that all of George's political enemies had gathered to whistle the play down. The author was inclined to agree with him when she described the event to her old friend and engraver, Luigi Calamatta. "I was hooted and whistled at with a ferocity I hardly expected. Every word that you and my friends admired and approved roused bursts of laughter and storms of indignation. Everywhere people shouted that the play was immoral. . . . I had no illusions that it was a work of art, but I'll insist to the end that it was completely honest."

Accustomed as she was to public acceptance, George, like Musset under similar circumstances, was shaken in her assurance by the play's "doubtful success or downright fiasco," as Heine described it. It took nearly a decade for her to try the stage again.

George and Chopin had meanwhile moved from the Rue Pigalle to a modern building on the Rue Saint-Lazare, in the Square d'Orléans where, still to preserve appearances, but also to allow of their working independently, they occupied two apartments, Nos. 5 and 9, with old Madame Marliani, an amiable buffer, between them at No. 7.

Besides performing her function of chaperone Madame Marliani also took it upon herself to simplify the housekeeping arrangements of her two famous neighbors by having their dinners served in her dining room and by helping them receive their acquaintances in her salon. Intimate friends George and Chopin entertained either in George's delightful parlor, or in Chopin's music room whenever he chose to play for them. Maurice had his bedroom and studio—he was studying painting with Delacroix

—above his mother's apartment; Solange's sitting room was next to George's. Solange used it only when she came home from the boarding school of Madame Ferdinand Bascans, who had been reluctant at first to enroll George Sand's daughter for fear of losing her *pensionnaires.* The girl was delighted with her little salon and exhibited it to overawe her cousin, Oscar Casamajou, Caroline's son, and Augustine Brault, a quiet, un-assuming girl, a distant relative of George's on her *côté de chez Delaborde,* whom she had taken to live with her to save her from the influence of a disreputable family. Oscar, too, George had half adopted in her all embracing motherliness, and sent to school at her expense. Solange and Chopin tolerated these common cousins, but wished George had cultivated her aristocratic acquaintance instead.

The Sand-Chopin union was working out better than officious parties on both sides had either anticipated or desired. Chopin's compatriots and titled patronesses had doubted that it would last. The novelist and the musician were the very reverse of the Goethean elective affinities. They had scarcely one friend in common, except perhaps for Liszt, Delacroix and Heine, and their interests were as opposed as those of the two classes to which they had elected to adhere. Even the household was one divided against itself, George and the long-haired Raphaelite Maurice forming a close communion against Chopin's partisanship with the snobbish, tempestuous Solange who, no doubt like the possessive Chopin, suffered from the obvious exclusiveness of George's sentimental affinity to her son. George had still to declare, "My true source of strength always came from my son," but the fact struck the two jealously vigilant stepchildren between the eyes.

Nevertheless, the union might have been counted successful. While far from the real-life romance which the uninitiate chose to make of it, it was sufficiently unconventional to lend the relationship a poetic nimbus. George accepted Chopin for what he was. She revered him for his genius and was humbly touched whenever he consulted her about his music—"For he came to me for advice as Molière went to his housekeeper." Although they shared no opinions outside of his art, although they were at opposite poles in politics and held entirely different views of life, George had too much respect for Chopin's individuality to seek to modify it in the least. She took him in with her nest of starlings like some wonderful bird of paradise whose ways were difficult, whose needs excessive, but whom, because he was at a disadvantage in an alien world, she must protect, sometimes even against himself.

Chopin, on his side, gave her the utter trust of the stranger who had at last found a home. Unsympathetic to her researches, her convictions and the proletarian swarm that buzzed noisily wherever she happened to be, he clung to her for her warmth and protectiveness. Her strength gave confidence to his weakness. Her energy drove away the phantoms which, after the death of his father, followed immediately by that of his closest friend, Jean Matuszinski, of consumption, had possessed him more tenaciously than the ghosts of Valdemosa. Because he had given himself to her as never before to any individual, he expected a reciprocal surrender and therefore suffered from George's unexclusive expansiveness. He wished to be the center of her life, but gradually found himself in the periphery, not so far removed as Solange, but certainly not so close as Maurice who, together with her work, came nearest to George's essential being.

Feeling excluded, Chopin sometimes turned sharply against whatever took precedence over him. Everyone could see, and many made note, how the rivalry deepened between the lover and the son, who knew the place he held in his mother's life and had no intention of relinquishing it. The Countess d'Agoult in her letters, described the youth as "very disagreeable, an out and out bad lot," which must be accepted with some allowance for the countess' usual causticity. Maurice was indeed spoiled and possessed of those faults of character that come of being indulged. Even though talented in painting and writing, and with an adoring presence constantly at his elbow providing encouragement and opportunity, Maurice never rose above the accomplishment of an amateur, even if the Sand influence ultimately obtained him a medal at the Salon and an honorary decoration. His novels never succeeded in being more than the scrub in the shadow of his mother's oaks. As a person he had none of her largeness and generosity. Chopin's entrance upon the scene in the crucial years of Maurice's development had inflicted a psychic trauma which seriously affected the man.

For the most part an outward cordiality existed between the rivals. Like his mother and Solange, Maurice called him Fritz, Chopinet, Chip-Chip, Chip-Chop and other absurd pet names. But he was of an age to resent the liaison, and even more the intruder who had authority and yet was not his father, who was part of the household and had no legal right to be there. Jealousy and hate took such a deep root that when Maurice edited his mother's correspondence he endeavored to omit all mention of Chopin.

On her side Solange contributed to the complexity. During the progress of the relationship she entered from girlhood into womanhood. At first she wooed Chopin as her ally by innocent coquetry and then by precocious wiles which George, in her astonishment, believed herself to be imagining. The young girl was handsome, fresh and fair-haired like her great-grandmother Aurore de Saxe and, like her, cold, though with a semblance of passion which deceived one on the frigidity within. She had always been a problem, rebellious, untamable, with the vanity and instability of Sophie, but with a desire to destroy which was wholly her own.

There is an account of her being taken through the garden of Pauline Viardot. As the young hostess, walking ahead with George, pointed out with pride the flowering borders which she had grown at great pains, she was aware of an intermittent swishing noise behind her. Turning about, she saw Solange systematically decapitating tulips and jonquils with lashes of her riding crop, her eyes shining in enjoyment of the destruction. "She was evil, evil for evil's sake," Pauline Viardot condemned when the words held still greater justification.

From childhood Solange had never known the security of undisputed affection, for neither George nor Casimir had ever made a pet of her, for reasons implicit in as yet unpublished correspondence, reasons with which Solange herself taunted her mother in subsequent years, when she declared herself not to be Casimir's daughter. Her irregular upbringing had contributed to her turbulent character: the early years with Casimir at Nohant, then with her mother in the Paris garret, among the bohemian crew who filled the place with smoke and noise; the vacations in the country and the ensuing scenes between Casimir and George, witnessed and heard by the children; finally the unexplained entrance into the family circle of a young man, not many years older than Maurice. Even a girl more fortunately endowed would have borne the marks of such influences.

With a shrewdness beyond her years, the child had known how to utilize the emotional crosscurrents arising from the complicated circumstances. Little by little she had insinuated herself into Chopin's reserve since, at bottom, they shared the same grievances. As the years passed the two stood solid against the common "enemy," Maurice.

At sixteen, Solange left Madame Bascans' boarding school without completing her courses. With her at home the situation grew more tense. George undertook to round out the girl's education by trying to interest her in social problems, perhaps to offset her *airs de princesse*. No doubt there was some such implication when she dedicated her socialist novel, *Le Meunier d'Angibault* "To Solange. . . . My child, let us seek together."

The offer was lost upon Solange. She knew what she wanted: money, position, independence—and as quickly as possible. George studied her daughter and son, and judged them with the unreasoning heart. "There's only one sex, really," she concluded. "I have watched the development of my son and daughter. My son was myself and therefore more of a woman than my daughter, who was only an unachieved man."

Visitors who called at the Square d'Orléans carried away their impressions and lost no time in setting them down for posterity. The reports are not without their bias, most of the callers arriving with preconceived notions which they immediately set about proving. Wilhelm von Lenz, a Petersburg pianist introduced by Liszt, started his researches with the concièrge.

"And what's the real name of the lady—is it Dudevant?" he prompted, bringing out the retort, good for a laugh in an anecdote, "Ah, sir, she has so *many* names!"

Monsieur von Lenz did not like Madame Sand. She was too silent, too withdrawn, which was not complimentary to a talented musician who played for her and Chopin. At one point, he recorded, "she produced an enormous *trabuco* cigar from the pocket of her apron, shouting across the room, 'Frédéric, a light!' I was outraged for my great master's sake . . . as he swung docilely toward her with a *fidibus* match."

Madame Juste Olivier, the poetess, who met George Sand and Chopin through Mickiewicz, wrote in her diary, "Mickiewicz thinks Chopin is her evil genius, her moral vampire, her cross, that he torments her and will probably end by being the death of her."

Karl Gutzkow, another caller, painted a Rembrandt interior of dim lights and tension wherein the ticking of the clock gave the only sign of life. George struck him as distant and ungracious, Chopin as unhappy.

The truth lay between the extremes. George could no longer love with the impulsiveness of thirty years. Moreover, she was concerned for Chopin's health, as she told Grzymala. Gradually she imposed virtual chastity. Chopin, suspicious, became embittered. He imagined that she was deceiving him with her numerous friends, and when he could prove nothing because there was nothing to prove, he consumed himself, like Musset before him, in retrospective jealousy. In him, for whom reality had no existence, suspicion grew out of all proportion. He would brood for days in a silence that even Solange could not break, until, in a fit of hysteria, he would tear his cuffs and handkerchiefs to ribbons.

But the picture was not uniformly somber. He had his playful moments when, after executing some of his sublimest compositions, he would disappear, to return in the disguise of an Englishman, a governess, some member of the Sand group, in a mimicry that must have reminded George too vividly of Musset. He was

YOUNG LISZT

"Liszt's angelic face whose burning eyes nevertheless bespoke passion. . . ."

very much in demand for charades and amateur theatricals at Nohant. In Chopin the transformations were as delightful as they were unexpected, as if one of a choir of angels should suddenly turn to Puck. But George had seen many other changes in that "angel fair of face as a sorrowing woman," changes which, when she described them in the thin disguise of Prince Karol of her *Lucrezia Floriani*, she called diabolic.

Sometimes Chopin seemed to have adjusted himself to the extent of falling into the fanciful *coteriesprache* of the Sand household, as in the letter he wrote George from Paris in December of 1844. "It is snowing heavily here. . . . Jean has put your flowers in the kitchen. Your little garden is all snowballs and sugar and swan's-down and ermine and cream cheese and the whiteness of Solange's hands. . . . Many letters have come for you . . . one from the Colonies, one from Prussia. . . . There are newspapers everywhere, some books, some cards. From your old, old Chopin," he closed the letter, "older than ever, terribly, incredibly old." They had been together for six years yet he employed throughout the formal *vous*.

There might have been a slight edge to his mention of letters, cards, papers—all for George. They spoke too much of the world that claimed her, a world in which he was not included because he kept out of it in wise self-protection. He had not the robust common sense of a Balzac who could utilize whatever had validity in George's reformism while puncturing her bright but air-filled bubbles.

One of his letters to Madame Hanska shows Balzac delightfully at work. He had recently returned from visiting his lady in Russia and, while dining at George's, he brought up the subject of the czarist government. "If you saw Czar Nicholas you'd be mad about him," he threw a tentative barb. "You'd turn at one bound from your *bousingotisme* to autocracy."

"She was furious," Balzac reported to Madame Hanska. "I went on to tell her that like all very corrupt people the Russians are very agreeable . . . and that it's the only country in the world where they've learned to obey. Oh! If you could have heard George Sand's blasts! . . . I dealt her a death blow right at dinner with this: 'How would you like it if at some critical time your servants began to deliberate on your instructions on the pretext that you were *brothers* and *compatriots* of the *Tour de la Vie?*' . . . You know the effect of a drop of water on the reasoning of a boiling kettle. The philosophico-republico-communistico-Pierre Lerouxico-germanico-Deisto-Sand train stopped dead . . . 'You're a horrid satirist,' she said. 'Go and write your *Comédie Humaine!*' "

Prior to this lively dinner party, Chopin had been present at a meeting of the Berrichon clan, Planet, Dutheil, Fleury, Néraud and Duvernet, to found George's newspaper, *L'Éclaireur de l'Indre*. "We taxed Chip-Chip's enthusiasm to the tune of fifty francs," George wrote Maurice, away from home. "He'll have to pay, willy nilly."

The paper, another organ for Leroux' ideas, had grown out of one of those local crimes which society perpetrates and forgets after a momentary shock, but which will not let those sleep who, like George, feel the misery of the least of human creatures as their own.

A young girl, no more than fourteen, very pretty but feeble-minded, was found wandering one spring day of 1843 in the woods of La Châtre. She had been roaming the neighborhood for some time. No one knew where she came from, or who her family were, nor could she tell. A doctor of the neighborhood took her out of the hands of a group of children who were badgering her. Since he could not care for her in his own house, he went with her to a home run by nuns who, most unchristianly, protested against having to take her in. The doctor thereupon made out a certificate that the child was sick, so they had no choice but to admit her.

The poor girl was delighted with her new home, the food, the warmth, as she showed by her smiles. The nuns, however, refused to keep her since they had enough children to take care of as it was, and placed her with a certain Mother Thomas. Three times the girl ran away and returned to the nuns, to the rejoicing of the other children who had grown fond of her. The mother superior then concocted a plan to rid herself of the unwelcome guest. With the help of two women in charge of the diligence service, and with the unwitting connivance of the coachman, the girl, who had not been listed among the passengers, was dropped and "lost" somewhere between La Châtre and Aubusson.

But as nothing can happen in a small town without everyone's knowing, the last unexplained disappearance of the girl brought about inquiries. Where was the child? What had become of her? The coachman, who began to suspect foul play, told all he knew to the authorities, and a search was conducted. It took four months before the girl was found, among a group of wandering mountebanks, and brought back to La Châtre. She was in a miserable state, and had lost what feeble wits she had. Medical examination found her pregnant and diseased.

George Sand rose up in pity and indignation. Under the assumed name and personality of "Blaise Bonnin," and in the direct language of the people, so that the simplest peasant would not be left ignorant of the facts, she told the story of Fanchette, as she called the girl, and published it in the *Revue Indépen-dante,* with a note to which she appended her own name as author.

The effect of the disclosures was tremendous. A roused public conscience clamored for the punishment of the guilty, who came forward to accuse George Sand of "making a novel."

In another issue of the *Revue Indépendante* George sub-stantiated her accusations. Moreover, she issued Fanchette's story as a pamphlet and sold it to raise a fund for the unfortunate child. The nuns and other interested parties endeavoured to prosecute George for stirring up a scandal. But her facts were unassailable. Furthermore she was in earnest and she would be heard. *L'Éclaireur de l'Indre* carried her words to the remotest hamlets.

Chapter XXIV: The Poem Ends

EVEN the friends of Chopin who disapproved most of the George Sand connection—for there are always those who will take it for granted that the woman destroys the man in such a relation—even they had to admit that his music gained by what George had to give. It was not alone that he consulted her on his work in progress (she returned the compliment by showing him her writings before they left for the printer's) , nor that she freed him of the financial worry that made him the most disagreeable of correspondents to Camille Pleyel, Probst and other publishers of his compositions; but that at her house he was brought in contact with the most brilliant minds of the day, a stimulating change from the inconsequential *Schwärmerei* of his prevalently feminine entourage. He had not abandoned those connections, however. The baronesses and countesses would still come to perfect their trills under the touch of his long, thin hands, or to sit by as he conducted their daughters up the grades toward Parnassus, hoping that at the end of the lesson he would favor them with an impromptu concert of his predilected Bach.

Heinrich Heine, Sainte-Beuve, Delacroix, Balzac, Joseph Dessauer, Berlioz, the violoncellist Auguste Franchomme, Lamennais, Louis Viardot and Pauline with whom Chopin went over the scores of *Don Giovanni* to the delight of all listeners; aspiring poets like young Leconte de l'Isle who hailed George as *poète éclatant* and compared himself to the torpid wintry insect awakened to life by the sunlight of her genius; Marie Dorval, men and women distinguished in the arts, political leaders like Louis Blanc, Emmanuel Arago, Mendizabal, Armand Barbès, all blew in, whether at Nohant or in Paris, on the invigorating breeze of their many activities. Amusement too was not wanting, as when at some of George's gatherings a florid blonde, very décolletée, preened herself, like one accustomed to adulation, in the center of a circle of men. She was Madame de Boissy by second nuptials, but she preferred to be called the Countess Guiccioli, a title celebrated, if not notorious, in connection with Byron. Whenever a newcomer, hearing the name and seeing her youthful face asked the inevitable question, "Is the countess related to that Guiccioli connected with the famous English—" Monsieur de Boissy would cut him short with a booming: "She's the countess herself, sir—Byron's mistress!" Sallies went back and forth in an intellectual battledore and shuttlecock. One, recorded by George in her journal, Chopin must have heard with some little satisfaction when Heine uttered it: "Musset, ah, Musset—there's a young man with a promising past."

Most of all Chopin enjoyed the talks with Delacroix who adored him. They were both more at ease with men than with women, both dandies who enjoyed discussing fashion—a bore to George—both fastidious in manners and friends and therefore intolerant of George's pet philosophers whose presence invariably reminded them of an appointment elsewhere. Delacroix, however, was the more intellectual of the two, as concerned as George with the world outside his art. He was, besides, an original thinker and a stimulating talker. Chopin paid him the tribute of listening to his conversation with the same absorption that Delacroix had for his music. The simpler Chopin could not always follow Delacroix' flights—on *la note bleue*, for example, on which Delacroix would hold forth as enthusiastically as Balzac on his *rose bleue*, through which he expected to make millions.

What was the *blue note* and how could Chopin find it? How could one relate the harmony of color as a painter used it, to the harmony of tone? It sounded plausible from Delacroix' lips. But could he produce it on the black and white keys of the piano? "I don't find anything at all," he would say, as his fingers wandered over the keyboard. "No color, no pattern. Only shadows and reflections of shadows." Delacroix, carried away by the music, was avid for more. "Try—try for the pattern and the color will come." And in the peace of the summer dusk Chopin would discover the magic and keep them all enchanted far into the night, when George, before sitting down to her work, would record in her journal that Chopin had found *la note bleue*.

But he had discovered it long since, when its subtleties had begun to shade his musical coloring at Valdemosa, and give depth to his musical conceptions. One has only to hear his compositions, published after 1840—some of them, it is true, written or planned before his meeting with George, but certainly perfected during his association with her—to know that the brilliant promise of the poet of the piano, the magician, as he was variously called, had ripened to powerful thaumaturgy. Even the *Préludes*, taken half finished to Majorca, reveal his more authoritative use of Prospero's wand, from the Ariel lightness of the fifth prélude in D, to the *B Minor*[1] which follows, whose dark magic, George rightly observed, "threw the soul into a terrible despair."

[1] It is believed by some authorities that this was the "raindrop" prélude Chopin was playing at Valdemosa. Others think it may have been the fifteenth,

Chopin, almost at a bound, had become master of his powers. The tentativeness of his early compositions was gone. He had tenderness, but it was now profound. Originality had become his personal expression, the perfume, as it were, that only he, through his music, could exhale. His power attained grandeur, his melodic richness, magnificence. Even the patriot fervor for Poland which had given passion to his music, found more intense and direct expression. "One prélude of Chopin," said George, "contains more music than all the trumpeting of Meyerbeer"—a judgment endorsed by James Huneker who described it as holding between its bars the sorrows of a nation.

Chopin found at Nohant more than in Paris the conditions he needed for composition. There, in his room, where he could be alone with his piano, away from the many activities of the family and also, alas, from the quarrels which broke out more frequently between him and Maurice, he enjoyed the solitude to compose or dream, the source of his profoundest happiness, as George well understood, even if the labor of composition was an agony. She had learned to bear with him when, after he had found a melody, like a gift of God, he would travail to set it down on paper. "For days he would shut himself up, groaning and pacing up and down in his room, breaking his pens, repeating and altering a measure a hundred times over, writing it down and blotting it out as many times, and beginning all over again the following day with infinite and desperate perseverance. He would spend six weeks on a page, only to end by writing it exactly as he had put it down in the first surge of inspiration." At the end of his stay, however, he would return to Paris with manuscripts for his publishers.

His *Sonata in G Minor,* for pianoforte and violoncello, published as *Opus 65,* he finished before leaving Nohant, late in the autumn of 1846. He had been composing it while George was writing her *Lucrezia Floriani,* which had begun to appear in the *Courier Français* that June and which Chopin had been reading, installment by installment, as it left George's desk. Did he see himself in Karol? Did he sense that although their affair was not yet over George had already written its history, even as he had composed his swan song in the violoncello sonata, the last major composition of his life?

For some time, especially since the adoption of Augustine Brault by George Sand, life had become increasingly strained in the family circle. Rumor had it that Augustine was Maurice's mistress, that George smiled on the affair and hoped her son

---

in *D*-flat major, for which Kleczinski contends that the sixth was a preparation.

would marry the girl, and that Chopin and Solange found the prospect intolerable. Rumor also had it—and the prying Mademoiselle de Rozières, Solange's tutor, had contributed more than a word to it—that the daughter was endeavoring to displace the mother in the lover's affections. That the eighteen-year-old girl might succeed in seducing Chopin George would not admit. It was too humiliating, too ungrateful a return for her devotion, and no consolation to know, that "all affection is a source of sorrow, and one must find solace in telling oneself that if the life of the heart is bitter, the life of those who do not know love is ugly and despicable." It was bitterer still, however, to see Chopin side with Solange in family disputes—and she did not underestimate the advantage of Solange's youth against her forty-two years.

The parting, while not definitive, was precipitated by one of the numerous altercations between Chopin and Maurice. Ever since he had come of age, Maurice had asserted himself as the master against Chopin who, he felt, often made his mother appear ridiculous by insisting on authority. Ordinarily Chopin would retire in hurt silence, and after waiting for the atmosphere to clear, return to the family as if nothing had happened. This time, however, something had been said and something, more important, left unsaid, which made it obvious to the wounded Chopin that the end was near. During the quarrel Maurice threatened to leave the house forever. Chopin saw George turn and cling to her son. In her fear that Maurice might carry out his threat, she took his part against Chopin, whose life had been linked with hers for nine years. Chopin lowered his head and murmured, "You do not love me any more." George, clinging to Maurice, made no reply.

During that fatal autumn Nohant had seemed to be under the dominion of evil spirits working turmoil everywhere. For some inexplicable reason George discharged her grandmother's gardener, Pierre, who had survived even the rule of Casimir, and her servant, Françoise, who had been with her since before Solange's birth. Chopin mentioned their dismissal in a gloomy letter to his family. He also predicted that Solange would marry in the spring but urged his relatives to keep the secret.

Solange had already had a number of suitors. One, the thirty-five-year-old Louis Blanc, had been proposed by George, whose admiration of Blanc's political activities made her wish to have him in the family. Solange, however, had other social views which did not include sympathy with the struggles of the people. Victor de Laprade, poet and future Academician, came next, but his family refused to sanction an alliance with the daughter of the notorious Madame Sand. Before Chopin returned to Paris, another had come wooing, Fernand de Préaulx, a young man of substantial Berry stock and some claim to rank which, though not lofty enough for Solange, nevertheless persuaded her into acceptance, much to George's relief, who found her headstrong daughter too difficult to manage.

De Préaulx was very much in love, and perhaps in apprehension of Solange's fickle temper, was anxious for them to marry quickly. But the terms of the contract had hardly been discussed when Solange pleaded for time. After all, she had barely touched on the marriage market, and if she could turn the head of a De Préaulx, she might as easily succeed higher up on the social scale. Men were basically the same; that wisdom Solange learned early.

Leaving the disconsolate suitor in the country, George, Maurice and Solange suddenly arrived in Paris, early in February, 1847, ostensibly to prepare for the impending marriage. During their stay an acquaintance of George's, a Monsieur d'Arpentigny, called to introduce a young sculptor who had recently created a furore by exhibiting a nude with a serpent twined about her legs. It was not that the arrangement was particularly novel; but the judges had found the posture of the unadorned statue so bold that they had insisted on the colubrine substitute for a fig leaf.

George consented to sit to the sculptor, and allowed him also to make a bust of Solange. Every day while they were in Paris, Jean Clésinger sent them some token of his appreciation—flowers, *bibelots*, even pet dogs. Before long Solange and Clésinger had fallen in love and De Préaulx was given his dismissal.

In no time all Paris knew about it, as George, in her solicitude for Solange, had enlisted Madame Marliani, Delacroix, Arago and others to find out what they could about Clésinger. The reports were deplorable. Clésinger was a scoundrel. He beat his mistresses. He had had to flee Italy, where he was studying art, to escape his creditors. He had no money, no influential connections. Nobody knew how he lived, and he had no expectations, for his father, a Besançon sculptor, hardly managed to feed his rabbit warren of a family. Of his mother, the less said the better, though George learned that she had the amiable eccentricity of wearing nothing but a shift all day. Clésinger's education had been rudimentary, and his graduation to the *cuirassiers*, which he had joined to assure himself of food and shelter, had only succeeded in giving him the manners of the barracks, unbecoming to a gentleman of thirty-four.

George tried to dissuade Solange, but the girl was obdurate. She loved Clésinger, she said, and she would marry him and no one else. When D'Arpentigny heard of the state of affairs, he was

260

conscience-stricken at having introduced Clésinger, and, instead of the polite letter of congratulation, he sent the distracted mother an apologetic note in which like Pilate he washed his hands of the consequences. Chopin was told as much as George and Maurice thought advisable for him to know, although for different reasons. George did not wish to give him further worries in the poor state of his health, while Maurice desired to continue keeping him at a distance from family intimacy.

In April George carried off Solange to the country. Clésinger had not yet received a definite answer; Solange might still change her mind. But Clésinger did not give her time to do so. In a few days he appeared at Nohant, insisting on a formal engagement. Solange accepted him. George, who believed in the individual's freedom of choice, had to submit. She wrote to Maurice, still in Paris, not to tell Chopin as yet. "It does not concern him," she said ominously.

Solange, who was really fond of him, wrote him of her coming marriage and her present joy. Chopin returned a friendly little note. "You are at the peak of happiness. I hope you will always be there." To his family, however, he confided his worries, dwelling on the dissoluteness of Clésinger, predicting that the marriage would not last, and betraying shocked concern lest at some future exhibition the world would see "Sol's little *derrière* in white marble."

Fearing a scandal from Clésinger's presence at Nohant, George set an early date for the marriage. Delacroix, mistrusting her future son-in-law, sent her sound advice: "You had better submit the precise material details of the contract to some of your good friends, so that the independence of your daughter may be assured as much as possible."

Meanwhile George was distressed about Chopin and their future relations. There had been no overt rupture, yet she knew that if she wanted peace at home she would have to choose between Chopin and her son. Now, more than ever, she needed Maurice, her source of strength. But how tell Chopin, who still confidently expected to come to the country for the summer as usual? She was feeling old and tired. If she needed a reminder that time was flying, there was Clésinger's portrayal of her, which made her look like the grandmother of that ardent girl whom Delacroix had painted in 1834. She no longer had the strength to cope with her many responsibilities and the constant drain of Chopin on her energies and emotions. Even now, while in the thick of her domestic troubles (which should have been joys) she had been made sick by a letter from Princess Marcelline Czartoryska, telling her that Chopin had been very ill. George's impulse was to fly to him—but how leave Solange alone with

261

Clésinger? (For the woman who had led the life of a man became the most solicitous of mothers as soon as Solange was of
age.) Count Grzymala had been helpful to her in Paris and was
still sending her comforting letters. Remembering his past assistance, she decided to soften the blow to the lover through the
friend.

The letter, written on the twelfth of May, 1847, while beginning with an announcement of Solange's impending marriage,
was in reality George's apology for her rupture with Chopin.
"Burn this letter," she begged at the close. Like most who receive such injunctions, Count Grzymala tucked away the document for posterity.

Chopin, she explained, must have been hurt at not being consulted on the family event. "But his advice on matters of fact
one cannot possibly take very seriously. He never sees things as
they are—his soul is so full of poetry and music. . . ." (Oddly,
Chopin was even then writing of her, "She is adorable, but she
hasn't a groat's worth of common sense.") Moreover, George
continued, Chopin's interference in her domestic affairs not only
menaced her authority but also the love between herself and her
children. "Try somehow to make him understand that he's not to
trouble himself about them any longer."

Then she came to the real purpose of her letter. "The malady
that has been gnawing at this unhappy being has long been
destroying me, and I see him go with a sense of never having
helped him at all, since the true source of his unhappiness is in
the anxiety, jealousy and bad faith of his affection for me." Her
"I see him go" spoke clearly to Grzymala, even without George's
further explanation that in torturing himself Chopin had
martyred her, and she could bear no more. It was the letter of
a tired woman, written in a moment of utter annihilation. She
lived to regret it, and even more, the tragedy which followed her
one selfish recoil from duty to a proud, sensitive, dying man.

Count Grzymala must no doubt have succeeded in making
Chopin "understand," for although invited to Solange's wedding,
set for the twentieth of May, Chopin did not go. Casimir
Dudevant, however, attended. He took an instant dislike to
Clésinger, to whom he referred as "that stonecutter" for the rest
of his life, but he was amiability itself to George whom he
affectionately called Aurore and to whom he showed numerous
little attentions—for a day. The wedding, rigidly conventional in
its legal forms, had its bizarre aspects. Nowhere in the announce-
ments did the name of the bride's father appear, nor was Solange
set down as Dudevant, but as Sand, after her mother's pseudonym.
If Casimir Dudevant made any objection, it is not recorded.

George's troubles had begun. No sooner had the newly married pair come to Nohant after the honeymoon than George had an opportunity of experiencing the truth of the rumors about her son-in-law. Although Solange had received a generous dowry in the property of the Hôtel de Narbonne, in Paris, which brought in a handsome income, she felt cheated, and in that Clésinger abetted her. They plagued George with demands for money and more money. They hated Maurice and despised Augustine.

The poor girl, in fact, was soon to become the victim of Solange's enjoyment of mischief for mischief's sake. Théodore Rousseau, a young painter and a friend of Maurice's, had fallen in love with Augustine and had become engaged to her. George was already making plans for the girl's wedding when the suitor withdrew. Solange had reported to him that Maurice had kept the girl as his mistress, and was now finding it convenient to palm her off on his friend. The scandal which ensued spread from Berry to Paris and reached Chopin, with whom Solange had been keeping up a not wholly disinterested correspondence.

The climax came when, in a quarrel between Clésinger and Maurice, the sculptor took up a hammer to strike him. George threw herself between them on seeing her son in danger, and in the general tumult Clésinger struck her a blow on the breast. Maurice made for Clésinger with a pistol. Had not the local priest who chanced to be there, intervened, there might have been murder at Nohant. After that, it was out of the question for the Clésingers to remain under the same roof with George. They took their departure, carrying off the silver candlesticks, the counterpanes, and everything else that they could smuggle away.

In Paris Solange filled Chopin's ears with grievances. Himself aggrieved, Chopin sympathized. He kept himself from writing to George who, fearing he might be ill, begged Mademoiselle de Rozières, "Tell me how he really is: no more. The rest holds no interest for me at all, and I have no reason to miss his affection." She had heard of Solange's maneuvering. The knowledge that he sided with her daughter against her, a fact which the intriguing Mademoiselle de Rozières had relished communicating, wounded her cruelly. She fell ill, always with her the consequence of mental anguish. "Thank God!" she cried. "I've had enough of life and I'll be glad to pack up and go."

In his journal, under July 20, 1847, Delacroix wrote of a recriminating letter from George to Chopin. "He came in the morning while I was having breakfast. . . . He talked about the letter he had received, but he had already read me most of it since my return to Paris. It is certainly atrocious. Cruel passions and impatience long pent-up, emerge and, in a contrast that would be ludicrous if it weren't such a tragic matter, the author, from time to time, gives way to the woman, and breaks out into tirades that sound like borrowings from a novel or a treatise on philosophy."

Lélia had made the mistake of unburdening her heart in real life, like any ordinary mortal, and neither her friend nor her lover would allow her that weakness. Chopin never wrote to her again. In a long letter to his sister Louise, he implied that the relationship was over. "I have no regrets that I helped her through the eight most difficult years of her life, when her daughter was growing up and her son was at home. . . . Some day, when Madame will reflect on the matter, she can only remember me kindly in her heart. . . . As for the rest, 'Even cypresses have their whims,' " he quoted.

Nevertheless, while adhering to his resolve, Chopin was inconsolable. Through complexities introduced by third parties he was cut off from the only person with whom he had found love and friendship, however agonizing they had sometimes proved. As he went to Delacroix with his grievance, he carried it to others of his friends who did their utmost to distract him, knowing the painful effect upon him of any allusion to the tragic break. But he was like one drunk with his own grief. Liszt, who carried to the end the guilt of having brought about the fatal meeting, declared: "He felt, and often repeated, that in putting an end to this long affection, in breaking this powerful bond, he had broken his life."

Chopin was nothing more than a shadow from the inroads of his disease. His sunken eyes looked out from a mask of pain. His cheeks were hollow. Under the thin, transparent skin the skeleton showed through. Only his wonderful brow and his hair, always meticulously arranged, death's alchemy had not touched.

Other torments were added to his physical ills. *Lucrezia Floriani,* upon its appearance, was read by his friends and all cried out at the shame of George's anatomizing him for the purposes of fiction. To the end George denied that Chopin had sat for Prince Karol, or that she had portrayed herself in the actress-author Lucrezia, but the evidence in the book gives the lie to her denials. It was enough that everyone who knew them recognized them in the book, and came to offer the suffering man the gall of commiseration. Chopin, whose ingenuous trust had neither sought nor found parallels in the novel as he read it, probably with mind occupied by his own compositions, added another accusation to the many already laid against George.

It was not alone from Chopin's intimates that criticism of George arose. Hortense Allart who had been in turn the mistress of Chateaubriand, Bulwer-Lytton and Jacopo Mazzei, and who might have detected some resemblance to herself in Lucrezia, mother of four children by as many fathers, was shocked by the book of the woman whom she had always admired. Her letter to Sainte-Beuve, written in May of 1847, expressed the outraged decorum of most impartial observers, and justified the comparison of *Lucrezia Floriani* to the Countess d'Agoult's novel *Nélida,* recently published under the name of Daniel Stern. (It is interesting to note the adoption of a masculine pen name and the resemblance of *Nélida* to *Lélia* which made Liszt say, "Had there been no *Lélia,* there would have been no *Nélida.*")

"I did not tell you how indignant I've been over *Lucrezia.* . . . Here's a curious how-do-you-do for women and their lovers! . . . Your Marie delivers up to the public a man to whom she owed a few reproaches but whose worst fault, really, had been the very common one of being no longer in love. The wrath, the hate, the frenzy of the book, however, betrayed that the woman was still susceptible and wounded. Well! Now, Madame Sand, after immolating all pianists, serves us up Chopin with mean kitchen details and a cold-bloodedness for which there can be no possible justification. . . . Women should not find words enough to protest against such betrayals of bedroom privacies. . . . Nélida was excusable in her fury; Lucrezia cannot be condoned in her icy irritation. How could such a noble genius allow itself to be so badly inspired?"

Oddly, *Lucrezia Floriani,* with *Consuelo* and *Jeanne,* won the cautious approval of Emerson in America.

"Like Goethe," remarked Oscar Wilde, "George Sand had to live her romances before she could write them." More than that, she had to have models for her characters who, in the process of re-creation, succeeded in gaining personal identity which made of the original a mere sketch, or, in another form of art, the armature under the finished statue. Many of her friends had been flattered to find themselves so translated. Pauline Viardot whose person and exquisite musicianship George had conferred upon her Consuelo, had lived in delightful suspense from installment to installment of the novel, and wrote to her from Madrid where she received the *Revue Indépendante:* "I have not yet the current number, but in the last you introduced me to a strange and wonderful family which I am very anxious to know better. . . ."

Of course Pauline Viardot could not but have been enchanted with her fictional counterpart, one of the best realized of George Sand's heroines as well as one of her most captivating. But not all of George's sitters had like reason for pleasure. One of the wonders of George's art was that in her self-portraits—and she executed many—she painted herself as objectively, and more unsparingly, than her other models.

In *Lucrezia Floriani,* she gave a full-length picture of her mature self. The heroine, a woman who had thrown herself into a life that rejected no experience, no emotion, for the supreme expression of her personality which, however, she always strove to keep in key with moral principle, met, when she was nearing forty, young Prince Karol who, in his almost sexless beauty, resembled "those ideal beings with which the poetry of the Middle Ages used to deck its churches. . . ." When she met him Lucrezia had had enough of love, whose living pledges remained to her in her children. Karol, on the other hand, "chaste, pious, poetic, fervent and fastidious in thought and affection," had, through profound self-engrossment, kept himself from surrendering to another. He succumbed to Lucrezia who yielded "maternally"— Musset would have said incestuously—as she had yielded to her former lovers "whom she had almost lifted to godhood, even if she had sacrificed herself too much for true success." "How could this beautiful youth have fallen, almost without a struggle," asks the author, "under the influence of a woman used up by so many passions, disillusioned in so many things, skeptical and rebellious in all that he most revered, believing, to the point of fanaticism, in all that he had always rejected? . . ."

On that question hangs a tale whose subjective import, once the attrition of the two personalities has begun, places *Lucrezia Floriani* among the masterpieces of the psychological novel.

How much is factual in the analysis of Karol's character? What incidents are taken from life in the accounts of his jealous rages, brought on by almost anyone, a beggar, a priest, a child, but most of all by the memory of Lucrezia's past lovers? How much is to be credited to Karol's sadistic "satisfaction in biting with deliberate gentleness, although the wound reached the very vitals?" Everyone who knew the two chief characters could not help wondering.

Like Hortense Allart, Heine, as well as others, partial to George Sand, deplored her literary treatment of the musician. Himself exacerbated by sickness and misfortune, Heine had scathing words for the woman with whom in his youth he had been half in love. "George Sand hasn't bothered herself about me since my illness. This emancipatrice, rather, emancimatrice, of her sex has outrageously maltreated my friend Chopin in a hateful novel divinely written." Some smiled wryly that in the book it was Lucrezia who succumbed, a martyr to her suffering.

Life, less artistic, is a greater respecter of truth.

From the outset of the alliance, sides had been fiercely taken. Emotions darkened to passions after the rupture and Chopin, declining steadily in health and spirits, showed too tragically that his days were counted. His intimates turned with hatred against

George Sand. She had killed him by letting him go. Biographers of Chopin, too much tempted by the effective drama of a villainess to be disinterested, repeated the accusation.

Chopin died of his disease. He would have died of it whether or not he had parted from George. But she was not without blame. She had committed the crime of sacrificing the weak to the strong in her exaggerated devotion to Maurice who would have been better off for going out into the world freed of her leading strings. She was inexcusable for breaking a bond with a man whom she knew to be dying. That she suffered in the cleavage her physical and moral anguish showed. As if to probe into her soul for the causes of her failure with every man she had loved, she began her *Histoire de Ma Vie,* placing before her the guiding principles: "Charity toward others, dignity toward oneself, honesty before God."

Chopin and George Sand met only once after their parting, at the house of Madame Marliani. Just as Chopin was about to leave, George entered. Always courteous, Chopin greeted her, then asked: "When did you hear from Solange last?"

"About a week ago," she said.

"You had no news yesterday or the day before?" he went on with the buffer caution of one careful to mitigate the effect of joy or grief.

"No," said George.

"Then let me tell you that you are a grandmother. Solange has a daughter, and I'm glad to be the first to tell you." Then with a bow he left her and went downstairs with his companion, Combes, an Abyssinian.

In the lobby Chopin remembered that he had omitted to tell George that Solange was doing well, and sent up the Abyssinian with the message, since he was too weak to climb stairs. George came down with Combes and asked Chopin countless questions. "And how are you?" she inquired.

"Well," he said, and turning to the *concièrge* pointed to the door. With another bow to George he went out into the street. They never met again.

"I thought she looked well," he wrote to Solange. "I daresay she's happy at the republican triumphs," he added, not without a little irony, alluding to the revolutionary events of February, 1848.

Solange's child, born six weeks too early, lived only a few days. The grief reconciled mother and daughter, but their differences were too basic for a lasting understanding.

"Chopin is in England," George Sand wrote in a letter of May 21, 1848. "He could not get lessons in Paris after the Revolution."

267

On the sixteenth of February, however, Chopin had been well enough to give a concert at the Salle Pleyel, with the assistance of Franchomme and Alard who played the cello and violin in a Mozart trio, to his performance at the piano. Mademoiselle Antonia Molina di Mondi sang a few airs, but the attraction was Chopin, who played several groups of his own compositions. The tickets sold at twenty francs, a high price for the day, and the attendance was limited to an audience of three hundred. "I shall have all the fashionable world of Paris," he wrote his sister Louise, and went on to tell that Louis Philippe, the queen, the Duchesse d'Orléans and the Duc de Montpensier had bought ten tickets each, although the court was in mourning and royalty probably would not attend.

The concert was a triumph. The people who had not heard him in many years marveled at the nuances that only Chopin could put into Chopin. "Had we at our command the pen that fashioned the delicate wonders of Queen Mab . . . we could scarcely convey an idea of a talent so purely ideal that matter scarcely enters into it at all," wrote the critic of the *Gazette Musicale*.

None knew that Chopin had had to summon all his strength to walk to the piano and that by the time the concert was over he was near collapse. Nevertheless, the volume of applause affirming that Chopin was still unequaled, gave him strength and confidence. In April, with the help of Jane Wilhelmina Stirling, a Scotswoman living in Paris and for several years his pupil, Chopin went to England to escape the rigors of the Revolution.

He gave two concerts, at Lord Falmouth's and at Mrs. Sartoris', as triumphant as the Paris appearance had been. At the Duchess of Sutherland's he played before Queen Victoria who did him the honor of twice addressing him—an unprecedented distinction, he was assured. The duchess paid him twenty pounds for his performance, a sum which old Lady Rothschild found too high, an opinion which she volunteered with the advice that he take less, as it was necessary for everyone to economize that season. He met Lady Byron—he remembered the buxom Countess Guiccioli at George's parties—and, being curious, talked with her, she in English, he in French. "I can understand why she bored Byron," he commented.

Jane Stirling carried him off to Scotland for his health. But the damp climate was the worst possible for the invalid, in spite of the care Jane Stirling and her relative, Mrs. Erskine, lavished upon him. "I'm about ready to give up the ghost," he confided to his friend Fontana. The letter, full of foreboding and discouragement, spoke of the drying up of his well of inspiration. "All I've left is a big nose and an undeveloped fourth finger," he jested.

After a number of concerts in Scotland, he returned to Paris, in January, 1849. Delacroix went to see him on the evening of the twenty-ninth and remained with him until ten. They talked, of course, of George Sand, whose autobiography had begun to appear serially, and deplored the admixture of faults with her many virtues. Delacroix predicted an unhappy old age for her. Chopin disagreed, saying, harshly for him, that her conscience never troubled her for the things her friends held against her. "Only one thing can afflict her," he added. "The loss of Maurice." Chopin had not forgotten.

"As for Chopin," Delacroix noted, "his sufferings keep him from taking an interest in anything, in work most of all."

He made the next to the last entry in his journal for the year 1849 under October 20: "I learned of poor Chopin's death. Strange, before getting up this morning, the thought struck me. It is one more instance, among others, where I've had such premonition. What a loss! What miserable wretches fill the market place, while that beautiful soul is burnt out!"

Chopin had died three days earlier, after receiving the last sacrament. His pupil, Adolph Gutmann, was with him at the end. No one had told George Sand that he was dying, or notified her of his death. Perhaps the Clésingers and others who had been near him toward the close had not wished it.

Clésinger made a death mask of Chopin, who seemed in the final repose to have regained youth and spiritual beauty. He also made casts of his hands. Nearly two weeks later they held the final services at the Madeleine, and Chopin's *Funeral March,* orchestrated by Reber, was played. Then the body was taken to Père Lachaise. Delacroix, Franchomme, Gutmann and Prince Alexander Czartoryski carried the bier. The handful of Polish soil which Chopin had treasured from the day he left his native land was buried with him.

"There were people full of ill will between us," George said in her *Histoire de Ma Vie.* "They did not tell me till all was over that he had called for me. . . . They felt they had to keep it from me. They felt they had to keep from him, too, that I was ready to fly to him. They did well if the emotion of our meeting would have shortened his life by a day, or even an hour."

Chapter XXV: The Cloak Embroidered with Golden Bees

ONCE again revolution had flared up in Europe in 1848. The first spark flashed in Palermo in the beginning of the year when the people rose up in a successful revolt against Ferdinand II, King of Naples and Sicily. The Sicilian triumph gave incitement to the northern towns of Italy. All of Tuscany demanded constitutional government. Venice proclaimed itself a republic against Austrian domination. In no time Poland was in revolt, while in Germany the streets swarmed with popular demonstrations which prompted King Frederick William of Prussia to declare himself in favor of a free, united Germany. Ultimately the union was accomplished. Freedom, however, remained an abstraction that not even the blood of revolutionary victims succeeded in vivifying. Across the Channel England endeavored to keep its house from burning by setting up protection in repressive measures which made seditious speeches a felony. In Ireland, the habeas corpus act was suspended after a revolutionary flare-up, quickly quelled.

Liberty chose the day of the Reform Banquet, set for the twenty-second of February, for her visit to France. The previous year Guizot had managed to stave off any large public demonstration. Now, in 1848, the parties of reform were confident that nothing would stand in the way of their meeting to make legitimate demands. On the eve of the banquet, the government suddenly threatened to put down by force any public manifestation on the stipulated day. In spite of the prohibition, the people of Paris milled by the thousands on the Place Royale and contiguous streets, shouting, "Long live Reform! Down with the Ministry!" through the ominous roar of the "Marseillaise."

Knowing the inciting effect of blood, the government forbore from carrying out its threat of violence. On the twenty-third however, when public feeling was keyed up to the pitch of insurrection, the National Guard was ordered out against the crowds. To everyone's amazement, they began marching through the roused quarters of Paris, shouting "Long live Reform!" It was the signal for the underground organizations to fly to arms behind the red flag. When the regular troops were sent out by Louis Philippe, horrified that his beneficent rule had brought forth such reward, the National Guard everywhere fought side by side with the people.

Guizot immediately resigned and a new Ministry was promised. Blood flowed in the inevitable skirmishes, with the people, as usual, bearing the greatest losses. The bodies of their dead, borne through the streets on open biers, united the proletarian ranks more solidly still. Even the soldiers abandoned their arms to the people and together with the National Guard marched behind the masses to the Tuileries.

Liberty had won. At least so it seemed for a time. Louis Philippe abdicated, while shrewdly planning to keep the crown in the family through his grandson, the Comte de Paris. When his scheme failed he fled to St. Cloud.

A provisional government was immediately nominated, with the Republicans at the helm and socialists like Louis Blanc and Arago to look after the rights of the workingman. Lamartine, who had been an eloquent spokesman for a constitution, became the contact between the provisional council which met behind locked doors, and the people massed outside, presenting their claims and offering suggestions. Blanc and Ledru-Rollin, listening to the common voice, signed a decree abolishing unemployment through the creation of national workshops, and pledged to distribute a million francs among the workers, as Napoleon had rewarded his faithful soldiers.

On the twenty-seventh of February, the Placé de la Bastille resounded to oratory and cheers proclaiming the Republic. From the stage of the Théâtre Français Rachel celebrated the event by singing the "Marseillaise." Meanwhile, at Honfleur, a Mr. and Mrs. William Smith waited in hiding for the arrival of the packet boat which was to carry them to England. It came at last, and hardly a week after the proclamation of the Republic, Mr. and Mrs. Smith landed safely at Newhaven. Mr. Smith had an unmistakably pear-shaped face. It is not recorded whether he carried an umbrella. It would, in any case, have done him no good against the storm of revolution which, appropriately, had made him assume the good bourgeois name under which he might have remained unsung and unlampooned and, perhaps, contented, had fate endowed him with it at birth.

George Sand, in Paris during the tremendous events, and counting many friends among the members of the provisional government, (Ah, if only Solange had married Louis Blanc!) threw herself heart and soul into the Revolution. The people's hour had at last arrived. She watched the men and women she loved, magnificent in their triumph, marching four-hundred thousand strong from the Madeleine to the Colonne de Juillet. "I saw them from Guizot's window while I talked with Lamartine," she wrote in a letter of March 5. "It was admirable! The people of Paris are the most wonderful people in the world. I saw Mazzini, Combes, friends I had made in Geneva. The whole world was gathered there and yet, at this very time, there are certain fine ladies who flee in disguise, thinking they're going through another Terror, whereas nobody gives them a thought."

"Long live the Republic!" she wrote to the people's poet, Poncy, in a rapturous outburst. "I have seen the last barricades opening under my feet. I have seen the people, grand, sublime, sincere, largehearted—the people of France united in the heart of France, in the heart of the world! . . . I have spent nights without sleep, days without rest. We're mad, we're drunk with joy, that after falling asleep in the mud we have awakened among the stars!" The letter had something of the republican oratory of the circulars and bulletins which she was writing for the government in her faith that at last the people's dream had been realized.

Solange, at Guillery, still mourning the death of her infant daughter, felt no such elation when Clésinger told her of the great events in Paris in which he claimed to have played a part. "The whole thing doesn't stir me as much as it does him," wrote George Sand's daughter, "for it doesn't mean very much. Unfortunately the French people are very fickle and they have, besides, little artistic sense. . . . There's moreover a *low* but sad truth to consider: it would be far better for Clésinger at this moment to have a well-garnished purse in his pocket than a laurel wreath on his head. Less glory and more money!" Besides its political cynicism the letter revealed that the rift which had begun as a gossamer line early in the marriage had become a perceptible crack.

In Berry, Maurice was reaping the fruits of his mother's republican activity. She lent her pen without remuneration, for it would never have occurred to her to seek rewards for herself. But for Maurice—that was different. At any rate, whether or not George pulled any strings among her political associates, Maurice, not quite twenty-five, was nominated mayor of Nohant. George even tore herself away from the excitement of Paris for a fortnight to see her son installed. But not even the celebrations at Nohant kept her from her duties to the Republic.

Alas, it did not take a person as aware as George to perceive that the general spirit of the Berrichons, minuscule landowners but colossal conservatives, was antagonistic to the Republic, even though, since the triumph of that government, they had been hailing one another as *citizen* and *brother*. Thinking back on her success in rousing her neighbors with her Fanchette pamphlet, she became again Blaise Bonnin, and wrote a simple history of France as the wise Bonnin would have understood and explained it. The brochure was published at La Châtre before George returned to Paris. At La Châtre too appeared her open letters "To the Middle Class" and "To the Rich."

Her style, direct and vigorous, dealt courageously with public issues. From the beginning she had had experience in the hortatory, but now the exhortations went beyond individual problems to the future destiny of the people. Because she loved that people, she exposed pitfalls, warned them of the danger in stubbornly clinging to prejudice, taxed them for making bugbears of words and, patiently, lucidly, tried to make all classes understand that in their union lay their strength.

"What are you afraid of?" she asked the rich, in the letter addressed to them. Of the phantom called Communism? And what was Communism?

She defined the thing and the fear in paragraphs which, although written nearly a century ago are equally, perhaps more, pertinent today. "By this word Communism one means the people, and their needs and aspirations. Let us make no mistake about it: the people are the people, and Communism is the future destiny, reviled and misunderstood, of the people. . . . You are terrified by an idea because there are groups who believe in that idea, and because it is a belief which must one day spread and gradually modify the social structure. Suppose its triumph were immediate. Don't you realize that by exhibiting such cowardice and aversion, by putting your hands before your eyes so as not to see it, you are giving it an importance, a coherence, a light which it does not yet boast of possessing? You are still men of yesterday. You have just witnessed the virtue, the grandeur of the people, and since you cannot possibly deny it, you express your reluctance to proclaim the rights of the people by pretending to fear that they are Communist. No, alas! The masses are not Communist. Yet France will be called to be Communist before a hundred years have passed. Among the people Communism claims a very small minority. You must know, however, that if the majority possesses the truths of the present, the minority holds the truths of the future. That is why you must respect and esteem the minorities, and give them freedom. If we refuse freedom, they will become hostile; they may even become dangerous. We shall be compelled to keep them in check by force. They will suffer persecution or they will exercise vengeance. Persecution as surely commits a moral murder on those who inflict it, as vengeance kills its own objects. . . . It is said that there are actual, *immediate* Communists who would destroy property and the family. Where are they? I, a Communist, have never seen such a one . . . Communism is the true Christianity, and a religion of brotherhood threatens neither the life nor the purse of anyone. . . ."

Henri Martin, who read her bold defense of Communism, reproved her for applying the "terrifying word" to herself. But George had the courage of her political convictions. As openly as she had declared herself a Socialist when Socialism seemed to promise the earliest accomplishment of the people's will, she now associated herself with the small and despised minority, giving no thought to the dangers incurred during a political tumult when feelings ran high and persecution was not unknown. She knew no such prudence as playing fast and loose with her political conscience. To Frédéric Girerd who wrote to her in commiseration of Michel who had not been suggested for the provisional government, she said: "Don't feel sorry for Michel. He is rich. He is what he wanted to be. He betrayed and abandoned us in our evil days. Now his pride and his spirit of domination have awakened. . . . If Michel and other deserters wanted my life, I would willingly surrender it, but my conscience, never."

The better to reach the masses she launched her own newspaper, *La Cause du Peuple*. It ran through three issues. The first and the second she penned in the enthusiastic tone of her letters hailing the Republic. The third and last issue was clouded with despair.

In the middle of April, when the second number went to press, as she had looked out on the government-sponsored celebration in which the people, united with no distinction of class or profession were marching side by side, she had seen and heard enough to startle her out of her optimistic dream. Far from solidarity, she had witnessed hate and disunion. The people proclaimed, "Long live the Republic!" But from two-hundred thousand mouths also issued the cries: "Down with the Communists! Death to Capet! Death to the Communists! *À la lanterne!*" She had almost expected the frenzied crowd to string up a few martyrs to the lampposts, so savagely did it repeat its shouts, and alas, with such ignorance of the aims of those whose death it cried for. "The Republic has been slain," she confided despondently to Maurice. "Today it was sullied by cries of *death.*"

Long before the wise politicos she had seen disaster looming. For that matter, they could not have stemmed a deluge which they themselves had started by well meant but impossible promises. Soon after the April celebration, the elections gave the conservatives such a large majority that Lamartine and his group seized the occasion to oust the radicals in the Cabinet. On the fifteenth of May a crowd of workingmen stormed the Chambers and installed their own government. But the conservatives, already entrenched, had strength on their side in the National Guard, no longer with the people. The radical leaders were arrested. To prevent similar insurrections through the implementing of hundreds of thousands of unemployed who had flocked to Paris on the promises of the national workshops, the government decreed that all beneficiaries of such workshops who were between the ages of seventeen and twenty-five must enlist in the army.

The desperate workers who had all to lose revolted, and barricading themselves in the eastern quarter of Paris, determined to fight it out. General Cavaignac, given supreme control of the government, called all available troops to the capital. From the twenty-third to the twenty-seventh of June a civil war was fought by uneven contestants. What chance had the poorly armed insurgents against field and siege artillery, against bayonets, grape and canister? Whole blocks where the workers had thrown up defenses were demolished. Finally they were driven to the northeastern quarter of the city and there those who did not make their escape were either arrested or shot down.

Asserting its victory, the government transported to its penal colonies hundreds of radicals without pretense of trial. Louis Blanc's workshops were shut down. Liberty, equality and fraternity, defined with inspiring eloquence by George Sand in her "Letter to the Commissioners," were abandoned as impracticable. The socialist, or as George Sand would have said, the Communist, dream was over.

As Minister of War General Cavaignac was given dictatorial power until a new constitution could be framed, and the conservative majority, satisfied with the results of the bloody holiday, slept safe from the Communist nightmare while waiting for a political savior to take France under his mantle.

Twice Louis Napoleon, inspired by the Eagle, had attempted a flutter of ambitious wings, at Strasbourg in 1836 and at Boulogne in 1840, in an effort to overthrow Louis Philippe and have himself proclaimed emperor. The second plot succeeded only in causing his detention in the prison of Ham from which he managed to escape disguised as a mason at the outset of the recent revolution. Although he was only the nephew of the first Napoleon, being the son of Louis Bonaparte and Hortense de Beauharnais, Josephine's daughter, the name of his illustrious uncle which he bore still cast a spell over France. It was a spell which the cunning Louis Napoleon well knew, for while writing sociological treatises in prison, he had seen to it that the followers he had been able to muster linked every utterance of his famous name with the still potent words, *"Vive l'Empereur!"*

By the pathos of his imprisonment, and by virtue of his humanitarian writings which he sowed generously where they would benefit him most, he had made influential friends. George Sand, after receiving his pamphlet, "The Extinction of Pauperism," in 1844, had been corresponding with him in the quality, however, of a propagandist of the Revolution. She left no doubt on that score. "There is a glory beyond that of the sword," she incited him, "and you know it, now that the calm of your misfortune has restored you to wisdom . . . They say that at present you have no ambition but to be a simple French citizen. It is a handsome rôle indeed for one who can appreciate it. . . . The terrible and magnificent name you bear might in itself have been enough to crush you. But we have at once diminished and grown as a people since those days of sublime intoxication which *he* gave us. His illustrious rule is no more for this world, and the inheritor of that name, bending over his books, meditates in pity over the lot of the proletariat. . . . Like you, the masses are in chains. The Napoleon needed today is the man who takes on the woes of the people."

Like George, other social idealists hoped to win the prisoner of Ham to their cause, and Louis Blanc even visited him in captivity. He found a small, stooped, withered man who had the eye and the profile of a caged eagle. "The eagle had gone," George remarked after she saw him. "The cage remained." And because Louis Napoleon was the prisoner of his uncertainties and frustrations, he had the lust to confine all France.

He accomplished his purpose with the ruses and psychologically perfect timing of sleepless ambition. He was the logical man of the hour, and the hour struck. Twice he was elected to the Assembly, and twice he modestly submitted. But that honor was not high enough. In December, he rose to the presidency by careful scheming, carrying a large majority over Lamartine and Cavaignac, the other candidates. The prince-president again accepted the people's confidence with humility. There was dancing in the streets. There were displays of fireworks that turned darkness into day. Political prisoners were deported by the boatload; the *bourgeoisie* felt safe again under the spell of the powerful name. Even the proletariat that had voted for the prince-president, felt it had not wholly lost. Louis Napoleon was better than the now hated Cavaignac and the untrustworthy Lamartine. Besides, the people could make their will known through the elections.

In 1850 Louis Philippe died in exile. "The king is dead, long live the prince-president" did not have the right ring, at least not to the erstwhile prisoner of Ham. Under the presidency his term of office would be over before he had enjoyed the full intoxication of power—and he wanted power. The people at large could be swayed by demagogy, but the radicals, while repressed, still had influence, as the elections showed. The prince-president therefore curtailed the privileges of suffrage and the liberty of the press. The people grumbled, but with the memory of bloodshed still fresh, submitted.

The third anniversary of the prince-president's inauguration was approaching; also December 2, memorable for the triumph at Austerlitz and the coronation of the first Napoleon. The prince-president knew the suggestive value of such red-letter days upon the popular mind. Again destiny was about to strike. He helped it along with the co-operation of his bastard brother, the Count de Morny, who always wore a tuft of hortensias in his buttonhole to signify his descent. As Minister of the Interior, De Morny knew what allies he might count upon in a well-planned *coup d'état* which, while it did not directly affect him was, nevertheless, a family matter.

On the night of December 1 Louis Napoleon and his co-plotters caused the arrest of the leading Republicans. At the crack of dawn troops filed out of the Paris barracks and occupied the danger points where previously the populace had set up barricades. Colonel Espinasse, it was said, received the promise of a general's rank and an immediate substantial bribe for his betrayal of the people. Meanwhile the troops occupied the government printing offices and, at bayonet point, ordered the printers to set up proclamations on which the prince-president had earlier exercised his literary skill. To assure the *coup,* sixteen members of the Assembly were arrested, together with the scores of known radicals already apprehended. Success was "in the bag," as De Morny laconically informed the prince-president next morning.

Louis Napoleon at once dissolved the National Assembly, which he branded as a focus of conspiracies. He dissolved also the Council of State, and convened the French people to "free elections," again re-established, so that by their vote they might be his judge against the Assembly. He called the elections for the week of December the fourteenth. The sporadic attempts to tear up the restless paving stones of Paris were quickly put down by the troops. The crowds were dispersed and the agitators carried off to prison. But with the arrest of their leaders the populace threatened to rise full force. Thereupon Louis Napoleon, who knew the effect of blood upon insurrection, commanded his soldiers to let it flow. On the fourth of December the toll of the victims rose to a thousand. The streets were cleared. The dark red stains hardened on the paving stones. In his private chambers the prince-president drew up two lists of names—of his friends and his enemies. The friends he marked for reward; the enemies, Victor Hugo, Thiers, Laboulaye, Théodore Bac and scores of others, for exile. At sunrise, in the barracks courtyards, other dangerous radicals were shot.

Meanwhile the prince-president, while loudly protesting his devotion to the Republic, secretly ordered a Napoleonic mantle on which skilled needlewomen were already embroidering the imperial golden bees.

George Sand, rushing to Paris at the first rumble of the new political storm, counted victims by the score among her immediate friends. Some had been arrested and awaited deportation, others were in hiding. Several had been killed, and many had a sentence of death hanging over them. Each day the families of the victims had graver reasons to mourn. Everyone, like Louis Blanc and Armand Barbès, with whom she had been associated in the events of 1848, was either in prison or in exile. She herself lived in daily expectation of arrest, but would not quit Paris in spite of the many warnings. She knew the profound dejection of equal guilt and unequal punishment—if it was guilt to strive for a better world.

"Here I am," she noted in her journal during the dread December days, "alone by my fire, on the night of the 3rd and 4th. . . . Ah, well-being, how necessary you are to man, and how bitter it is to think that most of mankind dies, deprived of everything. How have I deserved to sit quietly by my fire, warming my feet?"

On the twenty-first of December Louis Napoleon made public the results of the popular plebiscite. He had been elected for a term of ten years on an overwhelming majority. New Year's Day of 1852 saw his inauguration in Notre Dame. Celebration, at least on the part of the president, continued for a fortnight, as his most dangerous opponents were ceremoniously conducted to the French borders after the inaugural. Eighty-three members of the Assembly were sent to banishment, and six-hundred citizens, arrested for opposing the *coup d'état,* were herded at Havre, waiting for the penal boats to carry them to Cayenne.

The announcement of the new constitution fooled no one. The president assumed the absolute powers of a monarch; the senators appointed by him were nothing more than his highly remunerated hirelings. The presidency itself, as anyone could see, was a subsidiary part played by an ambitious actor in preparation for the starring rôle for which the costume was even then being designed. The very wiseacres were deprived of a wry, "I told you so," when in his address to the Senate, Louis Napoleon intimated that he would soon be asking France for a new title, to preserve her peace.

Meanwhile, unable to tolerate the persecution of the Republicans any longer, George Sand requested an interview with Louis Napoleon. She saw him on the twentieth of January, while he was still under the elation of his triumphs. The author of the "Extinction of Pauperism" took both her hands, and listened with moist eyes as she described to him the plight of the sufferers and their families. She pointed out, too, the likelihood of personal vengeances among the people heated by political frictions, especially in small communities which, in their conservatism, suspected of crime anyone who differed from the rest. He was victorious, she reminded him. Let the victor show mercy and declare an amnesty.

Louis Napoleon was too mindful of his imperial aims to risk a general pardon of his enemies. In some cases, however, he commuted the death sentence to life imprisonment and the penalty of deportation to voluntary exile. Encouraged by his clemency, George Sand renewed her pleas, till her frequent visits at the Elysée were marked and commented upon by the president's circle on the one hand, and on the other, by the aggrieved Republicans who, while accepting the benefits of George's intercession, condemned her for interceding. Some of her closest friends showed their disapproval by breaking off their relations. "One way or the other I'll be the one to have my throat cut at the first sign of trouble," she told Jules Hetzel. "I assure you it's all one to me, I'm so thoroughly disgusted with everyone and everything in this world."

Disgusted or not, she continued doing what her conscience prompted, sending money to the needy families of the exiles, and corresponding with them in England, Africa and Cayenne. She pleaded with the governors of penal colonies for better conditions; she sued the generals in charge of the prison forts for mercy. She was working out her expiation for the crime France had committed in destroying the Republic. For as surely as the words of freedom and equality were obliterated by government order from the public buildings, so surely had the people's rights been canceled by the new constitution.

The anniversary of the *coup d'état* was approaching and the Senate had a decision of such import to make that it turned it over to the sovereign people in another plebiscite. It was the question of the re-establishment of the Empire, already hinted at by Louis Napoleon.

The people expressed their will in another "overwhelming" majority: the counted votes showed eight million in favor of the Empire against a few hundred thousand nays. Louis Napoleon humbly submitted. On the second of December—he had faith in astrology—the president became Napoleon III, Emperor of the French. The title was made hereditary.

The better to ensure succession, Napoleon married, a month later, the beautiful Eugénie Marie de Montijo de Guzman, and followed the joyful event by an amnesty of more than five thousand political exiles previously banished by his regime.

George Sand had no more interviews with Louis Napoleon after he became Napoleon III. She also ceased all correspondence with him, although she worked as tirelessly as ever for her republican friends.

"I place great value on the esteem of my fellow men," Napoleon III had written her, "but most of all I value yours. I do not wish to forfeit the small token of *sympathie* you have shown me. I prize it as the priest prizes the lamp that burns before the altar, as one prizes the talisman that brings luck."

But he no longer needed talismans. He had his imperial cloak embroidered with golden bees.

And, magically, they worked for him, those golden bees, making and amassing gold till all of France was one vast, rich hive. The people must be made to forget their dream of liberty; prosperity would do it. The government became a busy apiary, mobilizing every resource of the nation for the making of gold and more gold. Roads crisscrossed hinterland that no trail had ever marked. Industrious subsidiary hives swarmed and produced where sleepy communities had been before. The banks utilized the golden hoard, making it yield greater treasure. Finance corporations sprang up. The Crédit Foncier, the gigantic Crédit Mobilier, founded by Jacob Émile Péreire as a joint stock company to finance the building of railways, encouraged speculation. Everyone, instead of wasting time in impossible visions, kept before him the realizable aim of a concrete golden private hive, known as a million. In the plethora of prosperity the spirit languished. The people had money to spend. They wanted amusement and they must have it loud, quick, effortless and lively. Offenbach was there, timely come, and ready to provide it, a jovial, long-nosed, goat-faced satyr leading the joy-mad crowd from the imperial bacchanal to the tragic "*Ça ira*" of 1871.

George Sand felt the world changing and suffered in the change. She was growing old, not so much in years as in heart. Many she had loved were dead—Chopin, Marie Dorval, both of the same disease. In 1850 that great and understanding heart, Balzac, the man she had loved as friend and brother, had died a cruel and untimely death. Musset, surviving both his genius and his health, was living a posthumous life crowned, the year of the Third Empire, by his election to the Academy. The honor fell upon a head jerking to the macabre rhythm of the nervous disorder that was soon to kill him. Heine, too, her "cousin," as he styled himself, was a sick man, suspicious and embittered, and constantly complaining of his neglect by his friends. He was to die before Musset. His published words, outlasting a temporary coolness toward George, made amends to her, the woman. "How beautiful is George Sand, and how little formidable, even to the spiteful cats that would stroke her with one paw and scratch her with the other, even to those dogs that barked at her most fiercely. Like the moon, she would look upon them placidly from above." Of George Sand's works he wrote with equal justice, although their author would have defended them against the charge that they had done as much harm as good. "They set the whole world on fire, lighting many a prison where no cheer had ever entered. But at the same time their pernicious flames consumed the peaceful temples of innocence."

Lamennais, too, that incandescent intellect, was gone. Even the Berrichon circle was narrowed by death and exile. Most of all she missed Leroux, fled, after the *coup d'état*, to England with his numerous clan. He had tried London for a time, lured there by the promises of John Stuart Mill who, when he saw himself in danger of being saddled with a whole refugee colony, turned a cold shoulder on the hopeful philosopher. George, as usual, stood by where others failed. Leroux was now in the Isle of Jersey, working out a plan to utilize human excrement for fertilizer, and writing a treatise, *The Circle,* in which he let his poverty dream so wishfully that he created another utopia out of manure.

At home there was little to give her joy. Maurice was still dependent upon her, and her writing had to support him as well as Solange. The Clésinger marriage had turned out badly. After the birth of their second child, Jeanne, Solange and her husband went their separate ways, each drawn by the impulses of an ungovernable nature. Scandal came when Clésinger surprised Solange's liaison with the nephew of a famous Italian poet, seized a bundle of incriminating letters and placed them in the hands of his lawyer. Solange had no choice but to submit to a legal separation.

During the lengthy proceedings in 1854 and 1855, Jeanne, who was not quite six years old, lived now with George at Nohant, now with Solange who loved her as she had never loved another human creature, and now in a boarding school where Clésinger, asserting his authority as the wronged party, insisted on keeping her, to save her from the influence of her mother. There, in the boarding school the poor child died, neglected and far from everyone who loved her, as a result of scarlet fever, too tardily diagnosed.

After Jeanne's death and the separation from Clésinger, it was as if Solange turned in rancor against society and led an openly scandalous life, outraging morality with an exultant defiance. Like her brother she wrote several novels and painted a few pictures. But she wasted a life which under other conditions, might have rewarded her and the world she defied. "Madame Sand used to allow her six thousand francs a year," noted Juliette Adam, who knew Solange, "so that she would not have the excuse of poverty for doing certain things." Solange's impulses, however, were as much her own as her provocative beauty. Before she died at the close of the century, she prepared her epitaph: "Solange Sand Clésinger, mother of Jeanne."

Clésinger, to the end, carried the hate of George Sand and her daughter in his heart. He lived a disordered life, but managed nonetheless to leave at least one good work, the statue of General François Marceau, hero of the Vendée. He also delivered himself of a scathing witticism on his mother-in-law. When someone remarked that George Sand would probably put Clésinger into a book where everyone would recognize him, he retorted: "She wouldn't dare, for I'd make a statue of her, without a head and without a fig leaf, and everyone would recognize her."

There was always a sure anodyne to the pains of living and George resorted to it like an addict. Her novels had been coming out steadily, engendered by her assimilation of experience revitalized by her force and energy. With *La Mare au Diable* which had appeared in 1846, foreshadowed two years earlier by her *Jeanne,* she entered into perhaps the happiest period of her art, as expressed in the pastoral novel. She had always possessed that intuitive kinship with nature which made her half a mystic, but now that empathy found all the meanings she sought in the things of the earth itself. She took joy in the recurrent seasons of her beloved Berry, and felt deeply with the peasants in their hardships and small tragedies, as great in their relative cause and effect as the catastrophes of the mighty. For who can measure the cosmic pangs of the infinitesimally minute insect we crush thoughtlessly underfoot?

She wrote, therefore, of the inarticulate people whom since childhood she had intimately known. But she painted a canvas so wide that it included all of life, and created characters of such reality that they became universal. For to George Sand the novel, however realistic, belonged to the domain of poetry, and poetry alone has the power to transmute fact to truth. Her Lucrezias and Consuelos, her Jeannes and Fadettes, her Spiridion and her foundling, François, were no mere shadows in the sun of her creativeness, no rigid photographs of an ephemeral expression but, within their limitations, characters capable of living beyond their fictive existence, like all vital productions from Oedipus to Hamlet.

In line with her new trend George wrote novel after novel, *François le Champi, La Petite Fadette, Les Maîtres Sonneurs,* and many other works of her inexhaustible imagination. Some of her novels, like *François le Champi,* she arranged for the stage. The play was presented so successfully at the Odéon that she was encouraged to continue writing for the theater. Between 1851 and 1856 there was scarcely a season without some play of hers on the boards of the Porte-Saint-Martin, the Gymnase, or the Gaieté. Two dramas besides her *François—Claudie* and *Le Pressoir*—followed her rustic trend. Her *Mariage de Victorine,* a society comedy, borrowed an effect or two from Musset's proficiency in the genre, as did also her much-acclaimed *Marquis de Villemer* of 1864. She also adapted Shakespeare's *As You Like It* for the French stage.

On the whole, however, as she grew in artistic stature, she was drawn even closer to common humanity. "For the aristocracy of the intellect she had always the deepest veneration, but the democracy of suffering touched her more," wrote the penetrating Wilde. "Of all the artists of this century she was the most altruistic. She felt everyone's misfortunes except her own."

Still, her own were often too painful to be ignored, so painful that sometimes even the anodyne failed, and in itself tormented her to the point of making her cry: "God grant that after my death I shall go to some planet where reading and writing are unknown!"

After the publication of her *Histoire de Ma Vie* she continued taking stock of her life. Some of her observations appeared as *Impressions and Souvenirs.* Before their publication, however, Louis Ulbach had asked her for a character sketch to include in his book, *Nos Contemporains.* She answered him in a long letter, on November 26, 1869, in which, as if in extenuation of past actions, she made the observation: "If one does good, one does not indulge in self-praise. . . . If one does ill, it is because one is not aware of doing it. Better enlightened, one would never do it again. . . . I don't believe it is due to wickedness but to ignorance."

Chapter XXVI: "Let green things . . ."

AS the years passed, George's "life of the heart" knew peace in the quiet devotion of Alexandre Manceau, a friend of Maurice's who had come to Nohant as a guest and remained as a member of the family. Manceau was very versatile and equally useful. He painted, he was a skillful engraver, he wrote a fair hand and he could mount entomological specimens better than any—no mean talent in a houseful of experts. He had a reverent admiration for George Sand the author, and a mute love of "the good lady of Nohant," as the Berrichons had come to beatify the Sataness of long ago. He arrived, a devoted Abishag to her tired David. She was touched and grateful, and her heart thawed in the warmth of his selfless affection.

George now lived vicariously through her son. She was proud of every sketch he made for her collected works, proud of every word he wrote and every picture he painted. Like a mirror Manceau faithfully reflected her. Maurice became his son as well as hers. When Maurice visited America with Prince Jerome Bonaparte, in 1861, Manceau was as much worried as George about the dangers that might befall him, and as relieved when the traveler returned with his accounts of the Great Lakes and the prairies and mountains of the United States. "He saw Niagara and the Northern Lights, the fogs of Newfoundland, the gardens of the South, filled with colibris, the battlefields, the encampments of the opposing armies." George's letters panted with excitement. "Maurice is working on his American notes," she retailed to Armand Barbès in prison. "He saw fleetingly but clearly this imperfect democracy which, while proclaiming equality and liberty, forgot one thing—fraternity, which makes the other two treasures ineffective, if not harmful." But America was even then learning that lesson in the agony of civil war.

Maurice's book eventually appeared as *Six Mille Lieues à toute Vapeur*. Manceau contributed the humble drudgery of preparing it for publication. George launched it with a preface.

In 1862, at forty, Maurice married the twenty-year-old Lina Calamatta, the daughter of George's Italian engraver and great-granddaughter of the sculptor Houdon. "A little Italian, *nera, nera,* who sings adorably in a lovely velvety contralto, a warm

284

CHOPIN
PAINTED BY EUGÈNE DELACROIX
"His sunken eyes looked out from a mask of pain. His cheeks were hollow"

generous nature," George described her. The girl was devoted to her mother-in-law. "I married *him* because I adored *her*," she would say only half in jest. As for George, she loved the simple, ingenuous girl whom she had watched grow up. "I mean my real daughter," she would say of Lina, "not *the other*, who is beautiful, which is all one can ask of her."

In time she became a grandmother again. She had felt the death of little Jeanne so deeply that she had had to leave France to try to forget. But the voyage to Italy had not cured her grief. She loved children, and only the laughter of another child could drive out of her mind the pathetic death of Jeanne. Marc-Antoine, a little grandson, was born in 1863. That miniature Maurice reawakened her maternal feelings. She doted on the infant, and even forgave him for being the innocent cause of his parents' submitting to a religious marriage, as if the legal formality before the mayor had not been sufficiently binding. But everything Maurice did was right, and George did not question aloud why he and Lina, ostensibly Catholic, had requested a Protestant ceremony.

Marc-Antoine did not live a year. While his parents were visiting at Guillery, he died suddenly in the night. They buried him the following day, beside Solange's first baby, in the tomb of old Colonel Dudevant. They had two more children subsequently, Aurore, born in 1866, and Gabrielle, two years later. George never recovered from her grief at the death of her first and only grandson. It was as if the line were destined to end. Maurice and his daughters, however, faithfully carried on her name.

George was still to know triumphs surpassing her early successes, even though the budding "new school" of naturalists, realists, or whatever they chose to call themselves, appeared in a hurry to put her into a neatly labeled pigeonhole as dated, in the fashion of those primitive tribes that periodically make a yet more summary end of the old for the surer survival of the new. George was not to be shelved so easily. Her pen had not lost its power, and she still had fight in her.

In 1863 she had taken up an old cause in her *Mademoiselle La Quintinie,* which might be called a sister novel to the earlier *Spiridion,* without, however, the fog of mysticism which, for those who did not know their gospel according to George's adopted philosophers, had obscured the clarity of the message. Her readers divided themselves into two angry camps on this controversial novel which attacked the clergy, the young hotheads reading into it the challenge of a militant anticlericalism, the others, the clatter of the cloven hoof against the stone on which St. Peter had builded.

It was at the height of the storm over *Mademoiselle La Quintinie,* late in February, 1864, that the première of the *Marquis de Villemer* was to be given and George, aware of the cabals that might arise, was understandably nervous. For although the play was a harmless society drama whose showing was to be graced by the imperial presence and its circle, she knew that a plot to hiss her down would be relentlessly carried out without the emperor's august functionaries deigning to burst their white gloves in her defense.

The day began ominously. At ten in the morning the students had been gathering in the square of the Odéon. By curtain rise the house was packed, and the overflow thronged the streets as far as the Rue Racine, where George had an apartment. Tense in her box, she held her breath, not daring to exchange looks with her friends. But the unexpected happened.

"My children," she wrote to Maurice and Lina at two o'clock in the morning. "I've just been escorted home by the students to shouts of 'Long live George Sand! Hurrah for *Mademoiselle La Quintinie!* Down with the clericalists!' It was a furious demonstration and at the same time a success such as they have never seen in the theater—or so they say. . . . The prince applauded like a claque of thirty, leaning out of his box and shouting at the top of his lungs. Flaubert, who was with us, cried like a woman. . . . There wasn't the shadow of a plot, although there were plenty of ill disposed persons. But they made everyone keep quiet, even people who were innocently blowing their noses. . . ." She had the students, the vanguard of progress, with her. She was not dated.

But her circle continued to narrow from year to year. Delacroix had died in 1863, of the scourge of the century, tuberculosis, and now his friends had arranged a sale for the benefit of his heirs. While George was attending the final rehearsals of her comedy, the Delacroix sale was creating a sensation. The canvases were fetching four and five times the prices Delacroix had received during his lifetime, while the merest sketch on a laundry bill brought as much as a painting, in that sudden irruption of recognition which the public undergoes when a living genius becomes a dead master.

George was amazed at the fabulous prices, and like the good *bourgeoise* she remained in financial matters—when they could benefit others—she sent Maurice letter after letter, urging him to take advantage of the unexpected providence. "The good man who used to give us his paintings so prodigally, who would sell them for next to nothing and had no fortune to speak of, is now leaving one to his heirs. Some canvases fetch as much as fifty-thousand francs! There's enough at Nohant to make money for you, especially the flower painting which, they say, would bring a fine price." Again she presented a lure: "The Delacroix sale has brought in two-hundred thousand francs in two days." Maurice must do something about it. "If you want to sell, *now is the time*," she said with finality. "Not in six months, not in a year, but *right away*. . . . I shall keep *"Le Centaure"* for myself while I live. It was his last gift, as *"La Confession du Giaour"* was his first. There are still *"Sainte Anne," "Les Fleurs," "Cléo-pâtre,"* two *"Lélias," "La Chasse au Lion," "Les Carrières,"* several sketches, horses, glimpses of the garden, drawings. . . . There's a tidy realizable sum for you—I can't say exactly how much—which you may acquire at once." And so the "poor man," no special prophet in the Nohant household—was it because Chopin had always disliked his painting?—changed, like Caesar dead and turned to clay, into a profit to keep the wolf at bay.

Casimir Dudevant was still flourishing like the green bay tree. A comfortable country squire, he noted from afar the changes in the government, the "sensations" created by his wife, and grew ambitious for himself. His son had received the Legion of Honor. Why should not he? After all, he had as many and as legitimate claims. He set them down in a petition to Napoleon III.

Certainly, for the originality of its arguments, it is unique in history. First of all, Casimir reviewed Colonel Dudevant's glories under the First Empire. Then he told of his own prowess with the army of the Loire. Moreover, he added, he had served faithfully "under the different powers that have ruled France, although for tradition's sake and from natural inclination I have been unalterably attached to the imperial dynasty and have never ceased praying for its return. The most personal and powerful claim he left for the last. "I also make bold to plead my domestic afflictions, which belong to history. After marrying Lucile (*sic*) Dupin, known to the literary world as George Sand, I was cruelly put upon in my affection as husband and father, and I trust I have deserved the sympathetic interest of all who have followed the melancholy events which have marked this portion of my existence. . . ." On that burlesque climax Casimir may well make his exit.

Did George ever see the petition? If she did, it was long after any hurt from men could affect her. She had suffered the last grief of her emotional life in the death of Manceau in 1865.

Long ago, he had bought her a tiny cottage in the region of Gargilesse. There they had passed the summers together, at peace with themselves and with each other, among the simple things they loved. In 1864 Gargilesse was abandoned for Palaiseau, not too far from Paris, since George's success as a playwright required her to make frequent visits to the city. The move, however, had also been made necessary by family friction. Maurice had not yet weaned himself emotionally from his mother; the jealousy he had vented on Chopin he directed toward Manceau. George, who had by now been sharing her life with Manceau for fourteen years, would not tolerate embittering his approaching end. She made it explicit to her son that she was contemplating a break. Maurice and Lina could keep Nohant; she would live at Palaiseau with Manceau.

On learning the decision of the good lady of Nohant, the whole community was in an upheaval. Who would take care of their sick and help the families of unemployed workmen? Monsieur Maurice was his mother's son, but who could equal her in generosity? George, however, was determined and she took her departure, even after the laborers' organization of La Châtre sent her a petition, pleading with her to stay, and pointing out the good she had done for the workingmen's cause with her novels. They tried finally to move her by her own eloquence by quoting a song from *Consuelo*. But she was prompted by her own sense of duty and listened to no other voice.

The house in Palaiseau, the last in the village, was bordered by a forest beyond a peaceful stretch of orchard. A stream slid almost silently among the willows of the garden. For days they would hear no living sounds but the chirping of the birds. They could have found no more tranquil place for their final communion.

At first Manceau, in the deceptive buoyancy of his malady, seemed to improve. But the disease had made its inroads. George saw that meek, uncomplaining man burning himself out, like Chopin before him, and she could do nothing. For three months she tended him alone, unwilling to share with anyone else the little time remaining. The spring gradually turned to summer. The gentle idyllicism of the countryside seemed one with Manceau's nature. He went from life to death as imperceptibly as one season flows into the other.

He was the only man she had ever loved, perhaps the only being she had ever known, who had given and not taken, with whom daily communion had meant much work and its reward in quiet enjoyment. With calm devotion he had companioned the lingering close of George's life of the heart, which, like all twilights, foreshadowed inevitable sadness. To George the months spent at Manceau's bedside meant atonement as well as love.

Her letter to Maurice communicating Manceau's death was stiff with reserve. In her loneliness she had to write freely to someone. She unburdened her sorrow to Oscar Casamajou, almost a son by adoption. "I have lost him, dear child. I have lost the wonderful companion of my last fifteen years. I have lost the devoted mainstay of my old age. He passed away without pain. . . . There he lies, my poor friend, calm, pale, and young again in death. I shall sit by him still another day—I have such dread of hasty burials. I've covered him with flowers, and I've been to choose a lovely spot for his final resting place."

Manceau was a good man. There had been nothing in their life together to trouble George's memory with regrets. Even by his last gesture Manceau had revealed his delicate understanding of her. He left his few personal belongings and his pathetic savings, derived from his skill as engraver, to Maurice, who had not always remembered to treat him as an equal.

George stayed on at Palaiseau alone. She needed the solace of an unshared consecration, in the house that had seen a good man die. "I am unhappy here nonetheless," she wrote to Flaubert, three months after Manceau's death. "This absolute solitude which has always given me peace and distraction is now shared by one who expired in this very room, like a lamp that goes out and yet is always there."

Gustave Flaubert could appreciate solitude. A bachelor of forty-four, he had devoted at least twenty of those years, except for two during which he traveled in the Orient with Maxime du Camp, to the cult of a hermitlike isolation. A nervous disorder akin to epilepsy which had afflicted him in early manhood had put an end to the law studies he hated. When his father, head of the city hospital at Rouen, bought a house at Croisset that had once belonged to the Benedictine monks, it was as if fate had mapped out the youth's career. Dr. Flaubert's death, followed immediately by his married daughter's at childbirth, removed the desolate family to Croisset, a little village of a dozen houses and a quay, leaving Gustave's brother Achille to succeed his father at the hospital.

The Croisset household might have come out of a tenebrous Gothic novel: a constantly mourning old woman, morbidly apprehensive of her sick son's death, the infant granddaughter whom Madame Flaubert was bringing up as her own child, and the large, outwardly robust young man who scarcely left the house. Flaubert adopted as the uniform of his invalidism and monkish seclusion a flowing robe tied with a cord about the middle, a pair of loose trousers and house slippers. The neighbors who sometimes caught a glimpse of him walking about the garden or the terrace, set him down as odd and prudently left him alone when rumors circulated that the strapping youth spent most of his time writing.

In spite of his studious sybaritism, Flaubert found time for a love affair with one of Paris' most notorious literary women.

When still an unpublished writer, Flaubert met Louise Colet in Pradier's studio, on one of his rare absences from home. Madame Colet was then the reigning, still beautiful, but somewhat shopworn Aspasia of the Academy whose prizes she had several times received, more, as everyone suspected, for her intimate rather than her poetic accomplishments. Victor Cousin, the middle-aged author of the spiritual-eclectic *Of the True, the Beautiful and the Good,* had been her lover for some seven years. His influence at the Academy had known how to turn the ballots for his mistress. When, after her liaison with the philosopher, Madame Colet had shown signs of becoming a mother, one of the journalistic gadflies of the day, Alphonse Karr, printed an unambiguous squib. Monsieur Colet, Karr wrote in his *Les Guêpes,* whom Madame Colet had so far presented only with Alexandrines, could not really claim the coming child. Pointed references to the kindnesses Victor Cousin had been showing the gravid Sappho left little doubt about Karr's meaning.

The irate Madame Colet whose husband was too timorous or perhaps too prudent to defend her honor, did it for herself by thrusting the point of her kitchen knife into Monsieur Karr's loins. The wound was slight but the scandal made up for it. An amusing side light—it was Sainte-Beuve who called on Karr as Victor Cousin's representative to find out whether or not a duel were in order. It was not.

The affair between Flaubert and Madame Colet quickly lost its intensity; their epistolary relationship had a longer and, for Flaubert, a more important life. Madame Colet wearied him with her tawdriness and superficiality which somehow disappeared in her letters, where she was at her best. Further, she terrified him with her threats to his privacy. She lived for sensation, physical, personal, tangibly rewarding. He was still the aspiring Benedictine of Art, capitalized but not abstract. Women, he tried to explain to Madame Colet, could not love the beautiful for its own sake but must always make it serve a personal end or purpose. In his temple Art was wholeness, perfection, an end in itself. "You ask if the few lines I sent you were written for you. . . . They were written for no one. I've always endeavored not to subject art to the satisfaction of a single isolated personality. I have written tender pages with no feeling of love, burning pages with not the least fire in my blood. I have imagined, I have remembered and combined. . . . You predict that some day I shall do great things. Who knows?"

By the time George Sand met Flaubert in 1863, Louise Colet's prediction had been verified. Flaubert's *Madame Bovary,* the result of his fidelity to Art and an unswerving adherence to reality, assimilated, however, by a prodigiously nurtured intel-

lect, ranked him, for the very tempests the book aroused in a
society that did not wish its soul exposed, with the great novelists
of the age.

The elder Dumas, abetted by Sainte-Beuve, had brought about
the meeting between George Sand and Flaubert at one of the
Magny dinners during which the incorrigible Gautier had whispered salacities in George's ear while the angelic Renan, more
than ever resembling Charles the Good, looked sweetly on. If
Sainte-Beuve had hoped for sentimental coruscations from the
meeting he was fated to disappointment. Flaubert had long since
consecrated body and soul to his only passion, Art, while George
Sand knew that she could love no more.

They initiated a friendship that was to last, uncomplicated,
to the day of her death, a friendship clearly defined by a vale-
tudinarian overtone in the title of the novel, *Le Dernier Amour,*
which George Sand dedicated to Flaubert, after a visit at Croisset.
What did it matter that as artists they stood at opposite poles;
that Emma Bovary was Flaubert's pitiless answer to George
Sand's Lélias and Indianas; that the one wrote with his father's
scalpel and the other "with the fire of the heart"? They understood each other and they respected each other's honesty.

After a severe illness George left Palaiseau and returned to
Nohant. Flaubert would come to see her there, and once so far
forgot his self-consciousness as to take part in the amateur theatricals which the Sand family had always enjoyed. They wrote
frequently to each other, a means of communication both preferred, Flaubert because he was always happiest with the word
unshadowed by the physical presence, and George for the opportunity it gave her to keep pace with the intellectual progress of
the younger generation from the privacy of her workroom.

He asked advice on Art, always on Art, with a respectful
humility that makes posterity smile ruefully. She gave it, scolding him for his preoccupation with the means rather than the
end, advising him to go out, to enjoy nature and people, to give,
not to hoard. He bowed to the *chère* maître, held his ground,
and resumed his complaints on the agony of arriving at the *mot
juste,* on the sacrifices, in terms of ascetic living which one must
make for the purity of one's creation. "I suspect you, obstinate
troubadour that you are. . . . (Troubadour was one of her
names for him.) In spite of all your protestations it is quite
likely that Art is your only passion, and that your seclusion,
which made me waste so much sympathy upon you, fool that I
am, is a state of absolute bliss."

The argument, begun early, continued late in their correspondence. "You love literature too much. It will kill you and
you will not kill the stupidity of humanity. Poor, dear stupidity.

. . . How much hate you have for it! What a war you wage against it! . . . That sacrosanct literature, as you call it," she wrote again, "is secondary in my life. I've always loved someone more than literature, and my family more than that someone."

Why did he wear himself out worrying about form? "You read, you delve, you work more than I do, more than a host of others. You have acquired such learning as I shall never attain. You are a hundred times better off than all of us. You are rich, yet you cry out like a beggar. Alms, give alms to a miserable wretch whose mattress is stuffed with gold but who won't feed himself except with well turned phrases and chosen words! Foolish man! Dig into your mattress and eat your gold! Nourish yourself with the ideas and the sentiments you've stored in head and heart. The words and phrases, the *form* you make so much of, will come naturally. . . ."

She was not blind to their respective merits, however, and knew the place each would occupy in the future—he with his books that could be counted on one hand, and she with her final toll of one hundred and twelve volumes. "You write for the future, but in fifty years I fear I shall be forgotten. That is the fate of what is not strictly of the first order. I aimed at influencing some of my contemporaries."

In February George Sand spent a few weeks in her Paris apartment on the Rue des Feuillantines for the opening of her play, *L'Autre*, at the Théâtre Français, with Sarah Bernhardt, a new young actress, playing the leading role. The play repeated the success of the *Marquis de Villemer* and George went back rejoicing to Nohant, her head filled with plans for future work in the medium that she found even more satisfying than the writing of novels. She was never to see another of her dramatic works performed, for all of France was that year involved in a drama of horror and blood.

It takes one small spark to start a conflagration. It took a slight to the French Ambassador at Berlin to precipitate the Franco-Prussian War. Between pretext and cause, however, lay the vacant throne of Spain which Prussia, arrogant in her military strength, proposed to fill with a Hohenzollern king. Bismarck, called to mediate, succeeded only in lighting the fuse. By July of 1870 the angry Paris mobs were shouting, "On to Berlin!"

France declared war.

The events of that disastrous year and the year that followed —the siege of Paris, the Communist uprisings, the famine, the bloodshed—have been recorded in history. Hugo's *L'Année Terrible* told them in verse. George Sand, no longer young enough to participate actively, wrote of them in her letters, in articles, in her *Journal d'un Voyageur pendant la Guerre*. She had no enthusiasm for the war and she could not feign it, even for her articles in which, because she had no conviction, chauvinism took the place of fervor. "I find this war infamous," she said truthfully in private, "and this compulsory *Marseillaise* a sacrilege."

The forests in Berry were being burned down. By the Prussians? By the French Army? She did not know. All she knew was that the wolves came prowling at night in the courtyard, where Maurice hunted them with a revolver while she held a lantern to light him. "The trees are losing their leaves, perhaps their very life," she lamented to Flaubert. "Our drinking water will soon give out. The harvest is almost nil. But we have a war —what luck!"

In Paris her apartment was wrecked by a shell. The neighborhood saw enacted in its small, concentrated area the larger tragedies of war, in an internecine conflict, more anguished and terrible, as brother shed his brother's blood. The Odéon became a hospital, the actresses nurses. Its pit and its cellars groaned with the wounded and dying. Out in the squares lay the bodies of Communists and soldiers, their blood equally red as it seeped through the cracks of the paving stones. There were corpses of women, too, the *pétroleuses,* whose task it had been to set fire to the Palais Royal, the Tuileries, the Luxembourg, the Hôtel de Ville.

Friends were lost by death, more bitterly lost by party feeling. "I cannot ask who are my friends or enemies," George Sand wrote. "They are where the storm has scattered them. The thoughtless blame of those who forsake me will not make me think of them as enemies."

But her comrades were not as forgiving. She despaired in disillusionment. Was this the end they had fought for in 1848 —this anarchy, this carnage? "Enough of bloodshed!" she cried in revulsion. "I'll have no more ill deeds to bring about good, no more of killing in order to create. No! No! My age rebels against the tolerance of my youth. . . . We must rid ourselves of the theories of '93. . . . A curse on all who dig charnel houses! No life ever rises out of them."

At the peak of the civil terror Pierre Leroux who had hurried to Paris at the first revolutionary flicker, died suddenly. Remembering his contribution to the cause, Jules Vallès proposed that the Commune buy Leroux a cemetery plot in perpetuity. The fanatical chiefs rejected that antirevolutionary and antidemocratic proposal and decreed a public grave good enough. One of a very small group who remembered, George Sand walked behind Leroux' coffin and saw it lowered into the ground. Leroux might have been a visionary, a charlatan, as some had called him, but he had kept faith with his ideal—justice to the people, that foolish, unreasoning, easily misled humanity, falling so readily into error, crawling so slowly toward its goal.

Even in the darkest days of fratricide George, too, kept faith. She knew that the people were not ready for the Commune; she despaired at seeing their leaders so mistaken. She still believed in the Republic, too briefly tried in 1848. The Republic alone could now save France and her great, her pitiful people.

"Humanity has always been the same. The people are despicable," Flaubert condemned from the perspective of Croisset. "Its irremediable wretchedness had embittered me since youth, therefore I feel no disillusionment today."

George was shocked at her troubadour. She berated him privately and, as in the days of Everard, answered his scorn of the people in letters, *Réponses à un Ami,* which were published in *Le Temps.*

"You say that the people have always been brutal, the priests hypocritical, the middle class invariably mean spirited, the soldiery brigands and the peasants fools? You have known that since youth, you say, and you rejoice that you are not trapped by maturity into false hopes. Then you have never been young. . . . No, no, you cannot isolate yourself. You cannot break the ties of blood. You cannot curse, you cannot despise your kind. Humanity is not an empty word. The people? you ask. But this people means you and me. Do what you will, you are still part of the people. . . . I will not believe that my country and my people have been stricken to death. By the grief and pain with which I feel myself responding, by the very hours that plunge me into despair, I know it is not so. I love therefore I live. Let us live, let us love."

Finally the civil strife was over. Factional differences were aired and settled in the assembly. To cries of *"Vive la République"* the Republic, once betrayed by imperial ambition, triumphed again. Empress Eugénie fled. In England, the sanctuary of fallen emperors and kings, Napoleon III put by forever his mantle strewn with golden bees.

Surrounded by her children and grandchildren, George Sand continued writing her novels year by year as inevitably as nature produced its fruit with every harvest. As each book appeared, Flaubert sent her his qualified praise. It was not till he read her *Marianne Chevreuse* in the *Revue des Deux Mondes* in August, 1875, that he wrote her in unbounded enthusiasm. The touching story of the dark-eyed melancholy girl who led her brave life among the uncomprehending gossips of her small village (George Sand had again drawn upon her girlhood) moved and fascinated the recluse of Croisset. "Two or three times I cried," he confessed to George. "I found myself in the person of Pierre, and some pages seemed almost fragments of my recollections—if I had had the talent to write them as you write. How charming, poetic and *true* it all is! The *Tour de Percemont* I had liked very much. But *Marianne* has literally enchanted me. . . . This time I admire you fully and without the least reservation."

The greatest compliment of all he paid her when he wrote his story of the old servant, Félicité, *"Un Coeur Simple"* in George's manner and on her repeated text of the greatness of the humble. George Sand never saw this, perhaps the nearest perfection, of Flaubert's masterpieces.

She became the grand old lady of literature, loved by the many whose youth her works had inflamed, hated by those whose hypocrisy they had exposed, adored by *la jeunesse* as the torn standard of brave causes, tolerated by the *moderns* who mistook new mannerisms for originality and, pouring their wine into the same old bottles, stood by delighted at the ferment they made. They were the last word. They were the future. Impatient, they waited for the past to go.

The past stood firm. Now and then one of its pillars crumbled. Sainte-Beuve died before he could witness the disasters that would have saddened his end. The loss of so brave a relic brought old and new together, the arts and sciences, youth and age. But no senators and no priests appeared, for it was a civil burial, and civil burials, even of the great, the prudent avoided.

The only woman attending, George Sand leaned on the arm of her friend Plauchut, as the old Dumas, who could no longer walk, leaned upon his son's. Count Grzymala was there, his white head bared. Sainte-Beuve, Musset. Grzymala, Chopin. The phantoms of her dead life stood with the gray-haired woman by the grave side. So little ecstasy, so much pain, all, in the end, covered by a spadeful of dust. What if she had been as careful in her life as Sainte-Beuve? But then, she reflected, she had had too much heart for her intellect, as Sainte-Beuve too much intellect for his heart. She had committed many sins. But, as time passes the world forgets, if it does not forgive. Perhaps it even forgives. She took it as forgiveness when, as she made her way to her carriage, the crowd parted and hats were raised to her in silent respect.

Every day time made her conscious of its passing. The world of her youth had changed, for better or for worse she did not know. Her unalterable faith made her hope, for better. Anchored as a rock in that faith, she had been touched by every current of progress, swept by every intellectual wind. She had herself altered with the changes. Asperities had softened, boldness toned down. She had lost much but she had also accreted, and those accretions were as the flowers that fill the clefts of ruins. She had suffered the buffetings of experience equally with the visitations of destiny, and remained firm. Weakness and strength had been alike drawn to her—weakness more than strength. The strong had gained by the contact; the weak had met ship-wreck. The rock bore lasting wounds from the disasters, but it was not shaken from its anchorage, grappled deep in the heart of the nature she had always loved.

She wrote until she could no longer hold her pen, and even then the active mind carried on the work of the useless hands. On the twenty-ninth of May, 1876 she left her novel *Albine* in the middle of a chapter. She was never to finish it. The cancer that had killed her mother had given her warning. She knew she was going to die. On the night of the seventh of June, she said good-by to her children, and struggled to make them understand some last wish. But unconsciousness came quickly. *"Laissez verdure . . ."* she said distinctly. The rest was unintelligible. "Let green things. . . ." They knew what she meant.

She died on the morning of June 8. Her body was prepared for burial by Solange and the women of the household. Prince Jerome Napoleon, Flaubert and the younger Dumas, with Harrisse, an English friend of George Sand's, came from Paris for the funeral. They had started out in the rain. It was still raining when they reached Nohant. Dumas alone went to take a last look at the dead. Flowers were strewn over the bed where George Sand was lying. The face was hidden by them. Only the right hand, perfect and smooth as if modeled in wax, the hand that had written so many books and helped so many wants, lay uncovered.

On the tenth of June, after the ceremonies which officiousness and mistaken filial piety had imposed, the coffin, a mound of flowers and laurel branches was laid under the yews of the family burial ground. The fragrant soil of the countryside that George Sand had always loved covered her. The rain continued to fall.

"Laissez verdure. . . ." The green things she had pleaded for would soon be growing over her. The grass, common as common humanity, would be her monument, and the epitaph of one, her spiritual brother, America's great Whitman, would be traced there in nature's hand, for all to read:

> The smallest sprout shows there is really no death
> And if there was it led forward life.

Forward. She had a little shown the way.

Bibliography

ADAM, ANTOINE. *Le secret de l'aventure vénitienne.* Paris, 1938.

ADAM, JULIETTE. *Le roman de mon enfance et de ma jeunesse.* Paris, 1902.

———. *Mes sentiments et nos idées avant 1870.* Paris, 1905.

AGEORGES, JOSEPH. *George Sand, paysan.* Paris, 1908.

ALLART, HORTENSE. *Enchantements de Prudence Saman L'Esbatx,* 3 volumes. Paris, 1872, 1873, 1874.

———. *Lettres inédites à Sainte-Beuve.* Paris, 1908.

ALTON-SHÉE, E. D'. *Mémoires du Vicomte d'Aulnis.* Paris, 1868.

AMIC, HENRI. *George Sand: Mes Souvenirs.* Paris, 1893.

ARAGONNÈS, CLAUDE. *Marie d'Agoult.* Paris, 1938.

ARNOLD, MATTHEW. "George Sand," in *Fortnightly Review.* January–June, 1877.

———. *Mixed Essays.* London, 1879.

BALZAC, ÉVELINE HANSKA. *La véritable image de Madame Hanska.* Paris, 1929.

BALZAC, HONORÉ DE. *Correspondance.* 1819–1850, 2 volumes. Paris, 1876.

———. *Lettres à l'étrangère,* 1833–1844, 2 volumes. Paris, 1899–1906.

———. *Œuvres complètes.* Edition définitive, 24 volumes. Paris, 1872–1879.

BARBEY D'AUREVILLY, J. *Les œuvres et les hommes au dixneuvième siècle.* Paris, 1878.

BARINE, ARVÈDE (CÉCILE VINCENS). *Alfred de Musset.* Paris, 1893.

BAUDELAIRE, C. *L'art romantique.* Paris, 1925.

———. *Œuvres posthumes et correspondances inédites.* Paris, 1887.

BENNETT, JOSEPH. *Frederick Chopin.* London. No date.

BIDOU, HENRI. *Chopin.* Paris, 1925.

———. "La Chartreuse de Valldemosa," in supplement of *Journal des Débats,* July 1, 1904.

BLANC, LOUIS. *Appel aux honnêtes gens.* Bureau Central, Paris, 1849.

———. *Historie de la Révolution Française,* 2 volumes. Brussels, 1847–1848.

———. *History of Ten Years,* 2 volumes. London, 1844–1845.

BONNEROT, JEAN (editor). *"Une grande amitié littéraire: Sainte-Beuve et George Sand."* (Lettres inédites de Sainte-Beuve.) *Revue de France,* Volumes 4 and 5, Paris, 1933.

BROWNING, ELIZABETH B. *Letters,* 2 volumes. London, 1898.

CAMP, MAXIME DU. *Souvenirs littéraires,* 2 volumes. 1892.

CHAMBON, FÉLIX. *Notes sur Prosper Mérimée.* Paris, 1904.

CHARPENTIER, JOHN. *George Sand.* Paris, 1936.

——. *La vie meurtrie d'Alfred de Musset.* Paris, 1928.

CHOPIN, FRÉDÉRIC. *Chopin Letters.* Collected by H. Opienski. Translated by E. L. Voynich. London, 1932.

——. *Lettres de Chopin.* Collection polonaise. Paris, 1933.

CLARETIE, J. *"Le mariage de Clésinger,"* in *Figaro,* January 8, 1883.

CLAUDIN, GUSTAVE. *Mes souvenirs: les boulevards de 1840–1870.* Paris, 1884.

COLET, LOUISE. *Lui.* Paris, 1880.

COURTHION, PIERRE. *La vie de Delacroix.* Paris, 1928.

DAVID, H. C. "Flaubert and George Sand in their Correspondence," in papers of the Chicago Literary Club. Chicago, 1924.

DAVRAY, JEAN. *George Sand et ses amants.* Paris, 1935.

DÉCORI, FÉLIX (editor). *Correspondance de George Sand et d'Alfred de Musset.* Bruxelles, 1904.

DELACROIX, EUGÈNE. *Correspondance générale.* Edited by André Joubin, 5 volumes. Paris, 1936–1938.

——. *Journal.* Edited by André Joubin. Paris, 1932.

DE QUINCEY, T. *Confessions of an English Opium-Eater.* Edited by Richard Garnett. London, 1885.

DEVAUX, A. *George Sand.* Paris, 1895.

DIMOFF, PAUL. *La genèse de Lorenzaccio.* Paris, 1936.

DONNAY, MAURICE. *La vie amoureuse d'Alfred de Musset.* Paris, 1926.

DOSTOEVSKY, F. *Pages from the Journal of an Author.* Translated by S. S. Koteliansky and J. Middleton Murry. Boston, 1916.

——. *Letters and Reminiscences.* Translated by S. S. Koteliansky and J. Middleton Murry. London, 1913.

DOUMIC, RENÉ. *George Sand.* Paris, 1909.

DUQUESNEL, F. *Souvenirs littéraires.* Paris, 1922.

ERCULEI, R. "Luigi Calamatta," in *La Vita Italiana,* Volume 5. November, 1895; January, 1896.

FAURE, GABRIEL. *Paysages littéraires.* Paris, 1917.

FERRÀ, BARTOMEU. *Chopin and George Sand.* Palma, 1932.

FEUGÈRE, ANATOLE. *Un grand amour romantique.* Paris, 1927.

——. "Le *Journal Intime* de George Sand arrangé par Paul de Musset," in *Revue d'histoire littéraire de France.* Paris, 1927.

FLAUBERT, GUSTAVE. *Éducation sentimentale.* Paris, 1869.

——. *Madame Bovary.* Paris, 1857.

——. *Trois Contes.* Paris, 1877.

FRANCE, ANATOLE. *La vie littéraire.* Paris, 1892.

FRYE, PROSSER H. *Literary Reviews and Criticisms.* New York, 1908.

GANCHE, ÉDOUARD. *Frédéric Chopin, sa vie et ses œuvres.* Paris, 1936.

——. *Dans le souvenir de Frédéric Chopin.* Paris, 1925.

GAUTIER, THÉOPHILE. *Honoré de Balzac.* Paris, 1859.

——. *Portraits contemporains.* Paris, 1874.

——. *Souvenirs romantiques.* Paris, 1929.

GIRAUDEAU, FERNAND. *Napoléon III intime.* Paris, 1895.

GOETHE, WOLFGANG VON. *Goethe und die Romantik; Briefe mit Erläuterungen,* 2 volumes. Weimar, 1898–1899.

GONCOURT, ÉDOUARD and JULES. *Journal.* Paris, 1912.

——. *Lettres.* Paris, 1885.

GOZLAN, L. *Balzac en pantoufles.* Paris, 1856.

GRIBBLE, FRANCIS. *George Sand and her Lovers.* London, 1908.

GROS, J. M. *Le mouvement littéraire socialiste.* Paris, 1904.

GUET, A. "George Sand inconnue; lettres inédites," in *La Vie Moderne,* June 22, July 29, 1882.

HEINE, HEINRICH. *Briefe,* 3 volumes. Hamburg, 1865–1866.

——. *Correspondance inédite,* Volume I. Paris, 1867.

——. *Heine Reliquien. Neue Briefe.* Berlin, 1911.

——. *Lutèce. Lettres sur la vie politique, artistique et sociale de la France.* Second edition. Paris, 1855.

——. *Sämmtliche Werke,* 7 volumes. Philadelphia, 1860–1865.

HOUSSAYE, ARSÈNE. *Les confessions; souvenirs d'un demi siècle, 1830–1890,* 6 volumes. Paris, 1855–1891.

HOWE, MARIE JENNEY. *George Sand: the Search for Love.* Garden City, 1927.

HUNEKER, JAMES. *Chopin: the Man and his Music.* New York, 1900.

JAMES, HENRY. *French Poets and Novelists.* London, 1908.

——. *Notes on Novelists.* New York, 1914.

——. "George Sand; the New Life," in *North American Review,* volume 174, 1902.

JONES, HOWARD MUMFORD. "American Comment on George Sand, 1837–1848," in *American Literature,* Volume 3, Durham, N. C., 1932.

KELLEY, EDGAR. *Chopin the Composer.* New York, 1913.

KENNAND, MRS. "Flaubert and George Sand," in *Nineteenth Century,* Volume 20, 1886.

KOMAROVA, V. D. *George Sand, sa vie et ses œuvres,* 4 volumes. Paris, 1899–1926.

LAMARTINE, ALPHONSE. *Portraits et salons romantiques.* Paris, 1927.

LEICHTENTRITT, HUGO. *Friedrich Chopin.* Berlin, 1920.

LENZ, WILHELM VON. *Die grossen Pianofortevirtuosen unserer Zeit.* Berlin, 1872.

LEROY, ALBERT. *George Sand et ses amis.* Paris, 1903.

LESCURE, M. F. *Eux et elles; histoire d'un scandale.* Paris, 1860.

LEVALLOIS, JULES. "Sainte-Beuve, Gustave Planche, George Sand. Souvenirs littéraires," in *Revue Bleue,* January 19, 1895.

LISZT, FRANZ. *Correspondance de Liszt et de Madame d'Agoult.* Paris, 1933.

——. *Frédéric Chopin.* Leipzig, 1852.

LOLIÉE, FRÉDÉRIC. *Le Duc de Morny et la société du Second Empire.* Paris, 1909.

MANN, HEINRICH. *Geist und Tat.* Berlin, 1931.

MARIÉTON, PAUL. *Une histoire d'amour.* Paris, 1897.

MARILLIER, LÉON. "La sensibilité et l'imagination de George Sand," in *Mercure de France,* Volume 64.

MAURRAS, CHARLES. *Les amants de Venise.* Nouvelle édition, Paris, 1916.

MAYNIAL, ÉDOUARD. *"Le procès en separation de George Sand,"* in *Mercure de France,* Volume 64.

MÉRIMÉE, PROSPER. *Lettres à une inconnue.* Paris, 1875.

MICKIEWICZ, ADAM. *Mélanges posthumes.* First series, Paris, 1872. Second series, Paris, 1879.

MURDOCH, WILLIAM. *Chopin: His Life.* New York, 1935.

MUSSET, ALFRED DE. *La confession d'un enfant du siècle.* (Edition Emile Henriot) Paris, 1887.

———. *Lettres d'amour à Aimée.* Paris, 1910.

———. *Mélanges de littérature.* Paris, 1867.

———. *Œuvres complètes.* (Édition Edmond Biré) 8 volumes. Paris, 1907–1909.

MUSSET, PAUL DE. *Biographie d'Alfred de Musset.* Paris, 1877.

———. *Lui et Elle.* Paris, 1860.

NORDAU, MAX. *Paris Studien und Bilder,* 2 volumes. Leipzig, 1881.

ODINOT, RAOUL. *Étude medico-psychologique d'Alfred de Musset.* Paris, 1906.

PAGELLO, PIETRO. Letter to Professor Ercole Mereni, in *Corriere della Sera,* March, 1881.

PAILLERON, MARIE LOUISE. *François Buloz et ses amis.* Paris, 1920.

———. *George Sand, histoire de sa vie,* Paris, 1938.

PITOLLET, CAMILLE. *"George Sand et le précepteur de ses enfants, Jules Boucoiran,"* in *La Grande Revue.* January, 1926.

POINSOT, ANTOINE. *La Fille de George Sand.* Paris, 1900.

———. *Rachel, d'après sa correspondance.* Paris, 1882.

PRAZ, MARIO. *La carne, la morte e il diavolo nella letteratura romantica.* Milano, 1930.

RAMANN, LINA. *Franz Liszt als Kunstler und Mensch,* 3 volumes. Leipzig, 1880–1887.

RENAN, ERNEST. *Feuilles détachées.* Paris, 1894.

REY, ACHILLE. *Agricol Perdiguier.* Avignon, 1904.

ROCHEBLAVE, SAMUEL. *"George Sand et sa famille pendant la guerre, 1870–1871,"* in *Revue des Deux Mondes,* Volume 24, 1914.

———. *George Sand et sa fille.* Paris, 1905.

ROYA, MAURICE. *Le plus grand amour de George Sand.* Paris, 1933.

ROYCE, W. B. *Balzac, Immortal.* New York, privately printed, 1926.

RUMMELSBURG-SULKE, GUSTEL. *Um George Sand.* Zürich, 1934.

SAINTE-BEUVE, C. *Correspondance.* Paris, 1877–1878.

———. *Nouvelle correspondance.* Paris, 1880.

———. *Vie, poésies et pensées de Joseph Delorme.* Paris, 1829.

———. *Volupté.* Paris, 1834.

SAND, AURORE. *George Sand et le théâtre de Nohant.* Paris, 1930.

———. *Le Berry de George Sand.* Paris, 1927.

———. *"Le roman d'Aurore Dudevant et d'Aurélien de Sèze,"* in *Revue des Deux Mondes,* Volume 32, 1926.

SAND, GEORGE. *Autour de la table* (Essays) . Paris, 1862.

——. *Correspondance,* 6 volumes. Paris, 1882–1884.
——. *Correspondance de George Sand et d'Alfred de Musset.* Bruxelles, 1904.
——. *Elle et Lui.* Paris, 1859.
——. *Histoire de ma vie,* 3 volumes. Paris, 1855.
——. *Impressions et souvenirs.* (Third edition) Paris, 1873.
——. *"Journal de Piffoël,"* in *Revue de Paris,* 1926.
——. *Journal d'un voyageur pendant la guerre.* Paris, 1871.
——. *Légendes rustiques. Fanchette.* Paris, 1877.
——. *"Lettres de George Sand à Emile Regnault,"* in *Revue de Paris,* Volume 3, 1937.
——. *Lettres d'un voyageur.* Paris, 1843, 1847, 1869.
——. *"Lettres inédites de George Sand et du Prince Napoléon,"* in *Revue des Deux Mondes,* Volume 7, 1923.
——. *Les Majorcains.* Paris, 1843.
——. *L'histoire d'un rêveur.* Paris, 1931.
——. *Œuvres,* 26 volumes. Paris 1855–1868.
——. *Questions politiques et sociales.* Paris, 1879.
SANDARS, MARY F. *George Sand.* London, 1927.
SANDEAU, JULES. *Marianna.* Paris, 1885.
SCHERMERHORN, ELIZABETH. *The Seven Strings of the Lyre.* Boston, 1927.
SÉCHÉ, LÉON. *Alfred de Musset,* 2 volumes. Paris, 1927.
——. *Sainte-Beuve,* 2 volumes. Paris, 1904.
——. *La Jeunesse Dorée sous Louis Philippe.* Paris, 1910.
——. *"Alfred de Musset à l'Arsenal et au Cénacle,"* in *Annales Romantiques,* Volume 3, 1906.
——. *"Sainte-Beuve et George Sand,"* in *La Revue des Revues,* Volume 51, 1904.
SEILLIÈRE, E. A. *George Sand, mystique de la passion.* Paris, 1920.
——. *"Le premier amour de George Sand,"* in *Revue hebdomadaire,* Volume 3. Paris, 1918.
SEYD, FELIZIA. *Romantic Rebel.* New York, 1940.
SHEPHARD, ESTHER. *Walt Whitman's Pose.* New York, 1938.
SPOELBERCH DE LOVENJOUL, CHARLES VICTOR, VICOMTE DE. *George Sand, étude bibliographique.* Paris, 1914.
——. *Études Balzaciennes.* Paris, 1896.
——. *Histoire des œuvres de Honoré de Balzac.* Paris, 1879.
SPULLER, ERNEST. *Lamennais.* Paris, 1892.
STAHL, P. J. (JULES HETZEL). *Le Diable à Paris.* Paris, 1845, 1846.
STEEGMULLER, FRANCIS. *Flaubert and Madame Bovary.* New York, 1939.
TAINE, HIPPOLYTE. *Derniers essays de critique et d'histoire.* Paris, 1894.
THOMAS, B. *George Sand.* London, 1883.
THOMAS, P. F. *"Pierre Leroux en exil,"* in *Revue de Paris,* December 1, 1903.
——. *Pierre Leroux, sa vie, son œuvre, sa doctrine.* Paris, 1904.
TOCQUEVILLE, ALEXIS. *Souvenirs,* Paris, 1893.
TOLDO, PIETRO. *"L'arte e la personalità di Alfred de Musset,"* in

studies of the R. *Accademia delle scienze dell'Istituto di Bologna*. Series I, Volume 10. Bologna, 1916.

TROMPEO, PIETRO PAOLO. *"Alfred de Musset à l'ombre des jeunes filles en fleur,"* in *Cultura*. Roma, 1932, Anno 11.

TURGENEV, I. S. *Lettres à Madame Viardot*. Paris, 1907.

———. *"Lettres de Turguéneff à ses amis d'Allemagne,"* in *Revue Politique et Littéraire*. Series 5, Volume 11, Paris, 1909.

ULBACH, LOUIS. *Nos contemporains*. Paris, 1883.

VALLÈS, JULES. *Les réfractaires*. Paris, 1866.

VIEL-CASTEL, COMTE HORACE DE. *Mémoires sur le règne de Napoléon* III, 3 volumes. Paris, 1883.

VIENS, PAUL (editor). *George Sand and Gustave Planche:* Unpublished correspondence. Providence, R. I., 1941.

WODZINSKI, COUNT. *Les trois romans de Frédéric Chopin*. Paris, 1886.

ZOLA, ÉMILE. *Les romanciers naturalistes*. Paris, 1890.

INDEX

Adam, Juliette, 282
Agoult, Count d', 210
Agoult, Countess Marie d', 173, 185, 205; with George Sand in Switzerland, 208-212; 213, 220, 228, 250, 265
Aimée, 96, 101
Alard, 268
Albine, 296
Alibaud, Louis, 204
Allan-Despréaux, Madame, 190
Allart, Hortense, 121, 210; on *Lucrezia Floriani*, 264-265; 266
Andrezel, Abbé d', 37
Anglais Mangeur d'Opium, L', 92
Année Terrible, L', 292
Antonia, 215
Antonio, Don, 1
Arago, Dominique, 194
Arago, Emmanuel, 194, 197, 247, 256, 260, 271
Arpentigny, Monsieur d', 260, 261
Artiste, L', (magazine), 101
As You Like It, 283
Aulnoy, Madame d', 27
Autre, L', 292

Babeuf, 193
Bac, Théodore, 278
"Ballad to the Moon," 93
Ballanche, Pierre, S., 200
Balzac, Honoré de, on Classicists and Romantics, 55-56; supports Hugo's Romanticism, 84; on the new adjectives, 87; and his literary "monsters," 104; on Gustave Planche, 118; his character and endearing traits, 120; his friendship with George Sand, 121; and George Sand on *Contes Drolatiques*, 149-150; on the Countess d'Agoult, 212; his *Béatrix*, 212-213; describes George Sand, 213; on George Sand's work, 214-215; on "her kind of male," 218; 239, 248; at George Sand's dinner party, 253; 256, 257

Barbès, Armand, 256, 278, 284
Bascans, Madame F., 249, 251
Battuécas, Les, 59
Bazard, Saint-Amand, 197
Béatrix, 212-213
Beauharnais, Hortense, 55, 275
Beau Laurence, Le, 215
Beaumont, Abbé de, 29-30, 36, 42, 58, 59, 60
Belgioioso, Prince, 135
Belgioioso, Princess, 212, 220
Béranger, Madame de, 36
Béranger, Mademoiselle, 136
Bérard, Frédéric, 91
Berlioz, H., 256
Bernhardt, Sarah, 292
Berry, Duchesse de, 112
Beyle, Henri. See Stendhal
"Bigarrure," 104
Bismarck, 292
Blacas, 55
Blaise Bonnin. See Sand, George
Blanc, Louis, 201-202, 247, 256, 259, 271, 275, 276, 278
Blanqui, Louis Auguste, 86, 103
Boissy, Monsieur de, 256-257
Bonnin, Louis, 55
Bonaparte, Louis, 55
Bonaparte, Prince Jerome, 284, 296
Bonnechose, Monsieur de, 220
Boucoiran, Jules, 97, 98-99, 104, 147, 150, 160, 172, 174, 175, 178, 180, 181, 188
Bougeaud, General, 193
Bourges, Michel de, defends workers in *procès monstre*, 194; description and character, 195; enlists George Sand for workers' cause, 196-197; becomes George Sand's lover, 198; 200; and the monster trial, 200, 202; as subject of George Sand's novels, 203-204, 206, 214, 218, 219, 243, 274
Brault, Augustine, 249, 259, 263
Brillant, the dog, 29, 58
Broadwood, James, 220
Broglie, Duc de, 83, 194